# Programming Windows Store Apps with C#

*Matt Baxter-Reynolds and Iris Classon*

Beijing · Cambridge · Farnham · Köln · Sebastopol · Tokyo

**Programming Windows Store Apps with C#**

by Matt Baxter-Reynolds and Iris Classon

Copyright © 2014 Matt Baxter-Reynolds. All rights reserved.

Printed in the United States of America.

Published by O'Reilly Media, Inc., 1005 Gravenstein Highway North, Sebastopol, CA 95472.

O'Reilly books may be purchased for educational, business, or sales promotional use. Online editions are also available for most titles (*http://my.safaribooksonline.com*). For more information, contact our corporate/institutional sales department: 800-998-9938 or *corporate@oreilly.com*.

| | |
|---|---|
| **Editors:** Maria Stallone and Rachel Roumeliotis | **Indexer:** Judith McConville |
| **Production Editor:** Melanie Yarbrough | **Cover Designer:** Randy Comer |
| **Copyeditor:** Rachel Monaghan | **Interior Designer:** David Futato |
| **Proofreader:** Charles Roumeliotis | **Illustrator:** Rebecca Demarest |

February 2014:      First Edition

**Revision History for the First Edition:**

2014-02-10:    First release

See *http://oreilly.com/catalog/errata.csp?isbn=9781449320850* for release details.

ISBN: 978-1-449-32085-0

[LSI]

# Table of Contents

# Preface

The computing industry is changing. PC sales are on the decline, and sales of post-PC devices (tablets and smartphones) are on the ascendancy. This change can be understood easily enough—computers are no longer something used for work, they are something used for *life*, and happily there is more to our society than just work.

The massive commercial success of post-PC devices suggests that this change works OK for most, but for companies like Microsoft it creates a big problem. The PC is not going to be as important over the next 20 years as it has been for the last 20 years. Windows 8.1 and Windows RT are Microsoft's first move to try to address that problem by making the Windows operating system "play more nicely" in the tablet space.

Microsoft has done this by introducing a new user interface paradigm called *Modern UI*. This new user interface paradigm is monochronistic (one thing at a time), rather than the polychronistic (many things at a time) nature of a normal windowing operating system. It is also optimized for touch.

As well as providing a new user interface, Microsoft has introduced a new API, called *Windows Runtime* (WinRT), and a new execution and packaging model for the apps, called *Windows Store apps*. We'll talk more about the actual construction of Windows Store apps in Chapter 2.

This book is designed to treat Windows 8.1 and Windows 8.1.1 RT equally—nothing we do in the book will exclude operation from either variant of the operating system. Similarly, everything we do can be used in apps that are distributed through the Windows Store.

Generally, we will be writing all the code ourselves, but from time to time we will be using third-party products. Virtually all of these are open source—there is only one exception, which is the Bing Maps component discussed in Chapter 11. Everything else is unrestricted.

So let's go! We'll start by learning about the app that we're going to build.

# Audience

What I've tried to do with writing this book is to tell a story that takes you, the reader, through the process of moving from .NET development over to Windows Store app development. There is a slight bias in the book in that I'm assuming most developers have day jobs developing web applications and have been asked to look into development tablet apps that run on Microsoft's tablet operating systems.

Some of you will also have done quite a bit of desktop development on Windows, particularly using Silverlight and/or Windows Presentation Foundation (WPF). This book isn't a primer on developing XAML, although you will see and work with enough examples that use XAML to become proficient.

I'll also tell you a bit more about the app we'll be discussing so you can judge if this is the right book for you. The app has within it the common sorts of functionality that you find in line-of-business apps (LOB) generally. At the time of writing, the Windows tablet story is not established, so the elements that we'll go through are those that apply to real applications on Windows Mobile, Android, and iOS that I've built over the past 10 years or so.

Although the application that we'll build is a LOB app, everything you'll see and do in this book applies equally well to a normal retail app that you might sell in a business-to-consumer fashion.

# The Application

As I mentioned, we're going to build a line-of-business app, rather than a "retail" app. The way that I distinguish between these two is that in a retail app, the software vendor typically doesn't have a strong relationship with the end customer. In retail, the end customer finds the app through indirect recommendations and/or through the app store catalog. In a LOB app, proactive marketing and relationship-building activities look to tie a client and vendor together through some sort of commercial offering. Technically, however, there isn't a big difference between retail apps and LOB apps.

The specific example I'm going to show you is a "field service" app. This type of app is a classic mobile working application. In field service you have a number of operatives whose operational control is within your remit. You send them out into the field to do something—either something specific ("go here, fix this"), or something reactive (e.g., someone "patrols" an area and reports back on problems).

The app we will build will be called StreetFoo, and it's a blend of those last two examples. I have created a simple server that is hosted on AppHarbor that will serve as the backend service for the app. When the user logs in to the app, it will download a set of "problem reports." Each report will be something that needs fixing—the sample data happens to show graffiti, but it could be anything. The concept of the app is that the user would then either fix the problem or could report new problems into the app. Updates to problems or new problems are then updated to the server.

That's the basic functionality. There are additional things that we'll look at, such as capturing photos and location information, as well as all of the various special user experience features in Windows 8.1/Windows 8.1.1 RT—sharing, snapped view, search, and so on.

# The Chapters

We'll start in Chapters 1 and 2 with a primer designed to get you up and running in terms of moving from .NET into this new world.

*Chapter 1, Making the Transition from .NET (Part 1)*
> Starts by explaining the "break" between .NET and associated technologies (specifically WPF) over to Windows Runtime (WinRT). You'll then build a basic user interface and implement a Model/View/View-Model (MVVM) pattern.

*Chapter 2, Making the Transition from .NET (Part 2)*
> Walks you through making the UI you built in Chapter 1 do something—specifically, calling up to the server to register a new user account. This chapter also has a detailed look at *asynchrony*—probably the most important thing that you will learn during your time with Windows Store app development.

The remaining chapters in this book each focus on a specific API feature area.

*Chapter 3, Local Persistent Data*
> Explores SQLite. The reason I've brought up this topic so early in the book is that you can't build a practically useful application without having some sort of persistent store. Although you can store information on disk easily enough using the Windows Store APIs, SQLite is the de facto relational database used in mobile solutions, and so we'll use it in our app.

*Chapter 4, The App Bar*
> Introduces the first of the special Windows 8.1 user experience (UX) features: the app bar. App bars are the small panels that pop in from the top and bottom of the screen and provide access to options and tabs. (The app bar is essentially analogous to toolbars.) We'll look at how to build an app bar and how to make up our own images for use on the buttons.

*Chapter 5, Notifications*
> Discusses notifications. Notifications in Windows Store apps can be used to update the tile on the Start screen, add badges to the tile, and display *toast* (the notifications that wind in from the top-right side of the screen). Notifications can be created locally and shown locally, or alternatively, created on the server and pushed out to

all connected devices using Windows Push Notification Services (WNS). In this chapter we'll look at both routes.

*Chapter 6, Working with Files*

Looks in detail at working with files. To be honest, when I first planned this book I didn't intend to include a chapter on files, as this tends to be a topic well served by the community whenever a new platform is introduced. However, I ended up adding this chapter to handle images. Each report that we track in the app will have exactly one image. Rather than storing these images in SQLite, which is impractical, we'll store them on disk.

*Chapter 7, Sharing*

Focuses on the Windows 8.1 sharing feature. Sharing is one of the key differentiators between Microsoft's tablet strategy and other platforms. Most platforms "silo off" apps and make it hard to share data. Windows 8.1 has a declarative model for sharing where apps indicate they can serve up certain types of data. That data can then be read in by another app that supports consumption of shared data. In this chapter we'll look at both sharing data from our app and consuming data from other apps.

*Chapter 8, Searching*

Looks at the Windows 8.1 UX feature of searching. The idea here is that, generally, all apps need some sort of search feature. In Windows 8.1 this is accessed from the charms or by using the SearchBox control. In this chapter we'll look at implementing a search feature that we can use to find problem reports.

*Chapter 9, Settings*

Concludes our look at Windows 8.1 UX specifics with a discussion of the settings charm, which—as its name implies—provides a common area where developers can put settings. It's also a common place to put links up for support information and privacy policies. In this chapter we'll go a little broad with this by using the `SettingsFlyout` control to load and render Markdown-formatted text.

*Chapter 10, Location*

Explores location, a very common requirement for mobile LOB apps because it's often helpful to have some "evidence" of where a particular activity took place, or to utilize the user's location as a way of creating new data. In this chapter we'll look at the basics of reading locational information from the device, and we'll also use the Bing Maps Windows Store apps control to present a map within the application.

*Chapter 11, Using the Camera*

Helps you discover how to use the camera. In mobile LOB apps it's often a requirement to gather photographic evidence of work done. (For example, if someone is asked to fix a sink, you may find it helpful to have a photo of the sink before and after it was fixed.) In this chapter we'll look at how to create new problem reports, starting with a photograph taken from the webcam.

*Chapter 12, Responsive Design*
Helps you master how to implement responsive design so the application can be resized in width to support even the smallest width size of 320 pixels, previously known as "snapped mode." Another Windows 8.1 UX feature that differentiates Windows from the other platforms is the ability to run apps side by side. The way this works is that you can have one app running in a thin strip on the left or right side of the screen, with another app taking up the remainder of the space. The only problem with this is that you need to build an entirely parallel UI to get your app running in this thin strip. In fact, this isn't as bad as it sounds, because the MVVM pattern that we'll use abstracts a lot of the work away. Specifically, in this chapter we'll build in the ability to run our application in different width sizes.

*Chapter 13, Resources and Localization*
Looks at resources and localization. By the time you get to this chapter, you will already have seen quite a few ways of working with resources, so some of this chapter is given over to covering the things that we haven't yet looked at in detail. In the other part of the chapter, we'll discuss how to implement proper localization of the app (i.e., how to add in support to present the app in different languages).

*Chapter 14, Background Tasks and App Lifetime*
Tackles *background tasks*, a special way of blocking off functionality that Windows will run on a schedule on the application's behalf. Common to all tablet platforms, Windows Store apps look to restrict what your application can do when it's not actually running in the foreground. In this chapter we'll look in some detail at implementing such background tasks—specifically, we're going to look at how to use this functionality to download new reports and upload local change reports back to the server in the background.

*Chapter 15, Sideloading and Distribution*
Details how you can actually package and distribute apps on the Windows Store. We'll look at using developer licenses to create *sideloading* packages for internal testing, and we'll also look at how to do proper enterprise sideloading. (Sideloading is the process whereby you distribute apps to a private audience rather than using the Windows Store.) We'll also look at the rules that you need to adhere to in order to get Microsoft to distribute your app on the Windows Store.

The book has two appendixes:

*Appendix A, Cryptography and Hashing*
Covers some common requirements related to cryptography and hashing that you'll likely either need or be asked about, but don't fit into the main body of the text.

*Appendix B, Unit Testing Basics for Windows Store Apps*
> Looks at how to unit test your code using the unit testing projects provided with Visual Studio. This will use the inversion of control containers that we built and used throughout the book.

And that's it! By the time you've been through the whole story, you should have a great understanding of how to build full-featured Windows Store applications.

# Prerequisites

The only thing that you will need in order to get working is Visual Studio 2013. Out of the box, this edition of Visual Studio comes with everything you need to build Windows Store apps. You can use either the Professional edition or the Express edition. I happened to use the Professional edition, but everything has been tested on Express.

You will need a Windows Store developer account if you want to actually get your apps listed on the store, although nothing in this book requires that level of paid account. You will need to create a free account in order to obtain a developer license, which is required to locally deploy any apps that you build.

# Source Code

The source code for this book is available on GitHub (*https://github.com/mbrit/Program mingWindowsStoreApps*).

The easiest way to work with this code is to grab the entire repo and put it on your local disk. Each chapter is represented by one folder, where the code in the folder is the same as the state of the application at the end of each chapter. (For example, the *Chapter8* folder includes everything from Chapter 2 up to and including Chapter 8. The *Chap ter9* folder builds on the *Chapter8* folder and also includes the work that we go through in Chapter 9.) From time to time, the code downloads may contain more than what we have specifically gone through in the book.

If you're not accustomed to using GitHub or git, here's a quick run-through.

## Using git

This section is intended to get you through the basics of installing git and using it to fetch the code from the repository. It's not intended to show you how to use git as a source control system, but GitHub offers a decent walkthrough (*http://learn.github.com/*) of that.

You'll need a git client to get started. You can download a client from the git website (*http://git-scm.com/*). Do this and install the package that's downloaded.

The installer will install both a command-line client and a GUI. Personally, when I'm actually using git I always use the command line. A lot of people use the GUI. If you're only interested in using git to get the code for this book, you might as well just use the GUI.

To open the GUI in Windows 8.1, access the Start screen by pressing the Windows key. Type **git** directly into the Start screen. You'll get options for Git Bash and Git GUI. Open up the Git GUI and select the Clone Existing Repository option.

You'll need to copy and paste the path of the repo from GitHub. To do this, access the repo using a web browser. The URL you want is *https://github.com/mbrit/Program mingWindowsStoreApps*.

On the page you'll find a "Quick setup" box that contains the actual URL of the repo. You'll need to copy this to the clipboard. The URL will look something like *https:// github.com/mbrit/ProgrammingWindowsStoreApps.git*. Figure P-1 illustrates.

*Figure P-1. The area of the GitHub page showing the actual repo URL.*

Back in the GUI, copy and paste the repo path into the Source Location field, and type the path to any local folder that you like into the Target Directory field. Figure P-2 illustrates.

*Figure P-2. Setting up the clone operation*

Click the Clone button, and the repo will come down to your local machine. You can then use Visual Studio to open the solution files contained in each folder.

## Contacting the Authors

Should you want to get hold of Matt directly, the best way is via Twitter (@mbrit). Alternatively, try his website (*http://mbrit.com/*). Iris Classon can be contacted via Twitter (@irisclasson) and her website (*http://www.irisclasson.com*).

## Let's Go!

And that's it. You should now be ready to get going building Windows Store apps.

## Conventions Used in This Book

The following typographical conventions are used in this book:

*Plain text*
> Indicates menu titles, menu options, menu buttons, and keyboard accelerators (such as Alt and Ctrl).

*Italic*
> Indicates new terms, URLs, email addresses, filenames, file extensions, pathnames, directories, and Unix utilities.

`Constant width`
> Indicates commands, options, switches, variables, attributes, keys, functions, types, classes, namespaces, methods, modules, properties, parameters, values, objects, events, event handlers, XML tags, HTML tags, macros, the contents of files, or the output from commands.

**`Constant width bold`**
> Shows commands or other text that should be typed literally by the user.

*`Constant width italic`*
> Shows text that should be replaced with user-supplied values.

 This icon signifies a general note.

 This icon signifies a tip or suggestion.

This icon indicates a warning or caution.

# Using Code Examples

This book is here to help you get your job done. In general, if this book includes code examples, you may use the code in your programs and documentation. You do not need to contact us for permission unless you're reproducing a significant portion of the code. For example, writing a program that uses several chunks of code from this book does not require permission. Selling or distributing a CD-ROM of examples from O'Reilly books does require permission. Answering a question by citing this book and quoting example code does not require permission. Incorporating a significant amount of example code from this book into your product's documentation does require permission.

We appreciate, but do not require, attribution. An attribution usually includes the title, author, publisher, and ISBN. For example: "*Programming Windows Store Apps with C# by Matt Baxter-Reynolds and Iris Classon (O'Reilly). Copyright 2014 Matthew Baxter-Reynolds, 978-1-449-32085-0.*"

If you feel your use of code examples falls outside fair use or the permission given above, feel free to contact us at *permissions@oreilly.com*.

# Safari® Books Online

 Safari Books Online (*http://www.safaribooksonline.com*) is an on-demand digital library that delivers expert content in both book and video form from the world's leading authors in technology and business.

Technology professionals, software developers, web designers, and business and creative professionals use Safari Books Online as their primary resource for research, problem solving, learning, and certification training.

Safari Books Online offers a range of product mixes and pricing programs for organizations, government agencies, and individuals. Subscribers have access to thousands of books, training videos, and prepublication manuscripts in one fully searchable database from publishers like O'Reilly Media, Prentice Hall Professional, Addison-Wesley Professional, Microsoft Press, Sams, Que, Peachpit Press, Focal Press, Cisco Press, John Wiley & Sons, Syngress, Morgan Kaufmann, IBM Redbooks, Packt, Adobe Press, FT Press, Apress, Manning, New Riders, McGraw-Hill, Jones & Bartlett, Course Technology, and dozens more. For more information about Safari Books Online, please visit us online.

# How to Contact Us

Please address comments and questions concerning this book to the publisher:

O'Reilly Media, Inc.
1005 Gravenstein Highway North
Sebastopol, CA 95472
800-998-9938 (in the United States or Canada)
707-829-0515 (international or local)
707-829-0104 (fax)

We have a web page for this book, where we list errata, examples, and any additional information. You can access this page at *http://oreil.ly/prog-win-store-apps-csharp*.

To comment or ask technical questions about this book, send email to *bookques tions@oreilly.com*.

For more information about our books, courses, conferences, and news, see our website at *http://www.oreilly.com*.

Find us on Facebook: *http://facebook.com/oreilly*

Follow us on Twitter: *http://twitter.com/oreillymedia*

Watch us on YouTube: *http://www.youtube.com/oreillymedia*

# Acknowledgments

Thank you to the technical reviewers, Oren Novotny, Stefan Turalski, Matt Fitchett, and Nathan Jepson, without whom this book would not have been possible.

This book would be fundamentally different, and nowhere near as good or complete, were it not for Twitter. Twitter is perhaps the most important learning resource for those involved in the computer industry that's ever been invented. This book has got quite a lot of advice in it, and the most important piece is this: if you're a professional software developer and you don't use Twitter, start.

Here's a list of my various Twitter friends who have given support, saved me hours upon hours of work, come up with new ideas, and provided invaluable input:

- Alex Papadimoulis (@apapadimoulis)
- Casey Muratori (@cmuratori)
- Chris Field (@mrcfield)
- Chris Hardy (@chrisntr )

- Craig Murphy (@camurphy)
- Daniel Plaisted (@dsplaisted)
- David Kean (@davkean)
- Duncan Smart (@duncansmart)
- Edward Behan (@edwardbehan)
- Filip Skakun (@xyzzer)
- Frank Krueger (@praeclarum)
- Gill Cleeren (@gillcleeren)
- Ginny Caughey (@gcaughey)
- Haris Custo (@hariscusto)
- Hermit Dave (@hermitdave)
- Iris Classon (@irisclasson)
- Jamie Mutton (@jcmm33)
- Joel Hammond-Turner (@rammesses)
- Jose Fajardo (@josefajardo)
- Keith Patton (@kpatton)
- Kendall Miller (@kendallmiller)
- Liam Westley (@westleyl)
- Mark Tepper (@binaerforceone)
- Matt Hidinger (@matthidinger)
- Matthieu GD (@tewmgd)
- Mike Harper (@mikejharper)
- Nic Wise (@fastchiken)
- Peter Provost (@pprovost)
- Ross Dargan (@rossdargan)
- Tim Heuer (@timheuer)
- Tomas McGuinness (@tomasmcguinness)

Finally, thank you to Rachel Roumeliotis, Maria Gulick, Melanie Yarbrough, and the rest of the O'Reilly team for their hard work and patience in making this book a reality.

# CHAPTER 1

# Making the Transition from .NET (Part 1)

In this chapter and the next we're going to start looking at the work that we have to do to move our .NET skills over to WinRT and start building Windows Store apps. Unlike the other chapters in this book, which focus on a particular API feature area, this chapter and the next are more mixed and intermingled, mainly because the changes that we have to make in order to achieve a transition are also mixed and intermingled.

Given Microsoft's history with .NET, you might have expected WinRT to be a direct evolution. In fact, it's not. WinRT represents a major shift in strategy from the team within Microsoft that "owns" the Windows API. It's coming to market at a time when considerable changes are happening within the broader world of software engineering. This is the "post-PC" age. Microsoft rose to dominance in the microcomputer/PC age.

## Why WinRT?

WinRT has emerged at the same time as Microsoft's "reimagining" of Windows into two new operating systems—Windows 8 and Windows RT—although the timing that brings the launch of the new OSes and a new API model together is more luck than judgment. WinRT is about fixing the fundamental limitations of writing software natively for Windows. Native applications in Windows are written using the Win32 API, which is a very old, non–object-oriented API. Alongside Win32 we also have COM, an object-oriented subsystem that allows for components to be plugged in and out of Windows. If you're a relative newcomer to writing software for Windows, there's a good chance you've never used either of these, or you've used .NET. If you're slightly longer in the tooth, there is a chance that you did use these technologies once, but—especially if you've selected this book—the likelihood is that over the past $n$ years you've been using .NET to write software that targets Windows OSes.

.NET is very different from Win32 or COM. .NET is a Java-inspired framework library and execution environment designed to make it easier to write software for Windows.

We call .NET a "managed code" environment because the runtime takes over a lot of the "management" of the code execution. Conversely, Win32 apps are "unmanaged." In its initial incarnation, .NET was built to let developers build websites in ASP.NET, or native applications with Windows Forms. (We'll ignore console applications or Windows services for the time being, as I want to talk about user interface technologies.) Both of these user interface technology tracks have evolved and changed over time, but regardless the more important thing about .NET was that it allowed developers to be more expressive. The Base Class Library (BCL) within .NET provided easy, object-oriented access either into Windows operating system features (e.g., `System.IO.File Stream`) or classes designed to save the developer time and effort (e.g., `System.Collec tions.Generic.List`). (The former set is relevant here, as a great deal of the BCL simply thunks down into Win32, which is how it provides access to OS functions.) In addition to the BCL, the CLR provides features like garbage collection so that under regular operations, developers don't need to worry about the mechanics of working with memory management and other important bits and pieces.

## Philosophical Differences

Where this starts to get untidy is that WinRT and .NET are *philosophically* very different. .NET is inspired by Java, and the big compromise with a system where memory is managed by garbage collection is that you inevitably cede control to the framework. If you're building an operating system (like the Windows Division—aka WinDiv—team within Microsoft), or building a major software product like Office, you wouldn't start with Java. Java, and by extension .NET, is too abstract, too "magical" for building that sort of software. But most of us don't build "that sort of software"; what most of us do is work within very small budgets to build relatively small-scale applications where the compromise of working within an execution environment like the CLR is much less keenly felt.

As .NET developers, we have to learn to play nicely within this philosophical difference imposed by a shift to WinRT, and therein lies the challenge. It should be said, though, that the general premise of this is, in my opinion, a bit broken. While the rationale for moving away from .NET and back to COM is understood, it's not necessarily a good idea. It would have been better in many ways if Windows Store apps had been built more squarely on .NET, and the oddities that come into play because Windows Store apps are fundamentally COM-based were negated. However, we are where we are.

In terms of the assumptions that I'm going to make, I'm assuming that the readers of this book are on the spectrum of "reasonably familiar" with .NET up to "very familiar" with .NET. I'll also assume that most of the modern .NET concepts up to and including .NET Framework v3.5 are understood—we're going to be seeing a lot of generics. We'll be seeing a bit of Linq (but I will go through that). I'll assume no knowledge of the Task Parallel Library (TPL)—which we'll be using a lot. As long as you can put together production-quality code in .NET, you'll be covered.

Most .NET developers will have been working on ASP.NET applications, so again I'm assuming that this is the user interface technology of choice for most readers of this book. For our Windows Store apps we're going to be using the XAML user interface track (more later). XAML is aligned with Silverlight and Windows Presentation Foundation (WPF), although I'm going to be assuming most readers of this book have little or no Silverlight/WPF/XAML experience.

# Objectives

In the next two chapters, our objective is to get a Windows Store app built, with a user interface, and some business logic that can call up to the server. We're also going to prove that we can build a unit test library to run alongside the application. Specifically:

- We'll build a new Windows Store app project in Visual Studio 2012. The purpose of this is to learn about the new project templates, and understand the difference in emitted outputs between the new-style Windows Store app projects and old-style .NET projects.

- Within that project, we'll build a new page in XAML, and from there we'll look at building in the infrastructure to support Model/View/View-Model (MVVM). (I'll explain what this is shortly.) We'll also look at building support for inversion of control. (Again, if you don't know what "inversion of control" is, you will find an explanation later.) The code will look to call up to a publicly accessible server. In the first instance, we'll fake this call and simulate the server.

- We'll take the view-model that we built and wrap a unit test around it, just so that we know that we can.

- Once we know we can test the model, we'll build the real implementation of our server communication. We can then test our app end-to-end and know that it's working.

# The New Project Templates

The first thing to get a handle on is that the version of .NET used in Windows Store apps is a cut-down, limited version of .NET referenced internally as .NETCore. There's precedent for Microsoft creating subsets of .NET; one example is the .NET Compact Framework used in Windows CE. Another is the Client Profiles introduced in v3.5 that are "optimized" for client applications. Likewise, the toolset for Windows Phone 8 is a cut-down version of the Silverlight libraries, which in turn is a cut-down version of WPF.

The motivation behind all of these "cutting down" operations is to limit what developers can do. There are a few reasons Microsoft might want to do this. One argument is that the Microsoft engineers might want to make a given API set more secure by removing exploit vectors. However, another important reason why Microsoft engineers will do this sort of thing is to "create a better experience." What this actually means is that Microsoft's engineers will control the API such that you as a developer can't do things that make Windows 8 look bad.

A good example of this is battery life. When you're using Windows 8 on a tablet, battery life is very important. The longer the battery lasts, the happier the user will be. If Microsoft designs the API so that it's hard for you as a developer to do things that use a relatively high amount of battery power, the battery life as the user perceives it will be better, and hence the user will perceive Windows 8 as being a good tablet operating system.

 You can see this idea exemplified in background tasks, which we'll look at in Chapter 14.

So we can only access the bits of the framework that happen to be in .NETCore. You should note that even if you could violate this rule, you probably wouldn't want to, as the app would not pass certification for inclusion in the Windows Store—something we'll talk about in Chapter 15.

## WinRT Metadata

A standout excellent feature of .NET available from introduction was the level of detail included within its metadata system. (Metadata at its most basic in this context is simply a description of how all the types and members within them are structured.) Each .NET assembly could describe itself to a hitherto unrealized level of detail. Conversely, normal Windows DLLs had very little metadata—essentially just an EXPORTS table of functions that could be called. COM sat somewhere in the middle by being mostly self-descriptive using IDL, but the level of detail was nothing like the .NET metadata. (Plus, consuming COM metadata was a chore, whereas consuming .NET metadata was a breeze.)

WinRT is, under the hood, COM with knobs on—COM++, if you will. (Although don't call it that because you will get looked at peculiarly.) Microsoft borrowed .NET's metadata subsystem for use within WinRT. Thus, when you compile a WinRT DLL you get a *.winmd* file that contains both the metadata and the binary executable code. The format of the metadata within that *.winmd* file happens to be compatible with .NET's.

The .NET behavior is unchanged—compile a .NET assembly, and the metadata gets embedded within as before.

What all this means is that the interoperability story between these two worlds is rather good. Because both parties understand each other well thanks to the shared metadata, Microsoft's job in getting actual calls going between the two is straightforward.

As most of you are likely familiar with the structure of .NET assemblies, I'll take you through the structure of the new assemblies using Reflector and we'll see how a Windows Store application references the central WinRT components. (If you don't know what Reflector is, we'll look at that in a short while.)

To begin with, we can create projects within Visual Studio in the usual way. Figure 1-1 illustrates adding a new C# Windows Store "Blank App" project to an existing solution. Notice how the Windows Store projects have their own entry in the tree away from the .NET projects that you're used to creating normally.

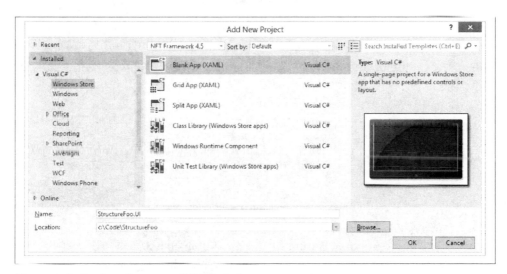

*Figure 1-1. Options for a new Windows Store app project*

If we create a new project—I'll create a Blank App type for this illustration—we can look under References in Solution Explorer and see something like Figure 1-2.

This looks quite different from the References view of a normal .NET project; what we're actually seeing here are placeholder references to the actual libraries and assemblies that the project will compile against. Specifically, these are references to the .NETCore assembly set and the core Windows WinRT libraries.

Because the rules are set in stone as far as what you have to reference in order to be a proper Windows Store app that gets through store certification, you can't change these references.

*Figure 1-2. Placeholders for the .NETCore assembly and Windows WinRT libraries*

What Visual Studio is doing here is representing bundles of referenced assemblies/ libraries as single items. In the normal .NET world, these would be a discrete set of explicit assemblies. We can use Reflector to get a better view of what's going on.

 For the uninitiated, Reflector is a popular .NET tool that allows you to see the structure of types and members within an assembly, and also decompile it. See the Reflector website (*http://www.reflector.net/*).

If you want to follow along, download a trial copy of Reflector if you don't have a licensed copy. If we point Reflector at the output assembly—which happens to be called `Struc tureFoo.UI.exe` in my example—we'll see something like Figure 1-3. What this is showing us is a bunch of regular .NET assemblies that make up .NETCore (`System.Col lections`, etc.) and a reference to `Windows`. (Looking back at Figure 1-1, we see something different. Visual Studio just showed us one item, ".NET for Windows Store apps." Reflector is showing us the actual references.)

The `Windows` reference isn't an assembly—it's a reference to the WinRT metadata file. With the information in that file, the runtime is able to bind through to the unmanaged, native code components that contain the implementations. When we get going, you'll see that under the hood this thunking[1] down to WinRT happens a lot, but you wouldn't even know it was happening unless you looked really hard.

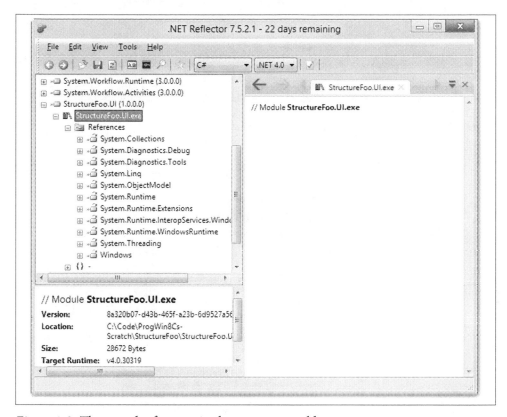

*Figure 1-3. The actual references in the output assembly*

If you select the Windows entry in Reflector, you'll see something like Figure 1-4. (The version of Reflector that I'm using at the moment cannot automatically reference the metadata.) Notice the version number of 255.255.255.255—this is a good hint that we are referencing WinRT metadata and not a .NET assembly.

The metadata file that it's looking for is stored in *C:\Program Files (x86)\WindowsKits \8.0\References\CommonConfiguration\Neutral\Windows.winmd*. That folder tree happens to be the WinRT development kit.

If we go into Reflector and tell it where to find Windows.winmd, we'd find something like Figure 1-5.

---

1. *Thunking* is the process of making calls across system boundaries. In this context, it refers to making calls from the "managed code" world of .NET to the unmanaged world of WinRT.

*Figure 1-4. Prompting for the Windows metadata*

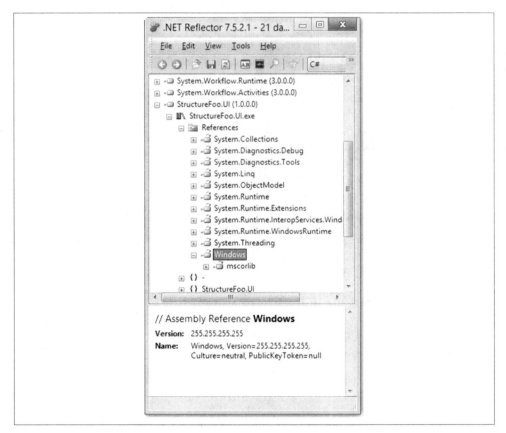

*Figure 1-5. Linking through to the Windows WinRT library reference*

You'll notice a reference to mscorlib, implying a reference back to .NET from WinRT. Ignore that—it's a red herring. It's an artifact of the metadata system being a .NET thing that's been repurposed for WinRT.

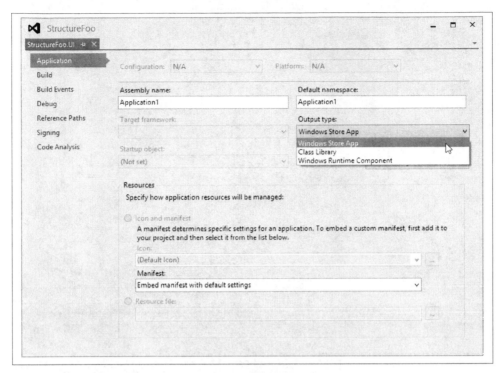

*Figure 1-6. Disabled target framework and selectable project types*

What I've tried to show here is how the worlds of .NET and WinRT interoperate. What we've done is created a more or less standard .NET executable assembly, and referenced a collection of normal .NET assemblies and also the WinRT libraries.

To close this loop, let's go back into Visual Studio and look at the project settings and adding references.

## Project Settings and Adding References

The first point of interest is that if we open up the properties for our project, you'll notice that we can't change the target framework. In a normal .NET project, we *would* be able to change the target framework and this option would not be greyed out. (Although obviously this is how it is at the time of writing, I'm actually expecting this to change as I assume that ultimately multiple framework versions will be supported on the various devices.) You'll also notice that the output types are different—we can create a Windows Store App, a Class Library, or a Windows Runtime Component. Figure 1-6 illustrates.

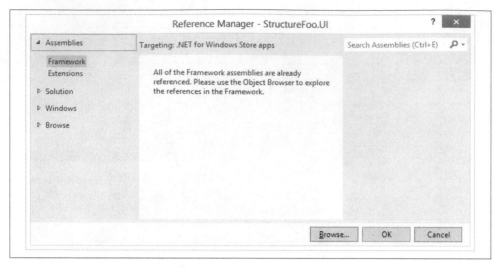

*Figure 1-7. With .NETCore selected, we can't choose any other assemblies in the way we usually can with normal .NET projects*

The Windows Store App is a normal, deployable-and-runnable executable. The Class Library is a .NET assembly that can be consumed from managed code. The WinMD File is used in scenarios where you want to consume the assembly/library from Java-Script or C++/CX. That latter case is out of scope for this book, although we will touch on it in Chapter 14 when we look at background tasks. Generally, in the work we do in this book we're going to create one executable and a support library to go along with it. Let's turn our attention now to references.

 In Visual Studio 2012, the dialog has changed for adding references. Thankfully, we now have a search option!

If you right-click on the project in Solution Explorer and select Add Reference, you'll see something like Figure 1-7. Note how we cannot add any Framework references. In Metro style we are given .NETCore, and that's all we're allowed to have. We can't add or remove any part of those references. Notice also at the top that it reads "Targeting: .NET for Windows Store apps."

Likewise, although I haven't included a screenshot of this, if you select Windows from the tree (i.e., "WinRT libraries"), you'll see a similar story.

The Solution option lists the projects in the solution. This works in the way that you would expect: simply select the projects whose output you want to reference, and you should be good to go. Use some caution, however, as there's nothing to stop you doing things such as adding a normal, full .NET class library project and trying to reference it. You'll get an error if you do this, but it's not a particularly descriptive error—it just reads "Unable to add a reference to project *<projectName>*."

You can use the Browse option to add any assemblies that you fancy, although your mileage will vary. I, for example, added a reference to a normal .NET 2.0 assembly. The reference went in fine, but it complained about classes missing from mscorlib. This makes sense if you consider that things will be missing from .NETCore.

# Building a Basic User Interface

Now that we've explored how the Windows Store projects are put together, we can look at how we build the user interface.

## UI Tracks

You can build Windows Store apps using one of three user interface *tracks*, which are a combination of a display technology and a coding language.

In this book, I'm going to be basing the work we do on XAML, and I'll talk about this in much more detail in a moment.

I've excluded DirectX/C++ from this book for the reason that it's more aimed at developing games, and this book isn't about building games.

### HTML

The HTML5/CSS3/JavaScript track is actually more interesting and in many ways hugely appropriate to developers looking to target Windows 8 and Windows RT. In the HTML5 scenario you build a self-contained, locally executing web application that runs inside of IE on the device. It's packaged up just like a normal Windows Store application. (We'll talk about application packaging in Chapter 15.) The language you use to build the application is JavaScript. Just for clarity, you don't get any backend, server-side execution (à la ASP.NET) with this—it's all done with JavaScript, although in this new world you have WinJS, which can get into the full WinRT library. (The prevailing wisdom is that it's this capability to thunk down from WinJS into WinRT that caused Microsoft's engineers to eschew basing Windows Store apps entirely on .NET.)

You might also be interested to know that the standard Mail, Calendar, and People apps in Windows 8 are based on the HTML5 track rather than the XAML track. However, that seems to be unusual. My informal analysis of the store at various points during the later half of 2012 shows that XAML tends to be much more popular, with about 70% of apps released into the Store being XAML-based. Moreover, there's a skew toward apps that repackage web content being more likely to be HTML5-based.

On paper, the ability to build apps using HTML5 is incredibly appealing and very sensible. With the market consolidation that's going on at the time of writing (early 2013), it's hard for people investing in software to know where to put their money. Targeting a platform-neutral technology like HTML5 seems like a winning plan because any investment you do make can be taken to other platforms in a way that follows profit without dramatically increasing complexity.

However, what that doesn't account for is that in the post-PC world, the user experience (UX) argument tends to be very strong, and it's typically the case that users demand apps that have a high degree of "slickness." It's counterintuitive to suggest that a platform that is inherently a compromise (i.e., HTML and the Web) can offer this slick user experience. (I tend to call this sort of approach "near native" as it tends to be good enough to be operational, but not classifiable as "native.") The iPad is a popular device because the apps are so good, and those apps tend to be based on the native toolset provided by Apple. Even though cross-platform technologies are available for iPad (in particular, Apache Cordova née PhoneGap), their adoption tends to be low, as developers understand that compromising UX is typically a move that harms the proposition in the post-PC world.

 There are other incidental problems with using HTML5 to gain cross-platform advantage with a Windows tablet strategy, the main one being that the UI metaphors used in the modern UI design aesthetic tend to be horizontally biased, whereas the Web itself is vertically biased. You have to wonder how much you really gain from going down an HTML5 route.

### Better experience

When we think about our UI track for Windows Store apps, it follows that the native experience should offer a better UX. This means using the XAML track, not the HTML5 track, given that the XAML track is the native UI technology for Metro style, as opposed to HTML5, which is the cross-platform, "near native" choice. You may choose to read the word *compromise* where I have written *choice* in that last sentence.

There are two ancillary considerations here. First, we know Microsoft can execute on native UI technologies better than it can execute on web technologies. The second argument is that Silverlight developers are likely to migrate to Metro-style development before other types of developers, and they will likely gravitate toward the XAML track because there's a natural evolution there. This will likely increase the volume and quality of community-created content around the XAML track. Working with technology where there is greater community involvement tends to be easier. You should note that it appears that building Windows Store apps in HTML5 seems to be more difficult than building the equivalent apps in XAML, although this statement in particular is relatively subjective.

But what actually *is* the XAML track?

During the development of Longhorn—the codename for what would eventually be called Vista—Microsoft had a new vision for replacing the subsystem that composed the user interface within Windows. This new vision was called Windows Presentation Foundation, or WPF. At the time, the existing Windows UI composition engine, GDI, was extremely old and old-fashioned. WPF was to be a new engine based on a declarative model rather than a programmatic model. (In GDI you have to write code to specifically place UI elements on the screen.) A declarative model would look much more like HTML, which was popular for obvious reasons. Thus, eXtensible Application Markup Language (XAML) was born. WPF was bundled into .NET 3.0 and happens to use DirectX to physically arrange pixels on the screen.

Internally within Microsoft, WPF did not get (and has not gotten) much traction, mainly because it was based on .NET. We've already spoken about how the Windows Division and the Office/Business Division don't like managed code—WPF is entirely a managed code proposition. In hindsight, that core division was never going to use it.

After WPF was released, Microsoft decided that it wanted to compete with Adobe Flash and created a new product called Silverlight to do just that. The idea of Silverlight was that it would run inside a web browser (the Microsoft engineers' vision of this was that it would run as an ActiveX control within IE). At this time, most of the interest in .NET was around line-of-business (LOB) applications that were either built as web applications (ASP.NET) or as desktop applications using Windows Forms; this happens to be a wrapper over GDI. Without internal adoption within Microsoft, or really much need to use it as a replacement for Windows Forms, Silverlight became a common delivery vector for WPF.

As a Flash competitor, Silverlight didn't gain much ground. The timing was off—by this time, Flash was looking past its best and HTML5 was getting much better. Some developers started to adopt Silverlight for internal LOB applications deployed as Silverlight applications running "out of browser" (OOB). What actually happened, though, in the end, was that by the time Silverlight and WPF were effectively deprecated, Silverlight's use as a foundation technology for private LOB apps was quite well established.

Now let's look at what happened with Windows Phone. When Microsoft junked Windows Mobile and moved over to Windows Phone, it needed a UI platform and chose Silverlight. More accurately, it chose Silverlight and cut it down as previously discussed.

"Silverlight for Windows Phone" is the only game in town for building nongame apps on Windows Phone.

So if you loop that in, you have native WPF being used hardly anywhere, Silverlight having no traction on the Web, Silverlight having some traction in private OOB applications, and Silverlight being the only option for Windows Phone.

The next thing is that we have Microsoft wanting to "reboot" the way that we build Windows applications, and to do this it takes WinRT and also takes WPF and divorces it from .NET. As part of this process, Microsoft dumps the WPF name and goes with XAML. XAML then becomes *unmanaged*—that is, native implementation built using WinRT components housed in WinRT libraries. This is why XAML is not called "WPF" in WinRT—the former is unmanaged and the latter is managed.

Importantly, the API remains roughly compatible. For example, in WPF there is a class called `System.Windows.Controls.Button` that represents a button on a page. It so happens that this class has a `Content` property available that can be used for setting the text, and a `Click` event available that is raised when the user clicks it. This is a managed code housed in the `System.Windows.dll` assembly. Over in WinRT/XAML, our button representing class is called `Windows.UI.Xaml.Controls.Button`. This is an unmanaged implementation of the same control—it supports `Content`, `Click`, and other members —but this time it's unmanaged and implemented via a WinRT control referenced through the `Windows.winmd` metadata. (You will find some rough edges to this model, but this "compatible API" approach is the general shape of the solution.)

## XAML Parsing Basics

The killer problem with coming to XAML cold is that if you're used to HTML, it's easy to look at it and wonder why on earth Microsoft didn't just use HTML. To understand why XAML exists, you need to understand the difference between it and HTML.

HTML is a document markup language. The original vision was that you start with some text and annotate it such that areas of the document appear different (e.g., bold, italics) or behave differently (e.g., link to another document). Over time, as a developer community using many different types of technology, we've taken that foundation and turned it into a way of declaring a user interface.

XAML is the other way around. It starts from the basis that you're not trying to describe a document, you're trying to describe a user interface. As it was born to support Windows, what you're actually looking to do is describe windows and user interface elements within. HTML is a document that needs to be parsed and interpreted. XAML is just an object graph expressed as XML.

The following is some sort of XAML. I've removed some of the attributes to make it easier to understand, so this code won't actually work:

```
<Page>

    <StackPanel>
        <Button Content="Foo" />
        <Button Content="Bar" />
    </StackPanel>

</Page>
```

The XAML parser works on a fairly simple basis. It walks the XML Document Object Model (DOM), creating instances of classes as it goes. Starting with the Page, the first element that it reaches is called StackPanel. The XAML parser will find a type with that name (given that it has a list of candidate namespaces to try, which is one of the things I've taken out of the XML in order to make it simpler), create an instance from it, and add it to the Content property of the current UI element under consideration—in this case, the page. This continues; the next element is a Button, which is added to the Children property of the panel. At this point we are looking at an element that has attributes, and the values in the attributes are set to properties found on the control. (This is as per ASP.NET's parsing behavior, incidentally.) The next element is another Button, and so on.

In many ways, this is how an HTML parser works in terms of creating its own internal HTML DOM representation, but seeing as HTML doesn't have to be valid XML, the XAML parser's job is much easier. (And there's very little ancillary information about scripts, alternate views, styles, and so forth like you get with HTML.)

 In this book, it's not my intention to tell you how to build beautiful and wondrous apps using XAML. That would involve going into too much detail on the construction of the user interfaces, whereas my goal is to show you how to get things happening, functionally. Therefore, I'll focus on pointing you to various helpful controls and looking at how to implement common constructs.

## Building a Basic Page

We'll now start building a basic user interface. Specifically we're going to build a registration form that will capture a username, email address, and password, and have a button. It'll look something like Figure 1-8.

*Figure 1-8. The intended layout of our registration form*

## App Bars

You should note that the Register button in Figure 1-8 is probably in the wrong place if we consider Windows 8 UX guidelines. The button should be positioned more properly on the app bar, which is the little panel that winds up from the bottom of the screen when you want to access more options. (You do this either by swiping up or down from the edge of the screen, or using the right mouse button.)

However, the situation is slightly complicated by the fact that if the action relates to the primary purpose of the form, you can put it on the main view. Oftentimes apps don't do this—they leave the button on the app bar but show the app bar rather than asking the user to show it.

This situation is complicated further by some apps—notably the built-in Mail app, which shows the New button, for example, in the top-right of the page.

We don't get into building app bars until Chapter 4. For now, we'll leave the button here. In Chapter 4 we'll discuss proper placement and grouping more fully.

Throughout this book, we're going to be using a publicly accessible service that I've created and hosted on AppHarbor. (If you're unfamiliar with AppHarbor, it's a .NET platform-as-a-service provider that I heartily recommend. You can find it at AppHarbor's website (*http://appharbor.com/*).) The business problem that the service solves was discussed in the preface—to recap, the idea that individuals can report problems in their local environment. For example, the individual might spot some graffiti or litter and wish to have it removed. My reason for choosing this "problem domain" is that it contains all of the common components of mobile apps—specifically, working with accounts, taking and uploading photos, reviewing historical data, and capturing location. What we'll implement in this next part of our work is the account registration. We'll capture the new user's details and send it up to the server, whereupon the user can perform other functions such as creating new issues. I'll be referring to the application as StreetFoo.

To get started, we need a new solution and project within Visual Studio. As a rule, I like to create a blank solution first, and then add projects into that solution. (I find this creates the most logical and natural folder structure on disk.) However you do it, create a new Visual C# by navigating to Windows Store→Blank App project and call it StreetFoo.Client.UI. Figure 1-9 illustrates.

*Figure 1-9. The structure of a newly created Windows Store→Blank App project*

In Figure 1-9, the assets are relatively obvious—these are the various graphics that we need to drive the application. (We'll look at these later.) We already discussed the References node earlier in this chapter. Properties and its attendant *AssemblyInfo.cs* are unchanged from .NET.

*App.xaml* is a cross between the *Global.asax* file in ASP.NET and the void static main method used to boot Windows Forms and console application executables. The boilerplate code in here responds to the Launched event and creates the first page to view. (We'll learn more about application lifecycle events in Chapter 14.)

*MainPage.xaml* is the default page that gets created. We'll delete this and replace it with *RegisterPage.xml* shortly.

*Package.appxmanifest* contains metadata about the application that affects how the application is deployed (i.e., installed) and what it can do. (If you happen to have done Android development, it's analogous to how manifests work on that platform.) We'll see various facets of this as we go, but for now we don't need to worry about it. Likewise, we also don't need to worry about the *.pfx* file down at the bottom. This is used for signing, but we'll talk more about that in Chapter 15.

Out of the box, a standard project template doesn't really do much—all you get is an app that will install and show a blank page. However, there is a sort of "subproject" that we can trigger, and when we do that we get a whole load of additional templates and functionality. This additional functionality does things like adding a set of default styles, creating a page layout that has a default header, and creating pages that supports even the smallest window size for this type of application. (We talk about this more in Chapter 12.)

To access this extra functionality, first delete *MainPage.xaml* and then add a new item to the project of type Basic Page and call it *RegisterPage.xaml*. Visual Studio will prompt you to add the missing files.

When we do this, the Windows Store app project template will add a new folder called *Common* to the project, and this folder contains a whole bunch of new stuff that supports the special templates. The *readme* file in this folder offers a stark warning that developers are not supposed to change the contents of the files in this folder, as it'll break the VS project template. You can take this with a grain of salt; like all these things, you have to tread relatively carefully, but it's hard to do any real damage.

I mentioned that the code in *App.xaml* was responsible for starting the application. The code that was created on project inception contains a reference to the `MainPage` class. However, we deleted the `MainPage` class from the project when we deleted *Main Page.xaml*. We need to replace the reference with a reference to `RegisterPage`.

Open up *App.xaml* and change the `OnLaunched` method to use `RegisterPage`:

```
        protected override void OnLaunched(LaunchActivatedEventArgs e)
        {

#if DEBUG
            if (System.Diagnostics.Debugger.IsAttached)
            {
                this.DebugSettings.EnableFrameRateCounter = true;
            }
#endif

            Frame rootFrame = Window.Current.Content as Frame;

            // Do not repeat app initialization when the Window already
            // has content, just ensure that the window is active
            if (rootFrame == null)
```

```
{
    // Create a Frame to act as the navigation context and navigate
    // to the first page
    rootFrame = new Frame();

    if (e.PreviousExecutionState ==
        ApplicationExecutionState.Terminated)
    {
        //TODO: Load state from previously suspended application
    }

    // Place the frame in the current Window
    Window.Current.Content = rootFrame;
}

if (rootFrame.Content == null)
{
    // When the navigation stack isn't restored navigate to the
    // first page, configuring the new page by passing required
    // information as a navigation parameter
    if (!rootFrame.Navigate(typeof(RegisterPage), e.Arguments))
    {
        throw new Exception("Failed to create initial page");
    }
}
// Ensure the current window is active
Window.Current.Activate();
}
```

If you run the project, you should see something like Figure 1-10.

The XAML for that page is quite verbose, so I won't reproduce it all here. However, here's an important part of the layout that we need to consider:

```
<Grid>
    <Grid.RowDefinitions>
        <RowDefinition Height="140"/>
        <RowDefinition Height="*"/>
    </Grid.RowDefinitions>

            <!-- Back button and page title -->
    <Grid>
        <Grid.ColumnDefinitions>
            <ColumnDefinition Width="120"/>
            <ColumnDefinition Width="*"/>
        </Grid.ColumnDefinitions>
        <AppBarButton x:Name="backButton" Icon="Back" Height="95"
                    Margin="10,46,10,0"
                    Command="{Binding NavigationHelper.GoBackCommand,
                    ElementName=pageRoot}"
                    Visibility="{Binding IsEnabled, Converter=
                    {StaticResource BooleanToVisibilityConverter},
                    RelativeSource={RelativeSource Mode=Self}}"
```

*Figure 1-10. Preview of our newly created page*

```
                              AutomationProperties.Name="Back"
                              AutomationProperties.AutomationId="BackButton"
                              AutomationProperties.ItemType="Navigation Button"/>
            <TextBlock x:Name="pageTitle" Text="{StaticResource AppName}"
                              Style="{StaticResource HeaderTextBlockStyle}"
                              Grid.Column="1"
                        IsHitTestVisible="false" TextWrapping="NoWrap"
                              VerticalAlignment="Bottom" Margin="0,0,30,40"/>
        </Grid>

    <!-- deleted for brevity... -->

    </Grid>
```

This is where we can start to see the divergence between XAML and HTML. Back in the day we would have laid out this HTML using TABLE controls, and if you look at that XAML from that perspective we don't have any TR or TD elements to help us. (Of course, now we're supposed to do that sort of layout using DIV elements and attendant CSS declarations, but I digress.) What we have instead is one Grid control inside of another. We also have some magic going on where we define RowDefinition values to lay out the rows, and ColumnDefinition values to lay out the columns. You'll also notice that we can put elements inside of grid cells by using Grid.Column attributes on the controls. HTML and CSS, this is not.

Before we go on to create the form, we want to change the header. At the moment, the header is defined in a TextBlock control, with a Text value that refers to a StaticRe source.

Here's a portion of the XAML markup that was created when *RegisterPage.xaml* was created:

```
<!-- Back button and page title -->
<Grid>
    <Grid.ColumnDefinitions>
        <ColumnDefinition Width="120"/>
        <ColumnDefinition Width="*"/>
    </Grid.ColumnDefinitions>
    <AppBarButton x:Name="backButton" Icon="Back" Height="95"
                  Margin="10,46,10,0"
                  Command="{Binding NavigationHelper.GoBackCommand,
                  ElementName=pageRoot}"
                  Visibility="{Binding IsEnabled, Converter=
                  {StaticResource BooleanToVisibilityConverter},
                  RelativeSource={RelativeSource Mode=Self}}"
                  AutomationProperties.Name="Back"
                  AutomationProperties.AutomationId="BackButton"
                  AutomationProperties.ItemType="Navigation Button"/>
    <TextBlock x:Name="pageTitle" Text="{StaticResource AppName}"
               Style="{StaticResource HeaderTextBlockStyle}"
               Grid.Column="1"
               IsHitTestVisible="false" TextWrapping="NoWrap"
               VerticalAlignment="Bottom" Margin="0,0,30,40"/>
</Grid>
```

When attribute values are surrounded by braces in that way, this tells the XAML parser that regular processing needs to stop and something else needs to happen. These are called *markup extensions*. StaticResource is one type of extension. In the next section, we'll meet Binding. (There's one of these references in the Button control in that snippet that happens to show or hide the default back button depending on whether the page is at the top of the stack or not.) For now, replace the Text value with Register. Here's the code:

```
<!-- Back button and page title -->
<Grid>
    <Grid.ColumnDefinitions>
        <ColumnDefinition Width="120"/>
        <ColumnDefinition Width="*"/>
    </Grid.ColumnDefinitions>
    <AppBarButton x:Name="backButton" Icon="Back" Height="95"
                  Margin="10,46,10,0"
                  Command="{Binding NavigationHelper.GoBackCommand,
                  ElementName=pageRoot}"
                  Visibility="{Binding IsEnabled, Converter=
                  {StaticResource BooleanToVisibilityConverter},
                  RelativeSource={RelativeSource Mode=Self}}"
                  AutomationProperties.Name="Back"
                  AutomationProperties.AutomationId="BackButton"
                  AutomationProperties.ItemType="Navigation Button"/>
    <TextBlock x:Name="pageTitle" Text="Register" Style="{StaticResource
               HeaderTextBlockStyle}" Grid.Column="1"
               IsHitTestVisible="false" TextWrapping="NoWrap"
               VerticalAlignment="Bottom" Margin="0,0,30,40"/>
</Grid>
```

 You'll see the WYSIWYG preview update as you make this change.

Next we'll restructure the page so that we have a single Grid control that occupies the whole page. The default layout is designed for views that scroll off the right side of the page. What we want for our form is just a place to enter some values underneath the caption. Therefore, if we redefine the grid with a row at the top 140 pixels high and a column on the left 120 pixels wide, we can put the back button in the top-left cell, the label in the top-right, and the form in the bottom-right. (We need the back button, as ultimately when we start the app we'll present the logon page and have a button that takes us into the registration page.)

This is now where we can use the StackPanel control. This is a very useful control for laying our controls vertically (the default) or horizontally. We'll also use TextBlock controls (which are labels), TextBox, PasswordBox, and Button controls. Here's the modified markup for our form. Figure 1-11 shows what we're aiming for.

```xml
<local:StreetFooPage
    x:Name="pageRoot"
    x:Class="StreetFoo.Client.UI.RegisterPage"
    xmlns="http://schemas.microsoft.com/winfx/2006/xaml/presentation"
    xmlns:x="http://schemas.microsoft.com/winfx/2006/xaml"
    xmlns:local="using:StreetFoo.Client.UI"
    xmlns:common="using:StreetFoo.Client.UI.Common"
    xmlns:d="http://schemas.microsoft.com/expression/blend/2008"
    xmlns:mc="http://schemas.openxmlformats.org/markup-compatibility/2006"
    mc:Ignorable="d">

  <Grid>

        <Grid.RowDefinitions>
            <RowDefinition Height="140"/>
            <RowDefinition Height="*"/>
        </Grid.RowDefinitions>
        <Grid.ColumnDefinitions>
            <ColumnDefinition Width="120"/>
            <ColumnDefinition Width="*"/>
        </Grid.ColumnDefinitions>

        <!-- Back button and page title -->
        <AppBarButton x:Name="backButton" Icon="Back" Height="95"
                      Margin="10,46,10,0"
                      Command="{Binding NavigationHelper.GoBackCommand,
                      ElementName=pageRoot}"
                      Visibility="{Binding IsEnabled, Converter={StaticResource
                      BooleanToVisibilityConverter}, RelativeSource=
                      {RelativeSource Mode=Self}}"
                      AutomationProperties.Name="Back"
                      AutomationProperties.AutomationId="BackButton"
                      AutomationProperties.ItemType="Navigation Button"/>
        <TextBlock x:Name="pageTitle" Text="Register" Style="{StaticResource
                   HeaderTextBlockStyle}" Grid.Column="1"
                   IsHitTestVisible="false" TextWrapping="NoWrap"
                   VerticalAlignment="Bottom" Margin="0,0,30,40"/>

        <!-- Registration form -->
        <StackPanel Grid.Row="1" Grid.Column="1">

            <TextBlock Text="Username"></TextBlock>
            <TextBox HorizontalAlignment="Left" Width="400" Text="{Binding
             Username, Mode=TwoWay}"/>

            <TextBlock Text="Email"></TextBlock>
            <TextBox HorizontalAlignment="Left" Width="400" Text="{Binding
             Email, Mode=TwoWay}"/>
```

```
<TextBlock Text="Password"></TextBlock>
<PasswordBox HorizontalAlignment="Left" Width="400" Password="
  {Binding Password, Mode=TwoWay}"/>

<TextBlock Text="Confirm password"></TextBlock>
<PasswordBox HorizontalAlignment="Left" Width="400" Password="
  {Binding Confirm, Mode=TwoWay}"/>

<Button Content="Register"></Button>

        </StackPanel>

    <!-- VisualStateManager element deleted for clarity ... -->

</Grid>
</local:StreetFooPage>
```

There are two things that are worth calling out in this code. We've used Binding extensions to supply values for the Text and Password properties of the edit controls. (An important part here is the specification of Mode=TwoWay. This pushes the data back from the UI into the view-model when it changes.) We'll come to that. Likewise we'll also cover how to make something happen when that button is clicked via commands.

Run the project now and you'll see the registration page appear. Figure 1-11 illustrates.

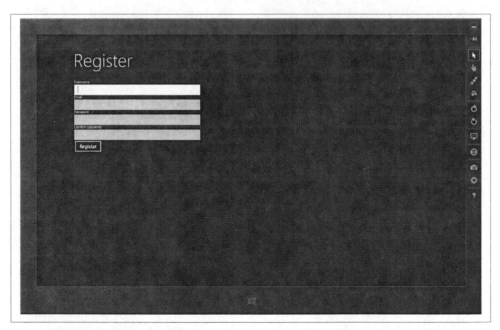

*Figure 1-11. Our registration form*

Now that we have the markup for our page, let's turn our attention to making it do something.

## Implementing MVVM

In this book, we're going to implement our user interface using the Model/View/View-Model (MVVM) pattern. The intention of MVVM is to create a separation of concerns between the data your application needs to manipulate and the view that's presented to the user.

The simplest way to build a user interface is not to introduce any separation of concerns at all. Imagine you have a database containing customer information and you have a form that allows you to edit a single customer. Without any separation of concerns, you can build one enormous and spaghettified class that has logic to load the data from the database, logic to display it on the screen, the ability to listen for a "save" button click, logic to validate the data, and logic to save the changes back, all mashed up together. This approach of lumping everything together is not clever for a number of reasons, not least of all because it doesn't promote reuse of the database and validation logic, and it doesn't support (straightforward) unit testing. By splitting up the capability into separate classes—such as one that knows how to get data in and out of the database, and one that knows how to drive the user interface—you get better reuse and more straightforward unit testing.

 Just in case it's not clear, don't mash together code without separation of concerns—it's almost always a really bad idea.

The first place you end up when you try to formalize an architecture to separate data persistence concerns and the user interface is a pattern called Model-View-Controller, or MVC. In MVC you have the persistent data part represented in the *model*. You then have the physical *view*. Finally you have the *controller* whose job it is to tie the model and view together. (For example, the controller might trigger the action "when this button is clicked, pull the input off of the UI, run this validation routine, and then update the model.") Figure 1 12 illustrates the structure. This diagram is simplified—usually you would have interfaces between the controller and the page class to abstract away the page's implementation.

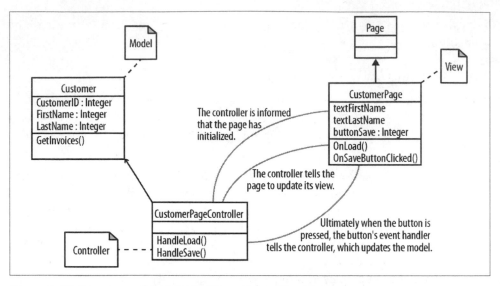

*Figure 1-12. Structure of the Model-View-Controller pattern*

Earlier I said that the model "knows how to get the data in and out of the database." Really the model is the in-memory representation of the persistent data that we're trying to manage. In an (old-fashioned) data-centric approach, the model would know how to drive the database. In a (more modern) object-orientated approach, the model is—as the name implies—a set of classes that "models" the application-specific problem domain. For example, if we need to represent a customer, we'll have a class called Customer. If a customer has orders, they'll be a method in the Customer class with the capability to return a collection of Order objects.

## WPF and Silverlight

With WPF, the various Silverlight implementations, and now XAML, Microsoft's recommendation is that we use MVVM. In fact, the Windows Store app community almost always follows this recommendation, and it's my recommendation, too.

The model part remains as it is in MVC—that is, a representation of the data that we're trying to manipulate. The view also remains as it is—that is, a representation of the UI elements that make up the display. The view-model is different. This is an amalgam of the controller functionality and a specialized façade on the model. In our basic "single page to edit a customer" example, it's likely our specialized façade will be a one-to-one mapping with a Customer instance, but it doesn't have to be. It could be that we need to invent an entirely new set of classes to represent a view's data by bundling and aggregating a number of pieces of data drawn from the model. (Incidentally, the view-model's data doesn't necessarily have to map to the persistent application data—in fact, in the first instance of looking at this, it won't, because we're going to use it to capture the registration details for our new account and that's something that won't exist in the local persistent dataset at all.)

A key motivation for introducing MVVM with WPF/Silverlight was to get around one of the really tedious aspects of programming user interfaces—namely, getting data out of the model and onto the controls on the screen. If you're trying to build a form, continually writing code like `textFirstName.Content = Customer.FirstName` and its reverse (`Customer.FirstName = textFirstName.Content`) is seriously boring. What we can do in WPF/Silverlight—more importantly, what we can do in WinRT's XAML implementation—is create bindings and allow the framework to do that for us. By setting the `Content` property of a `TextBox` control in XAML to `{Binding Customer.First Name}`, we don't have to write the tedious code to shuttle the data in and out of the view-model. This process is called *data binding*, and it's been around since the very first versions of Visual Basic. You mark up your UI with instructions as to where specific pieces of data come from and allow your framework to do the heavy lifting.

What any form of separation gives us in addition to this is the ability to do unit testing, which we'll talk about now.

---

## A Preliminary Discussion About Unit Testing

We've mentioned unit testing a lot, and I'm going to assume that readers of this book know what it is.

In this book, we're going to actually do some unit testing in the next chapter, but this isn't a "test-driven" book. When we do other work, we will be working in a non-test-driven way (i.e., just hacking code together until it works).

In the real world, my recommendation is that you always, *always* use unit testing in your work and get as close as possible to a fully *test-driven development* (TDD) mode of operation. In fact, I'd go further than that and say if you're not unit testing, you're not really writing software at all. If you haven't yet gone over to the "dark side" and really felt the benefits of unit testing, take some time out to do so as part of your professional learning.

In a book, however, unit testing is a pain because, as an author, you end up focusing more on taking the reader through building the unit tests than getting things working. (Unit testing isn't great for proof-of-concept work, and books are really about presenting a decent collection of interlinked proofs of concept.) Thus, I don't use unit testing when presenting development activities in a book. That said, it's important that whatever we do is unit testable, which is why in the next chapter we'll actually build some unit tests —as a proof of concept, as it were.

---

## MVVM Structure and Inversion of Control

In this section, we'll go through the process of building a basic pattern that we can reuse throughout our work whenever we need to implement a view.

The view itself will always be a XAML page. We'll always create our view classes by inheriting from the special `LayoutPage` implementation that Visual Studio gave us when we first created our *RegisterPage.xaml*. We've already built our `RegisterPage`, so that will represent the *V* in our MVVM implementation.

In each example of using this pattern in the book, the model will be different. In our specific `RegisterPage` case, we don't really have a model. What we're trying to do is collect a set of values that we can pass up to our server via an HTTPS call—specifically, we need to capture the username, email address, and password, and confirm password values as per the user interface shown previously in Figure 1-10. Thus—and hopefully not in a way that's confusing—our first MVVM implementation won't have a specific *M*. We'll assume the data stored in the view-model will be good enough. Properly, any model should map down to a persistent data store, but we won't see persistent data until Chapter 3.

Our view-model then will reside in its own class. The convention we'll use throughout is *ViewClass*ViewModel, so in this instance we'll create a class called `RegisterPage ViewModel`. This is the *VM* in our MVVM.

But there's more. Because I want to demonstrate how we can unit test our registration logic and attendant UI, I want to demonstrate a more complex and production-appropriate architecture.

Ideally, we want to create not just separation but isolation between the view and the view-model. The view should not really care what class it's driving. Likewise, the view-model should not care what view is driving it. This last point is particularly important because what we're actually going to do ultimately is build a unit test that fakes the view in order to exercise the function of the view-model. To achieve this, we'll design our architecture so that we have an `IRegisterPageViewModel` interface and insist that everything works with the interface rather than working with the concrete view-model instance directly. Because we're being all "enterprise architect" about it, we'll create `ViewModel` and `IViewModel` types—it's always helpful to have abstract base classes to help cement semantic understanding. (In fact, we are actually going to bake some important functionality into base types as we go forward.)

Another thing we'll need is a way to poke backward from the view-model into the view. For this reason we'll create an `IViewModelHost` interface. The view-model will be given an object that implements this interface on instantiation.

This is slightly against the "rules" of MVVM (as it breaks some of the abstraction), but we'll talk more about this when we get there. This bending of the rules makes life much more straightforward.

Altogether, we'll have a basic structure that looks like Figure 1-13. I've intentionally left attributes and operations out of this UML sketch, as we've yet to discuss details on behavior. What this diagram shows you are the basic pieces that we need to build.

There are two things to note about this diagram. First, there's no model—the left side shows the view-model, the right side the view. As `RegisterPage` doesn't need persistent on-disk storage, there is no model. Second, there appears to be a big disconnect between the view-model and the view. This is because the communication between these two components is done with XAML data binding magic, and this is not shown.

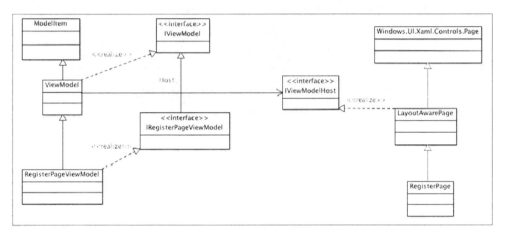

Figure 1-13. Static structure sketch of the view, view-model, and associated base types

 Throughout this book, whenever I present UML it's never intended to be complete. UML is always presented as a sketch with details omitted.

Next, we'll properly flesh out the `RegisterPageViewModel` class.

## RegisterPageViewModel

The most basic thing any of the view-model classes are going to do is store data. The most basic way for a class to store data is in an instance variable—in .NET parlance, this is, as we know, a *field*.

XAML's data binding subsystem is built on the idea that we should implement an interface on any object involved in data binding, the purpose of which is to provide a conduit through which the data binding subsystem can be notified of changes. This interface is called INotifyPropertyChanged and it contains a single member, which happens to be an event called PropertyChanged.

INotifyPropertyChanged means that you don't need to handle any of this yourself manually. So, one way to build a view-model is to do this:

```
// This code is just for illustration, you won't find it in the
// samples code...

public class FooViewModel : INotifyPropertyChanged
{
    // hold a value...
    private string _bar;

    // event for the change...
    public event PropertyChangedEventHandler PropertyChanged;

    // property...
    public string Bar
    {
        get
        {
            return _bar;
        }
        set
        {
            _bar = value;
            this.OnPropertyChanged(new PropertyChangedEventArgs("Bar"));
        }
    }

    public virtual void OnPropertyChanged(PropertyChangedEventArgs e)
    {
        if (this.PropertyChanged != null)
            this.PropertyChanged(this, e);
    }
}
```

The problem with this approach is that it's immensely tedious—unless you're using code generation, you're going to spend half your working day manually building properties and wiring up the event raising code.

---

A better approach—and the one we're going to use—is to create a base class with a `Dictionary<string, object>` instance to hold a "bucket" of values, and a generic way of handling the storage and the event so that we don't have to do all the tedious work involved in raising change notifications. In the view-model, we'll extend this base class and specialize it by adding properties to get and set the specific model implementation's data.

 In fact, what we'll end up doing is building a class called `ModelItem` that will contain this basic functionality and then extending that into `ViewModel`. We'll also use `ModelItem` at various other times in the book.

A really clever .NET capability we can use here is the `CallerMemberNameAttribute` class.

 As we go, I generally won't call out namespaces; it makes the discussion overly long. (As it happens, `CallerMemberNameAttribute` can be found in `System.Runtime.CompilerServices`.) If you're keying in the code in the book and can't find a reference, right-click on it and select Resolve from the context menu, and Visual Studio will tell you the namespace where it can be found.

This will automatically set the value of any optional parameter that it is decorated with to the member name of the caller. In the following contrived example, the value of the `magicArgument` argument passed to `ShowMeTheCallerName` will be set to the string value `"MagicCallingProperty"`:

```
private void ShowMeTheCallerName([CallerMemberName] string magicArgument = null)
{
  Debug.WriteLine(magicArgument);
}

private string MagicCallingProperty
{
  set
  {
    ShowMeTheCallerName();
  }
}
```

That's a silly example; a better one is to use `CallerMemberNameAttribute` to automatically generate keys into a dictionary of values. By adding helper methods to our `View Model` class that use `CallerMemberNameAttribute`, we can automatically generate keys that can be used to access the dictionary based on the names of properties that call those helper methods.

One thing we want to do is put all of our application logic in a separate "UI agnostic" assembly that we link into our main app project. I wanted to show how you could do this mainly so that you knew you could, but also so that we have an increased separation when we come to look at the unit testing.

First off, within the solution create a new Windows Store→Class Library project called StreetFoo.Client. Then, right-click on the StreetFoo.Client.UI project, choose Add Reference, navigate to the Solution "tab," and add a reference back to StreetFoo.Client. (This process is exactly how you always would have done it with normal .NET projects, but it's important to choose Windows Store→Class Library as the project type.)

First off, remember how we designed our architecture to have an `IViewModel` interface? This will need some mechanism by which it can initialize the view-model, which we'll achieve using an `Initialize` method. Here's the implementation that also happens to extend `INotifyPropertyChanged`:

```
public interface IViewModel : INotifyPropertyChanged
{
void Initialize(IViewModelHost host);
}
```

`ViewModel` is going to need to be able to understand `IViewModelHost`. We're going to add to this now and again as we work through the book, but for now the implementation can be empty:

```
public interface IViewModelHost
{
}
```

We're now at the part where we can create our base class that's able to handle ad hoc data storage and raise notification changes through `INotifyPropertyChanged`. We'll call this class `ModelItem`. Don't worry about the naming for now—it will become apparent why it has that name later:

```
// base class for holding ad hoc data and issuing notification changes...
public abstract class ModelItem : INotifyPropertyChanged
{
    private Dictionary<string, object> Values { get; set; }

    protected ModelItem()
    {
        this.Values = new Dictionary<string, object>();
    }

    public event PropertyChangedEventHandler PropertyChanged;

    protected T GetValue<T>([CallerMemberName] string name = null)
    {
        if (this.Values.ContainsKey(name))
            return (T)this.Values[name];
```

```
        else
            return default(T);
    }

    protected void SetValue(object value, [CallerMemberName] string name
    = null)
    {
        // set...
        this.Values[name] = value;

        // notify...
        this.OnPropertyChanged(new PropertyChangedEventArgs(name));
    }

    protected void OnPropertyChanged([CallerMemberName] string name = null)
    {
        this.OnPropertyChanged(new PropertyChangedEventArgs(name));
    }

    protected virtual void OnPropertyChanged(PropertyChangedEventArgs e)
    {
        if (this.PropertyChanged != null)
            this.PropertyChanged(this, e);
    }
}
```

Here's the first draft implementation of ViewModel. This extends ModelItem, but also maintains a reference back to the view-model host:

```
public abstract class ViewModel : ModelItem, IViewModel
{
    //  somewhere to hold the host...
    protected IViewModelHost Host { get; private set; }

    public ViewModel()
    {
    }

    public void Initialize(IViewModelHost host)
    {
                    this.Host = host;
    }
}
```

This will make more sense if we build RegisterPageViewModel, so here that is; then, I'll go through all three classes:

```
public class RegisterPageViewModel : ViewModel, IRegisterPageViewModel
{
    public RegisterPageViewModel()
    {
    }
```

```csharp
public string Username
{
    get
    {
        // the magic CallerMemberNameAttribute automatically maps this
        // to a hash key of "Username"...
        return this.GetValue<string>();
    }
    set
    {
        // likewise, CallerMemberNameAttribute works here too...
        this.SetValue(value);
    }
}

public string Email
{
    get
    {
        return this.GetValue<string>();
    }
    set
    {
        this.SetValue(value);
    }
}

public string Password
{
    get
    {
        return this.GetValue<string>();
    }
    set
    {
        this.SetValue(value);
    }
}

public string Confirm
{
    get
    {
        return this.GetValue<string>();
    }
    set
    {
        this.SetValue(value);
    }
}
```

```
        }
    }
```

Hopefully from that you can see the simplicity of this approach. The properties don't have to concern themselves with wiring themselves into the base ModelItem class's storage mechanism; .NET is doing that for us. When we call any of the SetValue methods, the dictionary key is inferred from the name; this is used in the first instance to set the value in the wrapped Values instance, and in the second instance it's used in the event signaling. GetValue is implemented such that it doesn't care whether the value is in the dictionary and will return a default value if the item is missing.

In the next chapter, we're going to start being clever about how we hook the view-model and the view together. (In this chapter, for simplicity we're just going to "new up" a RegisterPageViewModel and give it to the view to use.) Essentially we want a loose coupling between the view-model and the view. For this reason, we'll always create a companion interface for every view-model that we'll build—in this case, IRegisterPageViewModel. The rule with these interfaces is that they contain just a "map" of the public properties used in the binding operations. We've got four properties used for binding: Username, Email, Password, and Confirm. Such interfaces also need to extend IViewModel. Therefore, our interface has just those properties, specifically:

```
public interface IRegisterPageViewModel : IViewModel
{
    string Username
    {
        get;
        set;
    }

    string Email
    {
        get;
        set;
    }

    string Password
    {
        get;
        set;
    }

    string Confirm
    {
        get;
        set;
    }

}
```

Now that we've put that together, let's have a go at running some data through it.

## Handling errors

In this section we're going to build a helper class that will assist us in moving error messages around the system so that we can do something with them. In terms of what we actually do with errors when they occur, in this book we're typically just going to render them on the screen.

This particular functionality is reasonably contrived, as there are most likely better ways to do this in production applications; however, this is one of those things where we have to compromise in order to fit our work into a book. Be aware, then, that this is probably one of the rougher bits if you're looking to bring this work into production.

In the first go-through of this class we're going to use it to gather a collection of error strings. In the next chapter we're going to also use it to store an exception.

The class itself is simple:

```
public class ErrorBucket
{
    private List<string> Errors { get; set; }

    public ErrorBucket()
    {
        this.Errors = new List<string>();
    }

    public void AddError(string error)
    {
        this.Errors.Add(error);
    }

    public bool HasErrors
    {
        get
        {
            return this.Errors.Any();
        }
    }
}
```

How might we use this? Well, in relation to our `RegisterPageViewModel` we're going to use it as part of the validation. Here's the `Validation` method that needs to be part of the view-model:

```
// add method to RegisterPageViewModel...
private void Validate(ErrorBucket errors)
{
    // do basic data presence validation...
    if (string.IsNullOrEmpty(Username))
        errors.AddError("Username is required.");
    if (string.IsNullOrEmpty(Email))
        errors.AddError("Email is required.");
```

```
        if (string.IsNullOrEmpty(Password))
            errors.AddError("Password is required.");
        if (string.IsNullOrEmpty(Confirm))
            errors.AddError("Confirm password is required.");

        // check the passwords...
        if (!(string.IsNullOrEmpty(Password)) &&
            this.Password != this.Confirm)
            errors.AddError("The passwords do not match.");
    }
```

The functionality there is straightforward—as we find errors, we ask the `ErrorBucket` instance to store them for us.

Of course, storing the errors is no good unless we can show them to the user, so let's look at that now.

### Basic alerts

In the remainder of this chapter, all we're going to do is display a success message on the screen, or show the validation errors. The part where we actually make the call up to the server will be in the next chapter.

The Windows Store analog of a normal Windows message box is accessed via the `MessageDialog` class. Its basic usage is easy enough. However, to make it easier to access this method, I'm proposing creating extension methods in the base XAML `Page` class. These will then be accessible from any class that extends `Page`, including `LayoutAware Page`, the base class for our pages. We'll call the class that contains these extension methods `PageExtender`.

 Personally, I'm a huge fan of extension methods—they can really help you to build out standard framework functionality into your own specialized way of working. We'll be using them quite a bit in the work we do in this book.

One difference to consider between the `MessageDialog` class's behavior and a regular Windows message box is that the display operation is asynchronous. Typically we're used to these blocking so that execution of our program's code doesn't continue until the pop up is dismissed. This isn't the case with `MessageDialog`. We're about to go into a much deeper discussion about asynchronous calls, so don't worry about this behavior for now—just be aware of it.

In `PageExtender` we're going to build two overloads of the `ShowAlertAsync` method. One will take a string, and the other will take an `ErrorBucket` instance. Shortly we'll build a method in `ErrorBucket` that will return a string for display. Here's the code:

```
internal static class PageExtender
{
    internal static Task ShowAlertAsync(this IViewModelHost page,
ErrorBucket errors)
    {
        return ShowAlertAsync(page, errors.GetErrorsAsString());
    }

    internal static Task ShowAlertAsync(this IViewModelHost page,
    string message)
    {
        // show...
        MessageDialog dialog = new MessageDialog(message != null ? message :
        string.Empty);
        return dialog.ShowAsync().AsTask();
    }
}
```

The GetErrorsAsString method in ErrorBucket looks like this:

```
// add method to ErrorBucket...
public string GetErrorsAsString()
{
    StringBuilder builder = new StringBuilder();
    foreach (string error in this.Errors)
    {
        if (builder.Length > 0)
            builder.Append("\r\n");
        builder.Append(error);
    }

    return builder.ToString();
}
```

Now that we can in theory get something on the screen, let's pull all of the loose ends together and actually get something on the screen.

## Creating the View-Model and Running the App

The first loose end we have to tie up is the part that responds to the button click and then physically invokes a method in RegisterPageViewModel called DoRegistration. This will validate the data that's been keyed in by the user, and then display a message on the screen either showing the errors or confirming success. In the next chapter we're actually going to make the call to the server. In this chapter, we're going to fake the call.

The way that all of this is tied together using MVVM is via *commands*. The idea of commands is that rather than physically linking the view and the view-model together, you bind command objects that are invoked by user interface controls.

Somewhere on your view-model you will have a collection of private methods that actually do things. (Remember, the point of MVVM is to isolate code so that we're not using codebehind-style code in the pages.) As a foundation to building comments, WinRT defines an interface called `ICommand` with a method in it called `Execute`. Through some plumbing that I'll explain in a moment, you can rig your XAML such that when a button is clicked, that `Execute` method is called. You then defer down to your private methods, whereupon the magic happens.

For example, and with much code omitted for brevity, this code shows how we can create something called a `DelegateCommand`, which contains an anonymous method that refers to our concrete `DoRegistration` method. Ultimately, were we to actually run this example, something would invoke `RegisterCommand` from outside the view-model:

```
public class RegisterPageViewModel : ViewModel, IRegisterPageViewModel
{
    public ICommand RegisterCommand { get; private set; }

    public RegisterPageViewModel(IViewModelHost host)
        : base(host)
    {
        this.RegisterCommand = new DelegateCommand((args) =>
            DoRegistration());
    }

    // code omitted...

    private void DoRegistration()
    {
        // magic happens...
    }
}
```

We'll build `DelegateCommand` in a moment, but the idea of it is that it's a vanilla implementation of `ICommand` whose only function is to defer to our proper method.

In our XAML, we can use regular data binding operations like those we've already seen in order to associate the `Command` property of the button up to that `RegisterCommand` instance exposed by the view-model, like so:

```
<!-- Registration form -->
<StackPanel Grid.Row="1" Grid.Column="1">

    <TextBlock Text="Username"></TextBlock>
    <TextBox HorizontalAlignment="Left" Width="400" Text="{Binding
Username, Mode=TwoWay}"/>

    <TextBlock Text="Email"></TextBlock>
    <TextBox HorizontalAlignment="Left" Width="400" Text="{Binding
Email, Mode=TwoWay}"/>

    <TextBlock Text="Password"></TextBlock>
    <PasswordBox HorizontalAlignment="Left" Width="400"
Password="{Binding Password, Mode=TwoWay}"/>
```

```xml
<TextBlock Text="Confirm password"></TextBlock>
<PasswordBox HorizontalAlignment="Left" Width="400"
Password="{Binding Confirm, Mode=TwoWay}"/>

<Button Content="Register" Command="{Binding RegisterCommand}">
</Button>

</StackPanel>
```

For reasons that will become clearer when we get to unit testing, it's important that our interface keeps in step with our XAML, so we need to add `RegisterCommand` to the interface:

```csharp
public interface IRegisterPageViewModel
{
    string Username
    {
        get;
        set;
    }

    string Email
    {
        get;
        set;
    }

    string Password
    {
        get;
        set;
    }

    string Confirm
    {
        get;
        set;
    }

    ICommand RegisterCommand
    {
        get;
    }
}
```

So all of that would work if we had an implementation of `DelegateCommand`. Let's do that now.

The main capability of `ICommand` lies in the `Execute` method, but there is an ancillary capability in the `CanExecute` method. On more sophisticated UIs, this can be used to enable or disable UI elements depending on the state of the model. We're not going to worry about that—we're just going to implement the basics. Here it is:

```
public class DelegateCommand : ICommand
{
    private Action<object> Handler { get; set; }

    public event EventHandler CanExecuteChanged = null;

    public DelegateCommand(Action<object> handler)
    {
        this.Handler = handler;
    }

    public bool CanExecute(object parameter)
    {
        return true;
    }

    public void Execute(object parameter)
    {
        Handler(parameter);
    }
}
```

This code will compile with a warning—don't worry about that. In the version of the code you can download, I've smoothed out all the warnings. I've left that code out of the book for clarity, however.

And that's it. All we have to do now is get to a point where we can call our method.

## IViewModelHost

The important thing in MVVM is to work at keeping a separation between the view-model and the view. (Keeping a separation between the model and the view-model is also important.) Moreover, we need to ensure that the view-model doesn't actually become dependent on any user interface technology—it needs to instruct the application's view from time to time, but it can't have any direct control. (In a way, you can think about this as the view-model *hinting* that something needs to happen, but allowing the view architecture to decide what to actually do.) A prime motivation for this is that the view-models need to be fully unit testable and you have absolutely no user interface when running in a unit test container, but we'll get to that in the next chapter.

There are some who may not like this approach of being able to get back from the view-model to the view container. Admittedly, from a purist's perspective it's not ideal. The reason I chose to continue down this route was that pragmatically it felt appropriate.

In our architecture discussion we mooted the idea of using IViewModelHost. (We also accept one of these in the constructor for the abstract ViewModel class.) The first purpose of this will be to display a message box. Here's the interface; you'll notice that it maps onto the methods of our PageExtender class, which is intentional:

```
public interface IViewModelHost
{
    Task ShowAlertAsync(ErrorBucket errors);
    Task ShowAlertAsync(string message);
}
```

We'll implement this interface in our StreetFooPage class, as we'll need this throughout our work. However, because we implemented our alert methods as extension methods, we'll need to implement the methods of IViewModelHost explicitly, as follows. (The problem here is that the compiler can't see the methods resolve through cleanly, even though they do. We need to shim it.)

```
// add methods to StreetFooPage...
Task IViewModelHost.ShowAlertAsync(ErrorBucket errors)
{
    return this.ShowAlertAsync(errors);
}

Task IViewModelHost.ShowAlertAsync(string message)
{
    return this.ShowAlertAsync(message);
}
```

### Building out the DoRegistration method

In this chapter, DoRegistration in our RegisterPageViewModel won't do that much. It'll create an ErrorBucket instance and call the validation at first. If the validation is OK, it'll fake the call to the server, and then ask the host to display a message containing the ID of the newly created account. If errors occur during the validation process, we'll ask the host to display the errors. For clarity, I've reproduced the Validate method:

```
// add methods to RegisterPageViewModel...
private void DoRegistration()
{
    // validate...
    ErrorBucket errors = new ErrorBucket();
    Validate(errors);

    // ok?
```

```
            if (!(errors.HasErrors))
            {
                // the real call to the server will return an ID here—we'll
                //fake it for now...
                string userId = Guid.NewGuid().ToString();

                // call the success handler...
                this.Host.ShowAlertAsync(string.Format("Created user: {0}",
                userId));
            }

            // errors?
            if(errors.HasErrors)
                this.Host.ShowAlertAsync(errors);
        }

        private void Validate(ErrorBucket errors)
        {
            // do basic data presence validation...
            if (string.IsNullOrEmpty(Username))
                errors.AddError("Username is required.");
            if (string.IsNullOrEmpty(Email))
                errors.AddError("Email is required.");
            if (string.IsNullOrEmpty(Password))
                errors.AddError("Password is required.");
            if (string.IsNullOrEmpty(Confirm))
                errors.AddError("Confirm password is required.");

            // check the passwords...
            if (!(string.IsNullOrEmpty(Password)) &&
                this.Password != this.Confirm)
                    errors.AddError("The passwords do not match.");
        }
```

One small point on that: note how at the end of DoRegistration we check the errors instance again and display a message. Another way to build that would be to use an else after the first check. What I want to do, however, is introduce a pattern whereby we can continue to build up errors in the if block, but at the moment the code in the if block can't possibly create more errors. If that's not clear, don't worry; you'll see this again in a while.

## Running the application

The only thing that's missing from this is a way of creating the view-model and hooking it and the view up together. In the next chapter we're going to look at using an *inversion-of-control* (IoC) container to do this more properly. In this chapter we're just going to "new up" a RegisterPageViewModel instance and tell the view to use it.

As each view will need a way of setting up its view-model, I'm proposing that we create another extension method in Page that will take a view-model instance and bind it up to the view. The actual binding process is very easy—all we have to do is set the Data Context property of the page to be the view-model. This action will wire up all of the configured data binding, and in fact that's all we need to do in order to configure the two objects.

As I've mentioned a few times, in this chapter all we're going to do is create a new instance of the view-model. In the next chapter we're going to use an IoC container to do this more dynamically.

Here's the InitializeViewModel method that needs to be created in PageExtender. This will just "new up" a view-model instance and then use a (slightly dirty) hack to take our IViewModelHost instance and turn it into a Page instance so that we can access the DataContext property:

```
// Add method to PageExtender...
internal static void InitializeViewModel(this IViewModelHost page,
IViewModel model = null)
    {
        // create the model; ultimately we'll replace this with an
        // IoC container...
        model = new RegisterPageViewModel();
          model.Initialize(page);

        // set the data context...
        ((Page)page).DataContext = model;
    }
```

Here's the new property and the change to the constructor that's needed in Register Page:

```
    public sealed partial class RegisterPage : StreetFooPage
    public RegisterPage()
    {
        this.InitializeComponent();

        // initialize the model...
        this.InitializeViewModel();
    }

    // code omitted for brevity...
}
```

At this point, everything should run. Run the app, and you'll see something like Figure 1-14.

 Figure 1-14 shows the device simulator view. If you run the project using the standard options, your Windows Store app will run directly within your home environment. To change to the simulator, change the drop-down on the toolbar from Local Machine to Simulator.

*Figure 1-14. The running application*

To properly understand this part, I'd recommend setting a breakpoint in `DoRegistra tion`. Hit the `Register` button and use the call stack to confirm that the call has been routed through the command. If you step through, you'll see the validation collect errors because the fields are blank. Keep stepping, and you'll work your way back out of the view-model and into the view. Ultimately you'll see the message reporting the errors appear, as shown in Figure 1-15.

The next important thing to validate is that the binding is pushing the data back into the view-model. If you fill out some of the fields and break into `DoRegistration`, you should see the properties reporting back the values you keyed in. If the values pass validation, you'll see a successful result, as shown in Figure 1-16.

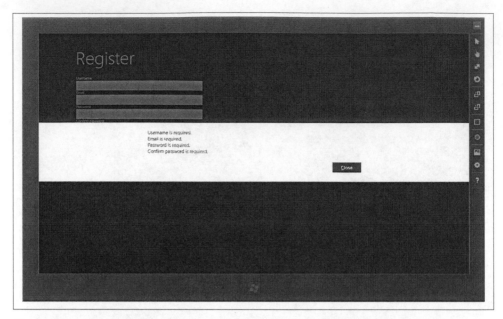

*Figure 1-15. Alert being used to show error messages in an ErrorBucket instance*

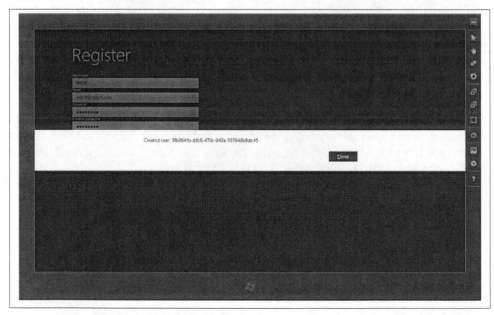

*Figure 1-16. A successful result*

# CHAPTER 2

# Making the Transition from .NET (Part 2)

We got most of the structural basics pinned down in Chapter 1. In this chapter, we're going to look at building up the functionality of the app in order to make it do something more than just putting a message on the screen.

Specifically, we're going to do the following:

- Introduce a basic inversion-of-control (IoC) container. The idea here is that rather than explicitly creating view-model instances as we did in Chapter 1, we'll ask an IoC container to pick one for us based on an interface that we provide.

- We'll build a set of classes that can call up to the service to register the user. This will use the `HttpClient` class available in WinRT to actually issue the call. We'll use the IoC container here, too, again to create a loose coupling between the service proxy interfaces and their concrete implementations.

## Inversion of Control

The idea of *inversion of control* is that rather than having "direct control" over object creation—as we did in Chapter 1 when we created concrete view-models for our view-model interfaces—you have some code that is structured so that if you ask it to create an object of type *X* in order to provide some service it'll choose the most appropriate concrete type for you. IoC "inverts control" by saying, "hey, give me an object that can do type *X* things, but I don't care what you give me," as opposed to direct control where you say, "give me an instance of object *X*."

Implementation-wise, the basic idea of IoC is you have a register of classes and interfaces. You ask for the handler of a given interface and get the appropriate class back in return. From there, you can swap out the underlying handler class without the requestor needing to know anything about the change. (This is the actual "inversion of control" bit.) The main benefit of this loose coupling is to create a clearer separation of concerns—and, in many cases, this is more of a process with mental benefits than tangible ones. A very common use is to—as I hinted at—replace real implementations with mocked, fake, or other implementations that support unit testing.

In Chapter 1, we welded the `RegisterPage` view to the `RegisterPageViewModel` by the expedient of having the view simply "new up" a view-model via the new keyword (e.g., `this.Model = new RegisterPageViewModel`), although we built `IRegisterPageView Model` as a step in the right direction of an architecture with looser coupling.

The particular form of IoC we want to use is *dependency injection*, which will replace a call like `this.Model = new RegisterPageViewModel(this)` with a call like `this.Model = SomeRegistryClass.SomeFactoryMethod<IRegisterPageViewModel>(this)`.

This is the first point in the book where we're going to use an external library. While I'm keen to see the use of external libraries in production code, they come with a danger. It's easy for developers to become dependent on using libraries, but unable to build them themselves. The problem here is that unless as a developer you know how to build, for example, an IoC container from scratch, you'll find it hard to make qualified judgments when it comes to selecting the library of your choice for use in a real application.

That's by the by—it's a little piece of advice that I think is really important for developers.

## Installing TinyIoC

In this book, we're going to use a lightweight IoC container called TinyIoC. You can find it on GitHub (*https://github.com/grumpydev/TinyIoC*).

We can install TinyIoC using NuGet. If you've never used NuGet before, it's pretty cool. The idea is that developers put packages up in the cloud that you can integrate into your product using a simple interface. NuGet is a *package manager*, an idea that's been around in other operating systems for some time. Windows is slightly odd in that it doesn't support such a thing.

If you're interested in that sort of thing, you can also get Chocolatey (*http://chocolatey.org*), which—as opposed to NuGet, which only works with development libraries that you can link or compile into your projects—will install packages onto servers. (By the way, it's NuGet→"Nougat"→Chocolatey. Get it?)

Steve Robbins, the developer who wrote TinyIoC, was kind enough to develop a WinRT version of the TinyIoC NuGet package so that I (and by extension, you) could use it in this book.

To get going, within Visual Studio right-click on the StreetFoo.Client project (what we'll typically call the "UI-agnostic" project going forward) and select Manage NuGet Packages. Under Online, look for TinyIoC. You will find one specifically called `Ti nyIoC.WinRT`. Select this one and install it. Figure 2-1 illustrates.

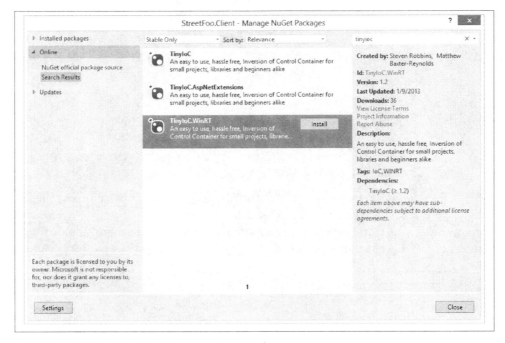

*Figure 2-1. Selecting the TinyIoC.WinRT package*

The installation process will create two C# files in the project. (Not all NuGet packages work this way; it's more typical that they will dynamically link rather than put source files into the project, although sqlite-net—which we'll use in the next chapter—installs source files in this way.) These files make up the TinyIoC container.

## Initializing IoC Defaults

The first thing we need to do is create a way of setting up the default mappings used by TinyIoC.

To that end we're going to build a class called `StreetFooRuntime` that will be responsible for "booting" the application. Its first job will be to ask TinyIoC to automatically configure itself. We'll add more functionality to `StreetFooRuntime` as we go.

One thing we're going to do is to pass in the name of a *module*. This is a pattern I've used for some time—the idea is that when you start the app, you provide some indication of why the app boots up. To be honest, this makes more sense when you're not building

Windows Store apps like this. For example, you might have some code shared by an ASP.NET website and a Windows Service application. Each needs to boot, but, for example, when you want to log information it's useful to know which module boots it; by writing the module name into the log, you know. I've decided to continue this approach here because it's a good illustration of the idea, even though it won't be much used.

 This also can be helpful when you're running background tasks (see Chapter 14), as these run in a separate process; thus, you can use the module name to indicate if logging information came from the main app process or from the background task service process.

From time to time, we will also use this class for storing global constants—`ServiceUrl Base` is an example of this, and we'll use that when we build up the service proxies. We'll also add some specific constants here ahead of time so that we don't have to worry about going back and doing this later.

Regardless, the important thing is to start up TinyIoC. We do so using the `AutoRegis ter` function on the singleton instance of `TinyIoCContainer`. (The result here is that TinyIoC will scan all of the types available within the code and look for things that look like pairings between interfaces and concrete types, and we can take advantage of that later.) Here's the code:

```
public static class StreetFooRuntime
{
    // holds a reference to how we started...
    public static string Module { get; private set; }

    // gets the base URL of our services...
    internal const string ServiceUrlBase =
    "https://streetfoo.apphb.com/handlers/";

    // starts the application/sets up state...
    public static void Start(string module)
    {
        Module = module;

        // initialize TinyIoC...
        TinyIoCContainer.Current.AutoRegister();
    }
}
```

The next move is to actually make the call into `Start` and boot up the application. We can do this from within the *App.xaml* implementation in the StreetFoo.UI.Client project. (If you remember, we modified this file in Chapter 1 when we had to change the page that was shown on startup from the default to `RegisterPage`.) Here's the change to `OnLaunched`:

```
// Modify OnLaunched in App.xaml...

protected override void OnLaunched(LaunchActivatedEventArgs args)
    {
        if (args.PreviousExecutionState ==
            ApplicationExecutionState.Terminated)
        {
}

        // start...
        StreetFooRuntime.Start("Client");

        // Create a Frame to act navigation context and navigate
to the first page
        var rootFrame = new Frame();
        rootFrame.Navigate(typeof(RegisterPage));

        // Place the frame in the current Window and ensure it is active
        Window.Current.Content = rootFrame;
        Window.Current.Activate();
    }
```

The value we pass in for the module is arbitrary—I've chosen "Client" as the string. Now we can actually use the TinyIoC container.

One of the things we'll need to do is enable the UI-agnostic view-models to call into the IViewModelHost-enabled containers and ask them to change the view. As I mentioned in Chapter 1, some people don't like the lack of purity involved in this approach of back-linking the view-models into the view implementations, as they would rather have complete separation. However, I think "muddying" the implementation in this way is pragmatic. Say we're on the logon page and we want to access the register page. How can the logon page ever direct the app to show the register page without saying something like "please show the register page"? Somewhere the coupling has to be such that that can happen.

The easiest way to do this is through *attribute decoration*. Our intention is to decorate the views such that there is a declarative understanding within the code as to the relationship between the view and the interface that describes their view-model. (It's important that this is a relationship between a view class and a view-model interface because we still want indirection and loose coupling between the view class and the view-model class.) The easiest way to achieve this is to create an attribute called ViewModelAttribute that we use to decorate the view classes.

Here's the definition of ViewModelAttribute. All it does is allow the developer to specify the type of the related view-model interface.

```
[AttributeUsage(AttributeTargets.Class)]
public sealed class ViewModelAttribute : Attribute
{
    public Type ViewModelInterfaceType { get; private set; }
```

```
        public ViewModelAttribute(Type viewModelInterfaceType)
        {
            this.ViewModelInterfaceType = viewModelInterfaceType;
        }
    }
```

From there, we can decorate the actual view class like this:

```
[ViewModel(typeof(IRegisterPageViewModel))]
public sealed partial class RegisterPage : StreetFooPage
{
    public RegisterPage()
    {
        this.InitializeComponent();

        // obtain a real instance of a model...
        // now done by dependency injection...
        this.InitializeViewModel();
    }
}
```

You'll note that the view class calls `InitializeViewModel` in its constructor. In Chapter 1 all this method did was create a concrete `RegisterPageViewModel` and assume that was the view-model. We can now change this method so that it uses TinyIoC to dereference a concrete class to use from the interface defined on the view class's attribute.

What I'm also proposing is that we make this a little more flexible by allowing the caller to pass in the view-model to use, as opposed to dereferencing one from the attribute. We won't actually use this in the book, but it's worth showing the approach. If we have to dereference it, the call to TinyIoC is easy and obvious enough. You'll recall that previously we called the `AutoRegister` method on application start. What this would have done is looked at all the types in the code and noted that `RegisterPageViewModel` happened to implement the interface `IRegisterPageViewModel`. Now if we ask TinyIoC to return a type for `IRegisterPageViewModel`, it just looks at that mapping and returns back an instance of `RegisterPageViewModel`. This is pretty easy stuff. Once we have the view-model, we call `Initialize` on it like we did in Chapter 1. Here's the new code:

```
    // Modify method in PageExtender...
  internal static void InitializeViewModel(this IViewModelHost host, IViewModel
model = null)
        {
            // if we don't get given a model?
            if (model == null)
            {
                var attr = (ViewModelAttribute)host.GetType().GetTypeInfo().
GetCustomAttribute<ViewModelAttribute>();
                if (attr != null)
                    model = (IViewModel)TinyIoCContainer.Current.Resolve
(attr.ViewModelInterfaceType);
                else
```

```
            throw new InvalidOperationException(
string.Format("Page '{0}' is not decorated with ViewModelAttribute."));
            }

        // setup...
        model.Initialize((IViewModelHost)host);
        ((Page)host).DataContext = model;
    }
```

Run the project now, and you should see nothing different from what you had before. However, this time you're using loose coupling and an IoC container to manage instantiation and initialization of the view-model. Figure 2-2 illustrates.

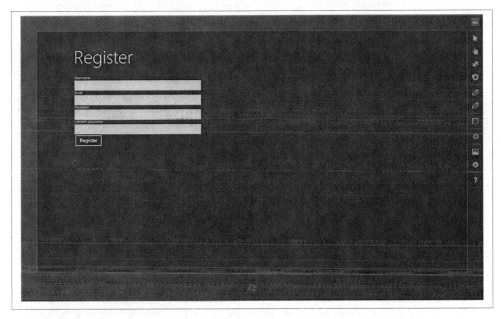

*Figure 2-2. The register page, as it was before, but initialized via the IoC container*

# Understanding Asynchrony

If you learn only one thing from this book, make sure it's this section on asynchrony. This is *the* thing to understand in order to be productive building Windows Store apps. Asynchrony is the way that programming practice in general is going, over and above direct control of threading. The general principles behind how asynchrony works apply to other development platforms and will only get more important as processors scale up their number of cores.

When working with XAML/C# Windows Store apps, you achieve asynchrony using the Task Parallel Library (TPL), which is a feature of .NET Framework 4.

Asynchrony is very hard to get your head around unless you experience it directly. The general principle behind it is that it tries to reframe how we developers think about threads and parallelism. In a normal approach, the OS will create a process, and one initial thread. As a developer you can create additional threads that do work in the background. In interactive applications—such as a Windows Store app, WPF app, or even a Java app—the developer is able to spin up separate threads, the advantage of which is that the main UI thread is responsive while other work is being done.

From a developer's point of view, having to manage separate threads is a pain. From an operating system design perspective, threads don't necessarily make the best use of system resources. This is especially true on constrained devices (think ARM-based tablets and smartphones), although in reality it applies to any device operating at any scale. Each thread requires RAM to store its state. Switching between different threads to perform processing is expensive (a problem known as *context switching*). Keep adding threads, and your program will become *less* responsive, not more.

Asynchronous programming is not in itself new. It has featured in a basic form from time to time in .NET since v1.0. For example, in `HttpWebRequest` you had both a `GetResponse` method that would not spin up a thread and block the calling thread, and a `BeginGetResponse` method that would use the .NET thread pool to service the request and not block the caller. As an aside, JavaScript in particular makes heavy use of asynchronous programming methods.

What's relevant about an asynchrony-based approach is that in neither case are you, the developer, responsible for doing anything proactive or intentional to manage the thread. The environment that is running your code manages the threads for you.

With WinRT, Microsoft's developers have gone all out on asynchrony. To keep the UI responsive, anything that could possibly block a calling thread for 50ms or more has been replaced by a version that is accessible only asynchronously. The whole API has been designed so that you can never, ever block a thread. (Actually, you can block a thread, but only by introducing a bug that deadlocks the whole app entirely—but that's a different thing.)

Continuing this idea, there are things that you simply cannot do in WinRT with threads. One of them is that you cannot create new threads. Similarly, you cannot control the lifetimes of existing threads—for example, you can't terminate a running thread. You still have threads, you just don't see them.

As we go through this book, you'll discover numerous places where restrictions in the API are designed to lodge control over the user experience with Microsoft rather than with you. This area of asynchrony is one of them, and probably the most important one. On the one hand, creating too many threads on constrained devices will "gum it up" and make it unusable. Microsoft's solution here is to stop you from creating too many threads. On the other hand, making calls that block the main UI thread makes apps unresponsive, leading the user to believe that the device is broken. Microsoft's solution here is to stop you from blocking.

But, as I alluded to, asynchrony does have benefits in that it's notionally a better way of putting applications together than using "old school" threads for *every* type of application—interactive desktop, web apps, and headless services.

## How Asynchrony Works in WinRT

Philosophically, the idea behind the asynchrony implementation in WinRT is tricky to explain. I've also failed in the past year and a half to find a decent diagram that explains it; hence, there are no figures in this section to explain the concept.

Imagine you have some code that calls a server, like so:

```
public void DoMagic()
{
    // build a request up...
    var request = (HttpWebRequest)WebRequest.Create("http://www.google.com/");

    // make the request - it'll block at this point...
    var response = request.GetResponse();

    // we'll only get here once the call is completed...
    Debug.WriteLine("Done!");
}
```

In theory, we're being wasteful when we make that GetResponse call. The calling thread at some point during that process won't be doing anything—it will have passed the request over the network and be waiting for a response to come back, and the thread that made the call will be blocking. Ideally, we want to be able to run other code during that blocking period. Ultimately, regardless of what asynchrony model we use, that's what we want to achieve—allowing something else to take advantage of processor cycles that we can't use because we're waiting.

 To add a little more complication to this, we won't be using the old-fashioned HttpWebRequest class in this book at all, other than in this illustration. We'll actually be using the more modern HttpClient class. I've left it in here, though, as statistically more of you will be familiar with HttpWebRequest than HttpClient.

The basic idea behind the way that asynchrony is implemented in WinRT is that we can "poke holes" in what is otherwise a synchronous procedure. Consider the code sample that we just saw. In the part where we call GetResponse, we don't actually need the thread, and if we wanted we could just "surrender" it up for use by other code that needed it. Specifically, we do this in WinRT by using Task instances. A Task is (sort of) like a token you hold that represents something that runs in the background. How it actually runs in the background (if indeed it does, because Windows can decide not to let it if it thinks it'll run in the foreground quickly enough) is something you'll never know.

The C# compiler now has specific and specialized support for working with Task instances. In a moment we'll meet the new async and await C# keywords—it's these two that make the asynchrony magic in WinRT happen.

 I've actually oversimplified this a little. The asynchrony model in WinRT can actually work with anything that implements IAsyncRe sult, and Task implements this. However, what's happened over the development of WinRT is that Microsoft's engineers have tried to consolidate their API designs to use Task instances rather than IAsyncResult. I digress, but for now, just think in terms of Task instances.

In WinRT, HttpWebRequest does not have GetResponse because it would block. It instead has GetResponseAsync, which returns a value of type Task<WebResponse>. This won't block, as all you're getting back is some token that references a background task. (This convention of suffixing with Async is very consistent within WinRT, and you'll notice that we'll do this too with our own code as we go through the book.)

It's at this point that things get clever. If you now consider the code we had before, we can in theory get the Task instance and wait. (However, you would never, ever do it like this, but I'll get to that.)

```
public void DoMagic()
{
    // build a request up...
    var request = (HttpWebRequest)WebRequest.Create("http://www.google.com/");

    // now we can get a Task back...
    var responseTask = request.GetResponseAsync();
    responseTask.Wait(); // but don't ever do this!

    // we'll only get here once the call is completed...
    Debug.WriteLine("Done!");
}
```

That code when it runs will make the call, get a Task instance, and then block. In fact, you don't ever, ever want to call Wait like this, or do any form of coding with intent to control the lifetime of tasks. (You'll find a specific note on this later.)

The proper way to use asynchrony in Windows Store apps is more subtle than this. What we actually do is get the C# compiler to do the heavy lifting for us by way of the new await and async keywords that I mentioned earlier. The await keyword is used to indicate that the compiler should pause the procedure and do something else while the Task is reaching a successful or failed completion state. The async keyword is used to indicate that a method contains the `await` keyword. Here's the proper way to write our method:

```
public async void DoMagic()
{
    // build a request up...
    var request = (HttpWebRequest)WebRequest.Create("http://www.google.com/");

    // make the request - it'll block at this point...
    var response = await request.GetResponseAsync();

    // we'll only get here once the call is completed...
    Debug.WriteLine("Done!");
}
```

It's through this approach that we can "poke holes" in our procedure. When we reach the `await` call, the system knows that something else can use the processor cycles available on that thread to do something else.

It's at this point that things, conceptually, get a little weird.

## State machines

You can, if you like, just take how it works as read and skip this next explanation as to what is actually happening. Some of you, however, might like to know what's happening when the compiler reaches a method marked as `async`.

The general idea here is to restructure at compile time the overall program flow so that threads are not, in principle, needed.

What the C# compiler does instead is rewrite the code into a *state machine* using the `async` and `await` keywords as clues. When the method is called, rather than it just hitting the method directly, the compiler would have rewritten the code such that a separate object instance that represents the method along with all its state as fields is created, and a method on that new "hidden" class is called instead.

The individual portions of the methods are broken up based on where the `await`-marked calls are. So it'll run the first part immediately, hit the first `await`, and then revert to the calling method. If the `async` method returns `void`, the calling method won't wait for it to finish—this can cause major headaches if you are expecting it to finish. (We'll talk about that in the next section.) If the `async` method returns a `Task` instance, the calling method would have had to invoke the called method using `await`, and thus the calling method would have to be `async` too. (If this seems hard, it actually isn't unless you make it so, which I'll also get to shortly. All you have to do is "rattle" the `async` markers up the calling tree.)

It's the "reverting to the calling method" that makes this work, and this is the "hole" that gets punched into the procedure. Nothing blocks because any `await` marked call simply results in the method returning. When the `Task` completes, either successfully or with a raised exception, the state machine is revived and resumes where it left off. So, in our case with our `HttpWebRequest`, `GetResponseAsync` returns an instance of type `Task<We bResponse>`; when the state machine resumes on a successful call, the `Task` is asked for its `Result` value (which happens to be of type `WebResponse` in this case), and off you go.

But, as I implied at the beginning of this section, you don't actually have to worry about how this works at all.

### Returning "void"

So far, we have our method returning `void`. Having a `void` method marked as `async` is usually bad because you have no way of controlling the lifetime. Say you have this code:

```
private int _magicNumber;

private async void SetupStateAsync()
{
    // some async stuff that sets up _magicNumber in the background...
}

private void DoSomeMagic()
{
    SetupStateAsync();

    // any code that uses _magicNumber may be unreliable...
    Debug.WriteLine(_magicNumber);
}
```

The problem with that code is that it contains a race condition. `SetupState` may not actually finish setting up the state before `DoSomeMagic` wants to use it. The way to get around this is to make `SetupStateAsync` return a `Task`. Interestingly, the compiler doesn't require you to return a `Task` instance. You can drop out of the end of the method without a `return` statement and the compiler just assumes you meant to return a task. (If you want to return a specific type, however, you can't do this—but I'll get to that.)

However, if we do this, we have to declare `await` when we call `SetupState`, we have to make `DoSomeMagic` `async`, we have to make that return a `Task`, and we have to change the method name in order to be consistent. Here are the changes:

```
private int _magicNumber;

private async Task SetupStateAsync()
{
    // some async stuff that sets up _magicNumber in the background...
}

private async Task DoSomeMagicAsync()
{
    await SetupStateAsync();
```

```
// any code that uses _magicNumber will now be reliable...
Debug.WriteLine(_magicNumber);
}
```

You'll notice from that code that Task return declarations tend to propagate up through your object models, as I alluded to before. This is certainly the case, and is something that you're going to have to get used to. It feels slightly wrong, but in practice is very workable, as you tend to always start operations from some user-driven event, such as a touch or click.

The exception to returning Task instances back is when you're programming event handlers. Event handlers already have a definition that in most cases is declared void. In these instances, if you wish to use await you have to simply return async void back. This is generally desirable, as the caller doesn't really know whether it needs to wait for you or not, or how much work you need to do in response. (And this principle in event-driven programming is as old as event-driven programming itself.)

Finally, you can return real values back by using Task<T>. If you actually use await in this sort of method, you can just return an object back—the compiler will wrap it in a Task instance for you:

```
private async Task<bool> DoYetMoreMagicAsync()
{
    await DoMoreMagicAsync();

    // the compiler will wrap this for us...
    return true;
}
```

### The trick of asynchrony

The one thing I'm very clear to impress on people when they're trying to understand asynchrony is this: don't fight it. Don't try to do anything clever with controlling the lifetime of operations or doing anything other than using the async and await keywords.

This can be a particular challenge to experienced developers who are used to being *allowed* to control the way in which operations run. With Windows Store apps, Microsoft has essentially taken the position that allowing you to have this level of control is a bad thing. To control the user experience presented by Windows, Microsoft wants Windows to be able to control background operations entirely and by itself. If you go around this rule, whatever you build will be more difficult to build, and is much less likely to be stable.

To reiterate, then, the best way to keep your head when working with asynchrony is to trust what it's doing and only use async and await. Although you can do clever things with Task instances—such as chaining on continuation handlers and blocking until completion—when it comes to Windows Store apps, doing so generally leads to problems.

# Calling the Server

With the background in asynchrony now covered, let's look at using it for the practical purpose of calling a server.

There's going to be quite a bit of work in this section, broken into two parts:

1. We're going to create an abstract base `ServiceProxy` class that knows how to call up to a function on the server. We'll specialize this class into other classes that understand discrete server functions (e.g., `RegisterServiceProxy` will know how to call the `Register` method). The way the server is designed is that every function the server can perform is accessed through a specific URL. The server accepts a request in JSON format, and returns data as JSON.

2. When the registration method completes successfully, we'll want to change the view to a logon page, so we'll have to build that mechanism. (The work to implement this mechanism was started when we built the attribute to associate a view class with a view-model interface.)

## Building the Service Proxies

When we looked at IoC/dependency injection in the first section of this chapter, we used the TinyIoC isolation-of-control container to decouple the view and view-model. We're going to use it again to decouple the service interfaces. This will be helpful if you want to add unit testing to your apps, which I strongly recommend (see Appendix B).

Firstly, let's create our `IServiceProxy` interface. This is just a stub/marker implementation for now—it doesn't have any actual members:

```
public interface IServiceProxy
{
}
```

When we built the UI for registering a user in the last chapter, we added four fields: username, email, password, and confirm password. The `Register` method on the server takes values for all four of those fields. (In this example I've removed the need to have client-side validation. Obviously, in a production app you could validate that the passwords match to save the effort, bandwidth, and time of asking the server.)

Here's the definition of `IRegisterServiceProxy`:

```
public interface IRegisterServiceProxy : IServiceProxy
{
    Task Register(string username, string email, string password,
    string confirm);
}
```

As I mentioned before, the service proxy calls work by shuttling appropriately organized JSON-formatted data to and from the server.

We're going to do JSON in two ways in this book. In this first instance we're going to manually build up a JSON representation using WinRT's `JsonObject` class. In the next chapter, we're going to use the popular JSON.NET library. In a production application, you'd likely use JSON.NET for both parts; I just wanted to show you the `JsonObject` implementation in WinRT, although it's worth remembering that WinRT's built-in implementation is far inferior to the JSON.NET implementation.

We've had JSON support in ASP.NET since the introduction of `JavaScriptSerializ` `er`. `JsonObject` is having another bite of that cherry, but the implementation is very different. `JavaScriptSerializer` worked by inspecting a received object—typically a `Dictionary`—and then emitting JSON (or vice versa). `JsonObject` is a `Dictionary` in and of itself, together with the attendant members you'd expect to see on a `Dictionary`.

`JsonObject` has keys of type `string` and values of type `IJsonValue`. This is where the implementation gets a bit weird, but interestingly this is the first place we've seen where you can actually "feel" a difference between the Windows DevDiv team (who build .NET and Visual Studio) and the WinDiv team (the ones that build Windows itself). This difference in approach—one team very good at building developer tools, the other team not very good at building developer tools but good at building Windows—is one of the reasons why I wanted to take you through `JsonObject`. It explains a certain amount of the stranger design decisions that you find in WinRT, `JsonObject`'s inferiority compared to the popular JSON.NET project being one of them.

With `JsonObject` you can't just add a string, you have to issue a call like this:

```
json.Add(key, JsonValue.CreateStringValue(value));
```

That is, you need to call that `CreateStringValue` factory method to get something you can add to the object.

Creating overloads of the method that took primitive types and deferred to the static helper methods would have been a better design. To get around this limitation, we'll build an extension method class that will add the desired overloads into `JsonObject`. Here it is:

```
public static class JsonObjectExtender
{
    // extension method that adds a primitive value...
    public static void Add(this JsonObject json, string key, string value)
    {
        json.Add(key, JsonValue.CreateStringValue(value));
    }

    public static void Add(this JsonObject json, string key, bool value)
    {
        json.Add(key, JsonValue.CreateBooleanValue(value));
```

```
        }

        public static void Add(this JsonObject json, string key, double value)
        {
            json.Add(key, JsonValue.CreateNumberValue(value));
        }
    }
```

 Extension methods are one of my absolute favorite features of C#. All I need now are extension properties, and I'd be an extremely happy man.

### Server protocol

The StreetFoo server protocol is straightforward: you send up some JSON, and you receive back some JSON. For basic interactions—such as registering a user or logging on—all that you need to send up is the name/value pairs captured in the view-model, plus an API key. (I'll get to the API key in a moment.) You then get back a similarly straightforward set of name/values.

Considering the request ("input") values first, as I just mentioned the only other thing you have to pass up is an API key. You can obtain an API key from the StreetFoo service's website (*https://streetfoo.apphb.com/*). It's important when you use the downloadable code that you get your own API key to use. Figure 2-3 illustrates where you can find your new API key.

*Figure 2-3. Getting an API key*

Here's an example of the JSON that the server needs to see to register a new user:

```
{
    "username":"mbrit",
    "email":"mbrit@mbrit.com",
    "password":"password",
    "confirm":"password",
    "apiKey":"4f41463a-dfc7-45dd-8d95-bf339f040933"
}
```

The server will signal the state of the request using the isOk value. This will be true or false depending on whether you passed in appropriate values or not. If it's false, you'll get back a value called error that contains more details. Here's an example of a successful response to the registration operation:

```
{
    "userId":"4fa973c1e7044a6fe4735119",
    "isOk":true
}
```

To round this off, if we were to encounter an error, we'd get an error back:

```
{
    "error":"Username already in use.",
    "isOk":false
}
```

 While I'm aware that we have WCF and WebAPI on the Microsoft stack, my StreetFoo service deliberately avoids using these so that we can prove we can make a call that's not dependent on having Microsoft's stuff at both ends. Otherwise, this book just becomes about using WCF at both ends of the problem, which I don't feel is necessarily representative of the real world.

## Building the Register Method

Each server method will have a distinct proxy object on the client. In this first instance, we'll build a specialized RegisterServiceProxy and a base ServiceProxy class. In addition, so that we can have a level of indirection as we did with the MVVM implementation that we've already discussed, we'll create IRegisterServiceProxy and IServiceProxy interfaces.

In all cases, a specific method will exist in IRegisterServiceProxy that takes the values required for the server call (username, email, password), packages it up, and then passes it to the base class for basic processing. The specialized version will then do specific processing.

As discussed previously, we need to pass up the API key with every call. The base ServiceProxy class will need to do this, and also need to form the URL of the service endpoint. Here's the code:

```
public abstract class ServiceProxy : IServiceProxy
{
    // the URL that the proxy connects to...
    private string Url { get; set; }

    // API key available from https://streetfoo.apphb.com/
    // *** YOU MUST CHANGE THIS FOR USE IN YOUR OWN APPS ***
    private const string ApiKey = "4f41463a-dfc7-45dd-8d95-bf339f040933";
```

```
protected ServiceProxy(string handler)
{

    this.Url = StreetFooRuntime.ServiceUrlBase + "Handle" + handler +
    ".ashx";
}

protected void ConfigureInputArgs(JsonObject data)
{
    // all the requests need an API key...
    data.Add("apiKey", ApiKey);
}
}
```

All this magic will happen when we call a method we'll build called `ExecuteAsync`. This method will take a `JsonObject` instance, add the API key, transform it into a JSON string, and then send it to the server. It'll wait for a response (using `await`), and then process the result. In the case of a success or failure (determined by checking the `isOk` value returned from the server), `Execute` will return a `ServiceExecuteResult` object. We'll build this `ServiceExecuteResult` object first.

The idea of `ServiceExecuteResult` is to containerize the JSON that we returned from the server, together with an error message if there was one. We can reuse the `Error Bucket` object that we built class in Chapter 1. Here's the code:

```
public class ServiceExecuteResult : ErrorBucket
{
    public JsonObject Output { get; private set; }

    internal ServiceExecuteResult(JsonObject output)
    {
        this.Output = output;
    }

    internal ServiceExecuteResult(JsonObject output, string error)
        : this(output)
    {
        this.AddError(error);
    }
}
```

The `ExecuteAsync` method itself will be very simple, as the `HttpClient` object provided by .NET 4.5 does all the heavy lifting for us. If you're used to using `HttpWebRequest`, `HttpClient` is much easier. It's *document-centric*, meaning you give it a document containing the content to send, and it'll return back a document containing the response.

This is really the first time that we've used asynchrony, and there are a couple of things to point out. First, note how this code is essentially just procedural. The two `await` directives "poke holes" into the procedural code to make it behave in a multithreaded, asynchronous fashion. Second, the method returns Task<ServiceExecuteResult> and is marked with the async keyword. Again, this tells the compiler that we're expecting that, when the whole thing is done and dusted, we'll be returning a ServiceExecuteResult instance back to the (a)waiting caller.

Here's the code:

```
// Add method to ServiceProxy...
public async Task<ServiceExecuteResult> ExecuteAsync(JsonObject input)
{
    // set the API key...
    ConfigureInputArgs(input);

     // package it us as json...
    var json = input.Stringify();
    var content = new StringContent(json);

    // client...
    var client = new HttpClient();
    var response = await client.PostAsync(this.Url, content);

    // load it up...
    var outputJson = await response.Content.ReadAsStringAsync();
    JsonObject output = JsonObject.Parse(outputJson);

    // did the server return an error?
    bool isOk = output.GetNamedBoolean("isOk");
    if (isOk)
        return new ServiceExecuteResult(output);
    else
    {
        // we have an error returned from the server, so return that...
        string error = output.GetNamedString("error");
        return new ServiceExecuteResult(output, error);
    }
}
```

We can now go ahead and create our specialized RegisterServiceProxy class. The first thing we need is the RegisterResult class. This will come about only as a result of a successful call to the server and will hold the user ID that the server provides. (Recall from earlier the examples showing what the JSON coming back from the server would look like for both a successful and an unsuccessful result.)

```
public class RegisterResult : ErrorBucket
{
    public string UserId { get; private set; }

    public RegisterResult(string userId)
    {
        this.UserId = userId;
    }
}
```

```
        internal RegisterResult(ErrorBucket bucket)
            : base(bucket)
        {
        }
    }
}
```

For the actual RegisterServiceProxy class, all we need to do is define the values that need to be placed into the JSON that goes up to the server via the base ServiceProxy class. We'll also need to interpret the results. The steps in the interpretation are limited to dredging the user ID out of the server response, creating a RegisterResult instance, and calling the success callback.

One last thing to note is that the specialized proxy needs to know what function on the server it's calling—you'll recall that when we build ServiceProxy we build up a URL in the constructor. In this case, the server method name happens to be Register.

Once we've done that, we can create a new JsonObject and put in the values that we want. We can defer to the ExecuteAsync method to call the server, and then process the results:

```
public class RegisterServiceProxy : ServiceProxy, IRegisterServiceProxy
{
    public RegisterServiceProxy()
        : base("Register")
    {
    }

    public async Task<RegisterResult> RegisterAsync(string username,
string email, string password, string confirm)
    {
        // package up the request...
        JsonObject input = new JsonObject();
        input.Add("username", username);
        input.Add("email", email);
        input.Add("password", password);
        input.Add("confirm", confirm);

        // call...
        var executeResult = await this.ExecuteAsync(input);

        // get the user ID from the server result...
        if (!(executeResult.HasErrors))
        {
            string userId = executeResult.Output.GetNamedString("userId");
            return new RegisterResult(userId);
        }
        else
            return new RegisterResult(executeResult);
    }
}
```

That's all we have to do to make the call to the server. Now we can look at how to get it wired up into the UI.

## Finishing the UI to Call the Register Server Function

This is where the various bits that we've done thus far come together. All we have to do is go back into our `RegistrationPageViewModel` class and change `DoRegistration` so that rather than faking the call to the server and displaying a message box, it actually makes the call to the server.

We're going to reuse the TinyIoC container to get a reference to the service proxy. This container doesn't care that there's a difference between view-models and service proxies, so the work we did to initialize the container in Chapter 1 will automatically work here, and we can use it in the same way to find service proxies as we did to find view-models.

Here's the revised implementation of `DoRegistration`. If registration succeeds, all we'll do in the first instance is display the ID of the user that was returned from the server:

```
// Modify method in RegisterPageViewModel...
private async void DoRegistration(CommandExecutionContext context)
{
    // if we don't have a context, create one...
    if (context == null)
        context = new CommandExecutionContext();

    // validate...
    ErrorBucket errors = new ErrorBucket();
    Validate(errors);

    // ok?
    if (!(errors.HasErrors))
    {
        // get a handler...
        var proxy = TinyIoCContainer.Current.Resolve
<IRegisterServiceProxy>();

        // call the server...
        var result = await proxy.RegisterAsync(this.Username,
this.Email, this.Password, this.Confirm);

        // ok?
        if (!(result.HasErrors))
        {
            // show a message to say that a user has been created...
(this isn't a helpful message,
            // included for illustration...)
            await this.Host.ShowAlertAsync(string.Format("The new user
has been created.\r\n\r\nUser ID: {0}", result.UserId));
        }
        else
```

```
                        errors.CopyFrom(result);
        }

        // errors?
        if(errors.HasErrors)
            await this.Host.ShowAlertAsync(errors);
}
```

I'd suggest what happens there is pretty obvious. When you run it, and you pass in valid parameters, you should see the result shown in Figure 2-4.

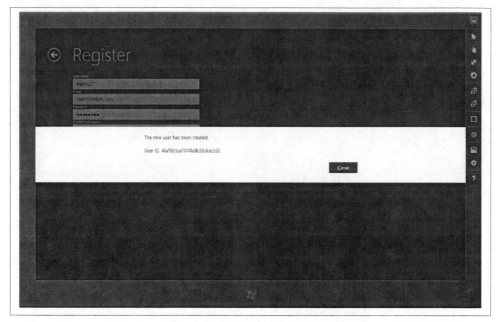

*Figure 2-4. A successful call to the Register function on the server*

That's it! We've now gone end-to-end through an entity example of an MVVM implementation, complete with inversion of control, pulling data back out of the UI with data binding, and then calling up to a server.

# Logon

In the final part of this chapter, I want to show you how to build the logon page—or rather, what I really want to show is how you can move between pages in the app. Another thing we'll cover in this section is how to display a progress indicator on the screen to show that the application is busy. (Specifically, we'll use the little "bumping dots" animation that's come from the original design work on Windows Phone over to Windows 8/Windows RT, which I personally think is rather cool.)

## Building LogonServiceProxy

Calling the server for a logon operation is very much like calling the server for a register operation. I'll go through this part quite quickly, as we've just done something similar.

Like the register operation, we'll need a class to capture the result of a logon call. Here's the code:

```
public class LogonResult : ErrorBucket
{
    public string Token { get; private set; }

    public LogonResult(string token)
    {
        this.Token = token;
    }

    internal LogonResult(ErrorBucket bucket)
        : base(bucket)
    {
    }
}
```

Then, here's the interface for the call. This will just take the username and password:

```
public interface ILogonServiceProxy : IServiceProxy
{
    Task<LogonResult> LogonAsync(string username, string password);
}
```

Finally, we arrive at the actual implementation. How the server works is that we'll be returned a token that we have to pass up to the server each time we want data. We won't actually use the token until the next chapter; for now, we'll just display the token if logging on was successful, which we'll do in the next section. Here's the code:

```
public class LogonServiceProxy : ServiceProxy, ILogonServiceProxy
{
    public LogonServiceProxy()
        : base("Logon")
    {
    }

    public async Task<LogonResult> LogonAsync(string username,
        string password)
    {
        // input..
        JsonObject input = new JsonObject();
        input.Add("username", username);
        input.Add("password", password);

        // call...
        var executeResult = await this.ExecuteAsync(input);
```

```
        // get the user ID from the server result...
        if (!(executeResult.HasErrors))
        {
            string token = executeResult.Output.GetNamedString("token");

            // return...
            return new LogonResult(token);
        }
        else
            return new LogonResult(executeResult);
    }
}
```

# Building the Logon Page

A lot of the work relating to building the logon form is basic copy and paste of the registration page and view-model, and I don't want to reproduce work we've already done in detail—I'd rather use the pages for something more interesting. As a result, we're going to go through some parts of this section quite quickly. Remember that you can refer to the downloadable code if you need to.

The initial problem that we need to solve is that XAML doesn't know anything about our view-model architecture, *but* when we want to change the page we have to give XAML the .NET type of the actual page implementation to which we want to navigate.

Specifically, we have to tell XAML "show typeof(LogonPage)" from within the Regis terPageViewModel, but RegisterPageViewModel can't see LogonPage.

Luckily, we've already done most of the work for this. Remember that at the beginning of this chapter, we built ViewModelAttribute so that we could create view-models automatically from a page. We can basically just flip that on its head so that we can say "find me the Page-derived type that has an attribute referencing the view-model type that we want." Thanks to .NET's reflection APIs, this is very simple. Here's the method to add to StreetFooPage; this just gets all the types that are in the assembly and walks each one, looking for an appropriate attribute:

```
        // Add to StreetFooPage...
        // shows a view from a given view-model...
        public void ShowView(Type viewModelType)
        {
            foreach (var type in this.GetType().GetTypeInfo().Assembly
            .GetTypes())
            {
                var attr = (ViewModelAttribute)type.GetCustomAttribute
<ViewModelAttribute>();
                if (attr != null && viewModelType.IsAssignableFrom
(attr.ViewModelInterfaceType))
                {
                    // show...
                    this.Frame.Navigate(type);
```

```
                }
            }
        }
```

We'll need this on `IViewModelHost`, as we'll need to call it from the view-models. Here's the code:

```
// provides a route back from a view-model to a view...
public interface IViewModelHost
{
    // show messages...
    Task ShowAlertAsync(ErrorBucket errors);
    Task ShowAlertAsync(string message);

    // shows a view from a given view-model...
    void ShowView(Type viewModelInterfaceType);
}
```

Of course, to make any of this work, you'll actually need a logon page. This should be called `LogonPage` and added to the StreetFoo.Client.UI project. I won't go through again how to actually build the page or show the XAML—just make it look like Figure 2-5.

*Figure 2-5. The logon page layout*

We've been trying to reach the point of being able to do very "light lifting" on new pages, pushing as much logic as possible into the view-model and using chunks of (hopefully) clever code to link it all together without having to think very hard about what's going on.

Thus, in terms of the code we have to add to `LogonPage`, all we have to do is add a couple of lines that look very much like the two lines we added to `RegisterPage`:

```
[ViewModel(typeof(ILogonPageViewModel))]
public sealed partial class LogonPage : StreetFooPage
{
    public LogonPage()
    {
        this.InitializeComponent();
```

```
        // obtain a real instance of a model...
        this.InitializeViewModel();
    }
```

In terms of a view-model, the ILogonPageViewModel has properties for the username and password, and commands for Logon and Register. Here's the code:

```
// exposes the map of public binding properties on LogonPage's view-model...
public interface ILogonPageViewModel : IViewModel
{
    string Username
    {
        get;
        set;
    }

    string Password
    {
        get;
        set;
    }

    ICommand LogonCommand
    {
        get;
    }

    ICommand RegisterCommand
    {
        get;
    }
}
```

ILogonPageViewModel will need an implementation. Here it is; I've omitted a lot of it for brevity. (You'll see how RegisterCommand is using a new NavigateCommand class. We'll build that in a moment.)

```
// concrete implementation of the LogonPage's view-model...
public class LogonPageViewModel : ViewModel, ILogonPageViewModel
{
    // commands...
    public ICommand LogonCommand { get; private set; }
    public ICommand RegisterCommand { get; private set; }

    public LogonPageViewModel(IViewModelHost host)
        : base(host)
    {
        // set RegisterCommand to defer to the DoRegistration method...
        this.LogonCommand = new DelegateCommand((args) => DoLogon(args as
CommandExecutionContext));
        this.RegisterCommand = new NavigateCommand<IRegisterPageViewModel>
(host);
```

```
        }

        // Username and Password properties ommitted for brevity...

        private void DoLogon(CommandExecutionContext context)
        {
            // validate...
            ErrorBucket errors = new ErrorBucket();
            Validate(errors);

            // ok?
            if (!(errors.HasErrors))
            {
                // get a handler...
                var proxy = TinyIoCContainer.Current.
                    Resolve<ILogonServiceProxy>();

                // call...
            var result = await proxy.LogonAsync(this.Username, this.Password);
                if (!(result.HasErrors))
                {
                    await this.Host.ShowAlertAsync("Logon OK!");
                }
                else
                    errors.CopyFrom(result);
            }

            // errors?
            if (errors.HasErrors)
                await this.Host.ShowAlertAsync(errors);
        }
    }
```

From time to time, it'd be helpful to have a command whose sole job it was to navigate
to another view. For this reason, we'll build NavigateCommand. We've just seen an example of how this will be used in the immediately preceding listing—note how we pass
through the type of the view-model to navigate to as a generic type argument, but our
ShowView method takes a type as a parameter.

Our ShowView method could have taken a type argument, but this causes "problems"
on interfaces with regards to method overloading. If you put both versions of the method
on the interface (the one that takes a type argument and the one that takes a type parameter), any implementer has to implement both methods. (This is the same argument
that you limit virtual methods to the most complex version of an overload.) As type
arguments are hard to pass dynamically, it's better to have the type-less method defined
on the interface and then use extension methods to create typed overloads, like this:

```
public static class IViewModeHostExtender
{
    public static void ShowView<T>(this IViewModelHost host,
object parameter = null)
```

```
        where T : IViewModel
    {
        host.ShowView(typeof(T), parameter);
    }
}
```

This approach allows you to build more complex interface implementations, reduces the amount of work that anyone implementing the interface has to do, and also provides an easier life for developers calling against your code. In this instance specifically, it helps make more defensive code because of the compile-time type checking that the value for <T> does indeed implement IViewModel.

Back to the main flow of the work: the NavigateCommand class is pretty straightforward, and all we need is a reference to the host and a reference to the type of interface to pass into ShowView. Here's the code:

```
public class NavigateCommand<T> : ICommand
    where T : IViewModel
{
    private IViewModelHost Host { get; set; }

    public event EventHandler CanExecuteChanged;

    public NavigateCommand(IViewModelHost host)
    {
        this.Host = host;
    }

    public bool CanExecute(object parameter)
    {
        return true;
    }

    public void Execute(object parameter)
    {
        this.Host.ShowView<T>();
    }
}
```

Before we look at the process of making the logon operation work, we'll dip back into *App.xaml* and change it so that the logon page is the one that's displayed first, as opposed to the register page. Here's the change:

```
// Modify OnLaunched in

    protected override void OnLaunched(LaunchActivatedEventArgs args)
    {
        if (args.PreviousExecutionState ==
ApplicationExecutionState.Terminated)
        {
}
```

```
        // start...
        StreetFooRuntime.Start("Client");

        // Create a Frame to act as navigation context and navigate
        // to the first page...
        var rootFrame = new Frame();
        rootFrame.Navigate(typeof(LogonPage));

        // Place the frame in the current Window and ensure that it is active
        Window.Current.Content = rootFrame;
        Window.Current.Activate();
    }
```

Now if you run the app, it should all hang together. The logon page should display first, and the Register button should take you to the register page. You can use the automatically provided "back" button to go back to logon. Although we didn't do this in the book, in the code that you can download for this chapter, a successful registration will return you to the logon page.

# Busy Indicators

Windows Phone introduced a novel and space-efficient way of indicating that a background operation was in progress—namely, a collection of dots right at the top of the screen that moves from left to right in a standing wave. That same progress indicator is available in WinRT, and in this section we're going to add it to our app.

 As background, that indicator is known as an "indeterminate" indicator. There is also a "not indeterminate" ("determinate"?) indicator, which works like a normal progress bar. There is also a spinning wheel indicator that we're not going to look at in this chapter, but if you want to use it, it's implemented in the `Windows.UI.Xaml.Con` `trols.ProgressRing` control and works in roughly the same way.

## Positioning the Indicator

The first thing to do is position the indicator on the display. If you're not familiar with XAML, this is actually much easier than it looks and a good example of just how different XAML and HTML are.

The document-centric nature of HTML implies that when new elements are positioned on the page, everything else gets pushed out of the way to accommodate it. However, in XAML, the layout is more explicit; and because it's not document-centric, if you happen to put controls on top of other controls, things just work. So, to put a progress indicator at the top of each page we can just add in the declaration of a control, and set it to render within the first row of the (existing) grid and span the two available columns. Here's the `ProgressBar` declaration for `LogonPage`; I've omitted the rest of the page for brevity. (For the time being, don't worry about the Visibility property—we're about to get to that.)

```xml
<Grid Background="{StaticResource ApplicationPageBackgroundBrush}">

    <Grid.RowDefinitions>
        <RowDefinition Height="140"/>
        <RowDefinition Height="*"/>
    </Grid.RowDefinitions>
    <Grid.ColumnDefinitions>
        <ColumnDefinition Width="120"/>
        <ColumnDefinition Width="*"/>
    </Grid.ColumnDefinitions>

    <ProgressBar Grid.ColumnSpan="2" VerticalAlignment="Top"
IsIndeterminate="true"
                 Visibility="{Binding IsBusy, Converter={StaticResource
VisibilityConverter}}"></ProgressBar>

    <!-- Back button and page title -->
        <AppBarButton x:Name="backButton" Icon="Back" Height="95"
                      Margin="10,46,10,0"
                      Command="{Binding NavigationHelper.GoBackCommand,
                      ElementName=pageRoot}"
                      Visibility="{Binding IsEnabled, Converter=
                      {StaticResource BooleanToVisibilityConverter},
                      RelativeSource={RelativeSource Mode=Self}}"
                      AutomationProperties.Name="Back"
                      AutomationProperties.AutomationId="BackButton"
                      AutomationProperties.ItemType="Navigation Button"/>
        <TextBlock x:Name="pageTitle" Grid.Column="1" Text="Logon" Style=
        "{StaticResource HeaderTextBlockStyle}"/>
```

I haven't provided a screenshot, as there's nothing to see until it runs! You'll need to go into the *App.xaml* and add the reference to BooleanToVisibilityConverter. This class is created by Visual Studio, but it's not referred where we need it.

Here's the change:

```xml
<!-- Modify App.xaml… -->
<Application
    x:Class="StreetFoo.Client.UI.App"
    xmlns="http://schemas.microsoft.com/winfx/2006/xaml/presentation"
    xmlns:x="http://schemas.microsoft.com/winfx/2006/xaml"
    xmlns:local="using:StreetFoo.Client.UI">

    <Application.Resources>
        <ResourceDictionary>

            <!-- TODO: Delete this line if the key AppName is declared
                 in App.xaml -->

            <local:BooleanToVisibilityConverter x:Key=
```

```
"BooleanToVisibilityConverter"/>

        </ResourceDictionary>
    </Application.Resources>

</Application>
```

# Showing the Indicator

The design we want to end up with is one where we don't necessarily have to worry about making the indicator visible or invisible explicitly. Another related feature is that we want any buttons on the page that may create additional background activities to disable themselves automatically. We can achieve both of these things by allowing the view-model to put itself into a "busy" state. The view can then decide *what* to do when the view-model goes into a busy state.

Implementing the busy state is actually pretty easy. All we need to do is create a property on the view-model called IsBusy and then configure bindings in the markup to display the progress indicator and disable the buttons when this is true. (I hinted at this earlier where the ProgressBar control has its Visibility property set to a binding.)

There's a deeper (and well understood) problem with an IsBusy flag in that if you have a collection of recursive methods that are all trying to control that flag (i.e., by setting it on before something happens and off when it's finished), a simple Boolean value won't cut it because the last one wins and the whole thing gets confused. What we need to do is have a counter incremented and decremented by calls to the methods EnterBusy and ExitBusy, respectively.

We then face a design decision. If you were designing this cold, you would create a field with a counter and then have the IsBusy property simply return _busyCounter > 0 when queried; however, to integrate with the binding subsystem we need it such that when IsBusy changes, the PropertyChanged event must also be raised. For this reason, I'm proposing having IsBusy as a normal view-model field (i.e., one that uses the GetValue<T> and SetValue methods and the underlying Dictionary) and explicitly setting that property in EnterBusy and ExitBusy. This is less sophisticated, but it means we don't have to make a specific effort to raise the property change notification.

As a final design point, all of the view-models are going to want to do this, so we'll change IViewModel and ViewModel to support it.

The first change is to IViewModel to add the IsBusy property:

```
// base class for view-model implementations...
public interface IViewModel : INotifyPropertyChanged
{
    // shared busy flag...
    bool IsBusy { get; }
}
```

Next, we can actually implement it. A neat pattern to use here is one that leverages the C# using keyword. If we create a method called EnterBusy, and have that method return something that returns IDisposable, we don't have to explicitly remember to undo the busy state when we're finished. For example, we can write something like this:

```
public void DoMagic()
{
    using(this.EnterBusy())
    {
        // busy flag is turned on here by "EnterBusy"...
    }

    // busy flag is "magically" turned off by the time we get here...
}
```

Here's the code change to ViewModel. I've omitted a lot of the code for brevity:

```
// base class for view-model implementations…
public abstract class ViewModel : IViewModel
{
    //  somewhere to hold the host...
    protected IViewModelHost Host { get; private set; }

    // somewhere to hold the values...
    private Dictionary<string, object> Values { get; set; }

    // support field for IsBusy flag...
    private int BusyCounter { get; set; }

    // event for the change...
    public event PropertyChangedEventHandler PropertyChanged;

    public ViewModel(IViewModelHost host)
    {
        this.Host = host;
        this.Values = new Dictionary<string, object>();
    }

    // code ommitted...

    public IDisposable EnterBusy()
    {
        this.BusyCount++;

        // trigger a UI change?
        if (this.BusyCount == 1)
            this.IsBusy = true;

        // return an object we can use to roll this back...
        return new BusyExiter(this);
    }
```

```
public void ExitBusy()
{
    this.BusyCount--;

    // trigger a UI change?
    if (this.BusyCount == 0)
        this.IsBusy = false;
}

private class BusyExiter : IDisposable
{
    private ViewModel Owner { get; set; }

    internal BusyExiter(ViewModel owner)
    {
        this.Owner = owner;
    }

    public void Dispose()
    {
        this.Owner.ExitBusy();
    }
}
```

It's neater with this pattern to return a vanilla IDisposable rather than returning a special object. (It makes it less likely that you'll force a breaking change if you have to refactor later.) The only behavior that you require in BusyExiter is the ability to let the compiler wire up a call to Dispose.

Going back to the actual implementation, the properties that we want to use this flag with to set properties on the XAML controls are as follows:

- On the ProgressBar we need to set the Visibility property to Visible when IsBusy is true, and Collapsed when IsBusy is false.

- On the buttons, we need to set IsEnabled to be the opposite of IsBusy.

XAML provides a mechanism for converting values when used with binding. In the last chapter, I called some of these out—specifically, Visual Studio will create a few converters for us when it creates the project. The ones we need to use here are BooleanToVisibilityConverter and BooleanNegationConverter. Although these are built for us, you have to wire them up manually in order to use them.

There are two ways to do this: you can put them into each page where you need them, or you can define them globally within the *App.xaml* file. They are not in the *App.xaml* file by default because it affects the application startup speed. However, it's a lot more convenient to map them in there because you only have to do it once.

Here's the *App.xaml* markup with the mappings defined:

```
<Application
    x:Class="StreetFoo.Client.UI.App"
    xmlns="http://schemas.microsoft.com/winfx/2006/xaml/presentation"
    xmlns:x="http://schemas.microsoft.com/winfx/2006/xaml"
    xmlns:local="using:StreetFoo.Client.UI"
    xmlns:common="using:StreetFoo.Client.UI.Common"
    >

    <Application.Resources>
        <ResourceDictionary>

            <local:BooleanToVisibilityConverter x:Key=
"BooleanToVisibilityConverter" />
            <local:BooleanNegationConverter x:Key="BooleanNegationConverter" />

            <ResourceDictionary.MergedDictionaries>
            <ResourceDictionary Source="Common/StandardStyles.xaml"/>
            </ResourceDictionary.MergedDictionaries>

        </ResourceDictionary>
    </Application.Resources>
</Application>
```

Next we can actually use them. Here's the markup for the new progress bar and the modification of the buttons to enable/disable them depending on the busy state (I've omitted other parts of the markup for brevity):

```
<local:StreetFooPage>      <!-- attributes omitted... -->

    <Grid Background="{StaticResource ApplicationPageBackgroundBrush}">

        <Grid.RowDefinitions>
            <RowDefinition Height="140"/>
            <RowDefinition Height="*"/>
        </Grid.RowDefinitions>
        <Grid.ColumnDefinitions>
            <ColumnDefinition Width="120"/>
            <ColumnDefinition Width="*"/>
        </Grid.ColumnDefinitions>

        <ProgressBar Grid.ColumnSpan="2" VerticalAlignment="Top"
                    IsIndeterminate="true"
                    Visibility="{Binding IsBusy, Converter={StaticResource
                    BooleanToVisibilityConverter}}"></ProgressBar>

        <!-- Back button and page title -->
        <Button x:Name="backButton" Click="GoBack" IsEnabled="{Binding
Frame.CanGoBack, ElementName=pageRoot}"
Style="{StaticResource BackButtonStyle}"/>
        <TextBlock x:Name="pageTitle" Grid.Column="1" Text="Logon" Style=
"{StaticResource PageHeaderTextStyle}"/>
```

```
<!-- Registration form -->
<StackPanel Grid.Row="1" Grid.Column="1">

        <TextBlock Text="Username"></TextBlock>
        <TextBox HorizontalAlignment="Left" Width="400" Text="
{Binding Username, Mode=TwoWay}"/>

        <TextBlock Text="Password"></TextBlock>
        <PasswordBox HorizontalAlignment="Left" Width="400"
Password="{Binding Password, Mode=TwoWay}"/>

        <StackPanel Orientation="Horizontal">
            <Button Content="Logon" Command="{Binding LogonCommand}"
                    IsEnabled="{Binding IsBusy, Converter={StaticResource
                    NegationConverter}}"></Button>
            <Button Content="Register" Command="{Binding RegisterCommand}"
                    IsEnabled="{Binding IsBusy, Converter={StaticResource
                    NegationConverter}}"></Button>
        </StackPanel>

    </StackPanel>
<!-- remainder of page omitted... -->
</local:StreetFooPage>
```

At this point, though, we still can't see anything different. However, it's a simple change
to DoLogon in LogonPageViewModel to actually use it. Here's the code:

```
// Modify method in LogonPageViewModel...
private async void DoLogon(CommandExecutionContext context)
{
    // validate...
    ErrorBucket errors = new ErrorBucket();
    Validate(errors);

    // ok?
    if (!(errors.HasErrors))
    {
        // get a handler...
        var proxy = TinyIoCContainer.Current.
            Resolve<ILogonServiceProxy>();

        // call...
        using (this.EnterBusy())
        {
            var result = await proxy.LogonAsync(this.Username,
this.Password);

            if (!(result.HasErrors))
                await this.Host.ShowAlertAsync("Logon OK!");
            else
                errors.CopyFrom(result);
        }
    }
```

```
// errors?
if (errors.HasErrors)
    await this.Host.ShowAlertAsync(errors);
}
```

Now if you run the code, you'll see the progress indicator appear when the logon request is being processed.

# CHAPTER 3

# Local Persistent Data

One topic I was keen to get deep into early on in this book was the subject of local databases. Every app that you will ever build will need some form of local storage, and if you need to store a decent amount of structured data, a database is the only way to go.

Back in the days of Windows Mobile (the version before Windows Phone), the local database story was actually really good. Because these devices were targeted at enterprises, Microsoft's approach was to put a cut-down version of SQL Server on the devices and build a synchronization framework that would let an enterprise's SQL Server push and pull data to the devices.

In Windows Phone, Microsoft got rid of all that, and the new device platform launched with no database support at all. You could write data to the filesystem, but that was about it. This strategy, however, is working fine because Windows Phone is a consumer play and not an enterprise play. Windows 8/Windows RT follows the same approach as Windows Phone—there is no built-in database that we can just use. We're going to use SQLite, a popular open source database that is used on all of the other mobile platforms.

We'll use the database in two different ways common to Windows Store apps:

- We're going to create a database table to store system settings. (An example of a setting that we'll build is the user's last logon username so that we can persist that between sessions.) This will be a simple name/value store that will store string values exclusively.

- We're going to create a database table for holding problem reports downloaded from the server. (To remind you, the idea behind the StreetFoo service is to store problems with a user's local environment—for example, graffiti, broken paving slabs, or dumped garbage. Each instance of a problem report is called simply a *report*.)

The more complex usage scenario is the problem reports, and my objective is to illustrate the following concepts:

- Most application sponsors will likely commission the application so that it is able to support "sometimes offline" capability. (This is a fancy way of saying that your Internet connection is likely to be a bit flaky, but your application still needs to more or less work when no network connection is available.) The way that we'll do this is by binding the frontend to a local cache of data that we update when we are able. In this chapter, we're not going to be handling updating the server—at the moment, this is a read-only cache.

- The StreetFoo service uses JSON as its data format, and so we're going to need some way of mapping between a .NET object (in this context, a *plain ol' CLR object*, or POCO) and some JSON data. We're going to use the popular JSON.NET library to handle these transformations.

To start, let's look at the libraries that we'll need to use to support SQLite.

# SQLite and sqlite-net

SQLite is a well-established, public-domain-licensed, tiny, high-performance, and generally wonderful embedded database. Apple bakes it into iOS, Google bakes it into Android, and RIM bakes it into BlackBerry. The only vendor that doesn't bake it into anything is Microsoft.

Luckily, though, the organization that maintains SQLite—SQLite.org—wants to make sure that developers targeting Windows 8/Windows RT can use SQLite, and hence there is a version of it available that works in Windows Store apps.

In Windows Store apps, you use SQLite via the open source sqlite-net library. This library is maintained by Frank Krueger, is licensed under the MIT license, and is available on GitHub. When we come to use the library in our project, we're going to use NuGet to install it into our project.

In addition to the sqlite-net code, you will need the SQLite engine itself. SQLite.org provides a version of the library that works with Windows Store apps. This is made available as a Visual Studio extension, which you can download from the maintainer's site.

As of the time of writing, you're looking for the version called Precompiled Libraries for Windows Runtime. When you install this, you'll see something like Figure 3-1.

*Figure 3-1. Installing the SQLite extension for Windows Store apps*

At the time of writing, the version of this library for Windows 8.1 was not finalized and was still in beta. The Windows 8 version will not work with Visual Studio 2013 and Windows 8.1. Make sure you get the latest and greatest.

# Working with SQLite

SQLite is a relational database like any other, but it includes some clever features for working with relational databases in a "looser" way. One example is that you have this extension to regular ANSI-92 SQL syntax for creating a table, but only if it doesn't exist. (In actual fact, when we do create tables we'll ask sqlite-net to do it for us, and it will be responsible for formulating the SQL—but we'll get to that.)

```
CREATE TABLE IF NOT EXISTS Customers (...)
```

In this chapter, I assume that you know your way around basic SQL syntax. It's not going to get any more complicated than the preced ing example!

This means that when using SQLite we don't need to check that a table does or does not exist before issuing a create call. Remember that the usage of SQLite is predicated on lightweight, on-demand, embedded use as opposed to structured and managed, enterprise-type use.

Another place where SQLite is different is that the data typing is very loose. In the first instance, data types are associated with a value, not with the actual column definition; so, we could store string values in numeric fields if we wanted. (The column "definition" is actually more of a column "recommendation.") In addition, there are only five types of data types that are supported: `null`, `text`, `integer`, `real`, and `blob`.

> We're not going to hit any issues with data typing here, and it's unlikely that you will either, given how SQLite is typically used.

As I alluded to, we're going to be using sqlite-net almost exclusively to retrieve, store, and change data in the database. sqlite-net has a micro-ORM (*object relational mapping*) that is used to do this.

I'll present a brief primer on object-relational mapping in the next section. If you're familiar with ORM, skip this bit and meet us back at "Using the Micro-ORM in sqlite-net" on page 87.

## A Primer on Object-Relational Mapping

I've always been something of a fan of ORM, but as of the time of writing, there's a trend where it's regarded as less relevant than it once was, and perhaps quite "old hat."

Most of you have heard of ORM, but just to frame the discussion the general idea is that you have classes in your code that map one to one with tables in your database. If you have a `Customers` table with `FirstName` and `LastName` fields, you might have a `Customer` class with `FirstName` and `LastName` properties.

Once we have the model you can then perform *CRUD* operations: create, retrieve, update, and delete. If you want to insert a customer you create a new `Customer`, set the properties, and then hand it over to the ORM, which then translates the object's state into an `INSERT` statement. Likewise, you can ask the ORM to return a collection of `Customer` instances. You do so by issuing a `SELECT` statement to the database, the results table of which is then used to construct a new set of actual `Customer` instances, with the properties of each populated with the data persisted in the database.

Once you have objects returned from the database, you can ask the ORM to issue `UPDATE` and `DELETE` statements on your behalf. The advantage in ORM is that you're not having to faff around building SQL statements.

There are all sorts of reasons why ORM is not attractive to use, the most common of these being that you likely don't want to model your domain in the same way that you might store data in a normalized fashion in a relational database, and it's really this point where in complex systems it struggles. What ORM *is* great for, though, is simply and cheaply persisting data. Whether or not ORM is appropriate in enterprise applications is (thankfully) beyond the scope of this book. We need to locally cache data so that we're not dependent on an Internet connection, and some form of ORM solution is a good fit for that scenario.

Part of the greater discussion around ORM has been the idea of a *micro-ORM*, which is designed to be a more lightweight way of working with ORM frameworks. Most ORM frameworks insist on a relatively high level of investment from the developer in terms of spinning up the framework, using specific base classes, and structuring code in a certain way. With a micro-ORM the only assumption is that you're expected to build classes and use public read/write properties.

A famous micro-ORM in the .NET world is Dapper (*http://code.google.com/p/dapper-dot-net/*). This is used by Stack Overflow as part of its technology stack. While it's a decent micro-ORM, it uses ADO.NET, which is not supported in WinRT, and hence we can't use it. What we can use instead is a micro-ORM not dependent on ADO.NET, and the one I've chosen to use in this book is sqlite-net.

sqlite-net has all the features you'd expect from a micro-ORM. You build your domain objects, decorate them with attributes, and use various methods in the sqlite-net classes to run CRUD operations. Now that you know the background, let's look at how we can use them.

## Using the Micro-ORM in sqlite-net

Here's an example of a class that models a customer setup for use with sqlite-net:

```
public class Customer
{
    [AutoIncrement, PrimaryKey]
    public int Id { get; set; }

    public string FirstName { get; set; }
    public string LastName { get; set; }
    public string Email { get; set; }
}
```

 We won't be storing "customers" in our database—this is just an example.

When using sqlite-net, you will find two versions of the API. One is designed to be used synchronously and the other is designed to be used asynchronously. We'll be using the asynchronous API.

When the application first runs, there likely won't be a database file on the disk. SQLite will create database files for you; all you'll need to do is tell it which tables you need, which you can do by using the sqlite-net `CreateTableAsync` method. You can call `CreateTableAsync` even if the table does already exist—unlike most SQL implementations SQLite is able to ignore instructions to create tables that do already exist. (We spoke about this special feature of SQLite earlier in this chapter.) As a bonus, if sqlite-net detects that new columns have been added to the table, it'll add these in for you. The upshot of this is that there's zero complexity in terms of synchronizing schemas in the store database even as you release new versions of the app.

Here's an example of using `CreateTableAsync`:

```
var conn = new SQLiteAsyncConnection("foobar.db");
await conn.CreateTableAsync<Customer>();
```

Once you've created the table, you can use `InsertAsync`, `UpdateAsync`, and `DeleteAsync`. For example, this code shows how we can create a new database, create a table within it, and then insert a new customer:

```
var conn = new SQLiteAsyncConnection("foobar.db");
await conn.CreateTableAsync<Customer>();

// create a customer...
Customer customer = new Customer()
{
    FirstName = "foo",
    LastName = "bar",
    Email = "foobar@mbrit.com"
};

// insert..
await conn.InsertAsync(customer);

// log...
Debug.WriteLine(string.Format("Created customer #{0}", customer.Id));
```

The final thing you need to understand when using sqlite-net is how to query data. You can do this using the `Table<T>` method.

The `Table<T>` method doesn't actually access the database (which is why it's not called `TableAsync<T>`). What it does is build up a query, which you can then access using `ToListAsync`, `FirstAsync`, or `FirstOrDefaultAsync`—these methods are inspired by the Linq extension methods that you're likely familiar with from traditional .NET work and, as their name suggests, do use asynchrony.

For example, here's how to select a list of customers:

```
var conn = new SQLiteAsyncConnection("foobar.db");
await conn.CreateTableAsync<Customer>();

// create a query...
```

```
    var query = conn.Table<Customer>().Where(v => v.LastName.StartsWith("A",
StringComparison.CurrentCultureIgnoreCase));

    // run...
    var list = await query.ToListAsync();

    // log...
    Debug.WriteLine(string.Format("List contains {0} elements(s)", list.Count));
```

Those are the basics of how sqlite-net works. The examples are all a little artificial, as each one calls `CreateTableAsync` at the top. In reality, it is better practice to get all of the tables set up when the application starts; that way, you'll know you have the database in the correct format when you need to use it and you can take that off of your radar. We'll see an example of how to do this shortly.

# Storing Settings

A typical usage pattern for using SQLite in mobile applications is to have one database for system data (such as global settings) and *n* databases for user data. The specific implementation we're going to see here will use the logged-on user's username as part of the filename of the user database. (The rationale for doing this is straightforward: if you have multiple people logging on to the same device, you want their data siloed off from other users. This is a quick and dirty way of solving that problem. Of course, if they are logged on to the *device* with a distinct account, their user data would be isolated anyway.)

In this first section we're going to look at how to store settings in a user-agnostic system database. Specifically, we'll store the last used logon name, and we'll tweak the operation of `LogonPageViewModel` to save and load this as appropriate.

## The SettingItem Class

The approach we'll use is a name/value pair table. I'm going to assume this is a fairly obvious pattern, but essentially what we're trying to do is use a relational database table to hold a list of values keyed off of a name. Specifically, we'll use the name `LastUser name` to store the value of the last used username.

As well as fields for name and value, we'll need a field to hold an integer ID. This is just my personal preference for building database tables—I always have a single integer primary key for everything, even though in this case keying the table off of the `Name` column is appropriate.

We can give sqlite-net instructions on how to create indexes using `IndexedAttribute` and `UniqueAttribute`. We'll use `UniqueAttribute` here. Here's the code:

```
    public class SettingItem
    {
```

```
    // key field...
    [AutoIncrement, PrimaryKey]
    public int Id { get; set; }

    // other fields...
      [Unique]
    public string Name { get; set; }
    public string Value { get; set; }
}
```

sqlite-net takes the name of a database by way of a *connection string*. It will detect when compiled against WinRT and will automatically put the database file in the correct location. Specifically, the path it will use is referenced via a call to `Windows.Storage.Ap plicationData.Current.LocalFolder.Path`. (We'll talk more about filesystem access in Chapter 6.)

"Connection string" in sqlite-net terms is probably a bit strong— it is simply the name of the database file. We can add a constant for storing this name, and a method for returning a connection based on it, to `StreetFooRuntime`. As we'll also need a "user connection string," I'm proposing creating a property and helper method for this too. Here's the code; I've omitted a good deal of code from `StreetFooRuntime` for brevity.

```
// add members to StreetFooRuntime...

public static class StreetFooRuntime
{
    // fields omitted...

    // holds references to the database connections...
    internal const string SystemDatabaseConnectionString =
"StreetFoo-system.db";
    internal static string UserDatabaseConnectionString = null;

    // defines the base URL of our services...
    internal const string ServiceUrlBase =
"http://streetfoo.apphb.com/handlers/";

    // starts the application/sets up state...
    public static async void Start(string module)
    {
        // omitted...
    }

    internal static SQLiteAsyncConnection GetSystemDatabase()
    {
        return new SQLiteAsyncConnection(SystemDatabaseConnectionString);
    }

    internal static SQLiteAsyncConnection GetUserDatabase()
    {
        return new SQLiteAsyncConnection(UserDatabaseConnectionString);
```

```
        }
    }
```

At this point, though, this won't compile because we haven't compiled in the sqlite-net classes. (Even if it did compile, it wouldn't run because we haven't included the SQLite reference.) Let's do this now.

## Linking in sqlite-net

Unlike most libraries, sqlite-net is intended to be compiled into your application as opposed to being referenced through an assembly or DLL. (Although you can do either of those if you wish. Personally, I like these small open source libraries that you can compile into your project directly; the self-contained nature of them is a big win. That said, complex libraries that require frequent updating don't lend themselves well to this model.)

To install the sqlite-net library, right-click on the UI-agnostic StreetFoo.Client project in Solution Explorer and select Manage NuGet Packages. Search the NuGet official package source for sqlite-net. You'll see something like Figure 3-2.

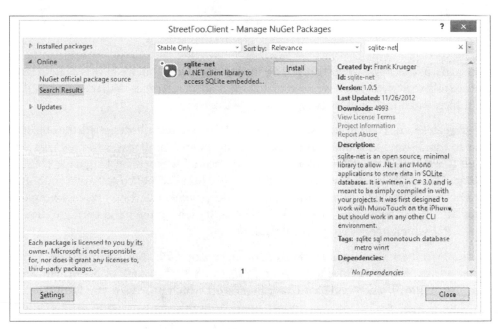

*Figure 3-2. Finding the sqlite-net package*

Click Install to install the library. Two files will be added to the project, as shown in Figure 3-3.

*Figure 3-3. The two sqlite-net files in situ within the project*

 The sqlite-net library is slightly unusual in that it doesn't install binary references in the project—it actually adds source code files.

To clarify, at this point we still don't have the SQLite *engine*—all we have is a client that's able to talk to SQLite. What we need to do now is add a reference to that engine. SQLite is implemented in C, and it's compiled into native code.

This creates some complications. Back when .NET was originally designed, the objective was to build something that was processor-agnostic in a similar way to how Java was. This is why .NET assemblies compile to Microsoft Intermediate Language (MSIL). When .NET code is actually executed, it is "just in time" compiled to native code. This works well in practical terms in the .NET world as you can create one assembly that runs on x86- and x64-based systems. You do so by setting the build configuration to Any CPU, which happens to be the default option.

In the Windows Store apps world, we still have Any CPU, but the meaning here is different. In Windows Store apps, Any CPU means x86, or x64, or ARM. However, because SQLite is native code, you have to indicate which processor you want it to run on. This doesn't really have any impact, apart from making packaging the app a little more complicated. If you have an "Any CPU" app, you can upload one package to the Windows Store and it'll work for everyone. If you can't use Any CPU, you'll need to create packages for each processor that you want to support. (I'll talk in a moment about why selecting x86 and ignoring x64 is likely good enough.) We talk more about packaging for the Store in Chapter 15. If you're wondering why the native core Windows

Runtime components work with Any CPU, it's because Windows is handling that part of the problem on your behalf.

Recall that previously you installed the Visual Studio extension that provided SQLite capability. You can now add a reference to the SQLite engine using the Add Reference dialog within Visual Studio. However, you need to select the Windows option from the list on the left, and the Extensions suboption within that. You then need to select both the SQLite for Windows Runtime option and the Microsoft Visual C++ Runtime Package option. (SQLite depends on that Visual C++ package—it's analogous to the Visual C++ Redistributables package from previous platform architectures.) Figure 3-4 illustrates.

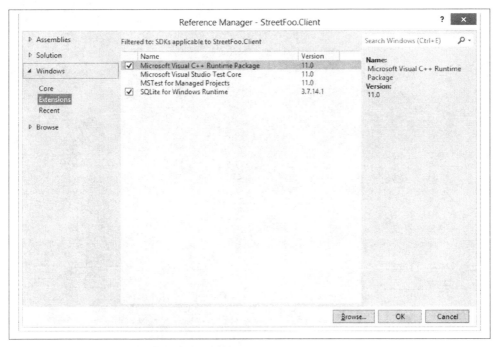

*Figure 3-4. Adding the SQLite reference*

If you accept those changes and compile, you'll see errors like this:

```
1>------ Build started: Project: StreetFoo.Client, Configuration: Debug Any CPU
------1>C:\Windows\Microsoft.NET\Framework\v4.0.30319\Microsoft.Common.targets
(1701,5): error MSB3779: The processor architecture of the project being built
 "Any CPU" is not supported by the referenced SDK "Microsoft.VCLibs,
Version=11.0". Please consider changing the targeted processor architecture of
your project (in visual studio this can be done through the Configuration
Manager) to one of the architectures supported by the SDK: "x86, x64, ARM".
1>C:\Windows\Microsoft.NET\Framework\v4.0.30319\Microsoft.Common.targets
(1701,5): error MSB3779: The processor architecture of the project being built
```

```
"Any CPU" is not supported by the referenced SDK "SQLite.WinRT,
Version=3.7.14.1". Please consider changing the targeted processor architecture
of your project (in visual studio this can be done through the Configuration
Manager) to one of the architectures supported by the SDK: "x86, x64, ARM".
2>------ Build started: Project: StreetFoo.Client.UI, Configuration: Debug Any
CPU ------
2>CSC : error CS0006: Metadata file 'C:\BookCode\Chapter04\StreetFoo.Client\
StreetFoo.Client\bin\Debug\StreetFoo.
Client.dll' could not be found
========== Build: 0 succeeded, 2 failed, 0 up-to-date, 0 skipped ==========
```

This is telling us that we need to be explicit about our choice of processors.

It's very important when you change this that you use the Configuration Manager option within Visual Studio and not just go into the per-project properties and change options in there. Right-click on the solution in Solution Explorer and choose Configuration Manager. Set the "Active solution platform" to x86. Figure 3-5 illustrates.

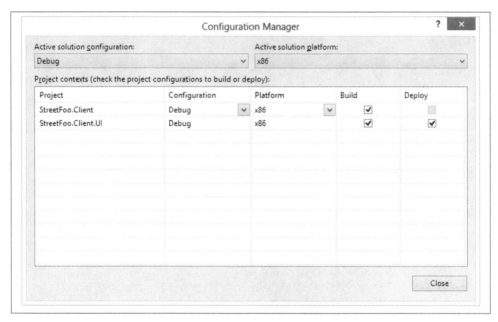

*Figure 3-5. Setting the solution platform to x86*

Confirm that this mostly works by compiling the project. You won't be able to test the ability to reference *sqlite3.dll* without running it, which you can't do yet because we haven't written the code to call it.

## Creating the Database Table for SettingItem

We already have a place for setting up our application on boot—it's the `Start` method of `StreetFooRuntime`. This would seem a good place to set up our system database.

One wrinkle is that if we want to access the database from that method, we'll need to make it `async` so that we can `await` the `CreateTableAsync<T>` call. This will involve rattling back through the methods that call `Start` to flow through the asynchronous nature of the call.

First, then, here's the modification to the `Start` method that will create our `Set tingItem` table. Note the change to the method declaration to include `async` and an adjustment of the return type from void to `Task`:

```
// starts the application/sets up state...
public static async Task Start(string module)
{
    Module = module;

    // initialize TinyIoC...
    TinyIoCContainer.Current.AutoRegister();

    // initialize the system database...
    // a rare move to do this synchronously as we're booting up...
    var conn = GetSystemDatabase();
    await conn.CreateTableAsync<SettingItem>();
}
```

Oddly, the compile won't raise a warning that the preexisting call to `Start` was not awaited. (The preexisting call happens to be within the `OnLaunched` method in *App.xaml*.) We should fix that, as we want things to happen in a predictable order—specifically, we don't want our logon form displayed before the application has started.

I won't show the code because it's just a simple change in a larger method, but you should find OnLaunched, declare it to be async, and add an await declaration to the call.

At this point you can run the application, although you won't see much. That said, having it not crash is a good enough indicator that the various bits are in the right place.

## Reading and Writing Values

Now that we have a database table that we can use, we can turn our attention to methods that read and write values to it. We'll start with SetValueAsync.

### SetValueAsync

The operation here is that given a key, we need to find an item with that key and create it if it does not exist. Either way, we need to set the value.

SetValueAsync will use the same convention used previously with regards to the three callbacks to business-tier methods (success, failure, and complete). Here's the code:

```
public class SettingItem
{
    // key field...
    [AutoIncrement(), PrimaryKey()]
    public int Id { get; set; }

    // other fields...
    [Unique]
    public string Name { get; set; }
    public string Value { get; set; }

    internal static async Task SetValueAsync(string name, string value)
    {
        var conn = StreetFooRuntime.GetSystemDatabase();

        // load an existing value...
        var setting = await conn.Table<SettingItem>().Where(v => v.Name
== name).FirstOrDefaultAsync();
        if (setting != null)
        {
            // change and update...
            setting.Value = value;
            await conn.UpdateAsync(setting);
        }
        else
        {
            setting = new SettingItem()
            {
                Name = name,
                Value = value
            };
```

```
                // save...
                await conn.InsertAsync(setting);
            }
        }
```

It should be fairly obvious what we're doing there. After we have a connection, we're querying the table to find out whether we have an item with that name already. If we do, we update it; if we don't, we create it.

### GetValueAsync

GetValueAsync will do the reverse. If we have it, it'll return it; otherwise, we'll return null. Here's the code:

```
// add method to SettingItem...
    internal static async Task<string> GetValueAsync(string name)
    {
        var conn = StreetFooRuntime.GetSystemDatabase();

        // load any existing value...
        var setting = (await conn.Table<SettingItem>().Where(v => v.Name
== name).ToListAsync()).FirstOrDefault();
        if (setting != null)
            return setting.Value;
        else
            return null;
    }
```

Now that we can get and set values, we can use these operations on LogonPageViewMo
del.

## Modifying LogonPageViewModel

Implementing this is very easy, as it should be because all we're doing is handling persistent settings values. If we've ended up making this difficult, we've mucked something up with the approach.

The only thing that's missing is that at this point we don't have a way of knowing that a view has been activated. This is where having base classes for the view-model types makes sense, as we can add an Activated method to the ViewModel class and override it whenever we need to know that we've been activated.

Here's the change to IViewModel:

```
// add method to IViewModel...

    // base class for view-model implementations...
    public interface IViewModel : INotifyPropertyChanged
    {
        // property to indicate whether the model is busy working...
        bool IsBusy
```

```
    {
        get;
    }

    // called when the view is activated...
    void Activated();
}
```

Here's the new method to add to `ViewModel`:

```
// add to ViewModel...

    // called when the view is activated…
    public virtual void Activated()
    {
    }
```

Now we need to call it, but that's a little more complicated.

`LayoutAwarePage` is given to use by Visual Studio on project inception, but we have refrained from making that understand view-models. Consider that thus far all we've done when we create a view based on our new `StreetFooPage` class is create a `Model` property and just set that to be whatever is returned from the view-model IoC container. We now need to change `StreetFooPage` so that when a page is displayed ("navigated to"), we find the view-model and call Activated. Plus, we could do with adding an extension method so that we can dereference a view-model from a page.

Here's the code to add to `PageExtender`:

```
// Add method to PageExtender...
    internal static IViewModel GetModel(this Page page)
    {
        return page.DataContext as IViewModel;
    }
```

Here's the implementation of `OnNavigatedTo` that needs to be added to `StreetFooPage`:

```
 // Add method to StreetFooPage...
    protected override void OnNavigatedTo
(Windows.UI.Xaml.Navigation.NavigationEventArgs e)
    {
        base.OnNavigatedTo(e);
        // ok...
        this.GetModel().Activated();
    }
```

To round this off, we need to call `SetValueAsync` and `GetValueAsync` to set and get the last known user. We'll do this in that order.

To set the last known user, we need to modify the `DoLogon` method in `LogonPageView Model` to save the username on success logon. Here's the code to do that:

---

```
            // Add a constant to hold the name of the value...
            internal const string LastUsernameKey = "LastUsername";

        // Modify DoLogon method in LogonPageViewModel...
            private async void DoLogon(CommandExecutionContext context)
        {
            // validate...
            ErrorBucket errors = new ErrorBucket();
            Validate(errors);

            // ok?
            if (!(errors.HasErrors))
            {
                // get a handler...
                ILogonServiceProxy proxy = ServiceProxyFactory.Current.GetHandler
<ILogonServiceProxy>();

                // call...
                using(this.EnterBusy())
                {
                    var result = await proxy.LogonAsync(this.Username,
this.Password);
                    if (!(result.HasErrors))
                    {
                        // logon... pass through the username as each user gets
                        // their own database...
                        await StreetFooRuntime.LogonAsync(this.Username,
result.Token);

                        // while we're here - store a setting containing the
                        // logon name of the user...
                        await SettingItem.SetValueAsync(LastUsernameKey,
this.Username);

                        // something happened...
                        await this.ShowAlertAsync("Logon OK.");
                    }
                    else
                        errors.CopyFrom(result);
                }
            }

            // errors?
            if (errors.HasErrors)
                await this.Host.ShowAlertAsync(errors);
        }
```

That's the setter. The getter is just as easy. Here's the change that uses the `Activated` method we built earlier:

```
            public override async void Activated()
            {
                base.Activated();
```

```
        // restore the setting...
        this.Username = await SettingItem.GetValueAsync(LastUsernameKey);
    }
```

You should now find that if you run the app and log on, then close the app and start it again, the username will be remembered. This shows that the whole loop is closed end to end—that is, you can create a new SQLite database, connect to it, and get data in and out of it.

# Caching Data Locally

Being able to store settings is a good introduction to working with data, but the much more interesting part in this is being able to store data locally to work with, rather than being dependent on a network.

Businesses typically take the view that Internet connections are inherently unreliable and building apps that deal with this inherent unreliability is typically worth the extra investment involved in syncing an offline cache of the data. Personally, I can't see this connection unreliability issue going away in anything but the long term—2023 or similar timescales.

The approach we're going to use here is to have the view-model and the attendant logic work exclusively with the local cached copy. We know that the local database is always available. Separate components will deal with getting data from the network and into the cache. Ultimately, we can then extend this model to synchronizing local changes back to the store on the server. We'll actually do this in Chapter 15.

## Local Caching

On our server we have a list of problem reports, and it's these that we need to get down onto the device. The data is not complex data—in fact, these are stored in one table and there is no related data (i.e., it's just a flat list). We'll create a `ReportItem` class to store reports, and structurally it won't be much more complicated than the `SettingItem` class that we just worked with.

The only difference is that whereas in `SettingItem` we created the entity and control its lifetime and values locally, for `ReportItem` the master copy of the data will reside on the server.

The server is going to return the reports as JSON, so we'll need to convert the JSON data returned into `ReportItem` instances. We're going to use a process called *mapping* to do this. It's a very straightforward idea: you nominate fields in your domain objects and tell them which values in the JSON they map to.

In the .NET world, the best framework to use for JSON mapping is JSON.NET. Micro-soft's engineers themselves even recommend using this library. To install JSON.NET, right-click on the UI-agnostic StreetFoo.Client project in Solution Explorer and select Manage NuGet Packages. Search the NuGet official package source for JSON.NET. (This is essentially the same process as when we installed sqlite-net previously.)

## Mapping JSON to Database Entities

The JSON that we're dealing with (i.e., the JSON describing an individual report) will look something like this:

```
{
    "ownerUserId":"4fb28003e7044a90803a3168",
    "title":"Remove damaged light",
    "description":"In malesuada vulputate ipsum sed posuere.",
    "latitude":0,
    "longitude":0,
    "apiKey":"4f41463a-dfc7-45dd-8d95-bf339f040933",
    "_id":"4fb2a0e1e7044a92bc693ac5"
}
```

We want to turn it into an object that looks like this:

```
public class ReportItem
{
    // key field...
    [AutoIncrement(), PrimaryKey()]
    public int Id { get; set; }

    // other fields...
    [Unique]
    public string NativeId { get; set; }
    public string Title { get; set; }
    public string Description { get; set; }
    public decimal Latitude { get; set; }
    public decimal Longitude { get; set; }
}
```

The advantage of not having a particularly sophisticated entity/domain model is it's really obvious to see what we need to do here. The description value in the JSON, for example, has to map to the Description field in the ReportItem class. The only strange one is NativeId, which has to map to the _id value in the JSON.

The server is using Mongo as its backing database, and _id is used as the unique object ID within Mongo. Overall, what we're trying to build here is a local cache of the remote data. It's a standard rule when doing this that you maintain your own IDs in the local cache, but maintain references to the real IDs on the server. (Maintaining your own local IDs allows the local database to do the heavy lifting for you and generally reduces brittleness.) Having the real IDs allows you to go back to the database to issue instructions for specific items.

In theory, then, we can further decorate our `ReportItem` class such that we know that properties are mapped to values in the fields, as follows. Because the convention with JSON is to camel-case the names, and in .NET we're supposed to Pascal-case the names, we need to provide that name mapping explicitly. Also, JSON.NET will map all of the properties that it finds, so we need to explicitly ignore the Id property using the `JsonIgnore` attribute.

```
public class ReportItem
{
    // key field...
    [AutoIncrement, PrimaryKey, JsonIgnore]
    public int Id { get; set; }

    // other fields...
    [Unique, JsonProperty("_id")]
    public string NativeId { get; set; }

    [JsonProperty("title")]
    public string Title { get; set; }

    [JsonProperty("description")]
    public string Description { get; set; }

    [JsonProperty("latitude")]
    public decimal Latitude { get; set; }

    [JsonProperty("longitude")]
    public decimal Longitude { get; set; }
}
```

## Creating Test Reports

The StreetFoo server has a feature whereby you can ask it to create test data for you, rather than your having to key in test data. You'll need to do this in order to run the rest of the project; otherwise, you won't have any data to store in your local cache, and therefore no data to put on the screen.

To do this:

1. Go to *http://streetfoo.apphb.com/*.
2. Click on Create Sample Data.
3. Enter your API key and the name of a user that you have already registered.
4. Click Ensure Sample Data.

The server will look to see if an account on that API key has any reports stored against it. If it does not, it will create 50 random reports for you.

# Setting Up the User Database

At the beginning of this chapter, we discussed having separate system and user databases, the idea being that we'd store system settings in one and user-specific data in the other. The reports are an obvious example of user-specific data; hence, the first thing that we need to do is get that database configured.

We're going to configure the user database when the user logs on. (This makes sense, as it's the first place that we know we have a valid user.)

The first thing that we need to do is modify LogonPageViewModel so that it sets up the database. As this operation to set up the database is a deep, application-level function, my proposal is that we build a method in StreetFooRuntime that handles a logon operation. One of the things that we're going to do is keep track of the logon token returned by the server, and it makes more sense to keep this global. We'll need to use this logon token when we ask for reports; otherwise, the server won't know which account the report is for.

We've already seen how to set up a database when we worked with SettingItem. This is essentially the same operation, just with a different POCO class.

 Again, a POCO class is a *plain ol' CLR object*, meaning a class that has nothing special about it in terms of integrating with an ORM (i.e., no special base class, interface implementations, etc.).

Here's the revised implementation of StreetFooRuntime, with some of the less relevant code omitted:

```
public static class StreetFooRuntime
{
    // holds a reference to how we started...
    public static string Module { get; private set; }

    // holds a reference to the logon token...
    internal static string LogonToken { get; private set; }

    // holds a refrence to the database connections...
    internal const string SystemDatabaseConnectionString =
"StreetFoo-system.db";
    internal static string UserDatabaseConnectionString = null;

    // starts the application/sets up state...
    public static async void Start(string module)
    {
    // omitted...
    }
```

```
internal static bool HasLogonToken
{
    get
    {
        return !(string.IsNullOrEmpty(LogonToken));
    }
}

internal static async Task LogonAsync(string username, string token)
{
    // set the database to be a user specific one... (assumes the
    //username doesn't have evil chars in it
    // -for production you may prefer to use a hash)...
    UserDatabaseConnectionString = string.Format(
        "StreetFoo-user-{0}.db", username);

    // store the logon token...
    LogonToken = token;

    // initialize the database-has to be done async...
    var conn = GetUserDatabase();
    await conn.CreateTableAsync<ReportItem>();
}

internal static SQLiteAsyncConnection GetSystemDatabase()
{
    return new SQLiteAsyncConnection(SystemDatabaseConnectionString);
}

internal static SQLiteAsyncConnection GetUserDatabase()
{
    return new SQLiteAsyncConnection(UserDatabaseConnectionString);
}
}
```

Of course, that won't work unless we actually call the LogonAsync method from within LogonPageViewModel. Here's the change:

```
// modify DoLogon within LogonPageViewModel...
    private async void DoLogon(CommandExecutionContext context)
    {
        // validate...
        ErrorBucket errors = new ErrorBucket();
        Validate(errors);

        // ok?
        if (!(errors.HasErrors))
        {
            // get a handler...
            ILogonServiceProxy proxy = ServiceProxyFactory.Current.GetHandler
<ILogonServiceProxy>();

            // call...
```

```
using(this.EnterBusy())
{
    var result = await proxy.LogonAsync(this.Username,
    this.Password);
    if (!(result.HasErrors))
    {
        // logon... pass through the username as each user gets
        // their own database...
        await StreetFooRuntime.LogonAsync(this.Username,
        result.Token);

        // while we're here, store a setting containing the
        // logon name of the user...
        await SettingItem.SetValueAsync(LastUsernameKey,
        this.Username);

        // something happened...
        await this.ShowAlertAsync("Logon OK.");
    }
      else
        errors.CopyFrom(result);
    }
}

// errors?
if (errors.HasErrors)
    await this.Host.ShowAlertAsync(errors);
}
```

We now have everything configured in terms of the database. Now we can turn to populating the local cache. Well, first we need a view to show the user.

## Creating ReportsPage

Visual Studio comes with lots of page templates that we can use in our project. The most relevant one to use here is the Items Page. This contains a scrolling grid of items where the scrolling runs off the right side of the page, as dictated by the Modern UI design language. Figure 3-6 illustrates where this template is in the Visual Studio Add New Item list.

*Figure 3-6. The Items Page template*

Add one of these to your project, now called `ReportsPage`, and you can get going.

As you can probably imagine, the objective of this page is to get a list of reports to display and then use data binding to present it. By default, you'll get some data binding directions, as per this automatically created one for `ReportsPage`:

```
<Page.Resources>

    <!-- Collection of items displayed by this page -->
    <CollectionViewSource
        x:Name="itemsViewSource"
        Source="{Binding Items}"/>



</Page.Resources>
```

One job we need to do is to get an `Items` property in the view-model that we'll build in a moment. (At this point, we just have a page and no attendant view-model.)

Before we do that, it's worth looking at the template that we are given along with the XAML.

## Using Templates

This book is based on Visual Studio 2013 and Windows 8.1, however the way this was done with Visual Studio 2012 and Windows 8 was slightly more refined. In Visual Studio

2012, each project was given a huge set of standard styles and templates to use. When Microsoft upgraded to Visual Studio 2013, they took these out. What happens in vanilla Visual Studio 2013 is each time you create a grid, inline with the grid's markup you get a template that defines how each item looks. In Visual Studio 2012, each grid would be created with a reference to a shared, standard style. What I'm going to do throughout of work is create a shared library of styles and keep reusing it as we go. This library is just a XAML file. To use it, we eventually need to alter App.xaml to reference that shared library. To start, create a new file in the Common folder called StandardStyles.xaml. Then add this markup:

```xml
<ResourceDictionary
    xmlns="http://schemas.microsoft.com/winfx/2006/xaml/presentation"
    xmlns:x="http://schemas.microsoft.com/winfx/2006/xaml">

    <Style x:Key="BasicTextStyle" TargetType="TextBlock">
        <Setter Property="Foreground" Value="{StaticResource
ApplicationForegroundThemeBrush}"/>
        <Setter Property="FontSize" Value="{StaticResource
ControlContentThemeFontSize}"/>
        <Setter Property="FontFamily" Value="{StaticResource
ContentControlThemeFontFamily}"/>
        <Setter Property="TextTrimming" Value="WordEllipsis"/>
        <Setter Property="TextWrapping" Value="Wrap"/>
        <Setter Property="Typography.StylisticSet20" Value="True"/>
        <Setter Property="Typography.DiscretionaryLigatures" Value="True"/>
        <Setter Property="Typography.CaseSensitiveForms" Value="True"/>
    </Style>

    <Style x:Key="BaselineTextStyle" TargetType="TextBlock" BasedOn=
"{StaticResource BasicTextStyle}">
        <Setter Property="LineHeight" Value="20"/>
        <Setter Property="LineStackingStrategy" Value="BlockLineHeight"/>
        <!-- Properly align text along its baseline -->
        <Setter Property="RenderTransform">
            <Setter.Value>
                <TranslateTransform X="-1" Y="4"/>
            </Setter.Value>
        </Setter>
    </Style>

    <Style x:Key="TitleTextStyle" TargetType="TextBlock" BasedOn="
{StaticResource BaselineTextStyle}">
        <Setter Property="FontWeight" Value="SemiBold"/>
    </Style>

    <Style x:Key="CaptionTextStyle" TargetType="TextBlock" BasedOn=
"{StaticResource BaselineTextStyle}">
        <Setter Property="FontSize" Value="12"/>
        <Setter Property="Foreground" Value="{StaticResource
ApplicationSecondaryForegroundThemeBrush}"/>
    </Style>
```

```
<DataTemplate x:Key="ReportItem250x250Template">
    <Grid HorizontalAlignment="Left" Width="250" Height="250">
        <Border Background="{StaticResource
ListViewItemPlaceholderBackgroundThemeBrush}">
            <Image Source="{Binding ImageUri}" Stretch="UniformToFill"/>
        </Border>
        <StackPanel VerticalAlignment="Bottom"
Background="{StaticResource ListViewItemOverlayBackgroundThemeBrush}">
            <TextBlock Text="{Binding Title}" Foreground="
{StaticResource ListViewItemOverlayForegroundThemeBrush}" Style="{StaticResource
TitleTextStyle}" Height="60" Margin="15,0,15,0"/>
            <TextBlock Text="{Binding Description}" Foreground=
"{StaticResource ListViewItemOverlaySecondaryForegroundThemeBrush}"
Style="{StaticResource CaptionTextStyle}" TextWrapping="NoWrap"
Margin="15,0,15,10"/>
        </StackPanel>
    </Grid>
</DataTemplate>

</ResourceDictionary>
```

The template that we're interested in is that last one—Standard250×250ItemTemplate.
We'll use that in our grid shortly. To reference our new bundle of styles, edit App.xaml
and add this markup:

```
<Application
    x:Class="StreetFoo.Client.UI.App"
    xmlns="http://schemas.microsoft.com/winfx/2006/xaml/presentation"
    xmlns:x="http://schemas.microsoft.com/winfx/2006/xaml"
    xmlns:local="using:StreetFoo.Client.UI">

    <Application.Resources>
        <ResourceDictionary>

            <!-- TODO: Delete this line if the key AppName is declared
                 in App.xaml -->
            <local:BooleanNegationConverter x:Key="BooleanNegationConverter"/>
            <local:BooleanToVisibilityConverter x:Key=
"BooleanToVisibilityConverter"/>

            <!-- shared styles... -->

            <ResourceDictionary.MergedDictionaries>
                <ResourceDictionary Source="Common/StandardStyles.xaml"/>
            </ResourceDictionary.MergedDictionaries>

        </ResourceDictionary>
    </Application.Resources>

</Application>
```

The activity surrounding the templates you are about to see happens a lot in WinRT. You ask some subsystem for a template, which is returned as XML. You'll then fill it in with your own data. (We'll see this specifically when we look at notifications in Chapter 4.)

Find the GridView that you were given when the page was created, remove the Data-Template element, then add this ItemTemplate attribute that references our common style:

```
<!-- Horizontal scrolling grid used in most view states -->
<GridView
    x:Name="itemGridView"
    AutomationProperties.AutomationId="ItemsGridView"
    AutomationProperties.Name="Items"
    TabIndex="1"
    Grid.Row="1"
    Margin="0,-4,0,0"
    Padding="116,0,116,46"
    ItemsSource="{Binding Source={StaticResource itemsViewSource}}"
    ItemTemplate="{StaticResource ReportItem250x250ItemTemplate}"/>
```

In terms of the actual XAML, we're done. This is really the point where Microsoft is driving the tooling for Windows Store apps. The Modern UI design language promotes an almost reductionist approach. As a result, the UIs are very easy to build.

It would be great to actually get some data on the page, so let's do that now.

## Building a Local Cache

We know that we have a user database that can store ReportItem instances once they have been created from the JSON returned from the server; the question is, how do we fill up the database?

Moreover, the question is, what sort of experience do we want for the user?

- If the user is logging in for the first time, the user's database will be empty. In this instance, we want to present the Reports page as blank, but update the cache in the background. When the cache update is finished, we want to update the UI.

- If the user is not logging in for the first time, we don't know how fresh the cached data is. However, the user will want to see a working UI as quickly as possible, so we'll present whatever data we have and still update the cache in the background. Again, when the cache update is finished, we want to update the UI.

Those distinctions are subtle, but important: get users to a point where they think that something is happening, while in the background actually do the work that needs to be done.

In actuality, this is pretty easy, given that async/await does all the heavy lifting for us with regards to the multithreading. We can structure our code as normal synchronous code and allow async/await to "streamline" it for multithreaded use. We can still drive the UI in a responsive fashion, despite the fact that we have to check local databases, drag data back from the network, update local databases, and so on.

This is reasonably complex to build, so let's enumerate the components:

- We'll need a new view-model called ReportsPageViewModel and its attendant IReportsPageViewModel.
- We'll need a service proxy that can return data from the server. This will be called GetReportsByUserServiceProxy.
- We'll then need some sort of cache manager. We'll have to make a decision about where to put that, but it will need to be able to indicate whether the cache is empty, fetch fresh data from the server, update its local store, and return its contents.

The first two are similar to things that we have built before, so when we do that I'll go through it quite quickly. The last part—the cache manager—is the novel part, so we'll take more time there.

So, the first decision we have to make about a cache manager is whether we roll it into its own class, or whether we simply put methods in ReportItem that manage the cache. My view on this is that if we were in a position where we were managing a lot of separate caches, creating a generic concept of a "cache manager" and then specializing it would make sense. I don't think we're in that place, though, so I'm going to invoke the idea of YAGNI and propose a simpler solution of putting cache management methods in ReportItem.

 YAGNI is short for "you ain't gonna need it." It alludes to the fact that developers are sometimes tempted to build overly complex systems containing features that aren't ultimately of value.

The first thing we'll tackle is the indicator of whether the cache is empty.

This is the first place where we see the subtleties of working with an "async-capable" database. We actually used this before, but didn't go into detail—so let's do that now.

The original version of sqlite-net (the access library we use for talking to SQLite databases) didn't have support for asynchronous access. However, asynchronous access is absolutely required if we want to create a good experience for the users of our app, and one of the beautiful things about our industry is the fact that we can all contribute to open source in order to fix things. Hence, sqlite-net now does have asynchronous support.

In the original library, you can create queries on the database using the `Table<T>` method. This method returns a `TableQuery<T>` instance and has a custom `Where` method. The regular `Where` extension method added to `IEnumerable<T>` in `System.Linq` walks objects that are already loaded in memory. The specific `Where` method on `Table Query<T>` actually changes the query that will ultimately be issued to the database. Here's an example of using `Where` in the synchronous sqlite-net API and the query that it maps to:

```
var query = GetConnection().Table<Foo>().Where(v => v.Bar == 27);
// issues to SQLite → SELECT * FROM FOO WHERE BAR=27
```

On the sqlite-net asynchronous API, exactly the same thing happens, but I'm laboring this point because of the confusion between the Linq methods and the specific methods added to sqlite-net.

`System.Linq` will give you methods like `First`, `Any`, and so on, but these methods will run *synchronously*. When you run `Table<T>` on the asynchronous API you will get an instance of `AsyncTableQuery<T>` back, which happens to implement `IEnumerable<T>`; therefore, you gain access to everything that Linq can do. However, if you use any of the underlying Linq methods, because Linq knows nothing about the asynchronous nature of the API those methods will run *synchronously*. Therefore, it's important that you use the special asynchronous methods in `AsyncTableQuery<T>`. Those methods specifically are `FirstAsync`, `FirstOrDefaultAsync`, `ElementAtAsync`, `CountAsync`, and `ToListAsync`. Whether the original Linq methods will remain accessible in `AsyncTa bleQuery<T>` remains to be seen, but as of the time of writing they are there

All of that is a longwinded way of saying that this method, which needs to be added to `ReportItem`, is correctly built to accommodate the asynchronous nature of the API:

```
// add to ReportItem...
    internal static async Task<bool> IsCacheEmpty()
    {
        var conn = StreetFooRuntime.GetUserDatabase();
        return (await conn.Table<ReportItem>().FirstOrDefaultAsync())
            == null;
    }
```

The `Table<ReportItem>()` method will run on the entry thread for the method (which may or may not be the UI thread—it depends what you've been called by). `FirstOrDe faultAsync` will definitely run on a worker thread.

Similarly, we can create `GetAllFromCacheAsync`, which returns everything from the cache using a worker thread:

```
// add to ReportItem...
// reads the local cache and populates a collection...
```

```
          internal static async Task<IEnumerable<ReportItem>>
     GetAllFromCacheAsync()
          {
               var conn = StreetFooRuntime.GetUserDatabase();
               return await conn.Table<ReportItem>().ToListAsync();
          }
```

## Updating the Cache

We'll do this next part backward—what we want to do is update the local cache, assuming that we have some class that can return ReportItem instances from the server. (We'll build that class in a moment, and it'll use JSON.NET to map the JSON to the POCO.)

When we update the local cache, we want to walk each item that we get and see whether we have an item with the given NativeId value in the database. If we do, then we have two options: we can either delete the item on the assumption that we'll insert it again, or we can update the item. In this instance I'm proposing deleting it. The upshot of this is that by the time we've run through everything, the local cache will be as per the set of data returned from the server. (In production software, you normally aim for more sophistication than "delete and recreate" in every instance.)

Here is the method that will get the reports from the server and update the local cache accordingly:

```
               // add to ReportItem...
               // updates the local cache of the reports...
               public static async Task UpdateCacheFromServerAsync()
               {
                    // create a service proxy to call up to the server...
                    var proxy = TinyIoCContainer.Current.Resolve
          <IGetReportsByUserServiceProxy>();
                    var result = await proxy.GetReportsByUserAsync();

                    // did it actually work?
                    result.AssertNoErrors();

                    // update...
                    var conn = StreetFooRuntime.GetUserDatabase();
                    foreach (var report in result.Reports)
                    {
                         // load the existing one, deleting it if we find it...
                         var existing = await conn.Table<ReportItem>().Where(v =>
          v.NativeId == report.NativeId).FirstOrDefaultAsync();
                         if (existing != null)
                              await conn.DeleteAsync(existing);

                         // create...
                         await conn.InsertAsync(report);
```

```
        }
    }
```

I hope you can see that working with the database is quite easy and that, in particular, async/await makes working with asynchronous code straightforward.

## Returning Reports from the Server

We've made server calls a couple of times already, so I'll do this quickly. The only interesting part is using JSON.NET to do the mapping. In previous examples, whenever we called the server we didn't do any automated JSON mapping on the results. As discussed, the server will give us back an array of reports as a string. We can use JSON.NET to transform that string into ReportItem instances.

One thing we need to cover first, though, is that we need to send the logon token up to the server so that the server knows who we are. We do this within the ServiceProxy class. We already passed up the API key; now we need to also pass up the LogonToken if we have one. The ConfigureInputArgs method was used previously to do this. Here's the change:

```
// Modify method in ServiceProxy class...
  protected void ConfigureInputArgs(JsonObject data)
  {
      // all the requests need an API key...
      data.Add("apiKey", ApiKey);

      // are we logged on?
      if (StreetFooRuntime.HasLogonToken)
          data.Add("logonToken", StreetFooRuntime.LogonToken);
  }
```

Finally, we can look at the actual service call. Here's the implementation of GetReportsByUserAsync. This is where we use the core class of JSON.NET—the JsonConvert class. All we have to do to use this is just tell it what type of object we think the JSON string contains. JsonConvert will then sort this all out for us. (It's really this that makes JSON.NET so appealing. Not only is it fast—and it is very fast—but also the usage pattern is significantly straightforward to make it almost magical. Give it the merest hint of what you want, and it seems to work it all out.)

```
// Add method to GetReportsByUserServiceProxy...
public async Task<GetReportsByUserResult> GetReportsByUserAsync()
{
    var input = new JsonObject();
    var executeResult = await this.Execute(input);

    // did it work?
    if (!(executeResult.HasErrors))
    {
        // get the reports...
        string asString = executeResult.Output.GetNamedString(
```

```
                "reports");

                // use JSON.NET to create the reports...
                var reports = JsonConvert.DeserializeObject<List<ReportItem>>
    (asString);

                // return...
                return new GetReportsByUserResult(reports);
        }
        else
            return new GetReportsByUserResult(executeResult);
    }
```

`GetReportsByUserResult` will hold a list of reports. This will also extend `ErrorBuck et` so that we can return any errors back to the caller. Here's the code:

```
public class GetReportsByUserResult : ErrorBucket
{
    internal List<ReportItem> Reports { get; set; }

    internal GetReportsByUserResult(IEnumerable<ReportItem> items)
    {
        this.Reports = new List<ReportItem>();
        this.Reports.AddRange(items);
    }

    internal GetReportsByUserResult(ErrorBucket bucket)
        : base(bucket)
    {
    }
}
```

We're almost there—we just need to define the interface and enroll the service proxy into the service IoC container. Here's the interface:

```
public interface IGetReportsByUserServiceProxy : IServiceProxy
{
    Task<GetReportsByUserResult> GetReportsByUserAsync();
}
```

We're actually now very close to getting this working. The only remaining step is to get the view-model to expose a list of items.

## The Items Property

The only slightly odd thing that we have to do is that in order to update the grid, we need to use a special type of collection that will signal to the XAML data binding subsystem whenever data in the list changes. A normal `List<T>` won't work, as this doesn't have any events that can be subscribed to. What we need to use instead is `Observable Collection<T>`, which does.

---

The way this works is that we have our model expose an `ObservableCollection<Re portItem>` called `Items`. From time to time, we'll load `ReportItem` instances from the cache and manipulate this collection.

To make this more manageable, we'll attack the problem in smaller chunks. The first step is to create a fake report and see if we can get it on the screen.

Here's the code for `ReportsPageViewModel` to put up a fake report:

```
public class ReportsPageViewModel : ViewModel, IReportsPageViewModel
{
    public ObservableCollection<ReportItem> Items { get; private set; }

    public ReportsPageViewModel(IViewModelHost host)
        : base(host)
    {
        // setup...
        this.Items = new ObservableCollection<ReportItem>();

        // add a fake report...
        this.Items.Add(new ReportItem()
        {
            Title = "Foobar",
            Description = "Hello, world."
        });
    }
}
```

If you run that code and log on, you'll see something like Figure 3-7.

*Figure 3-7. Our fake report*

Replacing the fake reports with real reports is relatively straightforward. All we have to do is override the `Activated` method on `ViewModel` and then update or load the cache. Because we're using `async/await`, the user interface will present itself and update the `Items` list while this is going on. This should create an impression of responsiveness, even if users don't actually have access to the data that they're looking for in the first few seconds of operation.

To close the loop and put this together, we need to build a mechanism to refresh the user interface. In the version of the code that you can download, you will find a specific Refresh button; however, we won't build the actual button here. (All the button does is call the DoRefresh method that we're about to build.)

That DoRefresh method will look to see if the cache is empty or if a flag is set. If either of those is true, it will defer to the cache management method in ReportItem called UpdateCacheFromServerAsync, which we built earlier. After the cache has been updated (or if it does not need updating), we'll load the items from the cache and update the collection referenced via our Items property. The standard XAML data binding subsystem, together with the functionality in ObservableCollection<T>, will result in the UI being updated.

Here are the three methods to add to ReportsPageViewModel:

```
// add methods to ReportsPageViewModel...
    private async Task DoRefresh(bool force)
    {
        // run...
        using (this.EnterBusy())
        {
            // update the local cache...
            if (force || await ReportItem.IsCacheEmpty())
                await ReportItem.UpdateCacheFromServerAsync();

            // reload the items...
            await this.ReloadReportsFromCacheAsync();
        }
    }

    private async Task ReloadReportsFromCacheAsync()
    {
        // set up a load operation to populate the collection
        // from the cache...
        using (this.EnterBusy())
        {
            var reports = await ReportItem.GetAllFromCacheAsync();

            // update the model...
            this.Items.Clear();
            foreach (ReportItem report in reports)
                this.Items.Add(report);
        }
    }

    public override async void Activated()
    {
```

```
        await DoRefresh(false);
    }
```

Now if you do that, the whole lot will work end to end—specifically, we'll grab the data from the server, update the local cache, and then update the screen. Figure 3-8 illustrates.

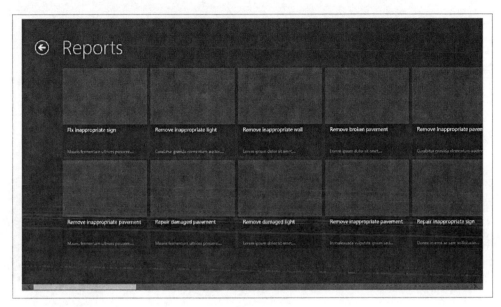

*Figure 3-8. Report sample data shown on the grid*

# CHAPTER 4

# The App Bar

We know that Windows 8/Windows RT represents a reimagining of Windows, and part of that work is to move Windows away from a windows, icons, menus, and pointer (WIMP) paradigm, and to one designed to be used by touch. In this chapter we're going to start looking at one of the tactics used to remove WIMP—specifically, the *app bar*.

Figure 4-1 shows an example of the app bar from the built-in Mail app.

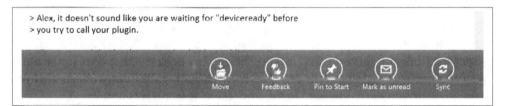

*Figure 4-1. The app bar in the built-in Mail app*

The app bar is designed to expose application commands to the user, but to move away from the tap-and-hold UI paradigm that was used in Windows Mobile and other early-generation touch interfaces.

If you go back a decade or so, mobile OS designers needed to implement a way of "right-clicking" on UI elements to display a context menu. A stylus has no modality in the way that a mouse does—the concept of "done with left" and "done with right" makes no sense when using a stylus or finger. The way that mobile OS designers "fixed" this was that if you tapped and held an item with your stylus or finger, a pop-up context menu appeared.

There are two problems with tap and hold. In the first instance, you are asking users to put their life on hold while the timeout period elapses for the operation. That is very much a "come on, come on!" moment for the user. The second instance is that there's no way of indicating to the user that something is right-clickable/tap-and-holdable. To put it another way, the *discoverability* of tap-and-hold functions is horrible. (For what it's worth, you get discovery issues with all gesture inputs.)

Although in the WinRT documentation you will find events that let you handle tap-and-hold, the UX principles ask that they not be used.

The replacement to tap-and-hold is the app bar. First, the app bar instantly reacts in a way that tap-and-hold does not, providing straightforward access to options without the wait. (Half the battle with UX lies in managing psychology.) Second, there is *always* an app bar, which reduces frustration. (Of course, you can still create confusion by the way you present the options. Also, games may not have app bars.)

The app bar is the first example of a UI feature common to all Windows Store apps. In later chapters we'll see other examples.

Like all things in software engineering, none of this is quite as easy as it sounds. While Microsoft has done a fantastic job of reducing the complexity of the APIs used to access Windows Store app functionality, making the app bar behave like it does in the built-in apps is not as straightforward as it could be. Also getting the button images that you want onto the app bar as opposed to the stock icons is strangely complex.

## Adding a Simple App Bar

You'll find that when you're building apps the basic behaviors that are required to achieve the desired UX are generally easy to implement, and app bars are no exception. Apart from a weird detail that we'll come to, getting your app bars to work like the ones in the built-in apps is straightforward.

In terms of implementation, the `Page` component exposes properties for `TopAppBar` and `BottomAppBar`. You are expected to place `AppBar` instances into these directly. (Although you can put them anywhere on the page, unless you put them in the two provided properties/locations-within-the-markup you will run into strange animation problems.)

You can put any control that you like into the app bar, but as you can imagine there are rules governing the controls that you *should* put in.

The top app bar should be dedicated to navigational functions, and at this point in the book we don't have any pages other than the Reports page that we built in the last chapter —hence, we won't be using a top app bar.

The bottom app bar should contain functions that act either on the page in general, the app, or the selected item/items.

In this section, we're going to add a button and rig it to refresh the page. In the next section, we'll go into far more detail on app bar behavior and rules about how app bars should be used.

## Getting Started with an App Bar

To get started with an app bar, it's best to define one directly in XAML rather than using the toolbox to drop an instance onto the design surface. If you drop an instance, it won't go into the TopAppBar or BottomAppBar property, which (as I just mentioned) is a requirement, so you'll have to move it.

To add an app bar, open up the XAML editor for the page, and anywhere on the page add the app bar as shown here:

```
<Page.Resources>

    <!-- Collection of items displayed by this page -->
    <CollectionViewSource
        x:Name="itemsViewSource"
        Source="{Binding Items}"/>

</Page.Resources>

<Page.BottomAppBar>
    <AppBar>
    </AppBar>
</Page.BottomAppBar>
```

 If you want, you can make the designer spring into life at this point. If you're in split mode and put the caret on the <AppBar> reference in the code, the designer will show the app bar with a deep black background as opposed to the dark gray of the remainder of the design surface.

It's typical with an app bar to put controls on the left and right sides. (We'll talk about this more later.) To this end, it makes sense to configure a grid together with StackPa nel instances to act as separate left and right control containers. Here's the modified app bar with a grid:

```
<Page.BottomAppBar>
    <AppBar>
```

```
            <Grid>
                <Grid.ColumnDefinitions>
                    <ColumnDefinition Width="*"/>
                    <ColumnDefinition Width="*"/>
                </Grid.ColumnDefinitions>
                <StackPanel Orientation="Horizontal">
</StackPanel>
                <StackPanel HorizontalAlignment="Right" Orientation="Horizontal"
Grid.Column="2">
</StackPanel>
            </Grid>
        </AppBar>
    </Page.BottomAppBar>
```

 I'm going a little slowly here for those without much WPF/Silver-
light experience.

Now that we have those two panels, we can put controls onto them. We'll create nicer-
looking buttons later—for now, we'll just use a normal button.

Specifically, we're going to add a Refresh button. To make this button do anything, we
need to create a command in the view-model. Make this change to IReportsPageView
Model first:

```
// Add member to IReportsPageViewModel...
public interface IReportsPageViewModel : IViewModel
{
    ICommand RefreshCommand { get; }

    ObservableCollection<ReportItem> Items
    {
        get;
    }
}
```

The command itself is easy to build—we created the DoRefresh function in Chapter 3,
so all we need is to rig the command to call it. Here's the change (I've omitted some code
for brevity):

```
public class ReportsPageViewModel : ViewModel, IReportsPageViewModel
{
    public ObservableCollection<ReportItem> Items { get; private set; }

    public ICommand RefreshCommand { get; private set; }

    public ReportsPageViewModel(IViewModelHost host)
        : base(host)
    {
```

```
            // setup...
            this.Items = new ObservableCollection<ReportItem>();

            // commands...
            this.RefreshCommand = new DelegateCommand(async (e) =>
            {
                    await this.DoRefresh(true);
            });
        }

        // code omitted...
    }
```

The final step is to add the button to the app bar, together with the command binding. Here's the code:

```
<Page.BottomAppBar>
    <AppBar>
        <Grid>
            <Grid.ColumnDefinitions>
                <ColumnDefinition Width="50*"/>
                <ColumnDefinition Width="50*"/>
            </Grid.ColumnDefinitions>
            <StackPanel Orientation="Horizontal" Visibility="{Binding
HasSelectedItems, Converter={StaticResource VisibilityConverter}}">
            </StackPanel>
            <StackPanel HorizontalAlignment="Right" Orientation="Horizontal"
Grid.Column="2">
                    <Button Content="Refresh"
Command="{Binding RefreshCommand}" />
            </StackPanel>
        </Grid>
    </AppBar>
</Page.BottomAppBar>
```

You can now run the app and summon the app bar. We're going to talk about touch and mouse interaction much more in the next section, but for now, in order to get the app bar to display, right-click on the blank area at the top of the page. (If you right-click on the grid, the app bar will not display.) If you have touch hardware, swipe your finger in from the top or bottom edges. Figure 4-2 illustrates the result.

*Figure 4-2. The Refresh button on the bottom app bar*

# App Bar Behavior

Since the very first versions of Windows, software developers have looked to mimic the operation of standard apps and controls. After all, it's logical to assume that if Microsoft puts out apps that work in a certain way, that way must be correct. (The exception to this rule is the perpetually broken copy and paste behavior in Excel!) Observing standard behavior from Microsoft's built-in apps and treating them as exemplars is just as important as reading the documentation.

The Mail app has a `ListView` for showing items, not a `GridView` like our app, but the principle of how the app bar works in the app should be the same regardless of how items are being presented.

Looking at the mouse first, if you use the left button and click on items on the list in the Mail app, you get single selection behavior. This mimics the standard Windows behavior. Likewise, you can use the Control button to select a single item and Shift to select a group. However, if you make a multiple selection, the app bar will automatically appear. Go back to zero or one selected items, and the app bar will disappear.

If you click with the right button, this emulates the behavior of a Ctrl+click operation in all but one case. If you right-click on a single selected item, the app bar will appear. The app bar will also appear if you click anywhere outside of the grid. This is as per the behavior of the app bar that we built in the last section.

You'll find this behavior—having the app bar appear when you click on anything in the app—throughout the built-in apps. Pick any at random; for example, right-click on the Weather app and the app bar will appear, even though you can't actually select things in that app.

Rigging the app bar to appear on right-click is a good way of getting around the problem of having a touch-centric OS running on nontouch hardware.

So it appears we know the rules. Now go and look at the Store app and navigate to the "Your apps" section. (Swipe in from the top, and you'll get a top app bar because you're going somewhere.) In the grid of apps that appears, the app bar is always visible—which shouldn't be the case, as the app bar is supposed to go away when it's not needed. (The app bar is being used here to fix a workflow problem—the user needs access to the Install Updates button, but this actually shouldn't be on the app bar because workflow-related activities should be on the main form.)

But in terms of the grid of items you have, you don't need to Ctrl+click or use the right button to multiselect. The modality of that page is predicated on multiple selection, whereas the modality of the Mail app is predicated on viewing a single mail item (i.e., it's more normal to select multiple items on the Store, whereas multiple items on the Mail app is an edge case).

We'll see in a moment how we can choose between these two multiple selection modes.

But what happens when we look at Calendar? That behaves like neither. I would expect that when you click items on the calendar, they appear as selected and then we can bring up the app bar. However, in actuality clicking on any item or on any blank space brings up an item details view, or a "new item" view. Personally, I think the Calendar app has the wrong design, so we'll place that app outside the discussion.

So what about the actual rules that Microsoft has laid out? There are lots of them, but these are the salient ones:

- Grouping should be such that items related to the selected item(s) are on the left, while items related to the whole page are on the right.

- A page can have a top app bar and a bottom app bar. The top one should be used for navigation, and the bottom for commands/options.

- The app bar should persist if whatever the user is doing calls for frequent access to the commands. There's a "right way" and a "wrong way" of doing this. You should always err toward hiding the app bar unless it creates a choppy user experience. For example, if the user is cropping and colorizing an image, having the options available probably makes sense. In most cases, it doesn't make sense to force the app bar to be visible. (You'd do this by setting the IsSticky property on the app bar, which has to be done before you force it to show with IsOpen, something that we'll do later.)

- That said, if the user has made multiple selections, showing the app bar is logical because this means the user is likely actually *doing* something as opposed to *looking for* something. Again, this is one of the options you'll need to feel your way through, but reflect on how the Mail app always shows the app bars when multiple selections have been made.

- Options pertaining to workflow should appear on the form, not on the app bar. A classical workflow in this scenario would be an ecommerce cart checkout.

- The guidelines do not call out specific rules about right-clicking, but I like the way the Mail app does it (i.e., simulating Ctrl+left-click).

Now that we know the rules, let's see what happens in our app with its default behavior.

## App Bar with Single-Select Grid

In this section, we'll look at app bar behavior with a single-select grid, which happens to be the selection mode of the grid we are given by Visual Studio when we add a grid page.

Leaving aside the built-in apps and going back to our app, we know that we can show the app bar with a swipe, and we also know that we can right-click on an area of the page not occupied with the grid.

If you click an item with the left button, you can select an item, but by default you can't deselect that item with the left button. If you click an item with the right button, the selection toggles between selected and deselected. In neither case does the app bar appear.

For me, what's broken here is that if you can right-click outside of the grid to display the app bar, right-clicking on an item in the grid should also show the app bar. Having it work when you click on void space and not work when you click on real items is horribly inconsistent.

If we want that behavior, we'd need to override the default behavior of the grid. But before we look at that, let's see what happens when we have a multiselect grid.

## App Bar with Multiselect Grid

The `GridView` control has two multiselect modes, one called `Multiple` and one called `Extended`.

`Multiple` is the operation shown in the Store app—that is, left-clicking on items toggles between selected and deselected. `Extended` behaves like the Mail app: left-clicking changes the selection, but you can use Ctrl+left-click to select multiple items. Likewise, right-clicking emulates Ctrl+left-click behavior.

By default, neither of them will display an app bar when multiple items are displayed, but in most cases it's likely that displaying the app bar with a multiple selection is a desirable behavior.

Your choice between `Multiple` and `Extended` is most likely driven by whether you need multiselect accessible when the user is in touch mode. In `Extended` mode, multiple selections are possible only if you have a Ctrl key or a right mouse button—or you do the hard-to-discover gesture of flicking lightly vertically on the item. `Extended` mode makes sense for the Mail app, as you can usually work with email with single selections —the multiselect capability is a "nice to have" bonus. Conversely, with the Store app, making users work hard to perform the same action on multiple loaded apps is asking too much of them; hence, multiple options is the default.

To choose between the two, reflect on the touch experience that you are looking to achieve (i.e., design such that the only input device you have is a finger). Don't be lulled by the assumption that Microsoft tablets have keyboards—to be a "proper" post-PC device, the only thing that you know you have is a screen with touch digitizer. If the modality of the operation suggests that the user will typically want to work with one item, use `Extended`. If the modality suggests that manipulating multiple items in one operation is the norm, use `Multiple`.

`Extended` mode makes some form of multiselection without a mouse a practical impossibility. In some edge cases, having a "multiselect mode" in touch apps—whereby you can let the user make multiple selections without a mouse—might be appropriate. There's actually a version of this on iOS; on its Mail app, for example, if you go into "delete mode," checkboxes appear next to each item. However, remember that in Modern style, checkboxes appear on the top-right corner of selected items; therefore, rendering checkboxes next to each item will run against expected behavior. I'll leave it to you as individuals, and the greater community, to work out the details on this!

Thus, when it comes to it, the only thing that's missing is the ability to automatically show the app bar when multiple selections are made. Also relatively easy is the modification to show the app bar on right-click. In the next section, we'll consider a more "full-on" implementation of our app bar.

# A More Complex App Bar Implementation

In this section, we're going to look at the following app bar implementation:

- We want our app bar to show when the user right-clicks on any grid option.
- We want our app bar to be able to display context-sensitive options.
- We want our app bar to automatically display when multiple selections are made, and hide when the selection is reduced.
- We want all of this to be compatible with the MVVM rules that we laid down in Chapters 1 and 2.

The question to answer first relates to the last point there—do we want to try to wire this behavior up as a one-off within the view/view-model, or do we want to make something more reusable?

In fact, wiring up the behavior within the view/view-model is actually quite difficult. The first problem is that the property that returns the set of multiple selection items—`SelectedItems`—is not data-bindable; hence, you need to address it directly from the codebehind in the view itself. This breaks the rule of having zero code within the view. (You can bind to the `SelectedItem` property, but that only holds zero or one items.) The approach I'm proposing here is that we can create a specialized version of `Grid`

View through inheritance and then bake our enhanced behavior into that. That will allow us to reuse this behavior whenever we fancy.

The first thing we'll look at is how to pass through this selection to the view-model, and then we'll see how to show the app bar.

## Showing the App Bar on Multiple Selections

For those who are unfamiliar with WPF/Silverlight, I need to explain the idea behind *dependency properties*. If you're familiar with them, you can skip the next few paragraphs.

As hinted at, dependency properties were a WPF/Silverlight invention, but they've found their way down into WinRT's XAML implementation. Understanding what they are and how they work can unlock a lot of the weirdness in WPF/Silverlight/XAML. (I'll now stop referring to WPF/Silverlight and just refer to XAML.)

If you go back to the original versions of Visual Basic (VB), the idea was that you would have a control, such as a button, and a set of properties on the control, such as Text. In VB, and in Windows Forms and ASP.NET Web Forms, such properties are generally backed by a private field. (I'm simplifying a bit here.)

In XAML, the idea is that control/component properties are not backed by private fields but are instead held in a dictionary of some sort. So, if you want to create a Text property on class Button, you tell XAML that you want to create a dependency property for that, well, property. This dependency property acts as a backing store, which you expose usually a normal CLR property.

So what's the meaning behind the name *dependency property*? I did a bit of digging on this and couldn't find a particularly compelling answer. The official version is along the line of "because other things depend on them." In XAML you can have styles, templates, bindings, and other things that can change your property underneath you. What this means is that you could set your Text property to "Foo", but something else could change that property to something else by the time you retrieve it. Although glib, it might be useful to think of a dependency property in terms of "*you* can't depend on it still having the value that *you* set."

 Later in the chapter we'll see how property values can change underneath us. Generally, don't worry about it—properties have their value changed for the greater good of the app's functionality, and this sort of operation normally won't come back and bite you.

In terms of our actual implementation, we need to create a new, specialized implementation of a GridView and then add OpenAppBarsOnMultipleSelection and Selection Command dependency properties.

Extending controls through inheritance is an idea as old as time, so I won't go into detail on this. The first step is to create a new class that extends `GridView` and then we can add in the properties.

Whenever we have a dependency property, we need two things:

- A static read-only field containing the metadata of the property
- An instance read-write property that gets or sets the value as appropriate

There is also a strange wrinkle with dependency properties in that you need to include a callback anonymous method within the metadata of the property that defers to the instance method. This is needed to support data binding. The data binding subsystem understands how to dereference and work with the static dependency property metadata, but doesn't know how to deference and work with the instance properties.

Here's the code showing the two properties together inside the new control:

```
public class MyGridView : GridView
{
    public static readonly DependencyProperty SelectionCommandProperty =
        DependencyProperty.Register("SelectionCommand", typeof(ICommand),
typeof(MyGridView),
            new PropertyMetadata(null, (d, e) =>
                ((MyGridView)d).SelectionCommand = (ICommand)e.NewValue));

    public static readonly DependencyProperty
OpenAppBarsOnMultipleSelectionProperty =
        DependencyProperty.Register("OpenAppBarsOnMultipleSelection",
typeof(bool), typeof(MyGridView),
            new PropertyMetadata(true, (d, e) => ((MyGridView)d).
OpenAppBarsOnMultipleSelection = (bool)e.NewValue));

    public MyGridView()
    {
    }

    public ICommand SelectionCommand
    {
        get { return (ICommand)GetValue(SelectionCommandProperty); }
        set { SetValue(SelectionCommandProperty, value); }
    }

    public bool OpenAppBarsOnMultipleSelection
    {
        get { return (bool)GetValue(
            OpenAppBarsOnMultipleSelectionProperty); }
        set { SetValue(OpenAppBarsOnMultipleSelectionProperty, value); }
    }
}
}
```

At the moment, the XAML in the `ReportsPage` is rigged to use the standard `Grid View` control. If we want to use our new control, we just have to change the declaration from `GridView` to `local:MyGridView`.

If you're unfamiliar with XML namespaces, `GridView` is declared in the default namespace and hence doesn't need a prefix. By default, the base XAML created by Visual Studio when we create the page contains an XML namespace declaration called `local` that maps to the default namespace of the project, which in my case happens to be `StreetFoo.Client.UI`. Thus `local:MyGridView` resolves to `StreetView.Client.UI.MyGridView`.

The modified XAML snippet looks like this (I've omitted the surrounding container code):

```
<!-- Horizontal scrolling grid used in most view states -->
<local:MyGridView
    x:Name="itemGridView"
    AutomationProperties.AutomationId="ItemsGridView"
    AutomationProperties.Name="Items"
    TabIndex="1"
    Margin="0,137,0,-1"
    Padding="116,0,116,46"
    ItemsSource="{Binding Source={StaticResource itemsViewSource}}"
    ItemTemplate="{StaticResource ReportItem250x250Template}"
    SelectionMode="Multiple"
    Grid.RowSpan="2"
      />
```

Note that I have gone ahead and changed the `SelectionMode` as well.

You can run the project at this point if you like. You won't see any different behavior from before in terms of the actual operation of the app bar. We've yet to build the new behavior into the grid. To do that, we need to subscribe to the `SelectionChanged` event within the `MyGridView` control itself.

Back in the world of .NET, controls/components were always designed to have an On*EventName* property that you could override whenever an event was declared. XAML appears to be more hit and miss—certainly `OnSelectionChanged` is not an overrideable method in `GridView`, and hence the only way to receive notifications is to subscribe.

When the selection does change, we want to do two things. First, we must decide whether we want to raise our `SelectionCommand` command based on whether we have a value for it, and whether the command is in a state where it can be executed. Second, we want to show the app bar. This is all pretty simple; here's the code, along with a stub that we'll fill out in a moment:

```
// modified constructor and related handler in MyGridView...
    public MyGridView()
    {
        // wire up the selection changes...
```

```
        this.SelectionChanged += MyGridView_SelectionChanged;
    }

    void MyGridView_SelectionChanged(object sender,
        SelectionChangedEventArgs e)
    {
        if(this.SelectionCommand == null)
            return;

        // pass it on...
        var selected = new List<object>(this.SelectedItems);
        if(this.SelectionCommand.CanExecute(selected))
            this.SelectionCommand.Execute(selected);

        // do we care about multiple items?
        if (this.OpenAppBarsOnMultipleSelection && selected.Count > 1)
            this.OpenAppBarsOnPage(true);
        else if (this.OpenAppBarsOnMultipleSelection && selected.Count == 0)
            this.HideAppBarsOnPage();
    }
```

The `OpenAppBarsOnPage` method is not implemented, so we have a choice: we can either implement it as a one-off inside our control, or we can implement it as a helper method. I propose implementing it as a helper method via the expedient of an extension method.

Extension methods are one of my favorite .NET features, and they are fantastic in this kind of scenario where you want to extend multiple classes without affecting the chain of inheritance. Although we want to open (and ultimately close) app bars on the grid view in this instance, we might want to be able to do this from other controls that we build or extend.

The control/component hierarchy in XAML is understandably complex, but near the base of the hierarchy is a component called `FrameworkElement`. This contains the baseline implementation for components that are supposed to have some presence on the UI. We'll add our extension methods to this.

First off, a standard rule of the UX is that you cannot toggle the top and bottom app bars independently—swipe in from the top or the bottom, and both will display. (For example, I, for some unknown reason, have a habit of swiping in from the top to get access to the bottom app bar.) The methods that we'll build will need to show or hide both the top and bottom app bars each time. Second, we'll need a method that, given a `FrameworkElement` instance, can find its containing page. We can easily achieve this by walking up the `Parent` properties until we find one with an appropriate type.

The third and final consideration relates to "sticky" app bars. The idea of a sticky app bar is that it doesn't hide when you click off of the app bar, whereas a nonsticky/normal app bar does. To stop the app bar from flicking around, we'll provide an option to display it in sticky mode.

Here's the code for `FrameworkElementExtender`:

```
internal static class FrameworkElementExtender
{
    internal static Page GetParentPage(this FrameworkElement element)
    {
        DependencyObject walk = element;
        while (walk != null)
        {
            if (walk is Page)
                return (Page)walk;

            if (walk is FrameworkElement)
                walk = ((FrameworkElement)walk).Parent;
            else
                break;
        }

        // nothing...
        return null;
    }

    internal static void OpenAppBarsOnPage(this FrameworkElement element,
bool sticky)
    {
        // get...
        var page = element.GetParentPage();
        if (page == null)
            return;

        if (page.TopAppBar != null)
        {
            page.TopAppBar.IsSticky = sticky;
            page.TopAppBar.IsOpen = true;
        }
        if (page.BottomAppBar != null)
        {
            page.BottomAppBar.IsSticky = sticky;
            page.BottomAppBar.IsOpen = true;
        }
    }

    internal static void HideAppBarsOnPage(this FrameworkElement element)
    {
        var page = element.GetParentPage();
        if (page == null)
            return;

        if (page.TopAppBar != null)
        {
            page.TopAppBar.IsOpen = false;
            page.TopAppBar.IsSticky = false;
        }
```

```
        if (page.BottomAppBar != null)
        {
            page.BottomAppBar.IsOpen = false;
            page.BottomAppBar.IsSticky = false;
        }
    }
}
```

If you want to set an app bar to be sticky, you need to set the IsSt
icky property before setting IsOpen.

Now you can actually run your project and it should work. Go into the Reports page
and click items on or off; your app bar should automatically show and hide them.

Remember, if you can't seem to make multiple selections, make sure
the MyGridView control's SelectionMode is set to multiple.

## Checking Touch Operations

One of the challenges of being an early adopter in Windows 8/Windows RT is that you
are supposed to be building touch-centric apps on old-style, WIMP-optimized hardware. For this reason it's very important that you check that your app's functionality
works well without a mouse.

You don't have to buy a tablet, though. Visual Studio 2012 comes with a simulator that
lets you simulate touch operations. This is accessible through Visual Studio. You can do
essentially what you can with your full machine, although I found many of the built-in
apps failed to run, as they could not load in time. (Windows will kill off Windows Store
apps if they are slow to load. We'll talk about this more in Chapter 15 when we look at
validating apps for the store.) The point of the simulator is that it has a touch mode that
simulates the mouse.

To run the simulator, in Visual Studio you will find a drop-down control next to the
Run toolbar button. Typically this shows Local Machine, as illustrated in Figure 4-3.
You can drop this down to select Simulator.

*Figure 4-3. Selecting the Simulator option*

By default, the simulator just forwards the mouse events. On the righthand "bezel," you will find an option for Basic Touch Mode. Check this on, and you'll get a crosshair with a circle around it. You've now lost the ability to right-click, but gained the ability to drag in off the edges in the normal way. Figure 4-4 illustrates (as well as I can without having video to show!).

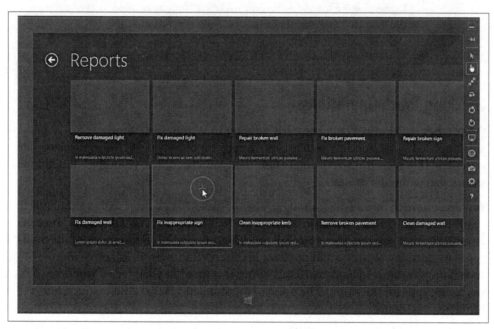

*Figure 4-4. The simulator in Basic Touch Mode*

Confirm for yourself that the operation of the form is roughly within the parameters you expect. Next, we'll look at how to show context options.

# Showing the App Bar on Right-Click

Determining how to actually handle a right-click requires a bit of digging around in the APIs, which makes sense if you consider that it's the old-style way of interaction compared to the new-style, touch-centric way. You can do it by responding to the Pointer Pressed event and digging around for a PointerPoint instance. This has properties on it to tell you what happened. (As a side note, you'll find throughout WinRT a level of agnosticism about what type of input device was used to initiate each event.)

We'll need a new dependency property so that the developer could turn off the behavior if desired. But apart from that, it's pretty simple. Here's the code—note that I have omitted some of the code we built in the last section:

```
// Add new members to MyGridView...
public class MyGridView : GridView
{
    public static readonly DependencyProperty SelectionCommandProperty =
        DependencyProperty.Register("SelectionCommand", typeof(ICommand),
typeof(MyGridView),
        new PropertyMetadata(null, (d, e) => ((MyGridView)d).
SelectionCommand = (ICommand)e.NewValue));

    public static readonly DependencyProperty
OpenAppBarsOnMultipleSelectionProperty =
        DependencyProperty.Register("OpenAppBarsOnMultipleSelection",
typeof(bool), typeof(MyGridView),
        new PropertyMetadata(true, (d, e) => ((MyGridView)d).
OpenAppBarsOnMultipleSelection = (bool)e.NewValue));

    public static readonly DependencyProperty
        OpenAppBarsOnRightClickProperty =
            DependencyProperty.Register("OpenAppBarsOnRightClick",
            typeof(bool), typeof(MyGridView),
            new PropertyMetadata(true, (d, e) => ((MyGridView)d).
OpenAppBarsOnRightClick = (bool)e.NewValue));

    public MyGridView()
    {
        // wire up the selection changes...
        this.SelectionChanged += MyGridView_SelectionChanged;
    } s

    public bool OpenAppBarsOnRightClick
    {
        get { return (bool)GetValue(OpenAppBarsOnRightClickProperty); }
        set { SetValue(OpenAppBarsOnRightClickProperty, value); }
    }

    protected override void OnPointerPressed(PointerRoutedEventArgs e)
    {
        // do we care?
```

```
            if (this.OpenAppBarsOnRightClick && e.GetCurrentPoint(this).
    Properties.IsRightButtonPressed)
                this.OpenAppBarsOnPage(false);

            // base...
            base.OnPointerPressed(e);
        }

    // code omitted for brevity...
    }
```

Now if you run the project, you'll find that you can use the right-mouse button to bring up the app bar, albeit in a slightly different way than the operation exemplified in the Mail app.

## Showing Context Options

At the moment, our app bar is just displaying one option. What we want to look at now is how we can show and hide options on the app bar depending on the selection. We'll add a button that will display a message. (We don't have much business logic that we can hook into at this point, and doing anything more inventive than a message would complicate the discussion.)

The (slightly) tricky element is that we need to show or hide context options depending on the selection state. We've already built a command so that the view can tell us when the selection changes. What we need to do is get the view-model to signal that app bar –based commands are available.

The way that we'll do this will be to put a `StackPanel` on the app bar and then put our context options in that. We can then rig a property (`HasSelection`) and set up data binding so that `StackPanel` is shown or hidden depending on that value. That's the simple, clunky route.

We're going to build commands called `SelectionCommand` and `DumpSelection`, plus a `HasSelectedItems` property in the `IReportsPageViewModel` interface. Here's the code:

```
    // Add properties to IReportsPageViewModel...
    public interface IReportsPageViewModel : IViewModel
    {
        ICommand RefreshCommand { get; }
        ICommand DumpSelectionCommand { get; }
        ICommand SelectionCommand { get; }

        ObservableCollection<ReportItem> Items
        {
            get;
        }

        bool HasSelectedItems
        {
```

```
        get;
    }
}
```

For the actual implementation, we just have to build handlers for those two commands:

- We'll need a property for holding a list of the selected items called SelectedItems.

- When we respond to SelectionCommand, we'll take the IEnumerable<object> instance that we'll be given, assume it contains ReportItem instances, and replace whatever is already held in SelectedItems.

- When we do respond to SelectionCommand, we'll be changing the meaning of the HasSelectedItems property. A "gotcha" on this is that we'll have to raise an appropriate INotifyPropertyChanged signal when we respond to SelectionCommand so that the XAML data binding subsystem knows that we've changed the value of HasSelectedItems. A corollary point is that for completeness we should tell it that SelectedItems has also changed.

- Finally, when we respond to DumpSelectionCommand, we'll render a message.

This is straightforward code, so I'll just present it. Here are the changes required for ReportsPageViewModel (I've omitted some of the other code for brevity):

```
public class ReportsPageViewModel : ViewModel, IReportsPageViewModel
{
    public ObservableCollection<ReportItem> Items { get; private set; }
    private List<ReportItem> SelectedItems { get; set; }

    public ICommand RefreshCommand { get; private set; }
    public ICommand DumpSelectionCommand { get; private set; }
    public ICommand SelectionCommand { get; private set; }

    public ReportsPageViewModel(IViewModelHost host)
        : base(host)
    {
        // setup...
        this.Items = new ObservableCollection<ReportItem>();
        this.SelectedItems = new List<ReportItem>();

        // commands...
        this.RefreshCommand = new DelegateCommand(async (e) =>
        {
            await this.DoRefresh(true);
        });

        // update any selection that we were given...
        this.SelectionCommand = new DelegateCommand((args) =>
        {
            // update the selection...
            this.SelectedItems.Clear();
            foreach (ReportItem item in (IEnumerable<object>)args)
```

```
                    this.SelectedItems.Add(item);

                // raise...
                this.OnPropertyChanged("SelectedItems");
                this.OnPropertyChanged("HasSelectedItems");
            });

            // dump the state...
            this.DumpSelectionCommand = new DelegateCommand(async (e) =>
            {
                if (this.SelectedItems.Count > 0)
                {
                    var builder = new StringBuilder();
                    foreach (var item in this.SelectedItems)
                    {
                        if (builder.Length > 0)
                            builder.Append("\r\n");
                        builder.Append(item.Title);
                    }

                    // show...
                    await this.Host.ShowAlertAsync(builder.ToString());
                }
                else
                    await this.Host.ShowAlertAsync("(No selection)");
            });
        }

        public bool HasSelectedItems
        {
            get
            {
                return this.SelectedItems.Count > 0;
            }
        }
    }
}
```

To wire this up, we just need to change the XAML. First, we need to alter the app bar so that the `StackPanel` control on the left side is bound to the `HasSelectedItems` property on the view-model. Second, we need to rig the `SelectionCommand` property on the `MyGridView` instance to call into the handler on the view-model.

I won't reproduce both together, as it'll be hard to see what's happening. First off, here's the change to the app bar:

```
<!-- Modify markup related to the app bar -->
<Page.BottomAppBar>
    <AppBar>
        <Grid>
            <Grid.ColumnDefinitions>
                <ColumnDefinition Width="50*"/>
                <ColumnDefinition Width="50*"/>
```

```
        </Grid.ColumnDefinitions>
        <StackPanel Orientation="Horizontal" Visibility="{Binding
         HasSelectedItems, ConverterBooleanTo={StaticResource
         VisibilityConverter}}">
            <Button Content="Dump Selection" Command="{Binding
             DumpSelectionCommand}" />
        </StackPanel>
        <StackPanel HorizontalAlignment="Right" Orientation="Horizontal"
Grid.Column="2">
            <Button x:Name="buttonRefresh" Style="{StaticResource
RefreshAppBarButtonStyle}" Command="{Binding RefreshCommand}" />
        </StackPanel>
        </Grid>
      </AppBar>
    </Page.BottomAppBar>
```

The last step is to rig up the binding for the command. This is just a matter of binding up SelectionCommand:

```
<!-- Horizontal scrolling grid used in most view states -->
<local:MyGridView
    x:Name="itemGridView"
    AutomationProperties.AutomationId="ItemsGridView"
    AutomationProperties.Name="Items"
    TabIndex="1"
    Margin="0,137,0,-1"
    Padding="116,0,116,46"
    ItemsSource="{Binding Source={StaticResource itemsViewSource}}"
    ItemTemplate="{StaticResource ReportItem250x250Template}"
    SelectionMode="Multiple"
    Grid.RowSpan="2"
    SelectionCommand="{Binding SelectionCommand}"
    />
```

That's all there is to it! If you run the project, you should find that the Dump Selection button is not available without a selection, but as soon as a selection is made it will become available. Clicking the button will result in a message being displayed, as illustrated in Figure 4-5.

*Figure 4-5. Message showing an example selection state*

# App Bar Images

Adding images to the app bar is an absolute requirement, but it's irritatingly difficult to achieve in the version of the tooling on which this book is based. Hopefully it will become easier, and perhaps it already is if you're using a later version of the tools.

On paper, the way images are done on the app bar sounds brilliant. Windows 8/Windows RT comes with a font called Segoe UI Symbol—a version of the standard Segoe font used in Windows Store apps, but with a whole bunch of glyphs that can be used as icons. You get, out of the box, a couple of hundred icons that you can use.

The genius of using fonts instead of images for icons is that they are vectorized, meaning that you can render them on any background and in any size, and they look exactly right. The downside of using fonts instead of images is that you can't change the set of icons that you have.

The Visual Studio template provides a set of styles that you can apply to buttons to produce an icon, but for some reason this tooling only works with the icons stored in font libraries. This means it's extremely limited. It also means that it's not straightforward to use your own icons, which in everything but the most basic of apps is going to be the case.

What we're going to do in this section is look at the way Visual Studio does it first, specifically by changing the Refresh button that we built previously to use the built-in Refresh icon. We'll then look at creating a parallel implementation of Visual Studio's implementation that will work with PNG files.

## The Glyph Method

You can see the icons that you get out of the box by using the Windows `charmap.exe` utility. If you start `charmap.exe` from the Run dialog and change the font to Segoe UI Symbol, you'll find the icons starting in the 0xE000 range. (In fact, 0xE000, as shown in Figure 4-6, is the standard "search" icon.)

I mentioned earlier that in the Windows 8 tooling, each project got given a large StandardStyles.xaml file. Among other things, this file contained the declarations of a massive collection of app bar buttons, based on the glyphs that we've been discussing. In the new Windows 8.1 tooling, for some reason there is no equivalent (at least as of the time of writing), so my proposal is to bring those styles forward manually into our new StandardStyles.xaml. There is an awful lot of it, but they do ultimately create a good effect. Here's the code:

```
<!-- Add to StandardStyles.xaml… -->
<Style x:Key="AppBarButtonStyle" TargetType="Button">
        <Setter Property="Foreground" Value="{StaticResource
AppBarItemForegroundThemeBrush}"/>
        <Setter Property="VerticalAlignment" Value="Stretch"/>
```

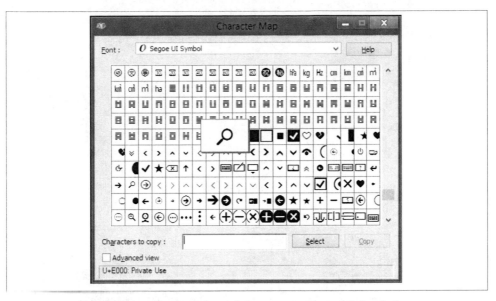

*Figure 4-6. Charmap.exe showing some of the icons in Segoe UI Symbol*

```xml
<Setter Property="FontFamily" Value="Segoe UI Symbol"/>
<Setter Property="FontWeight" Value="Normal"/>
<Setter Property="FontSize" Value="20"/>
<Setter Property="AutomationProperties.ItemType" Value="App Bar Button"/>
<Setter Property="Template">
    <Setter.Value>
        <ControlTemplate TargetType="Button">
            <Grid x:Name="RootGrid" Width="100" Background="Transparent">
                <StackPanel VerticalAlignment="Top" Margin="0,12,0,11">
                    <Grid Width="40" Height="40" Margin="0,0,0,5"
                        HorizontalAlignment="Center">
                        <TextBlock x:Name="BackgroundGlyph"
                        Text="&#xE0A8;" FontFamily="Segoe UI Symbol"
                        FontSize="53.333" Margin="-4,-19,0,0"
                        Foreground="{StaticResource
                        AppBarItemBackgroundThemeBrush}"/>
                        <TextBlock x:Name="OutlineGlyph" Text="&#xE0A7;"
                        FontFamily="Segoe UI Symbol" FontSize="53.333"
                        Margin="-4,-19,0,0"/>
                        <ContentPresenter x:Name="Content"
                        HorizontalAlignment="Center" Margin="-1,-1,0,0"
                        VerticalAlignment="Center"/>
                    </Grid>
                    <TextBlock
                        x:Name="TextLabel"
                        Text="{TemplateBinding
                        AutomationProperties.Name}"
                        Foreground="{StaticResource
```

```xml
                                         AppBarItemForegroundThemeBrush}"
                                Margin="0,0,2,0"
                                FontSize="12"
                                TextAlignment="Center"
                                Width="88"
                                MaxHeight="32"
                                TextTrimming="WordEllipsis"
                                Style="{StaticResource BasicTextStyle}"/>
                    </StackPanel>
                    <Rectangle
                                x:Name="FocusVisualWhite"
                                IsHitTestVisible="False"
                                Stroke="{StaticResource
                                FocusVisualWhiteStrokeThemeBrush}"
                                StrokeEndLineCap="Square"
                                StrokeDashArray="1,1"
                                Opacity="0"
                                StrokeDashOffset="1.5"/>
                    <Rectangle
                                x:Name="FocusVisualBlack"
                                IsHitTestVisible="False"
                                Stroke="{StaticResource
                                FocusVisualBlackStrokeThemeBrush}"
                                StrokeEndLineCap="Square"
                                StrokeDashArray="1,1"
                                Opacity="0"
                                StrokeDashOffset="0.5"/>

                    <VisualStateManager.VisualStateGroups>
                        <VisualStateGroup x:Name="ApplicationViewStates">
                            <VisualState x:Name="FullScreenLandscape"/>
                            <VisualState x:Name="Filled"/>
                            <VisualState x:Name="FullScreenPortrait">
                                <Storyboard>
                                    <ObjectAnimationUsingKeyFrames
                                      Storyboard.TargetName="TextLabel"
                                      Storyboard.TargetProperty="Visibility">
                                        <DiscreteObjectKeyFrame KeyTime="0"
                                         Value="Collapsed"/>
                                    </ObjectAnimationUsingKeyFrames>
                                    <ObjectAnimationUsingKeyFrames
                                      Storyboard.TargetName="RootGrid"
                                      Storyboard.TargetProperty="Width">
                                        <DiscreteObjectKeyFrame KeyTime="0"
                                         Value="60"/>
                                    </ObjectAnimationUsingKeyFrames>
                                </Storyboard>
                            </VisualState>
                            <VisualState x:Name="Snapped">
                                <Storyboard>
                                    <ObjectAnimationUsingKeyFrames
                                      Storyboard.TargetName="TextLabel"
```

```
                    Storyboard.TargetProperty="Visibility">
                        <DiscreteObjectKeyFrame KeyTime="0"
                        Value="Collapsed"/>
                    </ObjectAnimationUsingKeyFrames>
                    <ObjectAnimationUsingKeyFrames
                     Storyboard.TargetName="RootGrid"
                     Storyboard.TargetProperty="Width">
                        <DiscreteObjectKeyFrame KeyTime="0"
                        Value="60"/>
                    </ObjectAnimationUsingKeyFrames>
                </Storyboard>
            </VisualState>
        </VisualStateGroup>
        <VisualStateGroup x:Name="CommonStates">
            <VisualState x:Name="Normal"/>
            <VisualState x:Name="PointerOver">
                <Storyboard>
                    <ObjectAnimationUsingKeyFrames
                     Storyboard.TargetName="BackgroundGlyph"
                     Storyboard.TargetProperty="Foreground">
                        <DiscreteObjectKeyFrame KeyTime="0"
                        Value="{StaticResource AppBarItem
                        PointerOverBackgroundThemeBrush}"/>
                    </ObjectAnimationUsingKeyFrames>
                    <ObjectAnimationUsingKeyFrames
                     Storyboard.TargetName="Content"
                     Storyboard.TargetProperty="Foreground">
                        <DiscreteObjectKeyFrame KeyTime="0"
                        Value="{StaticResource AppBarItem
                        PointerOverForegroundThemeBrush}"/>
                    </ObjectAnimationUsingKeyFrames>
                </Storyboard>
            </VisualState>
            <VisualState x:Name="Pressed">
                <Storyboard>
                    <ObjectAnimationUsingKeyFrames
                     Storyboard.TargetName="OutlineGlyph"
                     Storyboard.TargetProperty="Foreground">
                        <DiscreteObjectKeyFrame KeyTime="0"
                        Value="{StaticResource AppBarItem
                        ForegroundThemeBrush}"/>
                    </ObjectAnimationUsingKeyFrames>
                    <ObjectAnimationUsingKeyFrames
                     Storyboard.TargetName="BackgroundGlyph"
                     Storyboard.TargetProperty="Foreground">
                        <DiscreteObjectKeyFrame KeyTime="0"
                        Value="{StaticResource AppBarItem
                        ForegroundThemeBrush}"/>
                    </ObjectAnimationUsingKeyFrames>
                    <ObjectAnimationUsingKeyFrames
                     Storyboard.TargetName="Content"
                     Storyboard.TargetProperty="Foreground">
```

```xml
                            <DiscreteObjectKeyFrame KeyTime="0"
                                Value="{StaticResource AppBarItem
                                PressedForegroundThemeBrush}"/>
                        </ObjectAnimationUsingKeyFrames>
                    </Storyboard>
                </VisualState>
                <VisualState x:Name="Disabled">
                    <Storyboard>
                        <ObjectAnimationUsingKeyFrames
                            Storyboard.TargetName="OutlineGlyph"
                            Storyboard.TargetProperty="Foreground">
                            <DiscreteObjectKeyFrame KeyTime="0"
                                Value="{StaticResource AppBarItem
                                DisabledForegroundThemeBrush}"/>
                        </ObjectAnimationUsingKeyFrames>
                        <ObjectAnimationUsingKeyFrames
                            Storyboard.TargetName="Content"
                            Storyboard.TargetProperty="Foreground">
                            <DiscreteObjectKeyFrame KeyTime="0"
                                Value="{StaticResource AppBarItem
                                DisabledForegroundThemeBrush}"/>
                        </ObjectAnimationUsingKeyFrames>
                        <ObjectAnimationUsingKeyFrames
                            Storyboard.TargetName="TextLabel"
                            Storyboard.TargetProperty="Foreground">
                            <DiscreteObjectKeyFrame KeyTime="0"
                                Value="{StaticResource AppBarItem
                                DisabledForegroundThemeBrush}"/>
                        </ObjectAnimationUsingKeyFrames>
                    </Storyboard>
                </VisualState>
            </VisualStateGroup>
            <VisualStateGroup x:Name="FocusStates">
                <VisualState x:Name="Focused">
                    <Storyboard>
                        <DoubleAnimation
                                Storyboard.TargetName=
                                "FocusVisualWhite"
                                Storyboard.TargetProperty=
                                "Opacity"
                                To="1"
                                Duration="0"/>
                        <DoubleAnimation
                                Storyboard.TargetName=
                                "FocusVisualBlack"
                                Storyboard.TargetProperty=
                                "Opacity"
                                To="1"
                                Duration="0"/>
                    </Storyboard>
                </VisualState>
                <VisualState x:Name="Unfocused" />
```

```
                        <VisualState x:Name="PointerFocused" />
                    </VisualStateGroup>
                </VisualStateManager.VisualStateGroups>
            </Grid>
        </ControlTemplate>
    </Setter.Value>
    </Setter>
</Style>
```

When we want a new button, we create a new style that uses the templates. Add this style for a refresh button to *StandardStyles.xaml*:

```
<Style x:Key="RefreshAppBarButtonStyle" TargetType="Button" BasedOn="
{StaticResource AppBarButtonStyle}">
    <Setter Property="AutomationProperties.AutomationId"
Value="RefreshAppBarButton"/>
    <Setter Property="AutomationProperties.Name" Value="Refresh"/>
    <Setter Property="Content" Value="&#xE117;"/>
</Style>
```

The `Content` entry does the magic of setting the font. `0xE117` refers to the Refresh icon, which you can confirm for yourself in `charmap.exe` if you want. The `AutomationPro perties.Name` entry is used for the label that will appear in the icon.

Using these is very simple. Here's the XAML for our existing Refresh button, but with the `Content` value removed and `Style` value added:

```
<Page.BottomAppBar>
    <AppBar>
        <Grid>
            <Grid.ColumnDefinitions>
                <ColumnDefinition Width="50*"/>
                <ColumnDefinition Width="50*"/>
            </Grid.ColumnDefinitions>
        <StackPanel Orientation="Horizontal" Visibility="{Binding
         HasSelectedItems, Converter={StaticResource
         VisibilityConverter}}">
            <Button Content="Dump Selection" Command="{Binding
             DumpSelectionCommand}" />
        </StackPanel>
        <StackPanel HorizontalAlignment="Right" Orientation="Horizontal"
         Grid.Column="2">
            <Button Style="{StaticResource RefreshAppBarButtonStyle}"
             Command="{Binding RefreshCommand}" />
        </StackPanel>
        </Grid>
    </AppBar>
</Page.BottomAppBar>
```

Run the app, and you'll see the "iconified" button on the app bar. Figure 4-7 illustrates.

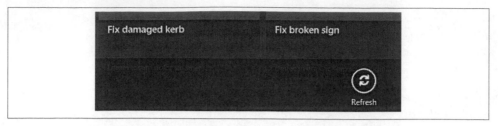

*Figure 4-7. The Refresh button with an icon*

You can likely see how fantastically straightforward this is. It's just a shame it's so limited —but we'll get to that.

# Using Images

Going through how to use images with your buttons is helpful in its own right, but for those of you new to WPF/Silverlight/XAML, it also serves as a way of going through styles and templates. If you are familiar with styles and templates, however, please keep reading, as we'll segue into looking at our own image implementation without a clean break.

### Styles in XAML

Have a look again at the style definition for our Refresh button:

```
<Style x:Key="RefreshAppBarButtonStyle" TargetType="Button" BasedOn=
"{StaticResource AppBarButtonStyle}">
    <Setter Property="AutomationProperties.AutomationId" Value=
"RefreshAppBarButton"/>
    <Setter Property="AutomationProperties.Name" Value="Refresh"/>
    <Setter Property="Content" Value="&#xE117;"/>
</Style>
```

In XAML, styles are a group of property set instructions expressed in XML. You can see here how we have three properties to set: `AutomationProperties.AutomationId`, `AutomationProperties.Name`, and `Content`. In fact, there's more than that because the style definition has a `BasedOn` attribute that tells XAML to go and set that style first before this one. The upshot is that just by our applying a style, XAML will change a whole load of our properties. This gets back to our conversation on dependency properties—you can't "depend" on the value you set directly staying current because, in this case, the style can co-opt the properties for its own purposes.

Where this gets a bit wacky is that the base style—`AppBarButtonStyle`—contains a directive that sets the `Template` property. I've chosen not to reproduce all of `AppBar` `ButtonStyle` here, as we saw previously. Here instead is the top part of the `Template` setter declaration in `AppBarButtonStyle`:

```
<Style x:Key="AppBarButtonStyle" TargetType="Button">
    <Setter Property="Foreground" Value="{StaticResource
AppBarItemForegroundThemeBrush}"/>
    <Setter Property="VerticalAlignment" Value="Stretch"/>
    <Setter Property="FontFamily" Value="Segoe UI Symbol"/>
    <Setter Property="FontWeight" Value="Normal"/>
    <Setter Property="FontSize" Value="20"/>
    <Setter Property="AutomationProperties.ItemType"
Value="App Bar Button"/>
    <Setter Property="Template">
        <Setter.Value>
            <ControlTemplate TargetType="Button">
                <Grid x:Name="RootGrid" Width="100"
Background="Transparent">
                    <StackPanel VerticalAlignment="Top" Margin="0,12,0,11">
                        <Grid Width="40" Height="40" Margin="0,0,0,5"
HorizontalAlignment="Center">
                            <TextBlock x:Name="BackgroundGlyph"
Text="&#xE0A8;" FontFamily="Segoe UI Symbol" FontSize="53.333"
Margin="-4,-19,0,0"
Foreground="{StaticResource AppBarItemBackgroundThemeBrush}"/>
                            <TextBlock x:Name="OutlineGlyph"
Text="&#xE0A7;" FontFamily="Segoe UI Symbol" FontSize="53.333"
Margin="-4,-19,0,0"/>
                            <ContentPresenter x:Name="Content"
HorizontalAlignment="Center" Margin="-1,-1,0,0" VerticalAlignment="Center"/>
                        </Grid>
                        <TextBlock
                            x:Name="TextLabel"
                    Text="{TemplateBinding AutomationProperties.Name}"
                    Foreground="{StaticResource AppBarItemForegroundThemeBrush}"
                            Margin="0,0,2,0"
                            FontSize="12"
                            TextAlignment="Center"
                            Width="88"
                            MaxHeight="32"
                            TextTrimming="WordEllipsis"
                            Style="{StaticResource BasicTextStyle}"/>
                    </StackPanel>
    <!-- etc... -->
</Style>
```

I've highlighted some of the important parts here. Ultimately what this is doing is setting up a stack of overlapping controls to form the image. The first two TextBlock controls are using the symbol font to render two circles, an outline circle and a solid circle. The solid circle is colored to match the background, the idea being that when clicked that color can be changed to give the user some visual feedback. The ContentPresenter control takes the Content property of the button and "re-presents" it.

Actually, that's an important point. In XAML, the templates work by totally replacing the rendering instructions of the base control—in this case, a button. This is a slightly odd concept to anyone who's done any UI programming from Win16 onward, as in most cases you extend behavior as opposed to presentation. If you're new to this, the key thing to remember is that with the `Template` property set, the `Button` control is no longer in charge of its rendering.

The last control to consider is the `TextBlock` control positioned underneath the image grid. This is used to render the caption under the icon.

You may have noticed references to `AutomationProperties` in there. If you're familiar with COM/ActiveX and unfamiliar with XAML, you may assume these are related to COM Automation. They are not—in fact, they have to do with automated testing and are a feature brought over from WPF. The principle is that they provide a more formally defined set of hooks for automated test harnesses. They can also be used for accessibility functions. What's relevant to us here is that we don't want to break this stuff when we add our images. The easiest thing to do with them is just not fiddle with that part of the existing implementation and steer clear.

So how do we add our images? Actually, the answer is pretty straightforward—we just need to replace the elements that render a glyph with elements that render an image. Let's see how.

### Creating images for app bar buttons

You'll need an image editor to create the images for the app bar. In fact, you'll generally need an image editor in your day-to-day work as a software engineer; it's a good thing to have in your toolkit. There are lots of them out there, but I happen to use Adobe Fireworks, and I'd go so far as to say that it would be my recommendation for web work, legacy desktop work, and Windows Store app development work.

 At the time of writing, I could not find any hard rules about the configuration of the images for app bars. I could for Windows Phone — it calls for a 48×48 image with a 26×26 area in the middle containing the actual image. Windows Phone also has this "circle surrounding the icon" look. The image is supposed to be big enough to accommodate the circle, meaning that the square in the middle is where you put your actual icon. Here, we'll pull the same trick with making the images large enough to accommodate the circle.

I took a screenshot of the Refresh button and measured the size. I then created a 40×40 image (which happens to be the size of the containing grid for the button declared in the template) and created a 24×24 "important part" in the middle. Figure 4-8 shows you what I got. (This jumps ahead to the part we haven't built yet—that is, actually being able to render an image in a button.)

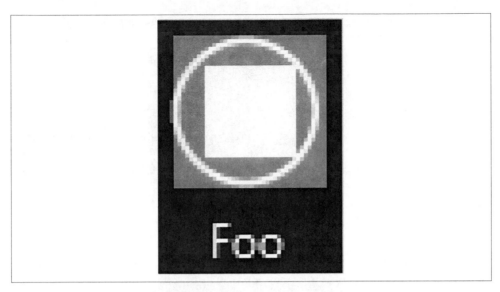

*Figure 4-8. Button image layout (zoomed in)*

What's throwing that off is the inexactness of the symbol font. It's all lining up, but it's not quite right in that it's skewed to the right and not aligned on the left. Another factor is that XAML will stretch the image to make it fit—in my experiments, it was impossible to do any better than that. (And if you actually zoom into the standard Refresh button, it's not evenly spaced or particularly neat.) Thus, my proposal is that for a "good enough" image, create a 40×40 box with a 24×24 area in the middle for the icon.

To make something more attractive for the download, I created a PNG based on one of the fonts in Segoe UI Symbol. By the way, there is a fantastic library of icons at the Noun Project (*http://thenounproject.com/*). I would have used one of those but did not, as some of them are copyrighted and it's easier not to risk using one of those in print.

When you create images, you need to render them on white and alias them onto a transparent background. This will give the renderer the best chance of making it look good regardless of the final app bar background color. You can see this for yourself in the code download. (It's difficult to render a white-on-transparent image in a book!)

To add the image to your project, all you have to do is add it to the *Assets* folder in the project. Make sure that you actually include the file in your project; otherwise, the AppX packager doesn't know to include it. You don't need to mark it as Embedded Resource, as it's not a resource in the traditional sense. The file should instead be marked as Content.

This packaging trick/feature is the same one used with *sqlite3.dll* in Chapter 3.

### Creating a template that uses an image

The magic part of the template is the `ContentPresenter`. All we have to do is override the default behavior so that it uses an image. (The default behavior renders the text stored in the `Content` property of the button.) Specifically, we want to pass the `Content` `Presenter` an `Image` control. If we set the `Content` property of the button to the URL of an image, with `ContentPresenter` rigged to use an `Image` control, everything should just work. (If that's not making much sense now, go with it—once you see this happen, it'll all become clear.)

This is the first time we've worked with images in the book. In my opinion, this is one of the standout great bits of WinRT development.

Just like every version of Windows from v1 onward, you can package static resources. Whereas in the past, these have always been baked into a single file, in WinRT they go into an AppX package, which is exploded onto the disk on installation. (We'll talk more about packaging in Chapter 15.) From within our apps, we can use URLs to refer to files included in the original package. Specifically, we can use the `ms-appx:` protocol handler.

Thus, if we have an image called *Foo.png* placed within the *~/Assets* folder of our project, we can refer to it with the URL *ms-appx:///Assets/Foo.png*. This is fantastically consistent with normal URI addressing and also very straightforward.

All we have to do then is create the following hierarchy:

- At the top we'll keep our `AppBarButtonStyle` as is.
- In the middle we'll create an `AppBarImageButtonStyle`. This will replace the `Tem` `plate` property created by `AppBarButtonStyle` with one that renders an image rather than a glyph.
- At the bottom we'll create our button-specific styles, as per the existing behavior in the template. We'll create a `FooAppBarButtonStyle`.

We'll do this in reverse order. You'll need to make these changes within *Standard Styles.xaml*. First, here is the definition of `FooAppBarButtonStyle`:

```
<!-- Add to StandardStyles.xaml -->
  <Style x:Key="FooAppBarButtonStyle" TargetType="Button" BasedOn=
    "{StaticResource AppBarImageButtonStyle}">
    <Setter Property="AutomationProperties.AutomationId" Value=
      "FooAppBarButtonStyle"/>
    <Setter Property="AutomationProperties.Name" Value="Foo"/>
```

```
    <Setter Property="Content" Value="ms-appx:///Assets/Foo.png"></Setter>
</Style>
```

You can see the `ms-appx:` protocol in play in that `Content` property setter. Hopefully it's obvious how the URL addressing is working.

 Note that we don't call this `FooAppBarImageButtonStyle`. Consumers shouldn't care about the underlying implementation—whether it uses an image or a glyph isn't directly relevant from their perspective.

`AppBarImageButtonStyle` is fairly easy (but long). I've highlighted where the `Content Presenter` is modified to use an `Image` instance, and also the base element where we tell it that it's based on `AppBarButtonStyle`.

```
<Style x:Key="AppBarImageButtonStyle" TargetType="Button" BasedOn=
"{StaticResource AppBarButtonStyle}">
    <Setter Property="Template">
        <Setter.Value>
            <ControlTemplate TargetType="Button">
                <Grid x:Name="RootGrid" Width="100" Background="Transparent">
                    <StackPanel VerticalAlignment="Top" Margin="0,12,0,11">
                        <Grid Width="40" Height="40" Margin="0,0,0,5"
                        HorizontalAlignment="Center">
                            <ContentPresenter>
                                <ContentPresenter.Content>
                                    <Image Source="{TemplateBinding
                                    Content}"></Image>
                                </ContentPresenter.Content>
                            </ContentPresenter>
                            <TextBlock x:Name="OutlineGlyph" Text="&#xE0A7;"
                            FontFamily="Segoe UI Symbol" FontSize="53.333"
                            Margin="-4,-19,0,0"/>
                        </Grid>
                        <TextBlock
                            x:Name="TextLabel"
                        Text="{TemplateBinding AutomationProperties.Name}"
                            Foreground="{StaticResource
                            AppBarItemForegroundThemeBrush}"
                            Margin="0,0,2,0"
                            FontSize="12"
                            TextAlignment="Center"
                            Width="88"
                            MaxHeight="32"
                            TextTrimming="WordEllipsis"
                            Style="{StaticResource BasicTextStyle}"/>
                    </StackPanel>
                    <Rectangle
                            x:Name="FocusVisualWhite"
                            IsHitTestVisible="False"
```

```
                                Stroke="{StaticResource
                                FocusVisualWhiteStrokeThemeBrush}"
                                StrokeEndLineCap="Square"
                                StrokeDashArray="1,1"
                                Opacity="0"
                                StrokeDashOffset="1.5"/>
                        <Rectangle
                                x:Name="FocusVisualBlack"
                                IsHitTestVisible="False"
                                Stroke="{StaticResource
                                FocusVisualBlackStrokeThemeBrush}"
                                StrokeEndLineCap="Square"
                                StrokeDashArray="1,1"
                                Opacity="0"
                                StrokeDashOffset="0.5"/>
                    </Grid>
                </ControlTemplate>
            </Setter.Value>
        </Setter>
    </Style>
```

You can now go ahead and add the new button to your app bar that uses that style. My
Foo button raises the refresh command, but you can make the button do whatever you
like. Here's the modified app bar:

```
<Page.BottomAppBar>
    <AppBar>
        <Grid>
            <Grid.ColumnDefinitions>
                <ColumnDefinition Width="50*"/>
                <ColumnDefinition Width="50*"/>
            </Grid.ColumnDefinitions>
            <StackPanel Orientation="Horizontal" Visibility="{Binding
             HasSelectedItems, Converter={StaticResource
             VisibilityConverter}}">
                <Button Content="Dump Selection" Command="{Binding
                  DumpSelectionCommand}" />
            </StackPanel>
            <StackPanel HorizontalAlignment="Right" Orientation="Horizontal"
             Grid.Column="2">
                <Button Style="{StaticResource FooAppBarButtonStyle}"
                 Command="{Binding RefreshCommand}" />
                <Button Style="{StaticResource RefreshAppBarButtonStyle}"
                  Command="{Binding RefreshCommand}" />
            </StackPanel>
        </Grid>
    </AppBar>
</Page.BottomAppBar>
```

That's it! Run the project, and you'll now have an image. Figure 4-9 illustrates.

*Figure 4-9. The PNG-backed Foo option in situ*

# CHAPTER 5

# Notifications

Notifications are one of the areas of the Windows Store app UX that have been extremely well implemented. They are used in situations where you want to reach out and inform users about something when they are not using the app. In retail scenarios they are commonly used to indicate that new messages are available. In line-of-business (LOB) scenarios they can be used to proactively reach out to your user audience in innovative ways.

There are four types of notifications in Windows Store apps: toast, tiles, badges, and raw. (In this book we won't be talking about raw notifications, as they are too niche.) Toast describes the messages that wind in from the right edge of the screen. (Prior to the implementation in Windows 8/Windows RT, these used to "pop up" from the bottom-right edge of the screen like toast from a toaster, hence the name.) Tiles are the most interesting way of handling notifications. Actually, tiles are perhaps *the* most significant UX feature in Windows Store apps. They are unique to the device-based/touch-centric Windows vision and allow apps to aggregate data in a single, easy-to-grasp view. First appearing in Windows Phone and brought over to Windows 8/Windows RT, they work like a "personal dashboard" for the user. In LOB scenarios they can be interesting, as they provide for new ways of interacting with your user base. Finally, badges apply to tiles. They allow you to attach numbers or a glyph to a tile. (A glyph, just in case the term is new to you, is basically an icon.)

The work in this chapter will be divided into two sections. We'll start off by looking at *local notifications*. These are notifications where the app uses the notification subsystem to initiate toast, badge, and tile updates on the same device. We're going to construct three "builder" classes, one for each type. As we'll see, when we work with notifications we ask WinRT to give us an XML-based template, which we then populate with data and give back to WinRT. This XML-based approach is fine, but challenging from a code maintenance perspective unless you happen to remember the structure of the various XML templates—hence the builders, which make the maintenance easier.

In the second half of the chapter we'll look at *remote notifications*. These are notifications that are initiated by a cloud-based server and that wend their way down to the device using the Windows Push Notification Service (WNS). This works by originating XML on the server in the same format as local and then passing it over to WNS. This requires an authentication step, followed by a transfer step.

# Local Notifications

Notifications work in two ways: they are either generated locally from the device and shown on that same device, or they are generated by an external server and pushed to all subscribing devices. In this section we're going to look at the former.

## Turning Notifications On and Off

It's possible to turn off toast notifications globally using the Change PC Settings option. You should make sure that notifications are globally available before you start this work to save frustration later.

## XML Templates

All three of the notification formats use the same approach. Each has its own manager class: `ToastNotifier`, `BadgeUpdater`, and `TileUpdater`. Each of the manager classes has a method that returns an XML template that you fill in with your app-specific data before returning it back to the manager for display. Each format has a variety of templates to choose from. (I'll go through some of the key templates as we look at each format, but MSDN should remain your definitive resource.) Here's an example of some basic toast XML that displays a "Hello, world" message. For clarity, this is an example of a toast template (specifically `ToastText01`) that has been populated with some data:

```
<toast>
  <visual>
      <binding template="ToastText01">
          <text id="1">Hello, world.</text>
      </binding>
  </visual>
</toast>
```

Easy, huh?

In fact, the only tricky thing about working with notifications is that from a code maintenance perspective, the XML-based approach is a bit of a pain. The code won't self-document because all you do is ask the notification manager to return the XML template, then use the DOM to update values.

For our work here, I'm proposing that we create some "builder" classes that are able to populate the template for us. They will also be able to send the populated XML through to the "managers." (The managers are the APIs supplied by WinRT that you give the notifications to.) This will let us create code that's more expressive and self-describing, and thus more maintainable. Although the schema information for notifications is documented on MSDN (look for "toast schema" on the MSDN site), it's much easier to abstract away the actual construction of the XML.

I'll start by sketching out the proposed object model. Let's look at the general structure of the templates first. (As we go through this I'm not going to create a detailed inventory of the templates, as these are all on MSDN. What I will do is call out some important templates with the expectation that you'll need to go to MSDN for the definitive list.)

- There are eight toast templates. Half of the eight templates allow for an image to be displayed on the left side of the notification. All of the templates have various text configurations—we'll learn more about that as we go.

- At the time of writing, there are 46 tile templates! (There are so many because Microsoft wants to provide maximum flexibility for this key feature. Plus, building your own tile formats is verboten.) There are two main types of tile template—one set that displays some static information, and another set that displays information that "revolves" between picture and text information. You can see this in action on the Start screen; the News app tile, for example, will display an image, and after a while it will be replaced with some text, and then it will go back to an image.

- There are two badge templates. Badges are overlays for tiles, and can either display a number (e.g., the number of unread items) or a glyph.

One of the strange API design decisions at play here is that there isn't a set of base classes in play. For example, WinRT provides `ToastNotification`, `TileNotification`, and `BadgeNotification`, but there is no base `Notification` class. Likewise, in the manager classes, there is no base implementation. While there will undoubtedly be good reason for this, our builder classes will be more obviously object-oriented. We'll have `Notifi cationBuilder<T>` and `NotificationWithTextBuilder<T>` classes that we'll specialize into `ToastNotificationBuilder`, `TileNotificationBuilder`, and `BadgeNotifica tionBuilder` classes.

Each of those classes will hold a static instance that keys into the notification system. For toast, this is called a *notifier*. For tiles and badges, this is called an *updater*. Regardless of the name, they do the same thing.

 The nomenclature inconsistency is because toast "notifies" the user something is happening, whereas tiles/badges are more passive. This inconsistency makes sense if you regard them in isolation, but seems strange if you regard them in terms of their construction and shared behavior. My advice? Don't worry about it!

Figure 5-1 shows a sketch of what we're looking to achieve.

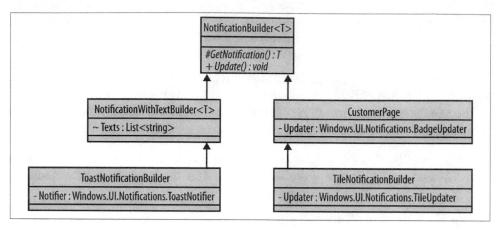

*Figure 5-1. Sketch of our notification builders*

Within our code, we'll create an instance of whatever builder we want and use an object model to define the notifications. As discussed, this will be easier and more maintainable in the long run than hacking around with the XML.

We'll start by looking at toast.

# Toast

The basic toast template—`ToastTemplateType.ToastText01`— displays a single line of text wrapped on three lines. In this section we're going to start with something a little more interesting by using `ToastText02`. This displays a single line of bold text, with the second and third lines being taken up with some wrapped content. Figure 5-2 illustrates.

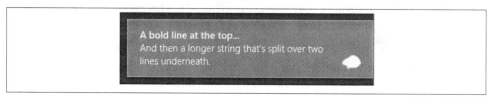

*Figure 5-2. A ToastText02 template example*

Let's look at how to create that notification.

### Setting permissions

The first thing we need to do to get toast working is to mark the app's manifest as "toast capable." If we don't do this, we won't see anything.

---

You should note that users can turn off the toast notifications using the always-available Permissions option within the settings charm. You shouldn't rely on toast to provide essential app functions—in fact, the store guidelines (which we'll see more of in Chapter 15) forbid it.

To do this, double-click the *Package.appxmanifest* file to open the manifest editor. On the Application UI tab you'll find an option called "toast capable" underneath the Notifications section. Change this to Yes. Figure 5-3 illustrates.

**Notifications:**

| | |
|---|---|
| Badge logo: | |
| | Required size: 24 x 24 pixels |
| Toast capable: | Yes |
| Lock screen notifications: | (not set) |

*Figure 5-3. Setting the app to be toast capable*

### Toast without an image

The XML used to create the previously shown Figure 5-2 looks like this:

```
<toast>
  <visual>
      <binding template="ToastText02">
          <text id="1">A bold line at the top...</text>
          <text id="2">And then a longer string that's split over two lines
            underneath.</text>
      </binding>
  </visual>
</toast>
```

We'll start at the top of our hierarchy with NotificationBuilder<T>. This is—as you can see—a generic class that will take the type of the notification that it's ultimately trying to create. (Specifically, we'll be creating a Windows.UI.Notifications.ToastNotification.) As I mentioned before, the notification classes do not have a common base type, so we can't constrain the type parameter. On a related note, because the manager classes don't have a base type either, we can't do much else than just add an abstract method to create a notification and another to update. (With more OO sophistication in the underlying API, we could make our builder base classes slicker.) Here's the code:

```
public abstract class NotificationBuilder<T>
{
    protected NotificationBuilder()
    {
```

```
        }

        protected abstract T GetNotification();

        public abstract T Update();
    }
```

Toast and tiles have shared behavior in terms of being able to show text and images. I'm therefore proposing creating a `NotificationWithTextBuilder<T>` class that will hold a collection of strings to display. When we come to build the notification, our specialized `ToastNotificationBuilder` and `TileNotificationBuilder` class will call up to us with the XML and expect us to populate any `text` elements that we find with the strings contained within the `Texts` property. This will be done via a method called `UpdateTem plateText`.

We haven't spoken much about XML so far, which tells us something about how popular XML is in 2012. Going back five years, this book would have been full of XML. Now it's far easier to work with JSON. However, we do need to talk about XML now.

The XML DOM API in the original version of .NET was a thing of beauty, especially compared to the way we used to work with XML in the days of COM. It was, and still is, easy to work with and expressive. With Windows Store apps we no longer use the `System.Xml.XmlDocument` class and its related types, but instead we use the WinRT version: `Windows.Data.Xml.Dom.XmlDocument`. This works in a very similar fashion to the "legacy" .NET version—in fact, I'd been using the new WinRT version for months before realizing that it had changed! Suffice it to say, if you're used to using the .NET version you're generally not going to come unstuck when working with the WinRT XML APIs.

Back to our `UpdateTemplateText` method: this just has to select out a list of all the `text` elements that are found in the DOM and replace the `InnerText` values with those stored in the `Texts` property. If we have more elements than strings, we'll set the elements to empty strings. Here's the code:

```
    public abstract class NotificationWithTextBuilder<T> :
        NotificationBuilder<T>
    {
        protected List<string> Texts { get; set; }

        protected NotificationWithTextBuilder(IEnumerable<string> texts)
        {
            this.Texts = new List<string>(texts);
        }

        protected void UpdateTemplateText(XmlDocument xml)
        {
            // walk and combine elements...
            var textElements = xml.SelectNodes("//text");
            for (int index = 0; index < textElements.Count; index++)
```

```
        {
            if (index < this.Texts.Count)
                textElements[index].InnerText = this.Texts[index];
            else
                textElements[index].InnerText = string.Empty;
        }
    }
}
```

With the base classes built, we can build `ToastNotificationBuilder`.

As discussed, we have these various template types to choose from when dealing with notifications. To add some color to our discussion, we'll design them so that they'll either infer the template type to use, or we can give it a specific template type if we want. In this case, we'll infer the type from a possible/limited set of `ToastText01` (one string, wrapped over three lines), `ToastText02` (two strings, bold first line), and `Toast Text04` (three strings, bold first line, normal weight for the other two). In the next section we'll look at images.

 How—or indeed if—you want to infer the template is up to you; this is just how I've done it based on how most readers of this book might end up using toast.

To start with, as we've also discussed, each notification type needs to be tied into its own manager. In the case of toast, we need to use the `ToastNotificationManager`. The first time that we want to use notifications, we need to ask this to provide a `ToastNotifi` er instance to us. We can store this in a static variable and use the static constructor to trigger its creation.

Here's the initial construction of the `ToastNotificationBuilder` class:

```
    public class ToastNotificationBuilder : NotificationWithTextBuilder
<ToastNotification>
    {
        // what we're trying to show...
        private ToastTemplateType _type;
        private bool TypeSet { get; set; }

        // the engine used to update it...
        private static ToastNotifier Notifier { get; set; }

        public ToastNotificationBuilder(string text)
            : this(new string[] { text })
        {
        }

        public ToastNotificationBuilder(IEnumerable<string> texts)
```

```
        : base(texts)
    {
    }

    static ToastNotificationBuilder()
    {
        Notifier = ToastNotificationManager.CreateToastNotifier();
    }
}
```

You'll notice that we have our template type stored in the _type field, and that we also have a TypeSet property. What we're going to do is infer the type to use if it hasn't been set (i.e., TypeSet is false), or use an explicit type if it has been set. Here's the implementation of the Type property:

```
// Add property to ToastNotificationBuilder...
public ToastTemplateType Type
{
    get
    {
        if (this.TypeSet)
            return _type;
        else
        {
            if (this.Texts.Count <= 1)
                return ToastTemplateType.ToastText01;  // just 1 line...
            else if (this.Texts.Count == 2)
                return ToastTemplateType.ToastText02;  // 1 - bold,
                next normal
            else
                return ToastTemplateType.ToastText04;  // 1 - bold,
                2-3 normal
        }
    }
    set
    {
        _type = value;
        this.TypeSet = true;
    }
}
```

Finally, we can implement the abstract methods defined on NotificationBuilder<T> that populate the template and send it through to the notifier for display. At this point, the only change that we need to make to the provided XML template is to populate the elements text, which we can do with the UpdateTemplateText method that we built earlier in NotificationWithTextBuilder<T>. Here's the code:

```
// Add methods to ToastNotificationBuilder...
protected override ToastNotification GetNotification()
{
    var xml = ToastNotificationManager.GetTemplateContent(this.Type);
    UpdateTemplateText(xml);
```

```
    // return...
    return new ToastNotification(xml);
}

public override ToastNotification Update()
{
    var toast = this.GetNotification();
    Notifier.Show(toast);

    // return...
    return toast;
}
```

To test this, we need to show some toast. I'm going to propose changing the behavior of the Refresh button that we put on the app bar in the last chapter such that when we explicitly choose this option, we'll see some toast. You should note that this is *not* a proper use of toast. Toast is supposed to be used in situations where external imperatives are affecting a system—such as receipt of an email, or an IM friend logging on. They are not supposed to be used to replace message boxes. (Moreover, you can turn off notifications globally, or even mute them so you can't rely on the user actually having seen them.)

Making this change is a matter of modifying the RefreshCommand handler on ReportsPageViewModel. Here is that change (I've omitted some code from the view-model's constructor for brevity):

```
// Modify anonymous method in ReportsPageViewModel constructor...
public ReportsPageViewModel(IViewModelHost host)
    : base(host)
{
    // setup...
    this.Items = new ObservableCollection<ReportItem>();
    this.SelectedItems = new List<ReportItem>();

    // commands...
    this.RefreshCommand = new DelegateCommand(async (e) =>
    {
        this.Host.HideAppBar();
        await this.DoRefresh(true);

        // toast...
        string message = "I found 1 report.";
        if (this.Items.Count != 1)
            message = string.Format("I found {0} reports.",
            this.Items.Count);
        var toast = new ToastNotificationBuilder(new string[] {
        "Reports refreshed.", message });
        toast.Update();
    });
```

```
            // code omitted for brevity...
    }
```

You can now run this code. Navigate to the Reports page and explicitly refresh. You should see the toast appear as shown in Figure 5-4.

*Figure 5-4. A successful toast notification*

That's great, but how do we display images?

### Toast with an image

As mentioned, half of the templates that we can use with toast display images. When we work with one of those templates, we'll get XML that's essentially the same as before, but happens to include an `image` element. Here's an example:

```
<toast>
  <visual>
      <binding template="ToastImageAndText02">
            <image id="1" src=""/>
            <text id="1">Reports refreshed.</text>
            <text id="2">I found 50 reports.</text>
      </binding>
  </visual>
</toast>
```

To handle this, we need to get a value into the `src` attribute that references an image, and change the template type. The image reference will most likely be an `ms-appx` resource URI, like the one we met in Chapter 4. What we need to do is grab an image and put it into the *Assets* folder within our project. You can take any image you want, but it has to be less than 200KB in size and smaller than 1024×1024 pixels. In the code downloads for this book, you'll find a *Resources* folder containing some images that are published under a Creative Commons license. I've called my image *Toast.png*. Do watch that 200KB size limit, however. If the image is too big you'll still get the notification, just without the image. The same applies to the tile images we'll see next.

 In the next chapter, we're going to do more work with images. The strange nature of the images in that folder will become clear in Chapter 6 when we talk about the problem domain from which they were taken!

To begin, add a new read/write property to ToastNotificationBuilder of type string called ImageUri. Then, depending on whether we have one of these, we can rig the Type property to infer a different type. Here's that change:

```
// Modify and add properties in ToastNotificationBuilder...
public ToastTemplateType Type
{
    get
    {
        if (this.TypeSet)
            return _type;
        else
        {
            if (this.Texts.Count <= 1)
            {
                if (this.HasImageUri)
                    return ToastTemplateType.ToastImageAndText01;
                else
                    return ToastTemplateType.ToastText01;
// just one line...
            }
            else if (this.Texts.Count == 2)
            {
                if (this.HasImageUri)
                    return ToastTemplateType.ToastImageAndText02;
                else
                    return ToastTemplateType.ToastText02;
// 1 - bold, next normal
            }
            else
            {
                if (this.HasImageUri)
                    return ToastTemplateType.ToastImageAndText04;
                else
                    return ToastTemplateType.ToastText04;
// 1 - bold, 2-3 normal
            }
        }
    }
    set
    {
        _type = value;
        this.TypeSet = true;
    }
}

private bool HasImageUri
{
    get
    {
        return !(string.IsNullOrEmpty(this.ImageUri));
```

```
        }
    }
```

The final step is then to set the image element within the template XML. Here's the code:

```
// Modify method in ToastNotificationBuilder...
protected override ToastNotification GetNotification()
{
    var xml = ToastNotificationManager.GetTemplateContent(this.Type);
    UpdateTemplateText(xml);

    // do we have an image?
    if (this.HasImageUri)
    {
        var imageElement = (XmlElement)xml.SelectSingleNode("//image");
        imageElement.Attributes.GetNamedItem("src").NodeValue =
            this.ImageUri;
    }

    // return...
    return new ToastNotification(xml);
}
```

Finally we need to change the command that creates the ToastNotificationBuilder to include the image URL. Here's a further change to the ReportsPageViewModel constructor. Again, I've omitted code for brevity:

```
// Modify constructor of ReportsPageViewModel...
public ReportsPageViewModel(IViewModelHost host)
    : base(host)
{
    // setup...
    this.Items = new ObservableCollection<ReportItem>();
    this.SelectedItems = new List<ReportItem>();

    // commands...
    this.RefreshCommand = new DelegateCommand(async (e) =>
    {
        this.Host.HideAppBar();
        await this.DoRefresh(true);

        // toast...
        string message = "I found 1 report.";
        if (this.Items.Count != 1)
            message = string.Format("I found {0} reports.",
                this.Items.Count);
        var toast = new ToastNotificationBuilder(new string[]
            { "Reports refreshed.", message });
        toast.ImageUri = "ms-appx:///Assets/Toast.jpg";
        toast.Update();
    });
```

```
        // code omitted for brevity...
    }
```

If you run that and do an explicit refresh, you'll see toast with the image shown in Figure 5-5.

*Figure 5-5. Toast with image*

### Asynchrony and notifications

Now that you've been through how notifications work, you may be wondering why when we hand an update over to Windows, the method we call is not marked as async. It would be typical to assume they would be; after all, they are calls that take some time to operate.

The reason they are synchronous is because they operate within the 50ms timescale rule. They pass over to the notification subsystem instantly and don't block or delay the UI thread. It just happens that from that point they take more than 50ms to rattle through the system but, as they say, that's not our problem.

# Badges

In this section, we'll quickly cover badge notifications. These are very straightforward. You can either have a number indicating the number of unread items, or you can have one of a small-but-decent number of glyphs.

You can choose from the following glyphs, and you can't define your own. The value listed beside each glyph is the value that's needed within the XML.

activity

alert

available

away

busy

newMessage

paused

playing

| | |
|---|---|
| ⊙ | unavailable |
| ⊗ | error |
| ⓘ | attention |

I'm not going to go through how to set the glyph because it's so similar to setting a number (which we will do), and I'd rather move on to explaining tiles, which is far more interesting. In the code download, you will find glyphs supported on the `BadgeNotifi cationBuilder` class that we're about to build.

As mentioned a few times, the notifications all work in the same way, so to set a badge value we need to get the template XML, populate it, and pass it back. Specifically, we'll get a template like this:

```
<badge value=""/>
```

We can set `value` to be any positive integer that we like. (Or we can set it to a glyph, as per the preceding table.) There is a high limit on that number of 99. If you specify 100 or greater, "99" will be rendered with a small plus sign next to it.

Seeing as `BadgeNotificationBuilder` is just a specialization of the `Notification Builder<T>` that we've already created, I'll simply present the code. Here's `BadgeNoti ficationBuilder`:

```
public class BadgeNotificationBuilder : NotificationBuilder
<BadgeNotification>
{
    // what we're trying to show...
    public int Number { get; private set; }

    // the engine used to update it...
    private static BadgeUpdater Updater { get; set; }

    public BadgeNotificationBuilder(int number)
    {
        this.Number = number;
    }

    static BadgeNotificationBuilder()
    {
        Updater = BadgeUpdateManager.CreateBadgeUpdaterForApplication();
    }

    public override BadgeNotification Update()
    {
        // create the notification and send it...
        var badge = GetNotification();
        Updater.Update(badge);

        // return...
```

```
        return badge;
    }

    protected override BadgeNotification GetNotification()
    {
        var xml = BadgeUpdateManager.GetTemplateContent
(BadgeTemplateType.BadgeNumber);

        // glyph?
        var attr = xml.FirstChild.Attributes.GetNamedItem("value");
attr.NodeValue = this.Number.ToString();

        return new BadgeNotification(xml);
    }
}
```

To test that this works, we can again change ReportsPageViewModel. In this case, whenever we update the view we'll set the badge. Like toast, this is *not* a proper use of badges in production information. They should be used solely to draw the user's attention to *new* information. Here's the change to ReloadReportsFromCacheAsync:

```
private async Task ReloadReportsFromCacheAsync()
{
    // set up a load operation to populate the collection from
    // the cache...
    using (this.EnterBusy())
    {
        var reports = await ReportItem.GetAllFromCacheAsync();

        // update the model...
        this.Items.Clear();
        foreach (ReportItem report in reports)
            this.Items.Add(report);

        // update the badge...
        var badge = new BadgeNotificationBuilder(this.Items.Count);
        badge.Update();
    }
}
```

Run the code, and the badge value will change as illustrated in Figure 5-6.

*Figure 5-6. Our tile with a badge showing the number of reports*

*Figure 5-7. All four possible views provided by the News app's tile*

Now that we can add a badge to a tile, let's see if we can make the tile even more interesting.

## Tiles

As mentioned, tiles are a big deal within the Windows Store app experience and are a great way for you to provide extra value to your user. While engagement is one of the things tiles offer, the most important thing they do is allow users to create a dashboard of all the apps they use, which puts timely information front and center. In LOB apps —especially when the enterprise has published many—this can be very helpful.

However, one thing you need to know about tiles is that the user can turn off the updates, in which case the tile just becomes a static presentation of whatever image you initially provide. This means that you cannot rely on presentation through a tile—or, to put it another way, a tile cannot be the only place where certain information is represented. It must bring forward information otherwise available in the app.

Another thing to consider with tiles is that they come in two varieties: normal and wide. They can also rotate between images and text (called *peeking* in the API). Figure 5-7 shows the News app tile in normal and wide mode, and I've presented both the text view and image view for all of these.

By default you get a normal width tile, but you can provide a wide tile. The wrinkle to this arrangement is that the user can select whether to view the narrow or wide tile, and you have no control over that. (Users do this via an option on the app bar within the Start screen.) Thus, when we're using wide tiles we have to provide both every time we do an update—that is, we need to tell the tile manager to change both the narrow tile and the wide tile. This is unlikely to be a problem, however, as in order to change one you likely have the information loaded and available to update the other. (Or, more specifically, there isn't going to be much horsepower wasted updating the one that the user doesn't want to see.)

## Tile template types

As mentioned, there are 46 tile template types. I won't repeat the MSDN documentation here, but in summary:

- Some of the templates are normal width, and some are wide.
- Virtually all of the templates display text information.
- Some templates are *peek* templates, which means they rotate between an image display and text display.
- Some templates show image *collections*. The People app tile does this—it'll display one large image and four smaller images next to it.
- Some templates include *block text*. For example, the Calendar app shows the current day of the month in large text, and upcoming calendar information in small text.

The tiles that we're going to use in this example are:

TileWidePeekImage01
> This is a wide, rotating template with an image on one side, and two lines of text on the other.

TileSquarePeekImageAndText02
> This is a normal-width, rotating template again with an image on one side and two lines of text on the other.

## Creating a wide tile

Before we update the tile with live information, we need to configure the wide tile. This is just a matter of creating a wide image and specifying it in the manifest.

Normal image files are 150×150 pixels. Wide images are—perhaps bizarrely—310×150 pixels in size. You can create an image in your favorite image editor.

 There's a wrinkle to working with images in that you need to provide a set of images to cover scaling on displays with a higher density. This is discussed more in Chapter 13.

We haven't spoken much about design of images for our apps (although you may have noticed that in the code downloads I've provided images based on the pica featured on the cover of this book). There are two approaches to designing them. The basic way of doing it is to create a transparent image and add design elements that are white aliased onto transparency. This allows you to change the background color for the app in the manifest and not have to change all of the images.

This isn't a design book, and I'm not expecting most readers to be design savvy, but this can be a little hard to get your head around. My recommendation is to use Adobe Fireworks or a higher-end design package. Although you can do this with free packages, it is much easier to buy the right tool for the job. In the code download for this chapter, you'll find my wide logo that was created using Fireworks.

 The built-in apps work using this transparency method. A lot of the apps currently in the Store, however, don't do this—they have more a designed, graphical look.

When you're done, add the logo to the ~/*Assets* folder within your project and remember to include it within the project. As a final step, open the manifest editor and set the "Wide logo" value on the Application UI tab. Figure 5-8 illustrates.

*Figure 5-8. Setting the "Wide logo" value in the manifest*

With the wide logo in place, find the tile on the Start screen, right-click on it, and choose the Larger option from the app bar. Figure 5-9 illustrates the wide logo.

*Figure 5-9. The StreetFoo wide logo*

As a side note, you should be aware that Microsoft's guidelines are that if you have a wide tile you must support tile updating. Specifically, Microsoft says that "content must always be fresh" when you're using wide tiles.

## Creating TileNotificationBuilder

`TileNotificationBuilder` will extend `NotificationWithTextBuilder<T>` and will be essentially the same as the others built so far. The only difference is that we're going to create a way to streamline the companion tile—specifically, we want to get to a position where we can create one and automatically create the other. We'll call this companion tile a *replica*.

`TileNotificationBuilder` will contain a collection of image URIs that can be patched into the template. If we were using a template that shows image collections (which we're not), we'll get multiple `image` elements in the XML in exactly the same way as we had a single `image` template in the toast XML. This, for example, is the template for `TileWidePeekImageCollection04`, which contains a collection of images:

```
<tile>
  <visual>
      <binding template="TileWidePeekImageCollection04">
          <image id="1" src=""/>
          <image id="2" src=""/>
          <image id="3" src=""/>
          <image id="4" src=""/>
          <image id="5" src=""/>
          <text id="1"></text>
      </binding>
  </visual>
</tile>
```

We're not going to be using that template type because we have only one image, but we'll make `TileNotificationBuilder` capable of populating any number of `image` elements in exactly the same way that `NotificationWithTextBuilder<T>` was able to populate any number of `text` elements.

Here's the basic implementation that doesn't take creating a replica into consideration. (We'll do the replica part next.)

```
    public class TileNotificationBuilder : NotificationWithTextBuilder
<TileNotification>
    {
        public TileTemplateType Type { get; private set; }
        public List<string> ImageUris { get; set; }

        private static TileUpdater Updater { get; set; }

        public TileNotificationBuilder(IEnumerable<string> texts,
TileTemplateType type)
            : base(texts)
```

```
    {
        this.ImageUris = new List<string>();
        this.Type = type;
    }

    static TileNotificationBuilder()
    {
        Updater = TileUpdateManager.CreateTileUpdaterForApplication();
    }

    public override TileNotification Update()
    {
        var tile = this.GetNotification();
        Updater.Update(tile);

        return tile;
    }

    protected override TileNotification GetNotification()
    {
        var xml = TileUpdateManager.GetTemplateContent(this.Type);
        this.UpdateTemplateText(xml);

        // images...
        if (this.ImageUrls.Any())
        {
            var imageElements = xml.SelectNodes("//image");
            for (int index = 0; index < imageElements.Count; index++)
            {
                var attr = imageElements[index].Attributes.
                    GetNamedItem("src");

                // set...
                if (index < this.ImageUris.Count)
                    attr.NodeValue = this.ImageUris[index];
                else
                    attr.NodeValue = string.Empty;
            }
        }

        // return...
        return new TileNotification(xml);
    }
}
```

The magic happens there with the population of the image. Like the text population we did earlier, we take any image elements that we can find and replace their src values with any image URIs that we've been supplied.

To handle creating the replica we'll add two methods. Replicate will create a new TileNotificationBuilder with a newly supplied template type. This would typically work by having you create the wide tile in the first instance with populated text and images and then creating a replica with a normal-width tile. By way of a shortcut, we'll create UpdateAndReplicate, which will do the first type and then the second type in turn. Here are the new methods to add to TileNotificationBuilder:

```
// Add methods to TileNotificationBuilder...
private TileNotificationBuilder Replicate(TileTemplateType newType)
{
    var newBuilder = new TileNotificationBuilder(this.Texts, newType);
    newBuilder.ImageUrls = new List<string>(this.ImageUrls);

    return newBuilder;
}

public TileNotification UpdateAndReplicate(TileTemplateType replicaType)
{
    // update this one...
    var result = Update();

    // then copy...
    var replica = this.Replicate(replicaType);
    replica.Update();

    // return...
    return result;
}
```

To get this to work, we'll modify the ReloadReportsFromCacheAsync method like we did when working with the badge builder to update the tiles. We'll add some text and an image URI. In this example implementation, just to show that we support multiple lines, I've repeated the word StreetFoo. In a production app you would not do this, because the name of the app always appears in the bottom-left corner of the tile.

Here's the change to ReloadReportsFromCacheAsync. For simplicity I've reused the same *Toast.jpg* image that we saw when we were working with toast.

```
// Modify ReloadReportsFromCacheAsync...
private async Task ReloadReportsFromCacheAsync()
{
    // set up a load operation to populate the collection
    // from the cache...
    using (this.EnterBusy())
    {
        var reports = await ReportItem.GetAllFromCacheAsync();

        // update the model...
        this.Items.Clear();
        foreach (ReportItem report in reports)
            this.Items.Add(report);

        // update the badge...
        var badge = new BadgeNotificationBuilder(this.Items.Count);
        badge.Update();
```

```
            // update the tile...
            string message = "1 report";
            if (this.Items.Count != 1)
                message = string.Format("{0} reports", this.Items.Count);
            var tile = new TileNotificationBuilder(new string[]
                { "StreetFoo", message },
                TileTemplateType.TileWidePeekImage01);
            tile.ImageUris.Add("ms-appx:///Assets/Toast.jpg");
            tile.UpdateAndReplicate(TileTemplateType.
TileSquarePeekImageAndText02);
        }
    }
```

Run the code and the tile will update. Wait long enough and the initial image will be replaced with text. Wait longer still and the text will rotate back. Right-click on the tile and use the app bar to toggle between the smaller and larger versions. Figure 5-10 shows the wide tile in picture mode.

*Figure 5-10. The wide tile showing a single picture (and badge)*

## Other Notification Features

There are some tile features that we haven't had space to talk about in this chapter. Here's a summary:

- Tiles and badges can both update themselves periodically by automatically calling up to a remote web server. The idea here is that this server will return the populated XML notification document that would be set on the tile. (This idea of servers creating notification XML is something that we talk about in the next section.) Some of the built-in Bing apps (News, Travel, and so on) do this. The periods are fairly conservative, ranging from 30 minutes to 24 hours. This sort of thing is useful for retail apps that want to keep content fresh, but it's unclear to me how this is useful in LOB apps.

- Tiles have a notification queue, which can be up to five items long. The idea here is that you can pile in a whole load of updates that will cycle through on the Start screen. The documentation describes the scheduling of the updates as being subject to "internal factors" and that they "cannot be controlled by applications." For retail apps, this is helpful for creating dynamic and interesting content. For LOB apps, I can't see how helpful this is, as the information would surely tend to become over-whelming.

- Secondary tiles are the final cool feature in the API that we haven't discussed. Each app has at least one tile (the "primary"), but apps can create any number of secondary tiles that allow shortcuts into the app. For example, say you were building an order-taking LOB app—you can let users create secondary tiles for their key customers. When this tile is clicked, the app could be rigged to view the order summary for that customer. Similarly, the app could update the tile with key information about that customer.

Now that we've been through local notifications in detail, let's look at how we can initiate notifications from the cloud.

# Push Notifications

A really fantastic piece of design in the Windows Store app APIs is that if you want your notifications to originate from a server in the cloud rather than from the local device, you take the same XML that we've just seen and hand it over to the Windows Push Notification Service (WNS), and eventually it will get routed to the device and displayed. The only complexity lies in the process of communicating with WNS, and it's these steps that we'll see in this section.

## WNS Process

To work with WNS, you need to have an account registered, and you need to tell it about your apps. There are two WNS systems—one production system and one test/sandbox system. In this section we're going to use the test system. A word of warning: these types of systems operated by Microsoft tend to change a lot, so the screenshots and steps I'll take you through here are for illustration only. Your mileage will undoubtedly vary.

Back to the steps: the principle is that on the client you need to obtain a notification URI and then pass that URI to your own cloud server. This process is called *opening a channel*. It's easier to think of this URI as an arbitrary "token," but we're going to talk about something else called an *authentication token*, and it will get confusing. When I talk about the "notification URI," it's just a string, nothing else.

Your cloud server will take that notification URI and attach it to some customer/account data in its database. When something happens that you want to tell that user about, you give the notification XML and the notification URI to WNS, and it deals with the problem of actually driving the notification down to whatever client it is applicable to. Note that's "client" singular—you'll have to handle multiple notification URIs per customer account, as each device's channel is unique. If one customer has three devices, that's three channels you need to record.

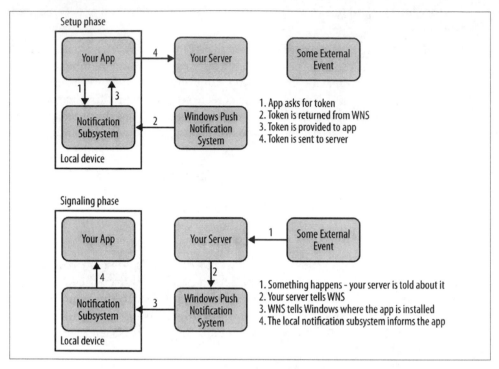

*Figure 5-11. Setup and signaling phases of the Windows Push Notification Service*

Sending the notification XML to WNS involves authenticating yourself using OAuth.

Figure 5-11 illustrates how this works. In the setup phase, the local Windows Store app calls an API to receive a notification URI specific to that application instance. That is then passed to the server. In the invocation phase, the cloud server calls through to WNS with that same notification URI. WNS then dereferences the client using that URI, and the call is passed to the client whereupon the notification is displayed.

In this chapter, we're not going to build the server, as it's way out of scope for the book. What we're going to do instead is build a Windows Forms client that acts as a simulator for a server. We'll plug the various values we need into this, it'll call WNS, and WNS will call down to Windows in our device, and from there into the Windows Store app client. The reason I wanted to do this in Windows Forms is that Windows Forms is notionally more similar to ASP.NET, which is the technology you'd most likely use for initiating the connections into WNS.

Because I felt it would be generally valuable, I wrote a small standalone library that I've put on GitHub for sending notification XML over to WNS and handling the authentication. You can find a version of this library in the download for this chapter within the *FakeCloud* folder. If you're following along, you should use the code in this folder.

You should be aware that as of the time of writing, you are only allowed to use WNS with apps that are distributed through the Windows Store. This means that you cannot use WNS with LOB apps that are sideloaded.

This is explicitly written into the certification requirements—we talk about this and sideloading in Chapter 15.

## Handling User Accounts

One big complication that we need to deal with here is that the WNS notifications know nothing about our user account model. Thus far, we've allowed users to register their own accounts and log on. The Windows notification system is based on the assumption that your app authentication is tied into the Windows authentication in some way. In a LOB app with single-sign-on, this makes plenty of sense, but generally for retail apps where you're going to want customer accounts, not so much.

I need to be clear on this—if you have *one* app where the user logs into *Windows* using two accounts, you're fine. You'll get two separate URIs and hence when you notify on those URIs it'll find its way to the correct user. But if you have one app where the user logs into the app on two separate accounts and you're only using *one* Windows account, this can be a real problem—if you're building an IM app and start surfacing updates to the wrong user, it could end up being extremely embarrassing.

There is an unwritten rule that when working in the Windows world you shouldn't necessarily allow this separate "subaccount" approach that is, user accounts should be tied one-to-one with the actual Windows account. Philosophically I don't agree with this, which is why the design of the app here provides an alternative view. It's easy for me to show you a more complex approach and allow you to simplify if you feel it necessary.

Even though we don't have the bandwidth to build a sample server within the book, I will take you through its design, as most of you will need to do this and some design elements are quite subtle.

- A notification URI is bound to a device, not to a user account.
- Your database will have a list of user accounts. As a user could have multiple devices, you need to hold multiple notification URIs per user.
- The Windows Store app on the client will from time to time send up a logon token and a notification URI. You can use the logon token to dereference the user.
- If the notification URI is not anywhere in your database, attach it to the user.

- If the notification URI is within your database, remove it from the old user, then attach it to the new user.

  This last step is key. Imagine you have Device X that User A and User B log on to. User B also logs on to Device Y. (The notification URIs we're about to see bear no resemblance to how real notification URIs look. You should treat the real ones as arbitrary in any case.)

- User A logs on to Device X and gets a URI like *https://myUriForDeviceX*. The server is updated with {UserA: `https://myUriForDeviceX`}.

- User B logs on to Device Y and gets a URI like *https://myUriForDeviceY*. The server is updated with {UserB: `https://myUriForDeviceY`}.

- If User B logs on to Device X, User A has to be logged off. The URI will be the same as the one User A got though, so you will have {UserA:(null)} and {UserB: `https://myUriForDeviceY, https://myUriForDeviceY`}.

What this last set of values tells you is that if you need to notify User A, you have no URIs, so you do nothing. If you need to notify User B, you have two URIs and need to call them both.

## Obtaining a Notification URI

You open a channel by calling the `CreatePushNotificationChannelForApplication Async` method on `PushNotificationChannelManager`. This will return a `PushNotificationChannel` object containing your URI.

You should ask for the URI whenever the app starts. The first time you get a URI, this needs to be sent to the server. On subsequent calls, you may or may not get the same URI back. If the URI changes, you should send it to the server, as this indicates that the one that you had is invalid.

Notification URIs have a natural life, which as of the time of writing was 30 days. However, various error conditions may cancel off a token, causing it to be replaced. Moreover, the 30 days isn't guaranteed; thus, this rule of "check whether it's changed and resend" will always apply. It's going to be better practice to only send up a new URI when it's changed for improved efficiency at both the client and server ends. While we're talking about best practice, you should transmit URIs over SSL, as anyone with both the URIs and the logon credentials for WNS can spam your users.

A wrinkle here is that your app may well end up running for more than 30 days, plus there's a chance it may end up being in a suspended state for more than 30 days. We're a little ahead of ourselves here, as we talk more about app lifetime in Chapter 14, but I need to explain some of this now.

If the user logs on explicitly, we need to ensure the channel is created, and transmit the notification URI up to the server if necessary. If the user opens the app and the logon is done implicitly through "remember me," we need to go through the same process. If the user resumes the app and we are logged on, we again need to go through that same process.

We can sort out the first two cases of explicit and implicit logon by calling our channel setup from within our existing LogonAsync method. For the other case we'll have to make a change to App to handle the Resumed event.

First, add this method to StreetFooRuntime. This will create the channel and use the SQLite persistent settings code that we built in Chapter 3 to track the state of various pieces of user settings data.

```
// Add method to StreetFooRuntime...
public static async Task SetupNotificationChannelAsync()
{
    // get the notification channel...
    var manager = await PushNotificationChannelManager.
CreatePushNotificationChannelForApplicationAsync();
    Debug.WriteLine("Channel: " + manager.Uri);

    // if either the URI we sent or the username we sent has changed,
    // resend it...
    var lastUri = await SettingItem.GetValueAsync("NotificationUri");
    var lastToken =
        await SettingItem.GetValueAsync("NotificationToken");
    if (lastUri != manager.Uri || lastToken != LogonToken)
    {
        // send it...
        Debug.WriteLine("*** This is where you asynchronously send it!
                    ***");

        // store it...
        await SettingItem.SetValueAsync("NotificationUri", manager.Uri);
        await SettingItem.SetValueAsync("NotificationToken", LogonToken);
    }
    else
        Debug.WriteLine("URI not changed.");
}
```

 We're writing the URI out to the debug console because we'll need to copy and paste it into our server simulator later.

Within App, we need to add a handler to the Resuming event and, if we have a logon token, call into SetupNotificationChannelAsync. Here's the code:

```
// Modify constructor and add method to App...
public App()
```

```
    {
        this.InitializeComponent();

        this.Suspending += OnSuspending;
        this.Resuming += App_Resuming;
    }

    async void App_Resuming(object sender, object e)
    {
        if (StreetFooRuntime.HasLogonToken)
            await StreetFooRuntime.SetupNotificationChannelAsync();
    }
```

That's really it as far as setting up the channel goes. Of course, there would be some additional complexity in transmitting the changes to the server, but we know that we can do that easily enough.

## Sending to WNS

Now we can turn our attention to the step where we transmit the notification to WNS, whereupon it would hopefully find its way down to our device.

As mentioned, I have built a Windows Forms client that we can use in this chapter. I'm not going to go through the construction of that at all. I will go through the construction of the MetroWnsPush library that we're using, as it illustrates some common patterns that you see when talking to third-party endpoints over HTTP, not least of all some basic OAuth stuff.

Figure 5-12 shows the client app. What we need to do is fill in the package security identifier (SID), security secret, and channel URI fields. The package SID and client secret fields will come from the Microsoft portal that you use to manage your apps. The URI comes from the Windows Store app itself when it registers the channel.

We'll now look at registering your app with the test/sandbox portal that Microsoft provides. As mentioned before, these screens are likely to change, but the steps should retain this general shape.

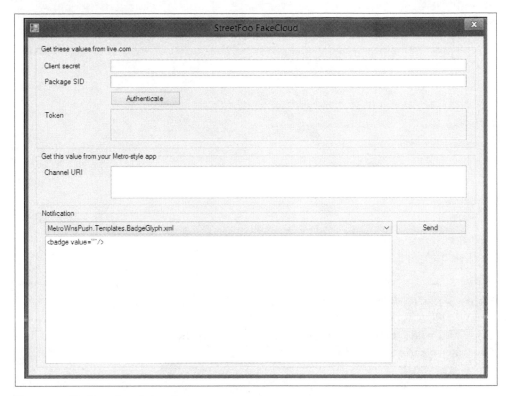

*Figure 5-12. Our cloud simulation app*

### Registering the app

To register the app, start by visiting *https://manage.dev.live.com/build*. You'll be asked to log in to your Microsoft Account. As of the time of writing, you will be shown a screenshot of the package editor within Visual Studio. You'll also be shown a form to complete asking for the "Package display name" and "Publisher." You'll find these within the Packaging tab of the manifest editor. Figure 5-13 illustrates.

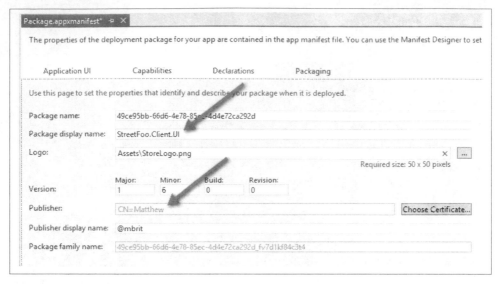

*Figure 5-13. "Package display name" and "Publisher" fields*

Copy and paste these into the form on the portal. Although it's obvious, Figure 5-14 illustrates clearly what to do.

*Figure 5-14. Filling out the form on the portal*

Click Accept, and you'll be given three pieces of information: the package name, the client secret, and the package SID. Figure 5-15 illustrates.

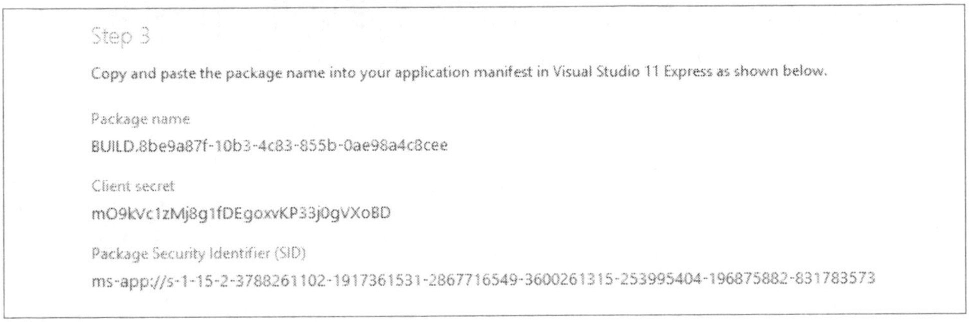

Step 3

Copy and paste the package name into your application manifest in Visual Studio 11 Express as shown below.

Package name
BUILD.8be9a87f-10b3-4c83-855b-0ae98a4c8cee

Client secret
mO9kVc1zMj8g1fDEgoxvKP33j0gVXoBD

Package Security Identifier (SID)
ms-app://s-1-15-2-3788261102-1917361531-2867716549-3600261315-253995404-196875882-831783573

*Figure 5-15. The values needed to hook into WNS*

Don't use these magic numbers—they're specific to my app and my account. Make sure you obtain your own using the steps detailed here.

The package name gets baked into the app. The client secret and package SID will get baked into your cloud server. These two values are used to authenticate you with WNS. The first value is used as part of the channel setup initiated by the Windows Store app and uniquely identifies your app out of the total universe of all Window Store apps.

Copy and paste the package name back into the Packaging tab of the manifest editor. Copy and paste the other two values into Notepad and keep them safe. Figure 5-16 shows the former.

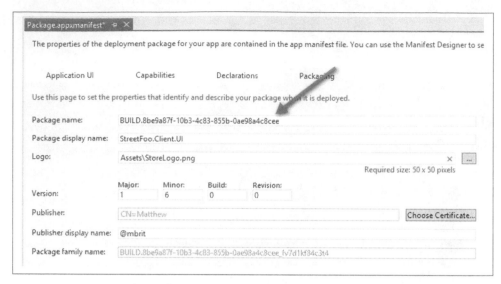

*Figure 5-16. Pasting the package name back into the manifest*

Now you can run the app. The channel will be created and the notification URI written to the debug console. Figure 5-17 illustrates. When you get the URI, copy and paste that into Notepad too.

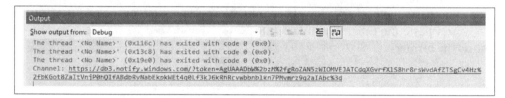

*Figure 5-17. Our new notification URI*

Now that we have all the data we need, we can make the call, starting with authentication.

### Authenticating

Authentication with WNS is done over OAuth. We use the client secret and the package SID to authenticate ourselves.

In this part, we're going to use the MetroWnsPush package that I described earlier; however, I will present code from it so that you can get a feel for how the actual communication works.

During authentication, a GET request is sent to *https://login.live.com/accesstoken.srf*, passing in the secret package SID, and some special values using the application/x-www-form-unencoded content type. The AuthenticateAsync method within WnsAu thenticator does this in the MetroWnsPush package. This uses the new HttpClient implementation that we've been using thus far in StreetFoo client. Ultimately, we'll receive JSON that contains token_type and access_token. Here's the code:

```
public async Task<WnsAuthentication> AuthenticateAsync(string sid,
string secret)
    {
        // create some content...
        var body = string.Format("grant_type=client_credentials&client_id=
{0}&client_secret={1}&scope=notify.windows.com",
                    HttpUtility.UrlEncode(sid).Trim(), HttpUtility.UrlEncode
(secret).Trim());
        var content = new StringContent(body);

        // set the type...
        content.Headers.ContentType.MediaType =
"application/x-www-form-urlencoded";

        // send it...
        var client = new HttpClient();
        var response = await client.PostAsync
("https://login.live.com/accesstoken.srf", content);

        // check...
        if (response.StatusCode == HttpStatusCode.OK)
        {
            // get it...
            string json = await response.Content.ReadAsStringAsync();
            var asObject = JObject.Parse(json);

            // get...
            string scheme = (string)asObject["token_type"];
            string token = (string)asObject["access_token"];
            return new WnsAuthentication(scheme, token);
        }
        else
            throw await CreateRequestException(string.Format("Invalid status
code received: {0}.", response.StatusCode), response);
    }
```

In terms of results, we'll get something like this:

```
{
    "token_type":"bearer","access_token":"EgAcAQMAAAAEgAAACoAAMgSg6vFTbLshYEo5VGPU
i+ph+uZ6G0w6bH+MFYwKIuGFHfeId77U4saX6DrfJ6GbzWBHcXPfPEo0P9OgywvqEhQjpduh7r7mJITC
5QLinGyE/FPJNTRNF9Lc5UuKOKyGQeBA61m1zU/KiEbt69dXXyJbrLRe+X6WZ95A/5in80GLAFoAiwAA
AAAAMeMMRBabEVAWmxFQ60gEAA8AODEuMTQ5LjI0Ny4yMzIAAAAAAFwAbXMtYXBwOi8vcy0xLTE1LTIt
Mzc40DI2MTEwMi0xOTE3MzYxNTMxLTI4Njc3MTY1NDktMzYwMDI2MTMxNS0yNTM5OTTU0MDQtMTk2ODc1
ODgyLTgzMTc4MzU3MwA=",
    "expires_in":86400
}
```

The `token_type` of `bearer` simply tells you what sort of OAuth request it is. At the time of writing, `bearer` is essentially the only OAuth methodology in use. It basically means that the "person who is bearing the token" has been authenticated.

To try this, run the Windows Forms client and paste in the secret and SID that you captured earlier. Click Authenticate, and you should see a token appear in the box. Figure 5-18 illustrates.

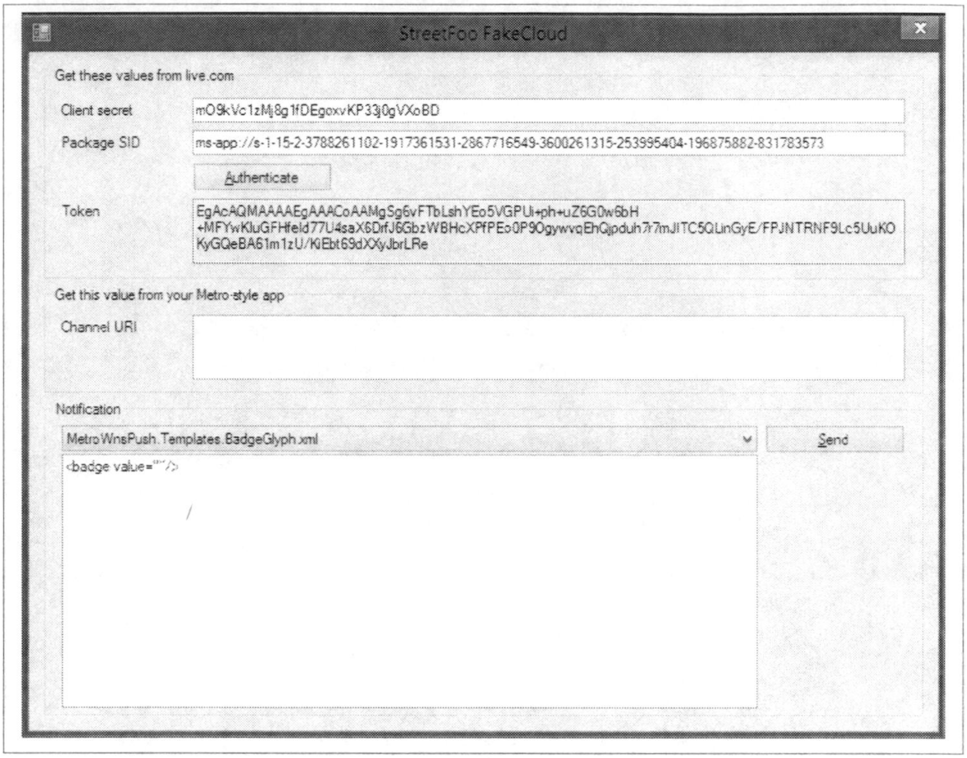

*Figure 5-18. The token appearing after successful authentication*

## Sending

Now that we've authenticated, we can push through our notification. We do so by creating a new `HttpClient` instance and providing it with an authorization header. In `MetroWnsPush`, the result of the call to `AuthenticateAsync` is a `WnsAuthentication` instance. The class of this instance contains the logic to do this. One wrinkle is that although `token_type` is provided as `bearer`, it has to be passed back to the server as `Bearer`.

```
public class WnsAuthentication
{
    public string Scheme { get; private set; }
```

```
            public string Token { get; private set; }

            internal WnsAuthentication(string scheme, string json)
            {
                // atm, this is fixed to understand bundle only...
                if(scheme != "bearer")
                    throw new NotSupportedException(string.Format("Cannot handle
'{0}'.", scheme));

                this.Scheme = "Bearer";
                this.Token = json;
            }

            internal HttpClient GetHttpClient()
            {
                // create a client and pass in the authentication...
                var client = new HttpClient();
                client.DefaultRequestHeaders.Authorization = new
AuthenticationHeaderValue(this.Scheme, this.Token);

                return client;
            }
        }
```

Passing up the XML is very easy. We just have to set the content type to text/xml, and make sure that we include special headers to indicate the notification type. In MetroWns Push we do this with the WnsPusher class.

One oddity of WNS is that the results come back in the response headers, not in the body. Specifically, we have to look in X-WNS-NOTIFICATIONSTATUS to see what happened if we get HTTP 200 back. If we don't get HTTP 200 back, there are other headers to look for. You can see these in the MetroWnsPush package within the CreateRequestExcep tion method.

If what we send up works, we'll get back one of these:

Received
> This means it looks OK, and it'll be queued for transmission. There is no guarantee of success given the vagaries of whether the device will ever be turned on, whether the user has uninstalled the app, etc.

Dropped
> This means there is an "error condition," or that you've sent a toast notification and the device is offline. This is a tricky one to deal with, because one of those is obviously an error condition, and the other (the toast one) isn't.

ChannelThrottled
> This means you are sending too many messages over too short a period of time.

With that covered, here's the code for sending the notification:

```csharp
        public async Task<WnsPushResult> PushAsync(WnsAuthentication
authentication, string uri, XmlDocument doc, NotificationType type)
        {
            // create...
            var content = new StringContent(doc.OuterXml);
            content.Headers.ContentType.MediaType = "text/xml";

            // if...
            if(type == NotificationType.Toast)
                content.Headers.Add("X-WNS-Type", "wns/toast");
            else if (type == NotificationType.Tile)
                content.Headers.Add("X-WNS-Type", "wns/tile");
            else if (type == NotificationType.Badge)
                content.Headers.Add("X-WNS-Type", "wns/badge");
            else
                throw new NotSupportedException(string.Format("Cannot handle
'{0}'.", type));

            // ok...
            var client = authentication.GetHttpClient();
            var response = await client.PostAsync(uri, content);

            // what happened?
            if (response.StatusCode == HttpStatusCode.OK)
            {
                // what happened?
                var all = response.Headers.Where(v => v.Key ==
"X-WNS-NOTIFICATIONSTATUS").FirstOrDefault();
                if(string.IsNullOrEmpty(all.Key))
                    throw new InvalidOperationException("'X-WNS-
NOTIFICATIONSTATUS' header not returned.");
                return (WnsPushResult)Enum.Parse(typeof(WnsPushResult),
all.Value.First(), true);
            }
            else
                throw await WnsAuthenticator.CreateRequestException("Failed to
post notification.", response);
        }
```

You can test this by running the Windows Forms client, authenticating, and then setting up the XML. Figure 5-19 shows a successful toast notification.

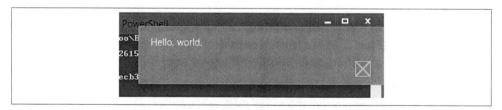

*Figure 5-19. A successful notification sent through WNS*

# Troubleshooting Tips

There are a few things to try if your notifications do not seem to be working.

- If you're sending toast notifications, make sure the app is marked as "Toast capable." (This may involve uninstalling and redeploying the app—see the last bullet in this list.) Also check the Permissions option in the settings charm to make sure you haven't switched off notifications.

- WNS will accept any XML, but the client side will decline to present XML if it doesn't fit the schema. Don't put additional XML in assuming you can use it as a channel for additional stuff. You can't.

- At the time of writing, the Dropped notification seemed flaky. Sometimes things that should be dropped (e.g., invalid XML) would return as Dropped or Received. The Received notification, however, was always correct.

- If you're struggling, try uninstalling and redeploying the app. The easiest way to do this is with PowerShell. Chapter 15 has more details on this. That can particularly affect the "Toast capable" flag, because if you create the channel with this flag off, the channel will be set not to support it and you'll need to uninstall.

# CHAPTER 6

# Working with Files

When I was first putting together the structure of this book, I intentionally left out a section on working with files. Whenever a developer faces a new platform, one of the first things that he or she does after "Hello, world" is to try reading or writing files on disk. As a result, you tend to get a lot of community-generated content early on in a platform's inception that comprises a million and one different rehashes on how to read and write files.

However, upon deeper reflection I decided to include this chapter, not necessarily to show you how to read or write files, but how to work with files within the restrictions imposed by WinRT and the Windows Store app UX. One aspect to this is sandboxing, which prevents abuse of the filesystem and its attendant data (a common activity of malware). Another aspect relates to how all the file access is done in WinRT, and so we have to deal with components that blend operations between WinRT and .NET.

In this chapter I'll take you through the various ways in which we can drive the filesystem. If you look in the download package for this chapter, you'll find some solutions/projects in addition to the StreetFoo ones that we have been working with thus far. Some of the examples we build will be "scratch" examples that don't fit into this greater body of work.

So, let's get going. First we'll look at the file picker.

## The File Picker

Sandboxed file access control in the world of Windows Store apps is generally limited to forcing one of two modes—you can either show a UI that lets the user explicitly give you a file, or you can programmatically access files within known folders.

In this first section we're going to look at the file picker, which, essentially, is the traditional "open file" and "save file" dialogs of yesterday rendered in a way that's touch-centric, but with some additional restrictions. For example, whereas in the old Windows file dialogs you can let the user choose All Files (*.*)—or in fact, the user can just nominate any file desired—you can't do that in the new pickers. The behavior is locked down to just the file types that you specify.

To separate some of this work from the core StreetFoo work, I'm proposing creating a new project. (The final StreetFoo app only uses files in a very limited way, and I don't want to confuse that implementation.) If you want to follow along, create a new solution containing a Visual C#—Windows Store—Blank App project. Mine is called FileScratch. In the code downloads for this chapter, you'll find a separate solution with that project in it.

For a scratch project, there's no point building out an entire MVVM subsystem, so we'll just bind event handlers to buttons in an old-school, VB-like manner. To get working, add a button to MainPage with content set to "Open File Picker for JPEG." Double-click it and add this code (note the need to change the handler to be async).

```
private async void Button_Click_1(object sender, RoutedEventArgs e)
{
    // create...
    var dialog = new FileOpenPicker();

    // set the types...
    dialog.FileTypeFilter.Add(".jpeg");
    dialog.FileTypeFilter.Add(".jpg");

    // show...
    StorageFile file = await dialog.PickSingleFileAsync();

    // show...
    if (file != null)
        await this.ShowAlertAsync(file.Path);
    else
        await this.ShowAlertAsync("No file chosen.");
}
```

Click the button and the picker will appear (Figure 6-1 illustrates). You may have already seen these as part of normal use of Windows 8. The key thing to remember is that this UI is all about touch access, not about mouse access.

This is a good example of where the Windows Store app APIs that relate to the new UX features tend to be very easy to use.

The only problem comes from adjustment of the types of files that you're trying to use. In the dialog that we've just seen, there is no way to change the file types, but as Figure 6-2 shows, there is a file of type *.txt* in the folder that we were looking at. The *.txt* file was not displayed, as it wasn't in the file type filter.

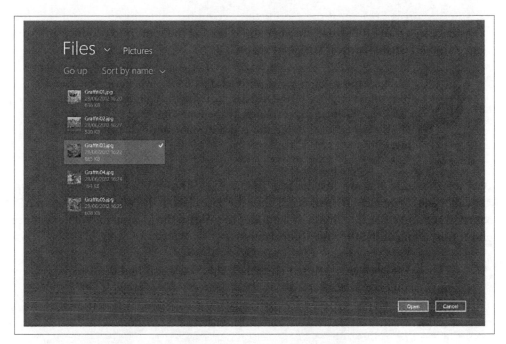

*Figure 6-1. The FileOpenPicker filtered for .jpg and .jpeg files*

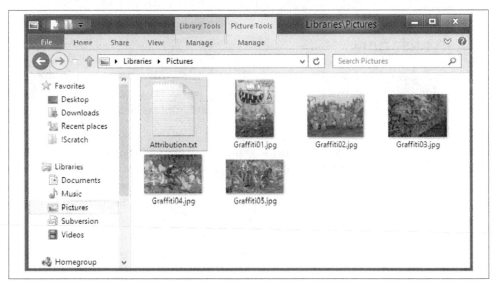

*Figure 6-2. Non-.jpg/.jpeg file shown in my Pictures library*

This limitation is because of the sandboxing. Windows is trying to control the user experience in a more "full trust" manner and is boxing the user in to produce an experience aligned with Microsoft's original vision.

 We'll see this a lot as we go through this book—whenever you see restrictions imposed by the API design, try not to fight them. You will feel hemmed in and constrained by the limits imposed by the operating system and APIs, but this is just the new world that we're dealing with.

Back to the code that we just looked at: the `PickSingleFileAsync` returns a `System.Storage.StorageFile` instance. This is the base class in the WinRT filesystem API for representing a file. It's essentially a pointer to a file on the filesystem. We'll see more about this, along with `StorageFolder`, later.

 Predictably, as well as `FileOpenPicker`, you'll also find a companion `FileSavePicker`.

That's all we need to see in terms of that basic functionality. Next we'll have a look at file associations.

# File Associations

The next feature that I want to take you through is the file associations. Although I suspect this feature will be rarely used, the way it works is interesting and it's a good demonstration of how complex Windows features are implemented very easily in Windows Store apps.

File associations in Windows allow the user to double-click a file in Windows Explorer and have an application execute and handle it. I suggest that in Windows Store apps this feature is unlikely to get heavy use because in a post-PC world, we tend to think more about apps than files and so it's unlikely you're ever going to be firing up Windows Store apps through document associations. (That said, how Windows 8/Windows RT handles files and sharing adds an interesting dimension to document-centricity when compared to the iPad, which has almost zero focus on documents as per its original design objectives.)

File associations are configured in the Declarations tab in the manifest editor in Visual Studio 2012. You can access the Declarations tab by double-clicking the *Package.appx manifest* file in Solution Explorer. This opens the manifest editor, and you can select the Declarations tab from there.

All declarations—not just ones related to files—allow you to say what special access your app requires to system features. I'm not going to enumerate them all here, but we'll see most of these as we work through the book. The one we're going to use here is the File Type Associations declaration. Add one of these and you'll see something like Figure 6-3.

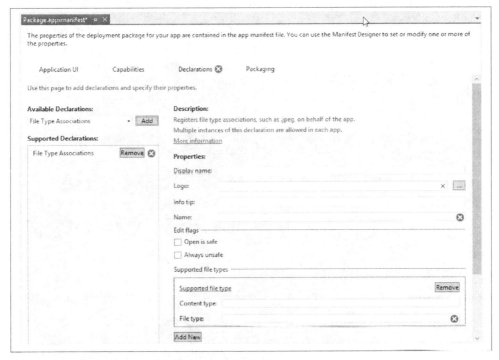

*Figure 6-3. Starting to add file type association*

In Windows, file type associations are stored in the Registry. Whenever your app is deployed, WinRT creates a whole bunch of Registry entries to register your app with the system. If you have file associations listed in your manifest, you'll get appropriate Registry keys configured that allow for your app to be launched.

Let's look at how the app is launched now.

## Launching the App

Interestingly, you can't launch the app from the Start screen via the file associations route. The only way to launch an app from the Start screen is to touch its tile. As I've hinted at, files are a legacy feature that belongs to the old WIMP metaphor in Windows.

Apps are launched from File Explorer in the legacy desktop only. That's not to say that file associations have no place in Windows Store apps. Consider the situation of "yesteryear," where lots of apps vie to be the default music player. It's certainly possible that some of those will be Windows Store apps. The same is true of PDF readers—these would actually benefit from running in a sandboxed environment.

You need to deploy the app to test it, and it's worth getting used to invoking Build – Deploy to do this. Whenever you have been running the project thus far, the deploy step is done implicitly. In this scenario, we want to explicitly do it.

If you create a file with a type of *.foobar* anywhere on your device, this will show up in File Explorer as associated with our app. (Use Notepad to do this—we don't care about the format of these files, only that they exist.) However, it won't have a usable icon yet, as the default icon created with a Windows Store app is a white icon on a transparent background. Figure 6-4 tries to show this, albeit it's hard to see in print.

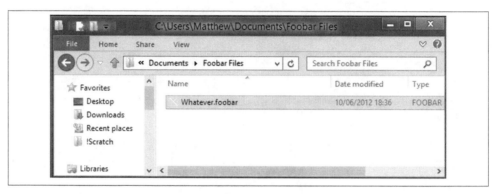

*Figure 6-4. A .foobar file ready for launch*

Setting the icon is very easy, and you may have already guessed how to do it. In the File Type Association editor (see Figure 6-3), you can assign a logo. Interestingly, this isn't a multiformat *.ico* file. I added an icon by creating a 64×64 PNG file. Whatever file you create, put it in the *~/Assets* folder within the project and then configure it in the File Type Association editor. Run/deploy the project and your icon will appear. Figure 6-5 shows my new icon.

*Figure 6-5. The .foobar file with an associated icon*

But what happens when the user opens the file? Let's find out.

## Handling the Launch

If you double-click the file in File Explorer, Windows will either activate your app if it's in the background, or start your app if it's not. (An interesting wrinkle about Windows Store apps is that you cannot have two versions of the same app running. We'll talk more about app lifetime in Chapter 14.)

What's missing is the part that actually responds to the file being opened. In this example we'll just render the name of the file on the screen. In fact, we can be given multiple files, so we'll need to handle this eventuality.

We can receive notifications of activation in this way via the OnFileActivated method on the Visual Studio-provided App class. The only wrinkle is that the notification will come into the app directly as opposed to the active view. We'll need to make sure we can react and display an appropriate view.

In this example we'll be clunky about this. If the app isn't showing the view that we want, we'll navigate to that view and then handle the file dropping. We won't nuance this by checking that the view is in a state where we're safe to navigate away without losing data —something that you'd want to do in a production app if you were in the middle of an edit.

To start with, create a new file in your project called FileActivationPage. Use the Basic Page template for this so that you get a caption and a back button; this will help you when experimenting with the behavior. It's this page that we'll go to in order to display our files. I should say that a separate page is *not* required if you want to handle file associations. I'm using a separate page here, as it's expeditious to our discussion.

In FileActivationPage add this code. The purpose of this code is simply to render the names of any provided list of files into a message.

```
            // Add to FileActivationPage...
    internal async Task FilesActivatedAsync(IEnumerable<IStorageItem> files)
    {
        // build a list of the files...
        var builder = new StringBuilder();
        foreach (var file in files)
        {
            if (builder.Length > 0)
                builder.Append("\r\n");
            builder.Append(file.Path);
        }

        // show...
        await this.ShowAlertAsync(builder.ToString());
    }
```

In the App class, you can now add this code.

```
        // Add method to App...
    protected async override void OnFileActivated(FileActivatedEventArgs
args)
    {
        base.OnFileActivated(args);

        // find the page and tell it...
        var frame = (Frame)Window.Current.Content;
        if (!(frame.Content is FileActivationPage))
            frame.Navigate(typeof(FileActivationPage));

        // if we did it...
        if (frame.Content is FileActivationPage)
            await ((FileActivationPage)frame.Content).FilesActivatedAsync
(args.Files);
    }
```

The purpose of this code is to attempt to navigate to our new page. The approach is to find the active window (of which there's only ever one), find the frame on that window (which convention says has to be held in the Windows instance's Content property), and then get the content of the frame. This last item will be our page. If that page isn't the page we want, we'll attempt to navigate.

Navigation may fail (for example, the page may be busy and refuse navigation away— see my point about having a more nuanced implementation in production); hence, we check to see if it worked before we call through to FilesActivatedAync.

You can try this for yourself now by going into File Manager and double-clicking one or more *.foobar* files. Figure 6-6 shows possible output if you select multiple files. Make sure that you confirm this works both when the app is running and when it is not. You may also want to check the behavior depending on whether FileActivationPage is the current page or not.

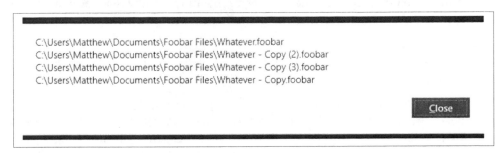

*Figure 6-6. Multiple file activations*

Now we know how to let the user give us a file; let's see what happens if we try to find files programmatically.

# Sandboxed File Access

In both of the examples that we've looked at, we've been given files to work with through direct user interaction. Whenever this user-driven action happens, WinRT assumes that we have explicit permission to access the files and that they are OK to work with. (You should note, though, that NTFS's security trumps all here—if Windows doesn't think you have access to the file, you can't have it regardless of how it was sourced.)

In this section we'll look at how we can work with lists of apps programmatically (in other words, how we can automate the operation of the user actually picking a file). For example, we might want to walk all TIFF documents in a certain folder within the user's *Documents* folder and OCR (optical character recognition) them.

You can only do programmatic work with folders that are within the sandbox. There are two sets of sandboxed folders: those given to your app for their private use, and those that are shared with other apps on the system.

In terms of your private folders, you get the following, which are accessed from special properties within the API. You can then use the storage APIs on these, which we'll get to in a moment. You can work with your private folders *without* specifying special manifest permissions. You can also work with any file type in these folders.

*Windows.Storage.ApplicationData.Current.LocalFolder*
> This is the private data store tied to the current machine (e.g., *c:\Users\<User>\AppData\Local\Packages\<id>\LocalState*).

*Windows.Storage.ApplicationData.Current.RoamingFolder*
> This is the private data store that is cloud synchronized (e.g., *c:\Users\<User>\AppData\Local\Packages\<id>\RoamingState*). (We'll talk about this more later, but for now you should note that this location is not in the Windows user profile

roaming folder. This is not the roaming profile functionality that's been managed by Active Directory for many years. It just happens to have the same name.)

*Windows.Storage.ApplicationData.Current.TemporaryFolder*
This is where you store temporary files (e.g., *c:\Users\<User>\AppData\Local\Pack ages\<id>\TempState*).

*Windows.ApplicationModel.Package.Current.InstalledLocation*
This is where your app is installed, which if you're developing will be the *AppX* folder underneath your *Debug* or *Release* folder. You cannot, unsurprisingly, write to this folder.

The following special folders exist in Windows Store apps, each of which is accessed through a special property. However, in order to use them, you need to switch on a specific permission in the manifest. You also need to nominate the file types that you wish to work with. Here's the list of folders, and the related manifest permission.

*Windows.Storage.KnownFolders.DocumentsLibrary*
Requires Documents Library Access

*Windows.Storage.KnownFolders.MusicLibrary*
Requires Music Library

*Windows.Storage.KnownFolders.PicturesLibrary*
Reqires Pictures Library Access

*Windows.Storage.KnownFolders.VideosLibrary*
Requires Videos Library Access

*Windows.Storage.KnownFolders.RemovableDevices*
Requires Removable Storage

*Windows.Storage.KnownFolders.HomeGroup*
Requires at least one of Music Library, Pictures Library Access, or Videos Library Access

*Windows.Storage.KnownFolders.MediaServerDevices*
Requires at least one of Music Library, Pictures Library Access, or Videos Library Access

 The inconsistent naming here isn't down to typographical errors— I've replicated how it currently is in Visual Studio 2012, which is inconsistent.

There's an additional folder called *Windows.Storage.DownloadsFolder* that allows write-only access to the system downloads folder. We'll talk about that in a moment.

What we'll do to demonstrate some of the file APIs is build some code that will copy files from your Pictures library into the private, local folder for your app.

## Walking and Copying Pictures

To get a feel for how the file API works, we'll have a look at actually running through the API. We'll create a simple function that will copy any pictures with the word *graffiti* in their name over to our private local data folder. We'll initially do this without setting appropriate manifest permissions so that you can see it fail the permissions check.

Whenever we access the filesystem in WinRT, we use its native filesystem API, as opposed to the .NET one in System.IO. This is a real shame, as the one in System.IO was fantastically put together, and the WinRT one is arguably not as good. It's also oddly incomplete, with no easy way to check for file existence and so on. (The official line is that checking for existence and then performing an action invites a race condition scenario, so you're supposed to check for exceptions. Personally, that argument seems flimsy, as since .NET v1 we've been told to design specifically against using exceptions to report ordinary ["nonexceptional"] failures.)

Coming back to my first point at the top of this chapter, I don't want to belabor the file API usage, as it's all basic stuff. To that end, you can add a button to your page and wire up this code, which will walk the files in your *Pictures* folder and copy them over to ~/ *LocalState*. It should be obvious to see what it's doing.

```
private async void HandleCopyGrafittiPicturesToLocal(object sender,
RoutedEventArgs e)
{
    await CopyGraffitiPicturesAsync(ApplicationData.Current.LocalFolder);
}

private async Task CopyGraffitiPicturesAsync(StorageFolder targetFolder)
{
    try
    {
        // copy...
        var files = (await KnownFolders.PicturesLibrary.GetFilesAsync())
.Where(v => v.Name.ToLower().Contains("graffiti")
                && (v.FileType.ToLower() == ".jpg" || v.FileType.ToLower()
== ".jpeg"));
            var builder = new StringBuilder();
        foreach (var file in files)
        {
            // get...
            var newFile = await file.CopyAsync(targetFolder);

            // add...
            builder.Append("\r\n");
            builder.Append(newFile.Path);
```

```
            }

            // show...
            if (builder.Length > 0)
                await this.ShowAlertAsync("Copied:\r\n" +
                    builder.ToString());
            else
                await this.ShowAlertAsync("No files were found to copy.");
        }
        catch (Exception ex)
        {
            this.ShowAlertAsync(ex.ToString());
        }
    }
}
```

If you run this code, you'll see an error similar to that shown in Figure 6-7. The problem occurs because we don't have rights to access the PicturesLibrary property in Known Folders. PicturesLibrary happens to be of type Windows.Storage.StorageFolder, and you should note that if some mechanism actually gave us a StorageFolder that mapped to the *same underlying folder*, this operation would not have failed. User selection via the FolderPicker, FileOpenPicker, or FileSavePicker always trumps the manifest setting.

*Figure 6-7. Failure to access the PicturesLibrary property*

You can change the manifest setting by double-clicking the *Package.appxmanifest* file in Solution Explorer and changing to the Capabilities tab. Once there, select Pictures Library Access. This is shown in Figure 6-8.

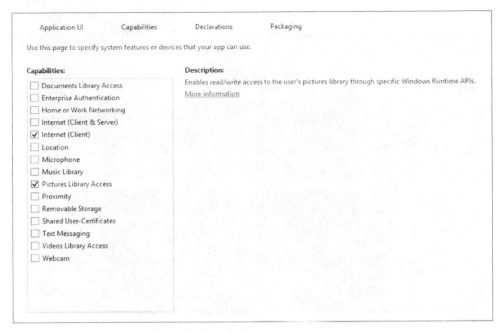

*Figure 6-8. Enabling Pictures Library Access*

Rerun the code and you'll get a successful result, as shown in Figure 6-9.

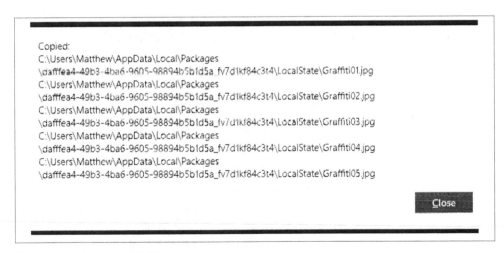

*Figure 6-9. A successful file copy operation*

This code works on the assumption that appropriately named files exist in the root of your standard Windows pictures library. You obviously may have to create some in order to see this operation work.

That's all I want to show you on the basic API. In the next section, I'll give a quick mention of the special `DownloadsFolder` property, and then we'll go on to talk about roaming files.

# Roaming Files

Now we're going to take a look at one of the neatest features in Windows Store app development: roaming data. In roaming data, certain data that's stored on one local machine is automatically propagated to any other device that the user operates.

Unless joined to the domain, Windows 8 and Windows RT devices have the option of being bound to a Microsoft account. (This process makes the device "Microsoft Account Connected.") When in this mode, apps are able to write data into a special *roaming folder*. Other devices on the same Microsoft account will receive synchronized copies of this data. In order for this to work, the device has to be "trusted." You may have noticed that when you installed Windows 8, you received an email asking for you to trust the machine. Those emails are part of this process.

 These same rules apply to Roaming Settings. I'll talk about that a little more toward the end of this section.

---

### Roaming Data Versus Roaming Profiles

There's likely to be some confusion with regard to the Roaming Profiles feature that's been in Windows since the very early days of Active Directory. This is *not* that feature. This is an entirely different feature that does something similar but has—basically—the same name (not a fantastic move by Microsoft there). *Floating* might have been better, but that's by the by. In short, just ignore anything related to Active Directory in this discussion.

---

There are some limitations. You have only a very small quota of data that can be used —you can and should ask WinRT to tell you how much your quota is (because it's not a fixed limit), but at the time of writing apps have 100KB of quota space. (When I say the space is not fixed, I mean that you should not *rely* on the amount, as Microsoft has the capability to change it either globally or in different scenarios going forward.) This 100KB limit is so small that you will need to carefully consider what file protocol you use. XML is particularly inefficient when it comes to space, for example. Alternatively, you may wish to compress the data.

The need for the device to be connected to a Microsoft account implies that this won't work for domain-connected devices; however, the documentation also states that you can use Group Policy to turn off this feature at a device level, which hints that it will work for domain-connected devices. But the fact that you can turn this off regardless tells us that this is not a mechanism that should be relied upon.

This sort of roaming feature is specifically designed to move around small amounts of data that is "nice to have"—for example, state information or preference information. It's impractical to make it work as a synchronization mechanism for sometimes-offline devices. (This last point is further militated against by the fact that you can't control when the synchronization happens.) We'll talk more about apps that synchronize changes with a server in Chapter 14.

All that said, I do want to take you through this feature, as it is pretty clever and can be helpful in certain cases.

## Multiple Devices

To test that your roaming data implementation works, you will need multiple devices. Using the simulator and your development machine won't work, as these are technically the same machine. (The simulator is just a remote desktop view into the machine it's running on.) If you don't have two devices, you'll have to follow along mentally rather than practically.

First we'll look at using the Remote Debugging tools. These allow Visual Studio to deploy, run, and receive debugger telemetry from remote devices. Remote Debugging has been a feature of Visual Studio since the very first editions (i.e., it's not a special Windows Store app thing).

## Setting Up the Remote Debugging Client

These are the same steps that you'll need to follow if you want to debug your apps on Windows RT. Visual Studio won't run on Windows RT, so this will be the only way to access debugging capability if you're troubleshooting software running on Windows RT.

To reiterate the requirements for the roaming data part: both devices must be on the same Microsoft account, and both must be trusted.

The easiest way to get the tools is to visit the Microsoft Downloads site and search for Remote Tools. This should yield installation packages for ARM, x86, and x64 machines. Install the one that matches the OS of your target.

Once you've installed the package, run the debugging client from the Start screen. When prompted, accept the firewall changes that it needs to make.

You can now connect to the machine from Visual Studio. On the toolbar, drop down the target selector and choose Remote Machine. Figure 6-10 illustrates the option, and Figure 6-11 illustrates selection of the remote device.

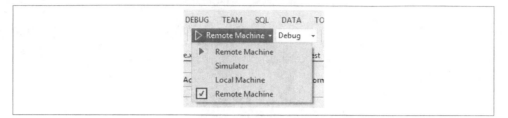

*Figure 6-10. Selecting the Remote Machine debugging option*

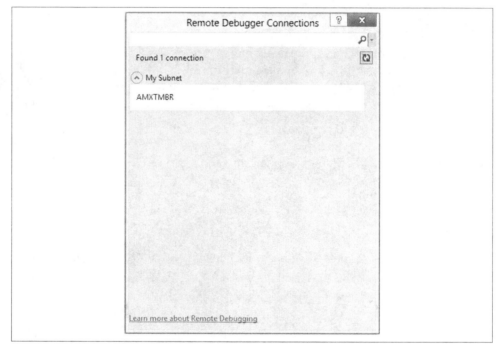

*Figure 6-11. Choosing the device to use as the debugging target*

With the remote device selected, run the solution from within Visual Studio to confirm that it operates as you expect. Now that we know that we can join the two halves of the problem together, we'll look at building our synchronization code.

If you need to change the target device, open the Properties window on the project that you're looking to debug, and select the Debug pane.

## Syncing Files

In an earlier section I called out example paths of folders used by apps to store their private data. I gave the path referred to by *ApplicationData.Current.RoamingFolder* as being of the following format:

*c:\Users\<User>\AppData\Local\Packages\<id>\RoamingState*

All we have to do to make this work is write data into that *~/RoamingState* folder. Windows will then do the rest. In this example, we'll drop a small text file into the folder on one device and then wait to see if it comes through on the other. It doesn't matter whether you create the file on your Visual Studio machine or the remote device, although if you want to try out the remote debugging firsthand, using the remote device to create the file would seem sensible.

Here's the code to create a file in the roaming folder—the intention here is to wire up a button that calls this code. Again, this is a simple example, so I'm just going to present it on the assumption that it's obvious.

```
        private async void HandleCreateFileInRoamingFolder(object sender,
RoutedEventArgs e)
        {
            // create...
            var file = await ApplicationData.Current.RoamingFolder.
CreateFileAsync(Guid.NewGuid().ToString()
+ ".txt");
            using (var stream = await file.OpenStreamForWriteAsync())
            {
                using(var writer = new StreamWriter(stream))
                    writer.WriteLine(string.Format("Hello, world. ({0})",
DateTime.Now));
            }

            // ok...
            await this.ShowAlertAsync(string.Format("Created file '{0}'.
Quota: {1}KB", file.Path,
                ApplicationData.Current.RoamingStorageQuota));
        }
```

There's one thing that is important to catch here. In .NET you don't *need* to wrap the StreamWriter reference in a using statement. In WinRT, if you don't wrap it in a using statement, the data won't be flushed out of the writer before the stream is closed, and your data won't be written. Of course, we should always wrap everything that implements `IDisposable`, but this caught me out so it may well catch you out too.

You'll also notice that in the message that's rendered when the file is written, I'm including the `RoamingStorageQuota` value. I've included this so that you know where it is. The upshot of going over quota is that *no* data will get synced for your app. I'd suggest, then, that if you have to keep track of and manage your storage within this quota, you're using this feature inappropriately.

If you run this code on the remote device, a file will be created that will eventually be synced up to the cloud and then down onto other devices where the app is installed. If you want to force the sync to run, lock the device, as this triggers all pending sync operations to flush. (It may still take a few minutes, however.)

## Roaming Settings

In Chapter 3 where we looked at SQLite, we used a local database to store system settings. WinRT has a built-in way of sharing a bucket of settings via the `ApplicationData.Current.RemoteSettings` member.

I chose not to use this in Chapter 3 because of the limitations outlined in this chapter (i.e., a required Microsoft account and the fact that domain administrators can just turn off this feature wholesale).

I said, perhaps enigmatically, at the top of this section that you might want to roll your own roaming implementation rather than using the one provided in the Windows Store app APIs. I'm not going to go through how you might do this in this book, but it's relatively easy. All you have to do is keep settings in SQLite as we first saw in Chapter 3. When they change, these settings just have to float up to your own cloud. When your apps activate, one thing they can then do is download the settings from the cloud. It's not rocket science, but it does involve more lifting than using the built-in features.

We'll talk more about background cloud synchronization in Chapter 14.

# Using Files with StreetFoo

Now that we've looked at the basics of the filesystem APIs, we can turn our attention back to the StreetFoo app. Philosophically, I'm a great believer in making examples in books as "real world" as possible. The examples that we have looked at thus far have explored some of the edges of the API, but as software engineers we know that it's only by fighting weird edge cases that we actually learn how things work. It was easier to show you those examples in isolation than to confuse the issue by adding spurious features to StreetFoo.

The objective of this section is to download photos from the StreetFoo server and display them on the Reports grid. These photos are obviously reasonably large, so fetching them on demand makes sense. Storing them on the filesystem as opposed to in the database also makes sense, as SQLite isn't particularly adept at storing large pieces of BLOB data.

We'll also make some improvements to our view-model story. At the moment, what we show on the view is a straight-through projection of what's in the database. What we'll do in this section is create a special `ReportViewItem` class that will hold both the core data in `ReportItem`, along with image data.

In summary, then:

1. We'll create a new service proxy called `GetReportImageServiceProxy`. This will take the native ID of the report and return a JPEG image as a base-64-encoded string.

2. We'll create a new `ReportViewItem` class and refactor our `ReportsPageViewModel` class to use instances of these as opposed to the `ReportItem` database entity.

3. We'll create a new `ReportImageCacheManager` class that will, as the name implies, manage getting the report's images cached onto the local disk.

Let's press on.

## Getting Report Images

The simplest thing to do first is create our service proxy that will get an image from the server. The server has a set of sample images, and will return these when presented with a report's native ID.

As we've built the service proxies many times, I'll just present the basic code. First, here's the result object that will contain either an array of bytes containing JPEG data, or error information:

```
public class GetReportImageResult : ErrorBucket
{
    public byte[] ImageBytes { get; private set; }

    internal GetReportImageResult(byte[] bs)
    {
        this.ImageBytes = bs;
    }

    internal GetReportImageResult(ErrorBucket errors)
        : base(errors)
    {
    }
}
```

Next, our service proxy interface:

```
public interface IGetReportImageServiceProxy : IServiceProxy
{
```

```
        Task<GetReportImageResult> GetReportImageAsync(string nativeId);
    }
```

The last class we have to create is the GetReportImageServiceProxy itself. The image will be returned as a base-64 string. We'll convert that and store it as bytes in the result. Here's the code:

```
    public class GetReportImageServiceProxy : ServiceProxy,
IGetReportImageServiceProxy
    {
        public GetReportImageServiceProxy()
            : base("GetReportImage")
        {
        }

        public async Task<GetReportImageResult> GetReportImageAsync
(string nativeId)
        {
            var input = new JsonObject();
            input.Add("nativeId", nativeId);
            var executeResult = await this.Execute(input);

            // did it work?
            if (!(executeResult.HasErrors))
            {
                // get the reports...
                var asString = executeResult.Output.GetNamedString("image");

                // bytes...
                var bs = Convert.FromBase64String(asString);
                return new GetReportImageResult(bs);
            }
            else
                return new GetReportImageResult(executeResult);
        }
    }
```

Remember that in order to use the proxy we need to enlist it in our IoC container, which has to be done manually. Add the mapping for IGetReportImageServiceProxy to GetReportImageServiceProxy to the Start method.

## Migrating to ReportViewItem

With that out of the way, we can start looking at the more interesting aspects of this problem.

As we know, the data binding subsystem in XAML works on this idea of listening to changes. In Chapter 4, we first looked at dependency properties—these are the foundation of XAML's data binding. We have seen already the ObservableCollection (used to hold our list of reports for presentation on the grid), and back in Chapter 1 when we first started looking at data binding we built our ModelItem class, which issued change notifications through `INotifyPropertyChanged`. When we built `ReportItem` back in Chapter 3, we also used `ModelItem` to get that same change notification.

As things stand at the moment, the grid view used on the Reports page just projects `ReportItem`. In terms of data, against each `ReportItem` we have to be able to dereference whether an image exists in the local cache or not. We can either update `ReportItem` and the attendant database schema to store a flag that records image presence, or we can look on disk. Avoiding changing the schema and relying on file existence as the definitive indicator seems more straightforward, at first glance. It also avoids polluting the schema with items that only relate to the client implementation.

This is where some of the advantages of MVVM come in. We can use view-model items that are a combination of data stored in SQLite and on disk. The nonimage data will be held in SQLite, and the flag to indicate whether we have an image and the URL will be determined by querying the disk. To that extent, we'll build a `ReportViewItem`.

Then comes the question as to whether we extend `ReportItem`, or whether we create a new class and encapsulate a `ReportItem` instance within it. Because we don't have any control over the creation aspects of the object (they are given to us by sqlite-net as part of the ORM), I'm suggesting encapsulation.

I also think it's not much of a stretch to risk a moment of YAGNI and build a new base class that supports encapsulation in this way. `WrappingModelItem<T>` will be a generic type of type `ModelItem`. One thing this will allow us to do is subscribe to notifications on the encapsulated instance and propagate them up as if they were our own. (We actually won't use that feature directly in this code, but it's a worthy illustration, as it shows how we can extend onto and enhance the preexisting notifications without having to do any specific work.)

Here's the code for `WrappingModelItem<T>`—although you'll be able to understand it more fully when we build `ReportViewItem` immediately after.

```
public abstract class WrappingModelItem<T> : ModelItem
    where T : ModelItem
{
    public T InnerItem { get; private set; }

    protected WrappingModelItem(T innerItem)
    {
        this.InnerItem = innerItem;

        // subscribe...
        this.InnerItem.PropertyChanged += InnerItem_PropertyChanged;
    }

    void InnerItem_PropertyChanged(object sender,
        PropertyChangedEventArgs e)
    {
        // re-raise this as our own...
```

```
            this.OnPropertyChanged(e);
        }
    }
```

Now we can turn our attention to implementing `ReportViewItem`. What we want to do here is expose our read-only versions of the relevant `ReportItem` data, and have a special property called `ImageUrl` that we'll set when an image is available. Only exposing our read-only versions of the properties is there for neatness—if we don't need setters for those properties, why expose them? Finer control of the surface area is another advantage of the MVVM model.

Here's the code for `ReportViewItem`:

```
public class ReportViewItem : WrappingModelItem<ReportItem>
{
    internal ReportViewItem(ReportItem item)
        : base(item)
    {
    }

    public string NativeId { get { return this.InnerItem.NativeId; } }
    public string Title { get { return this.InnerItem.Title; } }
    public string Description { get { return this.InnerItem.Description; } }

    public string ImageUrl { get { return GetValue<string>(); } set
{ SetValue(value); } }
}
```

It doesn't look like much yet, but it will shortly when we add some behavior. But before we do that, let's refactor our `ReportsPageViewModel` code to work with `ReportViewItem` instances rather than `ReportItem` instances.

### Refactoring to ReportViewItem

Refactoring involves changing both the `IReportsPageViewModel` interface and the mapped `ReportsPageViewModel` class. Here's the change for the interface:

```
public interface IReportsPageViewModel : IViewModel
{
    ICommand CreateTestReportsCommand { get; }
    ICommand RefreshCommand { get; }
    ICommand DumpSelectionCommand { get; }
    ICommand SelectionCommand { get; }

    ObservableCollection<ReportViewItem> Items
    {
        get;
    }

    bool HasSelectedItems
    {
        get;
```

```
        }
    }
```

There aren't many touch points in ReportsPageViewModel that need changing. The property definitions and the constructor need changing, as does the operation of Re loadReportsFromCacheAsync. Here's the code with the types changed in the constructor (I've omitted some code for brevity):

```
public class ReportsPageViewModel : ViewModel, IReportsPageViewModel
{
    public ObservableCollection<ReportViewItem> Items { get; private set; }
    private List<ReportViewItem> SelectedItems { get; set; }

    public ICommand CreateTestReportsCommand { get; private set; }
    public ICommand RefreshCommand { get; private set; }
    public ICommand DumpSelectionCommand { get; private set; }
    public ICommand SelectionCommand { get; private set; }

    public ReportsPageViewModel(IViewModelHost host)
        : base(host)
    {
        // setup...
        this.Items = new ObservableCollection<ReportViewItem>();
        this.SelectedItems = new List<ReportViewItem>();

        // commands...
        this.RefreshCommand = new DelegateCommand(async (e) =>
        {
            // omitted...
        });

        // update any selection that we were given...
        this.SelectionCommand = new DelegateCommand((args) =>
        {
            // update the selection...
            this.SelectedItems.Clear();
            foreach (ReportViewItem item in (IEnumerable<object>)args)
                this.SelectedItems.Add(item);

            // raise...
            this.OnPropertyChanged("SelectedItems");
            this.OnPropertyChanged("HasSelectedItems");
        });

        // dump the state...
        this.DumpSelectionCommand = new DelegateCommand(async (e) =>
        {
            // omitted...
        });
    }
```

```
    // omitted...
}
```

The change to `ReloadReportsFromCacheAsync` is more interesting because it's here that we key into the logic to update the cache. How this will work is that we'll ask SQLite for our list of `ReportItems` as usual, but we'll wrap them up in a `ReportViewItem` and then pass each `ReportViewItem` instance over to a manager class that will update the image in the background. We won't build `ReportImageCacheManager` immediately—we'll close off of the refactoring by editing the template XAML first. Here's the change to `ReloadReportsFromCacheAsync` that will defer over to `ReportImageCacheManager`:

```
// Modify method in ReportsPageViewModel...
  private async Task ReloadReportsFromCacheAsync()
  {
      // set up a load operation to populate the collection
      // from the cache...
      using (this.EnterBusy())
      {
          var reports = await ReportItem.GetAllFromCacheAsync();

          // update the model...
          this.Items.Clear();
          foreach (ReportItem report in reports)
              this.Items.Add(new ReportViewItem(report));

          // go through and initialize...
          var manager = new ReportImageCacheManager();
          foreach (var item in this.Items)
              await item.InitializeAsync(manager);
      }
  }
```

As mentioned, we need just a quick change to the template XAML and we're done.

### Modifying the grid item template

If you recall, in Chapter 3 we copied the `Standard250x250ItemTemplate` used on the grid to a new template called `ReportItem250x250Template`. This template has an `Image` control, but it's set up to bind off of the `Image` property on the view-model. We've called the property that refers to an image `ImageUrl`. (This makes more sense to me, as a property called `Image` should return an object that represents loaded image data, not a reference to a location on disk.)

Thus we have to change the XAML for `ReportItem250x250Template`. Here's the code:

```
<DataTemplate x:Key="ReportItem250x250Template">
    <Grid HorizontalAlignment="Left" Width="250" Height="250">
        <Border Background="{StaticResource
ListViewItemPlaceholderBackgroundThemeBrush}">
            <Image Source="{Binding ImageUrl}" Stretch="UniformToFill"/>
        </Border>
```

```
                <StackPanel VerticalAlignment="Bottom" Background="{StaticResource
ListViewItemOverlayBackgroundThemeBrush}">
                    <TextBlock Text="{Binding Title}" Foreground="{StaticResource
ListViewItemOverlayForegroundThemeBrush}"
Style="{StaticResource TitleTextStyle}" Height="60" Margin="15,0,15,0"/>
                    <TextBlock Text="{Binding Description}"
Foreground="{StaticResource ListViewItemOverlaySecondaryForegroundThemeBrush}"
Style="{StaticResource CaptionTextStyle}" TextWrapping="NoWrap"
Margin="15,0,15,10"/>
                </StackPanel>
            </Grid>
        </DataTemplate>
```

That's all we have to do for now. You can satisfy yourself that the refactoring "took" by running the project, although you won't see different behavior.

# Implementing ReportImageCacheManager

Now we come to the interesting part.

We know that we can store anything we like in the *~/LocalState* folder beneath our package folder. (As a reminder, this lives at *c:\Users\<User>\AppData\Local\Packages \<PackageId>*.) My proposal is that we create a separate folder called *ReportImages* under *LocalState*. Files will be named in the format *<NativeId>.jpg*. Don't forget that we can't use *RoamingState* because the quota allotment will be too small.

As well as seeing some real-world file behavior, this is also where we'll see some real-world async/await and multithreading behavior. All of the filesystem interaction that we do will run on a background thread, as will any network access.

One other thing we're going to see here is the ms-appdata URI protocol. This is a really clever part of WinRT and XAML. Like the ms-appx URI that we met in Chapter 4, ms-appdata allows us to reach into the *LocalState*, *RoamingState*, and *TempState* folders. By binding the Image control in our grid template to an ms-appdata protocol-based URI, we can bind directly to items on the filesystem.

To summarize our objectives for this section:

- When a new item is readied for the view, we'll pass it to the image cache manager.
- The manager will look on disk to see if a matching file already exists. If it does, it will calculate the URL of the image as an ms-appdata URI and set the item's Image Url property. This will rattle through the XAML data binding subsystem and the display will be updated.
- If a matching file does not exist, we need to go away, download it, and save it to disk. Here, rather than using async/await, we're going to create tasks directly within the TPL (task parallel library) by explicitly creating and scheduling background tasks. When those tasks are complete, they will update the ImageUrl property with

an `ms-appdata` URI. Again, notifications will be raised and the image will be displayed.

- If we do have to create tasks directly within the TPL, we'll need to manage the synchronization context. We'll dig into that in detail when the time comes.

Let's get on with that and build the code.

### Checking for file existence

When you go through this, it's likely that you'll reach the conclusion that working with the filesystem is quite fiddly in WinRT. That's to be expected—it *is* fiddly to work with!

We'll start with the method that returns to use a reference to the folder where we're going to store the cached files. This is where we start to run into some less good bits of WinRT. As mentioned before, we can't check to see whether a file or folder exists ahead of time. The mandated method is to capture any exceptions. As a wrinkle to this, if the exception isn't actually exceptional and you don't want to do anything with the exception data, it becomes a faff to hide the compiler warnings associated with ignoring the exceptions. To that end, I've created a `SinkWarning` method. This tricks the compiler into believing the reference to ex has been used and hides the warning. Apart from that, the method is straightforward. If the folder does not exist, it's created. Here's the code:

```
// Add members to ReportImageCacheManager...
private const string LocalCacheFolderName = "ReportImages";

private async Task<StorageFolder> GetCacheFolderAsync()
{
    // find...
    StorageFolder cacheFolder = null;
    try
    {
        cacheFolder = await ApplicationData.Current.LocalFolder.
GetFolderAsync(LocalCacheFolderName);
    }
    catch (FileNotFoundException ex)
    {
        SinkWarning(ex);
    }

    // did we get one?
    if(cacheFolder == null)
        cacheFolder = await ApplicationData.Current.LocalFolder.
CreateFolderAsync(LocalCacheFolderName);

    // return...
    return cacheFolder;
}

private void SinkWarning(FileNotFoundException ex)
```

```
    {
        // no-op - we're just getting rid of compiler warnings...
    }
```

In the modification to ReportsPageViewModel that we built previously, we called into a method called GetLocalImageUrlAsync. The purpose of this method is to return a preexisting cache URL. This method will use two helper methods that we'll also use in other functions. GetCacheFilename provides the filename used when given a Report ViewItem, and CalculateLocalImageUrl will return an ms-appdata format URI, again given a ReportViewItem. Here's the code:

```
// Add methods to ReportImageCacheManager...
private string GetCacheFilename(ReportViewItem viewItem)
{
    return viewItem.NativeId + ".jpg";
}

private string CalculateLocalImageUrl(ReportViewItem viewItem)
{
    return string.Format("ms-appdata:///local/{0}/{1}.jpg",
LocalCacheFolderName, viewItem.NativeId);
}

internal async Task<string>
    GetLocalImageUrlAsync(ReportViewItem viewItem)
{
    var cacheFolder = await this.GetCacheFolderAsync();

    // build a path based on the native id...
    var filename = GetCacheFilename(viewItem);
    StorageFile cacheFile = null;
    try
    {
        cacheFile = await cacheFolder.GetFileAsync(filename);
    }
    catch (FileNotFoundException ex)
    {
        SinkWarning(ex);
    }

    // did we get one?
    if (cacheFile != null)
    {
        Debug.WriteLine(string.Format("Cache image for '{0}'
was found locally...", viewItem.NativeId));
        return CalculateLocalImageUrl(viewItem);
    }
    else
    {
        Debug.WriteLine(string.Format(
"Cache image for '{0}' was not found locally...", viewItem.NativeId));
        return null;
```

```
        }
    }
```

You'll notice that I've put some `Debug.WriteLine` calls in there. This primarily is to help you see what's happening with the flow.

### Downloading and caching images

Now we can look at the method that actually does the downloading and storing to disk. I'll do this in parts so that you can follow the flow.

So far we've always used the `async`/`await` keywords in a very "vanilla" way. What I want to show you now if how you can work with tasks more directly. To load the images, we'll spin off separate tasks explicitly and use the standard asynchrony features to wait until they are completed and then update the UI.

In reality, you don't necessarily need to do this. You can just use `async`/`await` in the way we have been doing. In the experiments I did when writing this chapter, though, I got a slightly better effect doing it this way.

To run tasks explicitly, you can use the `Run` static method on the `Task` class. You can then use the `await` keyword as you usually would. Once the task has completed, we can set the `ImageUri` property of the `ViewItem`, and data binding will take over and display the image.

First we set up the task, passing in an anonymous method to run:

```
// Add method to ReportImageCacheManager...
internal async void EnqueueImageDownload(ReportViewItem viewItem)
{
    Debug.WriteLine(string.Format("Enqueuing download for '{0}'...",
viewItem.NativeId));

    // create a new task...
    var theUrl = Task.Run<string>(async () =>
    {
```

The first thing the task will do is use `GetReportImageServiceProxy` to download the image. This will be transferred over the wire as JSON, but returned to us as a byte array containing a JPEG file. We'll call `AssertNoErrors` to ensure that we have valid data.

```
        Debug.WriteLine(string.Format("Requesting image for '{0}'...",
viewItem.NativeId));

        // load...
        var proxy = ServiceProxyFactory.Current.GetHandler
<IGetReportImageServiceProxy>();
        var result = await proxy.GetReportImageAsync(viewItem.NativeId);

        // check...
        result.AssertNoErrors();
```

If the call is successful, we can write the image to disk.

```
// create the new file...
var filename = GetCacheFilename(viewItem);
var cacheFolder = await this.GetCacheFolderAsync();
var cacheFile = await cacheFolder.CreateFileAsync(filename,
    CreationCollisionOption.ReplaceExisting);
using (var stream = await cacheFile.OpenStreamForWriteAsync())
    stream.Write(result.ImageBytes, 0, result.ImageBytes.Length);
```

Note the use of `CreationCollisionOption.ReplaceExisting`. This is so that this method works if we're refreshing a cached version from the server, in which case a file would already exist.

Finally, we can work out what the URL will be given the name of the file and the standard name of the folder. This will be the result of the task. In a moment we'll build a continuation handler that takes this value and gives it to the `ReportViewItem` instance.

```
// get the URL...
string url = this.CalculateLocalImageUrl(viewItem);
Debug.WriteLine(string.Format("Image load for '{0}' finished.",
    viewItem.NativeId));
return url;
```

That completes the work that the anonymous method has to do. By the time we finish the awaited call, we'll have a URI that we can pass through to the `ViewItem`.

```
});

// set it...
viewItem.ImageUri = theUrl;
}
```

That's it! If you've managed to get everything lined up, when you run this the images will download and appear. Figure 6-12 illustrates.

If the images don't appear, it's likely that your exceptions are being masked by the TPL. (Exceptions in background operations don't crash the main app, so you have to explicitly look for them.) If you look in the Output window in Visual Studio, you may see exceptions being reported. You will get a lot of `FileNotFoundExceptions` during proper operations caused by the fact that we can't check for files. If you do see exceptions, go into Debug – Exceptions and check the Thrown option against Common Language Runtime Exceptions. That should help.

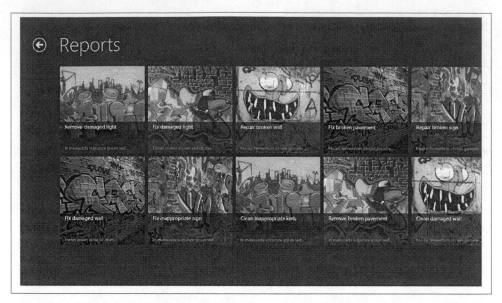

*Figure 6-12. The Reports page showing downloaded/cached images*

# CHAPTER 7

# Sharing

In this chapter, we're going to look at one of the key tenets of the Windows Store app user experience: sharing.

One of the key problems with iPad is that information is stored in each app's private silo. It's hard to share information between apps, and really the only tool that you have is the copy-and-paste feature. With Window Store apps, information sharing between apps is front and center. Apps can register themselves as a share target, or they can share information by acting as a share source.

Those of you who have been around the block a few times will see similarities in this feature with Dynamic Data Exchange, or DDE. DDE was a feature introduced in very early versions of Windows that was designed to work in a very loose and decoupled way. The idea was that an application, say Excel, could tell Windows that it had some text information to share. You could then choose an application that understood text, such as Word. Windows would then marshal the data from one to the other using some extra magic atop the standard system clipboard.

Sharing in Windows Store apps works in pretty much that exact way. An app can indicate that it shares data, and you'll receive a message asking for said data. You can provide a combination of text, HTML, URIs, bitmaps, files (storage items), and RTF data, or you can define custom formats. The OS will then find apps that are interested in receiving shared data (i.e., those that register as having a *search contract*) and present to the user a list of compatible apps. When the user chooses an app, it's activated and asked to provide a UI. The target app then acts on the shared data in some form (e.g., sending an email).

In this chapter, we're going to look at how we share data first. Then we're going to look at how we can implement a share contract and become a target for shared data.

In that first part we'll look at the fundamentals of pushing data out to other apps. This will include creating a *deferral* when handling requests that take a long time to fulfill (for example, in situations where we don't have the data in a state where it can be shared because we need to process or augment it).

In the second part we'll look at how to draw data in from other apps. This will also include some debugging tips that can be generally helpful.

# Sharing Data

The basic sharing data functions are tremendously easy to implement. Throughout the WinRT APIs, whenever Microsoft really wants you to include a feature in the Windows 8/Windows RT experience the APIs related to those features are always very straightforward. This is no exception.

In this section, we're going to look at the basics of sharing data first. We're then going to add more sophistication, particularly in dealing with share operations that take a long time and need to feed back information to the user.

## Basic Sharing

To tell Windows that we're able to share content, we need to use the `Windows.Applica tionModel.DataTransfer.DataTransferManager` class. This class doesn't understand anything about our view-model, so we need to close that loop.

### Hooking the DataTransferManager into the view-model

So that we know what we're trying to call into, we'll build the handling method in `IViewModel` and `ViewModel` now. The intention will be that view-models that wish to partake in sharing will override a new `ShareDataRequest` method on the view-model.

Here's the change to `IViewModel`. The two parameters to that method are in the `Win dows.ApplicationModel.DataTransfer` namespace.

```
// Add method to IViewModel...
public interface IViewModel : INotifyPropertyChanged
{
    // property to indicate whether the model is busy working...
    bool IsBusy
    {
        get;
    }

    // called when the view is activated...
    void Activated();

    // called when the view-model might have some data to share...
    void ShareDataRequested(DataTransferManager sender,
DataRequestedEventArgs args);
}
```

The implementation for the method will be a *no-op* call for now. (A no-op call means "no operation"—that is, it doesn't do anything. It's typically included to get things compiling, or as a placeholder for future work.) Here's the code:

```
// Add method to ViewModel...
public virtual void ShareDataRequested(DataTransferManager sender,
    DataRequestedEventArgs args)
{
    // no-op by default...
}
```

To call that method, we need to be able to dereference our view-model from a `Window` instance.

When our app boots, we have a single window, which can be referenced via `Window.Current`. The `App` class that's created as part of the Visual Studio project creates a `Frame` instance and tells it to navigate to the `Page` that we want to show. The frame is then attached to the window (via the `Window` instance's `Content` property) and everything springs into life.

In Chapter 5 we created a `FrameworkElementExtender` class specifically to allow us to show and hide the app bars on a page. One of the functions we added there walks the parents of a `FrameworkElement` instance to find one of type `Page`. Once it finds that, it casts it and returns it.

In the case we're about to look at, we have to walk down the tree as well as up. When we receive our message indicating that sharing needs to happen, the only thing we'll know about is the `Window`. We need to walk down the tree, examining any available `Content` properties. Hopefully we'll then hit the `Frame` whose `Content` property will be set to the `Page`. Once we have a `Page`, we can optimistically cast its `DataContext` property to `IViewModel`.

To implement this functionality, you'll have to add the new `GetViewModel` methods, and replace `GetParentPage` with `GetRelatedPage` in `FrameworkElementExtender`. Here's the code:

```
// Add methods to FrameworkElementExtender...
internal static class FrameworkElementExtender
{
    internal static IViewModel GetViewModel(this Window window)
    {
        if (window.Content is FrameworkElement)
            return ((FrameworkElement)window.Content).GetViewModel();
        else
            return null;
    }

    internal static IViewModel GetViewModel(this FrameworkElement element)
    {
        // walk up...
```

```csharp
                var page = element.GetRelatedPage();
                if (page != null)
                    return page.DataContext as IViewModel;
                else
                    return null;
        }

        internal static Page GetRelatedPage(this FrameworkElement element)
        {
            // up...
            DependencyObject walk = element;
            while (walk != null)
            {
                if (walk is Page)
                    return (Page)walk;

                if (walk is FrameworkElement)
                    walk = ((FrameworkElement)walk).Parent;
                else
                    break;
            }

            // down...
            walk = element;
            while (walk != null)
            {
                if(walk is Page)
                    return (Page)walk;

                if (walk is ContentControl)
                    walk = ((ContentControl)walk).Content as FrameworkElement;
                else
                    break;
            }

            // nothing...
                    return null;
        }

    // other methods omitted...
    }
```

The helper methods that we just added are generally helpful anyway, but they'll be of specific use as we go through the rest of this chapter.

Finally, we need to close the loop and register with the DataTransferManager. To do this, find the OnLaunched method in App and add a call to subscribe to the DataReques ted event. The event handler will dereference the view-model (if any) and then call through to the IViewModel interface's ShareDataRequested method. Here's the code— although I've omitted a chunk of OnLaunched for brevity:

```
protected override async void OnLaunched(LaunchActivatedEventArgs args)
{
    // code omitted...

    // Place the frame in the current Window and ensure that it's active
    Window.Current.Content = rootFrame;
    Window.Current.Activate();

    // register for data transfer...
    var manager = DataTransferManager.GetForCurrentView();
    manager.DataRequested += manager_DataRequested;
}

static void manager_DataRequested(DataTransferManager sender,
DataRequestedEventArgs args)
{
    // find the view model and dereference...
    if (Window.Current != null)
    {
        var viewModel = Window.Current.GetViewModel();
        if (viewModel != null)
            viewModel.ShareDataRequested(sender, args);
    }
}
```

At this point, we can go ahead and test that everything up to this point is working. Set a breakpoint in the `manager_DataRequested` handler method. Start the app and summon the charms from the right side of the screen. Select Share, and the breakpoint should hit.

Now that we know we can hook into the sharing subsystem, let's actually share some data.

### Sharing basic data

In Chapter 5 we built a mechanism for selecting items on the Reports page. This is what we'll use for sharing. Although that view-model supports selecting multiple items, we'll assume that the first item in that set is the one the user wants to share. That's a convenient shortcut here, but it would create a confusing experience in a production app, where it would be better to be able to share the entirety of the selected items in one operation.

Once we have an item to share, all we have to do is populate the `DataRequest` item that we get passed through in the request. To populate it, we have to set some metadata (a subject and description, basically) and then provide the data. You can supply as many formats as you like; Windows and the target apps will work out how best to interpret what's shared.

The simplest data to share is text and URI information, so we'll do that first.

In the `ReportsPageViewModel` class, override the `ShareDataRequested` method and add this code:

```
// Add method to ReportsPageViewModel...
public async override void ShareDataRequested(DataTransferManager
    sender, DataRequestedEventArgs args)
{
    // do we have a selection?
    if (!(this.HasSelectedItems))
        return;

    // share the first item...
    var report = this.SelectedItems.First();

    // set the basics...
    var data = args.Request.Data;
    data.Properties.Title = string.Format("StreetFoo report '{0}'",
report.Title);
    data.Properties.Description = string.Format("Sharing problem report
#{0}", report.NativeId);

    // set the text...
    data.SetText(string.Format("{0}: {1}", report.Title,
report.Description));

    // set the URI...
    data.SetUri(new Uri(report.PublicUrl));
}
```

We have to build that `PublicUrl` method before we can run it. All this does is format a special URL with which the user can review the report live on the StreetFoo server. Here's the code:

```
// Add property to ReportViewItem...
public string PublicUrl
{
    get
    {
        return string.Format
("https://streetfoo.apphb.com/PublicReport.aspx?api={0}&id={1}",
ServiceProxy.ApiKey, this.NativeId);
    }
}
```

You can now run that. Navigate to the Reports page, select an item, and then access the Share feature through the charms. You'll see something similar to Figure 7-1.

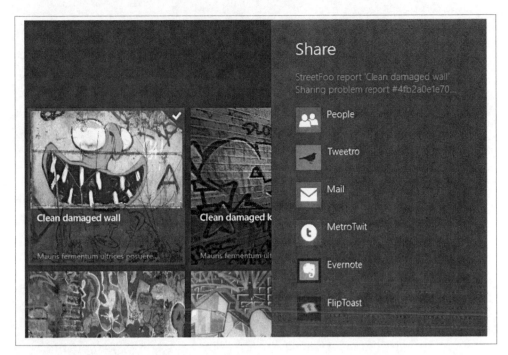

*Figure 7-1. Selecting an app to share with*

If you go ahead and select an app, you can see how the shared data flows into the other app. It's worth trying a few apps to get a feel for how they pick and choose from the available data. For example, Figure 7-2 shows the Mail app, which ignores the text value but takes the metadata and the URL.

### Sharing images

Now that we've got down the basics of sharing, the "edges" of this API are in the types of data that you can share, and in reporting progress back to the user. In this and the following two sections, we'll look at the other data types, and then we'll move on to reporting progress.

 We're not going to look at custom data types in this book, as that's an unusual niche requirement.

After text and URLs, the next most common thing you'll want to share is images. One problem we'll have to negotiate is that (as of the time of writing at least) none of the built-in apps receive image data. I'll present a workaround for this when we get to it.

*Figure 7-2. A problem report shared with the Mail app*

Sharing images is a matter of giving our `DataPackage` object a `RandomAccessStreamRe ference` instance. As its name implies, this is a helpful class that wraps a stream so that you can pass it around either within your own app or—as we're about to do—out into other apps. You can create `RandomAccessStreamReference` from a file, a stream you already have, or a URI.

We've already seen that we can use the special `ms-appx` and `ms-appdata` protocols to access resources that are part of the deployment and stored in the app's private data. Incidentally, you can reference `http` and `https` protocol URLs too, in which case WinRT will undertake some of the heavy lifting involved with setting up the network requests.

Anyway, we already have a URL for the image stored in the `ImageUrl`. All we have to do is provide that URL through to the share operation. One wrinkle we have to deal with is that we're supposed to provide a thumbnail image when we share. For simplicity here, I've just given it the main image for the thumbnail.

 As of the time of writing, some share targets will fail if you specify an image without a thumbnail. You can also find an example of how to scale images in Chapter 12.

Here's the modified version of `ShareDataRequested`:

```
// Modify method in ReportsPageViewModel...
public async override void ShareDataRequested(DataTransferManager
sender, DataRequestedEventArgs args)
{
    // do we have a selection?
    if (!(this.HasSelectedItems))
        return;

    // share the first item...
    var report = this.SelectedItems.First();

    // set the basics...
    var data = args.Request.Data;
    data.Properties.Title = string.Format("StreetFoo report '{0}'",
report.Title);
    data.Properties.Description = string.Format("Sharing problem report
#{0}", report.NativeId);

    // set the text...
    data.SetText(string.Format("{0}: {1}", report.Title,
report.Description));

    // set the URI...
    data.SetUri(new Uri(report.PublicUrl));

    // do we have an image?
    if (report.HasImage)
    {
        var reference = RandomAccessStreamReference.CreateFromUri
(new Uri(report.ImageUrl));
        data.Properties.Thumbnail = reference;
        data.SetBitmap(reference);
    }
}
```

As I mentioned, the challenge is now sharing the image. You may have an app on your device that acts as a target for images—the version on which I based this book's work didn't have a built-in app that supports being an image target. The one I'm using in Figure 7-3 is from the MSDN, "Sharing content target app sample." This dumps out information on shared data, and you'll be able to find it by searching the MSDN.

*Figure 7-3. Successfully sharing an image*

## Sharing other types of data

The other basic types of data are very easy to share. I won't take you through these in detail, but I will call them out.

- You can share one or more filesystem objects via the `SetStorageItem` method. This takes an array of `IStorageItem` instances. (Oddly, this means you can share entire folders as `StorageFolder` implements `IStorageItem`.)
- You can share HTML data by providing a string to `SetStorageHtml`.
- Finally, you can share RTF data by providing a string to `SetStorageRtf`.

As mentioned, we're not going to look at custom data in this book, as this is a niche requirement.

## Pull Requests/Deferrals

Sometimes you'll need time to prepare the data to share, in which case you need to set up a *pull request*. You can't just use `async`/`await` on the handler method that responds to the share request, as Windows doesn't understand you're doing a long-running operation and will just cancel you. You have to be more explicit.

In this section we're going to create a share operation that takes a reasonably long time. Specifically, we're going to download a static image off the StreetFoo server. We'll do this on demand, in the background.

 To keep the StreetFoo client "clean," I'm proposing that we create a new project for doing this. In the download for this chapter, you'll find a solution called `SharingScratch` and a project `PullRequest Scratch` that contains this work.

Pull requests are pretty easy to implement. All you have to do is tell the `DataRequest` object that you want to register a handler for a specific data type, and then within that handler ask for a `DataProviderDeferral` instance. In fact, the only work we have to do in this method relates to actually getting the image down from the server.

On the StreetFoo server, there are static versions of the graffiti sample files that we've seen so far. To download it, we create an `HttpWebRequest` (as we did when we set up `ServiceProxy` way back in Chapter 2), and then we'll copy the response into a `InMe moryRandomAccessStream`. `InMemoryRandomAccessStream` is a WinRT class, whereas the `Stream` object that we get back from the `HttpWebResponse` is a .NET class. Because `RandomAccessStreamReference` doesn't understand `Stream` instances (because that too is a WinRT class, not a .NET class), we have to use an extension method to gain a façade. This happens quite a lot when we're building Windows Store apps; although sometimes mapping between WinRT and .NET happens automatically through a project, on occasion we have to use a façade. In this case, we'll ask for a `Stream` façade in the WinRT `InMemoryRandomAccessStream` instance.

Here's the code, which I've placed into my `MainPage` class in the `PullRequestScratch` project:

```
// Add methods to MainPage...
protected override void OnNavigatedTo(NavigationEventArgs e)
{
    base.OnNavigatedTo(e);

    // subscribe...
    var manager = DataTransferManager.GetForCurrentView();
    manager.DataRequested += manager_DataRequested;
}
```

```csharp
        void manager_DataRequested(DataTransferManager sender,
DataRequestedEventArgs args)
        {
            // do the basics...
            var data = args.Request.Data;
            data.Properties.Title = "Deferred image";
            data.Properties.Description = "I'll have to be downloaded first!";

            // get a deferral...
            data.SetDataProvider(StandardDataFormats.Bitmap, async (request) =>
            {
                var deferral = request.GetDeferral();
                try
                {
                    // download...
                    var httpRequest = HttpWebRequest.CreateHttp
("http://streetfoo.apphb.com/images/graffiti00.jpg");
                    var response = await httpRequest.GetResponseAsync();

                    using (var inStream = response.GetResponseStream())
                    {
                        // copy the stream... but we'll need to obtain a facade
                        // to map between WinRT and .NET...
                        var outStream = new InMemoryRandomAccessStream();
                        inStream.CopyTo(outStream.AsStream());

                        // send that...
                        var reference = RandomAccessStreamReference.
CreateFromStream(outStream);
                        request.SetData(reference);
                    }
                }
                finally
                {
                    deferral.Complete();
                }

            });
        }
```

If you run that and access the share charm, it will work as per the sharing operation where we shared the image that we already had on disk. However, you should notice that the share target will load and after a time the image will appear. When we looked at this before from the main StreetFoo app, the image appeared immediately.

 This concept of a deferral comes up a few times in WinRT. You'll see it in other chapters.

# Acting as a Share Target

Now that we've looked at how we can share data, we'll turn our attention to how we can become a target for sharing.

This section is going to segue into work that we're going to do in Chapter 12 with regards to creating new reports. At the moment we've been relying on preexisting problem reports on the StreetFoo server. In Chapter 12 we're going to create reports on the device and upload them using background processes. (The background process itself will be covered in Chapter 15.)

In a production app, one way in which we might want to create reports is by receiving shared information from other apps (particularly images). Chapter 12 looks at using the camera to do this directly. In this chapter, we'll see in theory how we can receive both text data and photo data. In a real application, you'd likely want to create reports from both sources. However, given the constraints of having to put this book in a fixed order—and where I've happened to put this chapter before the camera chapter—you'll have to use your imagination as to how to ultimately create reports from shared images.

Setting up as a share target involves rigging your app with a share contract and then picking out the pieces of data that you're interested in. There are also some edge functions in terms of supporting long-running operations.

## Sharing Text

Visual Studio will do most of the heavy lifting for you in terms of implementing a share contract into your project. If you open up the Add New Item dialog, search for the Share Target Contract item. Give it a name (e.g., ShareTargetPage), and click OK.

This will do three things: it will create the new page in your project, override the On ShareTargetActivated method in your App class, and alter your manifest declarations to include a Share Target declaration. Figure 7-4 illustrates the manifest change.

*Figure 7-4. The Share Target contract/declaration*

 You'll see some inconsistency here in that in some areas these are called *contracts* and in others they are referred to as *declarations*. They're both the same thing—the naming is down to the fact that in the manifest you're "adding declarations of contracts."

By default we receive notification of text and URI formats. We're not interested in URI, so you can remove this from the declaration.

What we'll do to prove this works is run the app. If we share some text from another app, our icon will appear in the available apps list, and if we click our app we'll spring into life.

However, sharing text from the built-in apps is a little counterintuitive. In the version of Windows 8 on which this book is based, the Mail app doesn't act as a share source. IE does act as a share source, but will only share text data if you select a block of text on the page. Given those facts, using IE but making sure that we have a selection on the page seems to be the path of least resistance. (Don't forget you need to use the Windows Store app version of IE, as legacy desktop apps do not support share operations.)

If you are trying to troubleshoot share operations, using the Share Target Sample from MSDN—the one that we looked at before—can be a big help, as this dumps all of the information that's been shared.

Thus, if you go into IE, select some text, and then initiate a share, our app will appear in the list. Figure 7-5 illustrates.

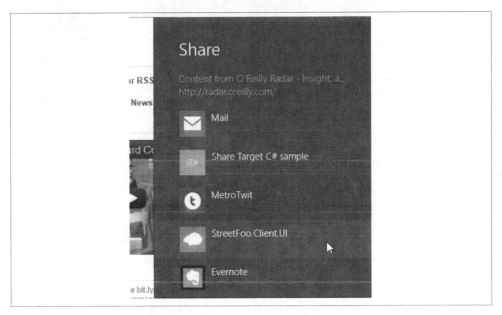

*Figure 7-5. StreetFoo as a share target*

 You should note, though, that as of the time of writing, there was an issue whereby if an app was already in the background, the share target UI would appear and then disappear instantly. If the app isn't in the background, the share target UI will appear and remain on the screen as expected.

If you go ahead and share that data, you'll get something like Figure 7-6. This shows the properties going across but none of the data. But as we'll see in the next section, we can use the opportunity of trying to share the text to learn more about how to debug interactions with Windows Store apps when things go wrong.

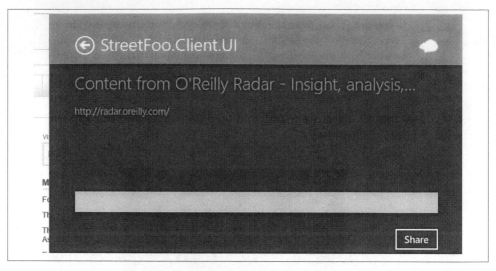

*Figure 7-6. Viewing share data properties in StreetFoo*

# Sharing Text (and Troubleshooting)

One of the problems with working with Windows Store apps is that because the system is designed to drive down user intimidation, you're not supposed to bamboozle users with errors. For example, if the app crashes and quits, you're not allowed (according to the rules) to show an error message. The idea is that the user will know that something went wrong by virtue of arriving at the Start screen.

 This seems like poor UX design, but this is in fact what the iPad does and is something I've never heard iPad users complain about.

What I want to show you in this section is a quick trick to dump out debugging information when you do hit problems.

We'll do this by breaking the share operation that we were given by Visual Studio. Well, I say "breaking," but what we're actually going to do is migrate the `ShareTargetPage` class over to the MVVM pattern of our other pages. In doing this, we're going to hit a problem that we have to fix, the symptom of which is to crash the app during the share operation. We'll then see how to view diagnostic information, and then fix the problem.

## Migrating ShareTargetPage to MVVM

As is the way with all of the Visual Studio templates, the provided implementation of ShareTargetPage uses the not-really-a-view-model DefaultViewModel "bucket" that's included by default in LayoutAwarePage. (Recall that in Chapter 2 one of the first things we did was to build a proper MVVM implementation to replace this bucket.)

If you look in the default code, you'll find lots of references to DefaultViewModel. Here's an example:

```
public async void Activate(ShareTargetActivatedEventArgs args)
{
    this._shareOperation = args.ShareOperation;

    // Communicate metadata about the shared content through the
    // view model
    var shareProperties = this._shareOperation.Data.Properties;
    var thumbnailImage = new BitmapImage();
    this.DefaultViewModel["Title"] = shareProperties.Title;
    this.DefaultViewModel["Description"] = shareProperties.Description;
    this.DefaultViewModel["Image"] = thumbnailImage;
    this.DefaultViewModel["Sharing"] = false;
    this.DefaultViewModel["ShowImage"] = false;
    this.DefaultViewModel["Comment"] = String.Empty;
    this.DefaultViewModel["SupportsComment"] = true;
    Window.Current.Content = this;
    Window.Current.Activate();

    // Update the shared content's thumbnail image in the background
    if (shareProperties.Thumbnail != null)
    {
        var stream = await shareProperties.Thumbnail.OpenReadAsync();
        thumbnailImage.SetSource(stream);
        this.DefaultViewModel["ShowImage"] = true;
    }
}
```

Note the async void declarations on that method. That's not recommended. async should in most cases return a Task; otherwise, you don't have any way of controlling the method's lifetime or responding to the method's lifetime changes.

What we need to do is create a new ShareTargetPageViewModel and IShareTargetPageViewModel so that we can deprecate the DefaultViewModel bucket approach.

We've done this a few times (see Chapter 2 for a basic run-through), so I'll go through this part quickly. What we need is properties for the basic items on the view (title and description labels, a comments, field, and a Share button), and some properties that the default page implementation needs to do its magic. These properties, all Booleans, are

Sharing (indicates that a share operation is in progress), ShowImage (indicates that we have image data, which isn't strictly needed, but I'm proposing leaving it in for consistency with the standard implementation), and SupportsComment (indicates that we want to capture a comment). We'll also need a command to indicate that the user wants to go ahead with the sharing. Ultimately from this we're going to share out a text value and an image value, so we'll create additional properties for SharedText and SharedImage.

Here's the interface code:

```
public interface IShareTargetPageViewModel : IViewModel
{
    string Title { get; }
    string Description { get; }
    string Comment { get; set; }

    string SharedText { get; }
    BitmapImage SharedImage { get; }

    bool ShowImage { get; }
    bool SupportsComment { get; }
    bool Sharing { get; }

    ICommand ShareCommand { get; }

    void SetupShareData(ShareOperation operation);
}
```

Now we can look at the view-model implementation.

You should be aware that a significant "gotcha" with regards to sharing operations is that the event that tells your app that you need to share (ShareTargetActivated) will pass over a ShareOperation. You *must* store this value in a field in your view-model; otherwise, the sharing operation will fail. What will happen if you don't do this is that the share operation will appear and disappear immediately. This is due to WinRT's COM-based nature. When you store a reference to a WinRT object in a .NET field, the COM reference count for that object is incremented. This "locks" your reference to the object. Without this locking, when the sharing mechanism releases its hold on the object, it's assumed that the sharing operation finishes, and the whole thing closes. (If you're not that familiar with how COM reference tracking works, don't worry about it too much, as the places where it has an impact are few and far between. This is the only place where it's important in this entire book, for example.)

For now, by way of a standard command handler, we're just going to put a MessageDia log on the screen. Here's the implementation for ShareTargetPageViewModel:

```
public class ShareTargetPageViewModel : ViewModel,
    IShareTargetPageViewModel
{
    private ShareOperation ShareOperation { get; set; }
```

```csharp
    public string Title { get { return this.GetValue<string>(); }
        private set { this.SetValue(value); } }
    public string Description { get { return this.GetValue<string>(); }
        private set { this.SetValue(value); } }
    public string Comment { get { return this.GetValue<string>(); }
        set { this.SetValue(value); } }

    public string SharedText { get { return this.GetValue<string>(); }
        private set { this.SetValue(value); } }
    public BitmapImage SharedImage {
        get { return this.GetValue<BitmapImage>(); }
        private set { this.SetValue(value); } }

    public bool ShowImage { get { return this.GetValue<bool>(); }
        private set { this.SetValue(value); } }
    public bool SupportsComment { get { return this.GetValue<bool>(); }
        private set { this.SetValue(value); } }
    public bool Sharing { get { return this.GetValue<bool>(); }
        private set { this.SetValue(value); } }

    public ICommand ShareCommand { get; private set; }

    public ShareTargetPageViewModel(IViewModelHost host)
        : base(host)
    {
        this.ShowImage = false;
        this.Sharing = false;
        this.SupportsComment = true;

        this.ShareCommand = new DelegateCommand(async (args) => await
HandleShareCommandAsync());
    }

    private async Task HandleShareCommandAsync()
    {
        await this.Host.ShowAlertAsync("Shared.");
    }

    public void SetupShareData(ShareOperation share)
    {
        // store the share operation - we need to do this to hold a
          // reference or otherwise the sharing subsystem will assume
          // that we've finished...
        this.ShareOperation = share;

        // get the properties out...
        var data = share.Data;
        var props = data.Properties;
        this.Title = props.Title;
        this.Description = props.Description;

          // we'll add code to read shared data later...
```

```
        }
    }
```

The final thing we need to do is add a mapping for the interface and implementation to `StreetFooRuntime.Start`. I won't show this here for brevity.

 Whenever Windows tries to invoke our app for a sharing operation, it will use the deployed version in our *~/Debug/AppX* folder. Thus, whenever we build, we also need to deploy by navigating to Build→Deploy.

### Tracking debug information

Once we've migrated the page over, if we run the share operation it will fail. (Remember, to run the share operation select some text in the Window Store app version of IE and use the share charm.) Figure 7-7 shows us what we can expect to see.

*Figure 7-7. Cryptic sharing failure*

The problem here is that because of the way that Windows manages lifetimes for Windows Store apps, we have to get Visual Studio to attach a debugger to our app before it actually runs. This is easy enough to do, as Visual Studio has a feature for handling exactly this.

However, what I want to do is go through some of the diagnostic bits and pieces that we can take advantage of when building Windows Store apps.

### Debugging share operations

This technique applies to both share operations and other places in which Windows may start your app to do something, such as searching (Chapter 8) and background tasks (Chapter 14).

In Visual Studio, open up the properties for the project and select the Debug tab. Select the "Do not launch, but debug my code when it starts" option. Figure 7-8 illustrates.

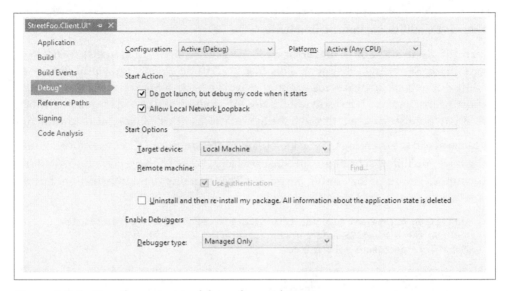

*Figure 7-8. Setting the project to debug when code starts*

Should you be working without a debugger, we have to be able to write error information somewhere so that we can actually see what's happening. Showing a `MessageDialog` is no good—on the one hand it's against the rules, and on the other hand its asynchronous nature will conflict with the startup process of the share operation and we'll hang. Luckily, since the very first versions of Windows there's been a shared debug message queue, which we can access.

The Windows event log is where this sort of crash information is supposed to be stored. In fact, in the standard Application log we do see a report of the error. Here's an example:

```
Faulting application name: StreetFoo.Client.UI.exe, version: 1.0.0.0,
time stamp: 0x4ffa029d
Faulting module name: Windows.UI.Xaml.dll, version: 6.2.8400.0, time stamp:
0x4fb6fcf4
Exception code: 0xc000027b
Fault offset: 0x0052967b
Faulting process id: 0x75c
Faulting application start time: 0x01cd5d54e800c69e
Faulting application path:
C:\BookCode\Chapter08\StreetFoo.Client\StreetFoo.Client.UI\bin\Debug\AppX
\StreetFoo.Client.UI.exe
Faulting module path: C:\Windows\System32\Windows.UI.Xaml.dll
Report Id: 25e22ff1-c948-11e1-9b91-e4ce8f131b41
Faulting package full name:
569e8a16-efb8-4992-ada5-7407fecb3dee_1.0.0.0_neutral__fv7d1kf84c3t4
Faulting package-relative application ID: App
```

This doesn't tell us anything that we don't already know—we know that we crashed and there's little additional information here.

Interestingly, in addition to that error we'll also get a report written to disk by the Windows Error Reporting subsystem. This turns out to be equally unhelpful, but worth calling out to mention that error summaries will go back to Microsoft via this standard reporting mechanism. Microsoft will use this information as part of its regular telemetry, but if you publish your app through the Store, Microsoft will share this data with you.

While we're in the event logs, if you look under *Application and Services Logs/Microsoft/Windows* you'll find subsystem-specific error logs. Some of them pertain to Windows Store apps. The Apps log does in particular. This contains more information, but still none that's of any help. Here's an example:

```
Activation of the app 569e8a16-efb8-4992-ada5-7407fecb3dee_fv7d1kf84c3t4!
App for the Windows.ShareTarget contract failed with error:
The remote procedure call failed..
```

The main reason this information is unhelpful is that it's all created from the WinRT side, not the .NET side. .NET's exception handling is generally "stronger" than WinRT's error handling, so if at all possible we want to track .NET's exception handling.

It turns out this is really easy—we just use `Debug.WriteLine`.

When the share target contract was added to the project, Visual Studio added an override to the `App` class, specifically `OnShareTargetActivated`. All we have to do is modify this so that it writes the error information through to `Debug.WriteLine`, like this:

```
// Modify method in App...
protected override void OnShareTargetActivated(Windows.ApplicationModel.
Activation.ShareTargetActivatedEventArgs args)
{
    try
    {
        var shareTargetPage = new StreetFoo.Client.UI.ShareTargetPage();
        shareTargetPage.Activate(args);
    }
    catch (Exception ex)
    {
        Debug.WriteLine(ex);
        throw ex;
    }
}
```

You'll be familiar with `Debug.WriteLine` as a .NET developer. When the debugger is attached, output is routed through to Visual Studio's Output window. What you might be less familiar with is that this also keys into a standard Win32 API called `OutputDebugString`. Windows maintains a piece of globally shared memory for debugging text. We can use an application called DbgView to show the output.

`Debug.WriteLine` is pretty limited. If you want a more fully featured logging system for your app, have a look at MetroLog (*https://github.com/mbrit/MetroLog*).

DbgView can be downloaded from Microsoft's website; go to the Microsoft Download Center (*http://download.microsoft.com*) and search for DbgView. When it's downloaded, make sure you run it as administrator, and select Capture – Capture Global Win32 from the menu.

Now if you run the share operation again, it will still fail, but you will be able to see why. Figure 7-9 illustrates.

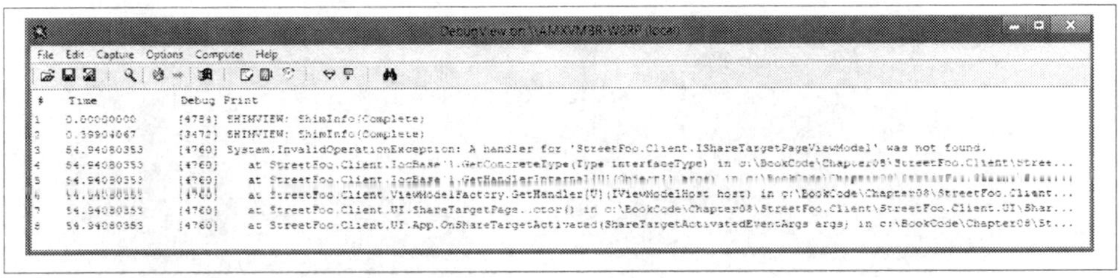

*Figure 7-9. DbgView reporting exception information*

So that's great! We can now actually see the problem. We just need to fix it.

### Fixing the runtime startup problem

The problem that we have here relates to the fact that our app is dependent on the `ViewModelFactory` being initialized whenever we need to obtain an instance of a viewmodel. At the moment, we configure this in the `OnLaunched` handler in `App` by calling `StreetFooRuntime.Start`. When our app is started from the share operation, `OnLaunched` is not called and hence `Start` is not called. The fix, then, is to make sure that `Start` is called when sharing starts.

An additional thing we have to deal with is that we need to automatically log on the remembered user when we start a share operation. Luckily, we can do this using the `RestorePersistentLogonAsync` method that we built in Chapter 4.

Reporting back to the user that there was an error is slightly more complex, however. The Windows Store app experience as it relates to displaying error messages is asynchronous in nature. The share UI will disappear, and a few seconds later toast will be used to tell the user that a problem occurred. What we want to do is put a message on screen immediately, front and center, telling the user that he or she needs to log in.

To fix this, we'll create a new page called `NotLoggedOnPage`. This will display a simple message asking the user to go into the app via the Start screen and log in. (This isn't a great user experience; I've taken a shortcut, as this operation is not central to this discussion. What you should do in a production app is get the user to log on through the `NotLoggedOnPage` UI.)

Create your new `NotLoggedOnPage` and add a couple of `TextBlock` instances to display a message. Figure 7-10 gives an example of what such a thing looks like when running. I haven't bothered adding a view-model for this page, as it's not interactive. If you did want to build this out properly, you could use the existing `LogonPageViewModel` class and simply wrap a new UI around it. Remember, though, that you need to hold a reference to the provided `ShareOperation` in a field; otherwise, the share UI will disappear. (See the previous discussion on this.)

*Figure 7-10. The "Not logged in" message*

Now we can turn our attention to the code. Remember, our goal here is to call `Street FooRuntime.Start`. The easiest place to do this, and to add in the capability to show the logon prompt, is in `OnShareTargetActivated` itself. Here's the code—note that I've changed the signature of this method to indicate that it is now async:

```
// Modify method in App...
protected override async void OnShareTargetActivated
(Windows.ApplicationModel.Activation.ShareTargetActivatedEventArgs args)
{
    try
    {
        // start...
        await StreetFooRuntime.Start("Client");

        // logon?
        var logon = ViewModelFactory.Current.GetHandler
<ILogonPageViewModel>(new NullViewModelHost());
        if (await logon.RestorePersistentLogonAsync())
        {
            var shareTargetPage = new ShareTargetPage();
            shareTargetPage.Activate(args);
```

```
                }
                else
                {
                    var notLoggedOnPage = new NotLoggedOnPage();
                    notLoggedOnPage.Activate(args);
                }
            }
            catch (Exception ex)
            {
                Debug.WriteLine(ex);
                throw ex;
            }
        }
```

Now if you retry the share operation (remember that you'll need to deploy it from within Visual Studio, close it, and then try to share from within IE), you'll either get the old `ShareTargetPage` or the new `NotLoggedOnPage`. However, we still haven't reached the point where the shared text is being displayed, so let's look at that now.

### Handling shared text

Sharing the text is very straightforward. In the page that Visual Studio built, you'll find a `Grid` control that's positioned in the middle of the form. All we have to do is add a `TextBlock` control bound to the `SharedText` property that we stubbed out earlier:

Here's what the markup in `ShareTargetPage` looks like before we make our changes:

```
<Grid Grid.Row="1" Grid.ColumnSpan="2">
            <!-- TODO: Add application scenario-specific sharing UI -->
        </Grid>

        <TextBox Grid.Row="1" Grid.ColumnSpan="2" Margin="0,0,0,27"
            Text="{Binding Comment}"
            Visibility="{Binding SupportsComment, Converter={StaticResource
BooleanToVisibilityConverter}}"
            IsEnabled="{Binding Sharing, Converter={StaticResource
BooleanNegationConverter}}"/>

        <!-- Standard share target footer -->
```

In the version of the template I used to write this book, there seemed to be a bug in that the "comments" form overwrote whatever content was added. I replaced this grid with a `StackPanel` control, and then brought up the editing code into that new `StackPanel`. Here's my markup, but you may well find it easier to refer to the code download to get a handle on exactly what I've done. The highlighted parts are new or changed items —I've moved the `TextBox` from lower down in the page.

```
        <StackPanel Grid.Row="1" Grid.ColumnSpan="2">
            <TextBlock Text="{Binding SharedText}" Style="{StaticResource
BodyTextStyle}"
                Margin="0,0,0,15"></TextBlock>
```

```
<Image Source="{Binding SharedImage}" Margin="0,0,0,15"
        Visibility="{Binding ShowImage, Converter={StaticResource
BooleanToVisibilityConverter}}"></Image>
        <TextBox Margin="0,0,0,27" Text="{Binding Comment}"
Visibility="{Binding SupportsComment, Converter={StaticResource
BooleanToVisibilityConverter}}"
            IsEnabled="{Binding Sharing, Converter={StaticResource
BooleanNegationConverter}}"/>
    </StackPanel>
```

To extract the text from the share operation, we need to go back to our view-model. (We'll cover the image sharing in a later section.)

When we want to extract data from the view-model, we use async calls. This means that we need to use async/await on the method that sets up the sharing operation. Previously I presented this method as synchronous. We're now going to change it, but the reason I've left it so that we have to change it is to help you get a feel for the "fiddlyness" of working with async/await. This happens a lot in Window Store app development—you build something one way, and then you discover that you have to rattle through a whole bunch of calls to put in async functionality.

In this case, we need to change the name and the return type of the SetupShareData method, change its return type, map that through to the interface, and change the operation of the caller.

Here's the first set of changes to SetupShareData. This also includes a call to GetText DataAsync. Note that we need to check whether or not the shared data package contains text data. The call to GetTextDataAsync will fail if we try to load a format that is not within the bucket.

```
// Modify and rename SetupShareData in ShareTargetPageViewModel...
public async Task SetupShareDataAsync(ShareOperation share)
{
    // store the share operation - we need to do this to hold a
    // reference or otherwise the sharing subsystem will assume
    // that we've finished...
    this.ShareOperation = share;

    // get the properties out...
    var data = share.Data;
    var props = data.Properties;
    this.Title = props.Title;
    this.Description = props.Description;

    // now the data...
    if(data.Contains(StandardDataFormats.Text))
        this.SharedText = await data.GetTextAsync();
}
```

The interface will need changing, which I won't present, but I will present the change to the caller. Here's the modification to the `Activate` method on the `ShareTarget Page` itself. Note that we've had to add the `async` modifier to the method.

```
public async void Activate(ShareTargetActivatedEventArgs args)
{
    // give it to the view-model...
    await this.Model.SetupShareDataAsync(args.ShareOperation);

    // show...
    Window.Current.Content = this;
    Window.Current.Activate();
}
```

So that's it! We've managed to create a share target based on a property MVVM implementation and handle the situation where the app is both logged in and not logged in. Let's now look at long-running operations.

## Long-Running Operations

Although a lot of share operations are likely to be quite quick to execute—after all, the likelihood is that the data will be local to the device and in a state where it can be shared —from time to time, we may have to handle data that takes a long time to process. We can use a bunch of methods in `ShareOperation` to tell Windows what's going on if it will take a long time to get the data to a point where it can be shared. (Note that this process is for situations where the *target* is taking a long time. If the *source* is taking a long time, then we create a deferral. Recall that we looked at that aspect earlier in the chapter.)

Here are the methods that you can use:

- `ReportStarted` is used to tell Windows that you have started the operation. Windows will take this as an indication that the user interface is now finished with. The UX angle on this is that the UI doesn't need the modality of the share operation if the share operation has been kicked off.

- Similarly, `ReportDataRetrieved` is used to tell Windows that you've grabbed the data that you need from the source app. For this, imagine a situation where you grab a whole load of files but then you need to upload them. The source app is not needed for the period of time that the upload happens, so Windows can swap it out of memory if needed. You can retrieve all the data and call `ReportDataRetrieved` before the user confirms the share operation and initiates `ReportShared`. (Windows will obviously work out the user experience flow here.) In fact, that's what we'll do in a moment.

- `ReportSubmittedBackgroundTask` is used to tell Windows that you have deferred processing of the shared data to a background task. We'll talk more about background tasks in Chapter 15, although we won't be discussing this particular point.

- `ReportError` is used to tell Windows that something went wrong with the share operation.

- `ReportCompleted` is used to tell Windows that you have finished the share operation.

Although our operation isn't going to take a long time, I will illustrate how to do this properly.

We should handle the `ReportDataRetrieved` scenario first. In `SetupShareDataAsync` we have all the data we need; hence, it's valid to call that method. Here's the change:

```
// Modify method in SearchTargetPageViewModel...
public async Task SetupShareDataAsync(ShareOperation share)
{
    // store the share operation - we need to do this to hold a
    // reference or otherwise the sharing subsystem will assume
    // that we've finished...
    this.ShareOperation = share;

    // get the properties out...
    var data = share.Data;
    var props = data.Properties;
    this.Title = props.Title;
    this.Description = props.Description;

    // now the data...
    this.SharedText = await data.GetTextAsync();

    // tell the OS that we have the data...
    share.ReportDataRetrieved();
}
```

Calling the other three methods is just an issue of handling the `ReportStarted`, `ReportError`, and `ReportCompleted` calls. Here, I've used `Debug.WriteLine` to render some error information to the system debug view as we did before. Here's the change to `HandleShareCommandAsync`:

```
private async Task HandleShareCommandAsync()
{
    try
    {
        // tell the OS that we've started...
        this.ShareOperation.ReportStarted();

        // placeholder message...
        await this.Host.ShowAlertAsync("Shared.");
    }
```

```
        catch (Exception ex)
        {
            Debug.WriteLine("Sharing failed: " + ex.ToString());
            this.ShareOperation.ReportError("The sharing operation failed.");
        }
        finally
        {
            this.ShareOperation.ReportCompleted();
        }
    }
```

If you run that and share some text, you'll see the result shown in Figure 7-11. The long-running reporting stuff that we just did won't have a discernable effect on the presentation.

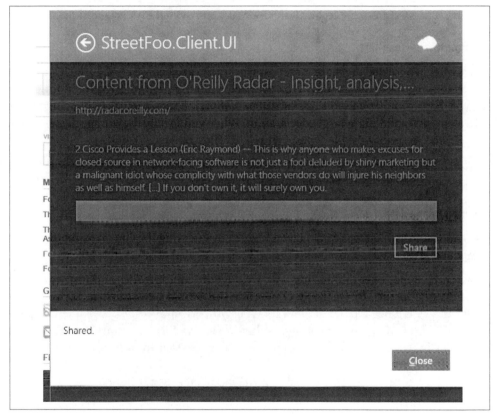

*Figure 7-11. The final share operation*

With that done, let's look at the process of sharing images.

# Sharing Images

As I mentioned at the top of the chapter, the requirement to work with images comes up very often when you're building LOB apps for mobile work, which is why I wanted to cover this topic in this chapter. What we're going to do here is look at capturing images that are shared by the built-in Photos app, and images from other sources.

Perhaps counter intuitively, the built-in Photos app actually shares files—or more specifically, it shares `IStorageItem` instances, all of which happen to be files. Other apps that share images are likely to actually share image data directly. Thus, we need to build our code such that we can handle either eventuality.

Way back when we first built `ISharePageViewModel`, we added a `SharedImage` property of type `BitmapImage`. All we need to do is set that, as well as the `ShowImage` property that we inherited from the legacy implementation provided by Visual Studio.

### Configuring the manifest

Back when we created the share target contract in the project, we configured it such that it was looking for text data only. We now need to configure it to listen for storage files and bitmaps. Double-click the *Package.appxmanifest* file and modify it to include those two elements in the Share Target declaration. When you specify the storage files element, you'll need to specify the file types. Figure 7-12 illustrates.

If you deploy that and try to share an image from the Photos app, StreetFoo will appear in the candidate list. Next we need to read in the data.

### Reading image data

We can test for which type of data we are given by querying the `Contains` method with `StandardDataFormats.StorageFiles` or `StandardDataFormats.Bitmap`.

If we receive files over the sharing link, we'll ignore multiple files and just work with the first one in the set. (In production code this would be confusing, so avoid this shortcut—you'll need to handle multiple files properly and/or display some UI to the user to explain what was happening.) When we have a file, we can use `RandomAccess` `StreamReference` as we've done before, and then use that to initialize a new `Bitmap` `Image`. If we get an image, we'll actually be handed an `IRandomAccessStreamRefer` `ence` interface—and we can use that to initialize a real `Image` instance.

We've already changed the XAML to show an image bound to the `SharedImage` property on the view-model, so all we have to do is modify `SetupShareDataAsync` to initialize the image. Here's the code:

```
public async Task SetupShareDataAsync(ShareOperation share)
{
    // store the share operation - we need to do this to hold a
    // reference or otherwise the sharing subsystem will assume
```

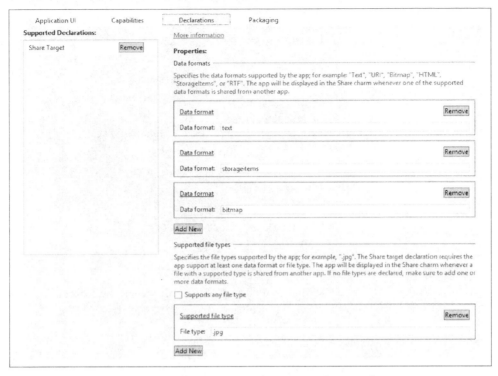

*Figure 7-12. Configuring the additional data formats in the manifest*

```
// that we've finished...
this.ShareOperation = share;

// get the properties out...
var data = share.Data;
var props = data.Properties;
this.Title = props.Title;
this.Description = props.Description;

// now the text...
if(data.Contains(StandardDataFormats.Text))
    this.SharedText = await data.GetTextAsync();

// do we have an image? if so, load it...
if (data.Contains(StandardDataFormats.StorageItems) || data.Contains
(StandardDataFormats.Bitmap))
{
    IRandomAccessStreamReference reference = null;

    // load the first one...
    if (data.Contains(StandardDataFormats.StorageItems))
    {
```

```
                    var  file = (IStorageFile)(await data.GetStorageItemsAsync())
.FirstOrDefault();
                        reference = RandomAccessStreamReference.
                            CreateFromFile(file);
                    }
                    else
                        reference = await data.GetBitmapAsync();

                    // load it into an image...
                    var image = new BitmapImage();
                    using(var stream = await reference.OpenReadAsync())
                        image.SetSource(stream);

                    // set...
                    this.SharedImage = image;
                    this.ShowImage = true;
                }

                // tell the OS that we have the data...
                share.ReportDataRetrieved();
            }
```

Run the code and share an image from the Photos app. You'll see something like
Figure 7-13.

### Testing sharing an image via GetBitmapAsync

To make it easier for you to find a share source that works with bitmap data as opposed
to storage files, in the code download for this chapter I've created a project called ImageShareScratch. You'll find it within the SharingScratch solution.

Run this project and you'll be able to pick an image using the FileOpenPicker. It will
automatically start a share operation (which is against the Windows Store app rules,
incidentally, but it's a good illustration). Share with the StreetFoo client to check that
the image loading works from this side too.

# Quick Links

The one feature of sharing that we haven't looked at is *quick links*. The idea here is that
you set up "shortcuts" for common sharing operations on a per-app basis. For example,
you might configure a quick link to email to quickly address an email to the same person.

I've skipped this topic in this chapter mostly because of space, but also because it's not
a central function that we would need for the StreetFoo client. It's relatively easy to do
—you create a new QuickLink object and pass it into the ReportCompleted method in
ShareOperation. The next time you run that same sort of share operation, the quick
link will appear in the share charm UI.

*Figure 7-13. A photo shared from the Photos app*

# CHAPTER 8

# Searching

Searching is a core Windows Store app UX feature. Because most apps have a search function, Microsoft decided that in Windows Store apps it would be best for search to be implemented in two common ways.

If the user wants to find something in your app, he or she will either swipe in the charms, access the Search feature, type in the keywords, and touch the search button, or use the SearchBox control, which will let the user search from within the application. It's your responsibility to present to the user the results and any UI elements needed to refine the search. (These refinement UI elements are called *filters*.)

What we're going to do in this chapter is add search through the charms bar, and then take a look at the SearchBox. The guidelines for search recommend strongly that you use only one of the two. The hardest part of the implementation is rendering the search results and this is done the same way for both solutions. While we have chosen the charm search, replacing it with the SearchBox won't require a lot of work, as you will see later. Since this is one area that has undergone a lot of change, I would keep my eye on the documentation and the guidelines in case one of the two methods becomes the preferred one. When the user wants to search, we'll present a user interface that will use the MyGridView control that we built previously, together with a custom item template designed to render ReportViewItem instances in *search results mode*. If you remember we built MyGridView in Chapter 4 to support the selection mode required for the app bar. This class extends the regular XAML GridView control to add extra functionality that's helpful when working in an MVVM mode. As part of the work in this chapter, we'll add a command that is raised when an item is selected. This is, of course, a normal aspect of a search function—when you can see the item that you want, you need to select it.

One important element of all this is that the search results page that gets created by Visual Studio doesn't fit into our proper MVVM pattern. We'll reconfigure the one supplied with one that does fit our MVVM pattern.

In the final part of the chapter, we'll run through a couple of additional best-practice features that apply when working with search.

# Implementing Search

The first thing we are going to do is add a `SearchResultsPage`. Whether you choose to use the charm search or the search control, you will need this page to render the search results. When using the charm search, we need to add a search contract, and this is done in the app manifest under declarations.

## Creating the Search Results Page

Right-click on the project within Solution Explorer, open up Add New Item, and add a new search contract called `SearchResultsPage`.

This page, like all the standard pages, has a region at the top containing the caption. It also contains a label showing what we're going to call the *query narrative*—that is, an explanation of what was searched for. (In Figure 8-1, the query narrative reads "Results for 'broken.'") Underneath this will be a list of filters ("all (19), wall (1)," and so on), and underneath that will be the list of items. The filters in our implementation will work by aggregating the last word that appears in the set of found titles. (Given the nature of the test data provided by the server, these all happen to be nouns. However, this approach is a bit ropey for a production implementation.) As well as creating this page, when we add a search contract, Visual Studio will also alter the app manifest to include a reference to the contract.

Figure 8-1 shows what we're ultimately aiming for.

## Creating SearchResultsPageViewModel

The easy part of all this is setting up the `SearchResultPageViewModel` class and `ISearchResultsPageViewModel`.

When we are told to perform a search, we will be told via the `SearchPane` class. We need to create a subscription to search notifications via an event on this class. The most important thing that we are told here is the *query text*—this being the string that the user entered into the search charm. We will make it so that this string will ultimately find its way through to the `Activated` method in our `ViewModel` class.

The search process will work like this:

- From within `SearchResultPageViewModel`, we'll take the query text and use a regular expression to split it into words.
- If we have any words to look for, we'll ask `ReportItem` to query SQLite and return `ReportItem` instances containing those words.

*Figure 8-1. What we're aiming for*

- If we don't have any words (i.e., the user didn't key anything in), we'll ask ReportItem to return everything from the cache. (We'll talk about the rationale for this later.)

- We'll store that master set of items in a property called MasterItems. However, we'll expose the list of items to display through a property called Results. Results will use ObservableCollection<ReportViewItem> because we need to bind to it. MasterItems will use List<ReportViewItem> because we do not want to bind to it.

- We have a master list and a display list because of the filtering. Once the master list has been used, we'll walk the items and build up a list of distinct nouns—the rule being that the last word in the report item's title will be the noun. We'll create a new class called SearchFilter to represent filters. We'll extend this new class from ModelItem because we want to use all of the property notification goodness that this class has. We'll store our filters in a property called Filters, and again because this is bindable we'll use an ObservableCollection<SearchFilter> instance for storage.

- The filter set will be built only when the search text changes, and this can only happen by the user reopening the search charm and keying in new data. When the user clicks a filter, the Results collection will be cleared, and a new collection built by taking each item in the master set and seeing if it passes the filter. Ultimately, in your own production apps, you'll need to decide on the best way to do your searching and filtering. What I'm presenting here is just one way of doing it.

Our view will end up binding two sets of data—the actual results using a `MyGridView`, and the filters using `RadioButton` controls hosted within an `ItemsControl`. In your apps, you may find a list of radio buttons too restrictive. You should feel free to design a (touch-friendly) implementation of your own.

In terms of the view-model members exposed off of the `ISearchResultsPageViewMo del`, we'll need:

- `QueryText`, which will be the actual text that the user enters into the search charm.
- `QueryNarrative`, which will be the message presented at the top of the view. If the user doesn't enter anything, this will be a blank string; otherwise, it will display "Results for <queryText>."
- `Results` and `Filters`, which we've already discussed.
- `HasResults` will be a Boolean value that indicates whether there are any items. This will be used to hide the grid and filter views and to show a message to indicate that there are no items.

All that gives us an implementation of `ISearchResultsPageViewModel` that looks like this:

```
public interface ISearchResultsPageViewModel : IViewModel
{
    string QueryText { get; }
    string QueryNarrative { get; }

    ObservableCollection<ReportViewItem> Results { get; }
    ObservableCollection<SearchFilter> Filters { get; }

      bool HasResults { get; }

    ICommand SelectionCommand { get; }
}
```

The base implementation of `SearchResultsPageViewModel` looks like this:

```
public class SearchResultsPageViewModel : ViewModel,
ISearchResultsPageViewModel
    {
        // the master list and filtered list...
        private List<ReportViewItem> MasterItems { get; set; }
        public ObservableCollection<ReportViewItem> Results { get;
            private set; }

        // filter options...
        public ObservableCollection<SearchFilter> Filters { get;
            private set; }

        // issued when an item is selected...
        public ICommand SelectionCommand { get; private set; }
```

```
          // track whether we've done a search...
          private bool SearchDone { get; set; }

          public SearchResultsPageViewModel(IViewModelHost host)
              : base(host)
          {
              this.MasterItems = new List<ReportViewItem>();
              this.Results = new ObservableCollection<ReportViewItem>();
              this.Filters = new ObservableCollection<SearchFilter>();
          }

          public string QueryText { get { return this.GetValue<string>(); }
              private set { this.SetValue(value); } }
          public string QueryNarrative { get { return this.GetValue<string>(); }
      private set { this.SetValue(value); } }

          public bool HasResults
          {
              get
              {
                  // if we haven't done a search—be optimistic or otherwise
                  // we'll flicker...
                  if (!(this.SearchDone))
                      return true;

                  // ok...
                  return this.Results.Any();
              }
          }
      }
```

A quick note on that `HasResults` option: because of the way the view will launch, `HasResults` will be called before the view-model has finished setting up. If we return `false` initially, the "no results" message will display and then be replaced by the grid. What we want to do is be more optimistic and assume that we do have results before we actually check whether we do or not. If we don't do this (i.e., if we're not optimistic), we'll get an ugly flicker as we go from "no data" to "some data."

At this point we should compile OK, but so that we know it works I propose adding an `Activated` method that will display the query text in a `MessageDialog` instance. This will let us track whether the basics work. (And remember the "basics" in this case is the code created by Visual Studio that will activate our view and pass in the query text.) Here's the implementation of `Activated`:

```
          SearchResultsPageViewModel public override async void Activated
      (object args)
          {
              base.Activated(args);

              // show the query text...
```

```
                await this.Host.ShowAlertAsync((string)args);
        }
```

In order to run the operation, we need to wire up the view in SearchResultsPageView
Model. We've done this a few times, but just for clarity:

```
        public sealed partial class SearchResultsPage : StreetFooPage
        {
            private UIElement _previousContent;
            private ApplicationExecutionState _previousExecutionState;

            private ISearchResultsPageViewModel ViewModel { get; set; }

            public SearchResultsPage()
            {
                this.InitializeComponent();

                            this.InitializeViewModel();
            }

            // code omitted for brevity...
        }
```

To make this work, we need to subscribe to the event on the WinRT-provided Search
View class. We'll dereference the current frame (creating one if necessary), and then pass
the search instruction over to the page. Here's the code:

```
// Modify App.xaml.cs:
            protected override async void OnLaunched(LaunchActivatedEventArgs e)
            {
                // start up our runtime...
                await StreetFooRuntime.Start("Client");

// code omitted for brevity...

                // Ensure the current window is active
                Window.Current.Activate();

                // register for data transfer...
                var manager = DataTransferManager.GetForCurrentView();
                manager.DataRequested += manager_DataRequested;

                // search...
                var search = SearchPane.GetForCurrentView();
                search.PlaceholderText = "Report title";
                search.QuerySubmitted += search_QuerySubmitted;
            }
```

Now you can run the code and try searching from the Reports page. You'll see something
like Figure 8-2 if you type the text **some search terms that I entered** into the search
charm. Part of how Windows 8.1 works is that you need to direct the search to the
StreetFoo app. Make sure StreetFoo.UI.Client is selected in the search charm, otherwise

you'll just be searching your machine for any instances of the string you entered rather than the app.

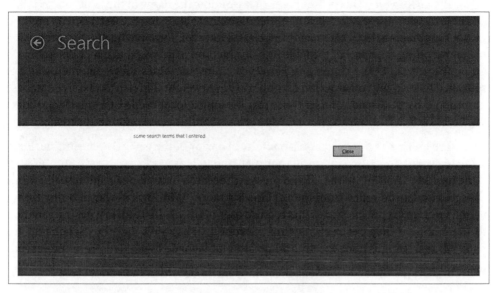

*Figure 8-2. The search terms displayed by SearchResultsPageViewModel*

# Implementing the Search Operation

What we're going to do in the remainder of this chapter is actually make the search operation do something. We know at this point that Windows will pass in search requests. Toward the end of this chapter, we're going to look at refining the basic operation so that it's a bit slicker.

### Searching SQLite

The basic search operation involves issuing a statement to SQLite that issues a `WHERE` clause based on the keywords that we type in. What we're going to do with the keywords is use a simple regex to split up the string and force an `AND` between each one. Thus, if the user enters "broken light," we'll issue:

```
SELECT * FROM ReportItem WHERE TITLE LIKE '%BROKEN%' AND TITLE LIKE '%LIGHT%'
```

Obviously, because it's not the late 1990s and we understand about SQL injection attacks, we'll use a parameterized query. In SQLite, parameters are simply presented as question marks in ordinal order, like so:

```
SELECT * FROM ReportItem WHERE TITLE LIKE ? AND TITLE LIKE ?
```

Since introducing the SQLite functionality in Chapter 3, we haven't done much with it. This is where we go slightly outside of the micro-ORM functionality provided by sqlite-net and build up a SQL string ourselves. (Generally, the idea of an ORM of any type is that you don't build up SQL yourself but instead rely on the library to do the heavy lifting for you.) This presupposes that we know the name of the table. It's certainly possible to ask sqlite-net to tell you the details of the table using the `GetMapping` method in the synchronous `SQLiteConnection` class. However, for expedience, I'm proposing just hardcoding the name of the table into our method. And yes, that query does contain an inefficient `SELECT *` statement. However, sqlite-net issues these statements all the time, just to keep the construction of the library lightweight. This isn't a massive database hammered by thousands of users—it's just keeping a local cache of a small set of data on a relatively well-powered device. My view is that this is a workable approach.

There are two more things to note about the behavior of the basic search routine. First, if no keywords are passed in, it will return all items. This works on the assumption that if the user keys nothing in the UI and presses the search button, he or she actually wants to see all items and refine from there. (This is a more "Windows 8" way of doing things —don't put up cryptic messages that require users to think. Instead, just get information to them so that they can keep moving.) Secondly, it assumes that the cache is up-to-date. All searching is done locally and no attempt is made to get data from the server.

With that, here's the code for `SearchCacheAsync` to be added to `ReportItem`:

```
// Add method to ReportItem...
internal static async Task<IEnumerable<ReportItem>> SearchCacheAsync
(string queryText)
{
    // run a regex to extract out the words...
    var words = new List<string>();
    var regex = new Regex(@"\b\w+\b", RegexOptions.Singleline |
RegexOptions.IgnoreCase);
    foreach(Match match in regex.Matches(queryText))
    {
        var word = match.Value.ToLower();
        if(!(words.Contains(word)))
            words.Add(word);
    }

    // do we have anything to find?
    if(words.Count > 0)
    {
        // build up some sql...
        var sql = new StringBuilder();
        var parameters = new List<object>();
        sql.Append("select * from reportitem where ");
        bool first = true;
        foreach(var word in words)
        {
            if(first)
                first = false;
            else
```

```
                sql.Append(" and ");

            // add...
            sql.Append("title like ?");
            parameters.Add("%" + word + "%");
        }

        // run...
        var conn = StreetFooRuntime.GetUserDatabase();
        return await conn.QueryAsync<ReportItem>(sql.ToString(),
parameters.ToArray());
    }
    else
    {
        // return the lot...
        return await GetAllFromCacheAsync();
    }
}
```

 For those of you who are not familiar with regular expressions, don't worry too much about the regex at the top of this method. All it does is select groups of at least one alphanumeric character delineated by word boundaries.

Now that we can search the SQLite database, let's go back and think about our search routine.

### The search routine proper

As mentioned previously, our full search routine in the view-model has some complexity.

When the user keys in new search terms, we'll go out to SQLite and get back all the ReportItem instances that match using the SearchCacheAsync method that we just built. We'll then build up a list of filters from those search results and present them to the user. By default, the user will have the All filter selected, which means "apply no filter." The master set of items returned from SQLite will be held in the MasterItems collection. The set presented to the user will be held in the Results collection.

If the user selects a filter, we'll take the values in the MasterItems collection, run them through the filter, and update the Results collection. The magic of XAML data binding will result in the view being updated automatically.

The filters will be held as a collection of SearchFilter instances owned by the Sear chResultPageViewModel. The SearchFilter class will have an Active property so that we know which one has been selected. To handle the selection, we'll have to implement a command that gets executed when the user clicks on one of the checkboxes.

We'll look at `SearchFilter` first. This will extend `ModelItem` because we want the data-binding-capable property notifications. When we create a `SearchFilter` we'll need a description, the number of items, the bound keyword, and an indicator as to whether it's active. The All filter will have a description but no keyword, which is why we break those two out.

Juggling the operation of listening for the user touching a filter and having our view-model react is reasonably complex. Each filter will be bound to exactly one checkbox. (They won't look like checkbox controls, but they are.) MVVM tells us that we're supposed to use commands to get actions on the UI "felt" in the view-model. Thus, to the `SearchFilter` class we'll add a command called `SelectionCommand`. When we build `SearchFilter` instances from within `SearchResultsPageViewModel`, we'll set this command to invoke a method that changes the filter.

When it comes to actually matching the keyword, if we don't have a keyword (i.e., we're using the All filter), we'll always return `true`. If not, we'll look for our keyword at the end of the string. (This isn't strictly accurate, as really we need to use a regex to match a word boundary before the keyword string, but this is good enough for our purposes.)

Here's the code:

```
public class SearchFilter : ModelItem
{
    // holds the keyword that we're bound to...
    internal string Keyword { get; private set; }

    // command to raise when we're selected...
    public ICommand SelectionCommand { get; internal set; }

    public SearchFilter(string description, int numItems, string keyword,
bool active = false)
    {
        this.Description = string.Format("{0} ({1})", description, numItems);
        this.Keyword = keyword;
        this.Active = active;
    }

    // holds the description...
    public string Description { get { return this.GetValue<string>(); }
        private set { this.SetValue(value); } }

    // holds a flag to indicate that we were active...
    public bool Active { get { return this.GetValue<bool>(); }
        internal set { this.SetValue(value); } }

    internal bool MatchKeyword(ReportViewItem item)
    {
        // if we have a keyword, match it, otherwise assume it's ok...
        if (!(string.IsNullOrEmpty(this.Keyword)))
            return item.Title.ToLower().EndsWith(this.Keyword);
```

```
        else
            return true;
    }
  }
}
```

Now we'll move on to the SearchResultsPageViewModel implementation.

The first thing we need to change on the view-model is the Activated method, which will be called when the search results page is shown. This will replace the one that thus far shows a message box:

```
// Modify method in SearchResultsPageViewModel...
public override async void Activated(object args)
{
    base.Activated(args);

    // do the search...
    await SearchAsync((string)args);
}
```

Let's look at the SearchAsync method. The first thing this does is set the internal flag so that we know at least one search has happened. (Before, I mentioned that this was to stop the "No results" message from appearing prematurely.) We'll also set the query text, as well as the narrative.

```
// Add method to SearchResultsPageViewModel...
private async Task SearchAsync(string queryText)
{
    // flag...
    this.SearchDone = true;

    // set...
    this.QueryText = queryText;

    // set the narrative...
    if (string.IsNullOrEmpty(queryText))
        this.QueryNarrative = string.Empty;
    else
        this.QueryNarrative = string.Format("Results for '{0}'",
queryText);
```

The next move is to update the MasterItems collection from the results drawn from SQLite.

```
// load...
var reports = await ReportItem.SearchCacheAsync(queryText);
this.MasterItems.Clear();
foreach (var report in reports)
    this.MasterItems.Add(new ReportViewItem(report));
```

Once we have the master items, we need to build the filters. As mentioned, this will pull the last word off of the title of each report and add each to a distinct list of nouns. First, though, we need to add the All filter. Note here how the `SelectionCommand` property is set to a lambda expression that defers to `HandleFilterActivated`. We'll create this handler method in a moment.

```
// do we have anything?
this.Filters.Clear();
if (this.MasterItems.Any())
{
    // all filter...
    var allFilter = new SearchFilter("all", this.MasterItems.Count,
null, false);
    allFilter.SelectionCommand = new DelegateCommand((args) =>
HandleFilterActivated(allFilter));
    this.Filters.Add(allFilter);
```

To build the list of nouns, we use a regex and `Dictionary<string, int>`. This dictionary keeps track of the hit count for each noun.

```
var nouns = new Dictionary<string, int>();
var regex = new Regex(@"\b\w+$", RegexOptions.Singleline |
RegexOptions.IgnoreCase);
foreach (var report in reports)
{
    var match = regex.Match(report.Title);

    // word...
    string noun = match.Value.ToLower();
    if (!(nouns.ContainsKey(noun)))
        nouns[noun] = 0;
    nouns[noun]++;
}
```

Finally, as far as the filters are concerned, we create exactly one filter per discovered noun.

```
// add the filters...
foreach (var noun in nouns.Keys)
{
    var filter = new SearchFilter(noun, nouns[noun], noun);
    filter.SelectionCommand = new DelegateCommand((args) =>
HandleFilterActivated(filter));
    this.Filters.Add(filter);
}
```

And finally, as far as the operation is concerned, we return to the `ReportImageCache Manager` that we built in Chapter 7 and initialize the images.

```
// update...
var manager = new ReportImageCacheManager();
foreach (var report in this.MasterItems)
    await report.InitializeAsync(manager);
```

That completes the branch where we actually got some items back. In either case, whether we did or didn't get items back, we need to apply the selected filter. Here is that call, and then we'll move on to building that method.

```
        // apply the filter...
        this.ApplyFilter();
}
```

To find the active filter, we just walk the list of filters and return the one that's marked as active. Here's the code for the ActiveFilter property:

```
    // Add property to SearchResultsPageViewModel...
    private SearchFilter ActiveFilter
    {
        get
        {
            return this.Filters.Where(v => v.Active).FirstOrDefault();
        }
    }
```

Next, remember how in our SelectionCommand handler on the filter we called the HandleFilterActivated method? The job of this handler is to mark all the filters as inactive, apart from the one we clicked on. Once it's done that, it calls HandleFilterActivated to update the user interface. Here's the code:

```
    // Add method to SearchResultsPageViewModel...
    private void HandleFilterActivated(object args)
    {
        // walk...
        foreach (var filter in this.Filters)
        {
            if (filter == args)
                filter.Active = true;
            else
                filter.Active = false;
        }

        // update...
        this.ApplyFilter();
    }
```

At this point, we can look at the method that ties it all together. ApplyFilter will take the master set of items held in MasterItems, mash it together with a filter, and update the Results property. After it's done all that, it'll ask the ModelItem base implementation to raise a change notification against the HasResults property. Here's the code:

```
        private void ApplyFilter()
        {
            // reset...
            this.Results.Clear();

            // do we have a filter?
```

```
            var filter = this.ActiveFilter;
            if (filter != null)
            {
                // match...
                foreach (var report in this.MasterItems.Where(v =>
    filter.MatchKeyword(v)))
                    this.Results.Add(report);
            }
            else
            {
                // copy in every thing...
                foreach (var report in this.MasterItems)
                    this.Results.Add(report);
            }

            // update...
            this.OnPropertyChanged("HasResults");
        }
```

At this point, the view-model will work, but if you run the app it won't work because we need to make some minor changes to the default XAML provided by Visual Studio. Let's do that now.

## Adjusting the presentation

The work to change the default supplied page layout to one that works with our view-model will make you wonder why we don't just create a layout from scratch! I haven't done this because the grid layouts are fiddly to organize, plus we want to grab the default "snapped" view. (We'll talk more about snapped view in Chapter 12.)

Recall how in Chapter 3 when we first started looking at the GridView we created a specific template for the view. We need to do this again here. Visual Studio will give us a view based on a template called StandardSmallIcon300x70ItemTemplate. What we're going to do first is create ReportItem300x70ItemTemplate. This continues the approach that we've taken thus far (i.e., creating distinct-yet-reusable templates for each type of view-model data).

 The first thing you need to do is go through and remove the template code that Visual Studio has added to *SearchResults Page.xaml.cs*. By default, you get a bunch of default view-model logic and other display logic in here that you don't need. You can comment all of this out, apart from the constructor that we changed earlier to call our InitializeViewModel method. The reason we have to do this is that we want Visual Studio to give us the basic XAML for the page, but the logic that it creates to support a default implementation doesn't fit into how we've architected the app.

The first thing you need to do is remove the template code that Visual Studio has added to *SearchResultsPage.xaml.cs*. By default, you get a bunch of default view-model logic and other display logic in here that you don't need. You can comment all of this out, apart from the constructor that we changed earlier to call our `InitializeViewModel` method. The reason we have to do this is so Visual Studio will give us the basic XAML for the page, but the logic it creates to support a default implementation doesn't fit into how we've architected the app. Within the *StandardStyles.xaml* file, add this XAML. This will display a thumbnail image together with the title and description fields on the bound item:

```
<DataTemplate x:Key="ReportItem300x70ItemTemplate">
  <Grid Width="294" Margin="6">
      <Grid.ColumnDefinitions>
          <ColumnDefinition Width="Auto"/>
          <ColumnDefinition Width="*"/>
      </Grid.ColumnDefinitions>
      <Border Background="{StaticResource
ListViewItemPlaceholderBackgroundThemeBrush}" Margin="0,0,0,10" Width="40"
Height="40">
              <Image Source="{Binding ImageUri}" Stretch="UniformToFill"/>
          </Border>
      <StackPanel Grid.Column="1" Margin="10,-10,0,0">
              <TextBlock Text="{Binding Title}" Style="{StaticResource
BodyTextStyle}" TextWrapping="NoWrap"/>
              <TextBlock Text="{Binding Description}" Style="
{StaticResource BodyTextStyle}" Foreground="{StaticResource
ApplicationSecondaryForegroundThemeBrush}" TextWrapping="NoWrap"/>
          </StackPanel>
      </Grid>
  </DataTemplate>
```

To use this template, locate the `GridView` declaration within `SearchResultsPage` and change its template. Remove any existing inline template references as well. Here's the change:

```
<GridView
    x:Name="resultsGridView"
    AutomationProperties.AutomationId="ResultsGridView"
    AutomationProperties.Name="Search Results"
    TabIndex="1"
    Grid.Row="1"
    Margin="0,2,0,0"
    Padding="110,0,110,46"
    SelectionMode="None"
    IsItemClickEnabled="True"
    ItemsSource="{Binding Source={StaticResource
resultsViewSource}}"
        ItemTemplate="{StaticResource ReportItem300x70ItemTemplate}">

        <GridView.ItemContainerStyle>
            <Style TargetType="Control">
```

```
                    <Setter Property="Height" Value="70"/>
                    <Setter Property="Margin" Value="0,0,38,8"/>
                </Style>
            </GridView.ItemContainerStyle>
        </GridView>
```

The good news is that at this point we can run the project and perform a search. Before we do that though, we need to change the header. As we've seen, all of the pages provided by Visual Studio have My Application as the header. Change this, and change the queryText control's binding to QueryNarrative. Here's the revised XAML:

```
        <Button x:Name="backButton" Grid.Column="0" Click="GoBack" Style=
    "{StaticResource BackButtonStyle}"/>
            <TextBlock x:Name="pageTitle" Grid.Column="1" Text="Search" Style=
    "{StaticResource PageHeaderTextStyle}"  />
            <TextBlock x:Name="queryText" Grid.Column="3" Text="{Binding
    QueryNarrative}" Style="{StaticResource PageSubheaderTextStyle}"/>
```

Run the code now, access the search function, and type some keywords. You'll see something like Figure 8-3.

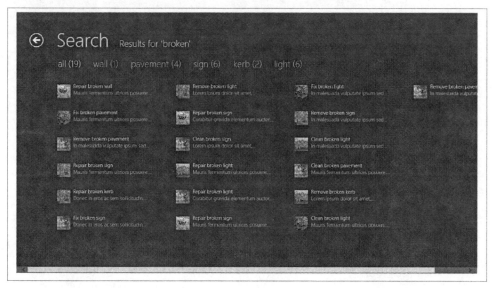

*Figure 8-3. Search results*

Now we know that everything hangs together and that the search function works. Next we need to get the filters working and remove the codebehind implementation provided by the Visual Studio template.

To do this, our main task is to wire up the Command property of the checkbox control to hook into our SelectionCommand exposed by the SearchFilter class, and remove the supplied event binding to `Filter_Checked`. (This `Filter_Checked` method was provided by Visual Studio so that we could do a codebehind handler to change the active filter.) We also have to change the `IsChecked` binding from a two-way to a one-way binding. (The two-way binding was provided by Visual Studio before we did our own implementation of this feature.) You'll find the definition of the checkbox within an `ItemsControl` instance called `filtersItemsControl`. Here's the revised XAML:

```
<ItemsControl.ItemTemplate>
    <DataTemplate>
        <RadioButton
            Content="{Binding Description}"
            GroupName="Filters"
            IsChecked="{Binding Active}"
            Command="{Binding SelectionCommand}"
            Style="{StaticResource TextRadioButtonStyle}"/>
    </DataTemplate>
</ItemsControl.ItemTemplate>
```

Now if you run the app, you'll find that the filter selection works and the view will be updated. To test this properly, enter an adjective rather than a noun (e.g., *broken*). Also, test that the SQLite selection works by entering multiple words in different order (e.g., "pavement broken" should yield results for "broken pavement." Figure 8-4 illustrates filter selection.

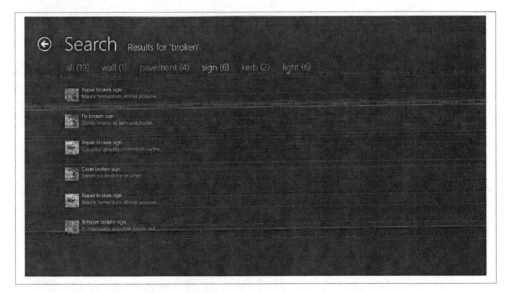

*Figure 8-4. Filter selection in action*

To round off this basic section, and before we start looking at refinements to the search operation, we'll add the functionality to react when the user actually selects an item. We don't do anything particularly sophisticated here—if we had a singleton view that displayed the details for a single report, we could navigate to that. (We'll build this in Chapter 11.) For now, we'll just put up a message box.

## Handling item clicks on the grid

Reacting to a selection borrows from the work we did in Chapter 4. If you recall, we created a new control called MyGridView that extended GridView. This established a command called SelectionCommand. (For reference, the command that we added to SearchFilter was also called SelectionCommand. I chose this name specifically to match the one in MyGridView.)

Selections on GridView controls are supposed to be reserved for situations where you select something, and then do something (for example, selecting a command from the app bar). Where you want to react to a click, you need a different command. On the stock GridView control, you get an IsItemClickEnabled property that "arms" an event called ItemClick. To reprise the work we did in Chapter 4, we need to convert this event into a command so that it can be used with the MVVM pattern. We'll do this now.

The first thing we need to do is modify MyGridView so that it supports a new command called ItemClickedCommand. Like the SelectionCommand from before, we should do this using a dependency property. (Recall that a dependency property is a special property that's held in a "bucket" of values and can be updated by styles and other runtime operations.) Here's the change to MyGridView to incorporate the new property (I've removed quite a lot of code from MyGridView for brevity):

```
        public class MyGridView : GridView
    {
        public static readonly DependencyProperty SelectionCommandProperty =
            DependencyProperty.Register("SelectionCommand", typeof(ICommand),
typeof(MyGridView), new PropertyMetadata(null));
        public static readonly DependencyProperty ItemClickedCommandProperty =
            DependencyProperty.Register("ItemClickedCommand", typeof(ICommand),
typeof(MyGridView), new PropertyMetadata(null));
        public static readonly DependencyProperty
OpenAppBarsOnMultipleSelectionProperty =
            DependencyProperty.Register("OpenAppBarsOnMultipleSelection",
typeof(bool), typeof(MyGridView), new PropertyMetadata(true));
        public static readonly DependencyProperty
            OpenAppBarsOnRightClickProperty =
            DependencyProperty.Register("OpenAppBarsOnRightClick",
            typeof(bool), typeof(MyGridView), new PropertyMetadata(true));

        public MyGridView()
        {
            // wire up the event to command mapping...
            this.SelectionChanged += MyGridView_SelectionChanged;
            this.ItemClick += MyGridView_ItemClick;
        }
```

```
        // code omitted...

        void MyGridView_ItemClick(object sender, ItemClickEventArgs e)
        {
            if (this.ItemClickedCommand == null)
                return;

            // ok...
            var clicked = e.ClickedItem;
            if (this.ItemClickedCommand.CanExecute(clicked))
                this.ItemClickedCommand.Execute(clicked);
        }
    }
```

With that done, all we have to do now is change the XAML. This is a matter of changing the type of the grid to local:MyGridView and adding the command binding. Here are the changes:

```
<local:MyGridView
    x:Name="resultsGridView"
    AutomationProperties.AutomationId="ResultsGridView"
    AutomationProperties.Name="Search Results"
    TabIndex="1"
    Grid.Row="1"
    Margin="0,2,0,0"
    Padding="110,0,110,46"
    SelectionMode="None"
    IsItemClickEnabled="True"
    ItemClickedCommand="{Binding SelectionCommand}"
    ItemsSource="{Binding Source={StaticResource
resultsViewSource}}"
    ItemTemplate="{StaticResource ReportItem300x70ItemTemplate}">

    <GridView.ItemContainerStyle>
        <Style TargetType="Control">
            <Setter Property="Height" Value="70"/>
            <Setter Property="Margin" Value="0,0,38,8"/>
        </Style>
    </GridView.ItemContainerStyle>
</local:MyGridView>
```

The final step, then, is to rig up a command handler in the view-model. Modify the constructor of SearchResultsPageViewModel to show a message, and you're done:

```
// Modify constructor of SearchResultsPageViewModel...
public SearchResultsPageViewModel(IViewModelHost host)
    : base(host)
{
    this.MasterItems = new List<ReportViewItem>();
    this.Results = new ObservableCollection<ReportViewItem>();
    this.Filters = new ObservableCollection<SearchFilter>();
```

```
        // command...
        this.SelectionCommand = new DelegateCommand(async (args) =>
        {
            await this.Host.ShowAlertAsync("Selected: " +
((ReportViewItem)args).Title);
        });
    }
```

Run the code and you should be able to select items. Figure 8-5 illustrates.

*Figure 8-5. Handling a selection on the search results page*

And that's it! The basic search operation is done. We've looked at a lot here. We've implemented the actual search routine to get information from the local database. We then looked at building on some of the UI work that we'd done in previous chapters to make it more flexible and deal with search data.

Now all we need to do is look at the extra features that Windows gives us that can improve the search experience.

# Refining Search

There are four refinements that we need to make to our search function to bring it in line with the Windows Store app UX guidelines. These are:

*Placeholder text*
    This displays a message in the search chart to indicate what the user is supposed to be able to type in.

*Query and result suggestions*
    These are intended to make it easier to enter queries and find results.

*Hit highlighting*
    This is where items in the search results are displayed such that you can see where the queried text appears in each item.

*Remembering where we were*
    This is where when we reenter the search function, we keep context with where we last were.

## Placeholder Text

Placeholder text is the easiest refinement to make. All we have to do is get hold of a `SearchPane` instance for our view and then set the `PlaceholderText` property. We can do this within the `OnLaunched` method of our App class. Here's the code. (I've omitted a lot of this method for brevity. I've also added a stub implementation for returning search suggestions. We'll need this in a moment.)

```
protected override async void OnLaunched(LaunchActivatedEventArgs args)
{
    // Do not repeat app initialization when already running, just
    // ensure that the window is active
    if (args.PreviousExecutionState == ApplicationExecutionState.Running)
    {
        Window.Current.Activate();
        return;
    }

      // code omitted...

    // search...
    var search = SearchPane.GetForCurrentView();
    search.PlaceholderText = "Report title";
    search.SuggestionsRequested += search_SuggestionsRequested;
}

    void search_SuggestionsRequested(SearchPane sender,
SearchPaneSuggestionsRequestedEventArgs args)
    {
        // TBD...
    }
```

Run the app now, and you'll see the placeholder text in the query window. This is helpful in that it avoids doubt as to what the user can type in. For example, in a LOB app this could be something like "Customer name or code." Figure 8-6 illustrates the effect in StreetFoo.

*Figure 8-6. Placeholder text in the search charm*

You'll notice that you get some other behavior here too. Requesting the `SearchPane` switches on the suggestion behavior—you'll see suggestions appear underneath the text box. We'll look at implementing this properly now.

## Suggestions

There are two kinds of suggestions: query suggestions and query recommendations. Query suggestions are the classic autocomplete approach, where you start typing and the app will present guesstimates of what you're ultimately trying to enter. With a real keyboard, this is a convenience, but with an on-screen keyboard this is an absolute requirement. Query recommendations—well, "query recommendation" *singular* really —is where you can identify a single hit in the results ahead of time and want to present that in the search pane.

Within the search pane, according to Microsoft's UX guidelines, you are allowed five "lines" to present your findings. You can present five query suggestions, or you could present three query suggestions, one separator, and one recommendation. Although in this example we're going to go back to our SQLite database to find the suggestions, in practical apps you can go out to disk, or a network—or anywhere, really—to get the information that you need. Figure 8-7 illustrates.

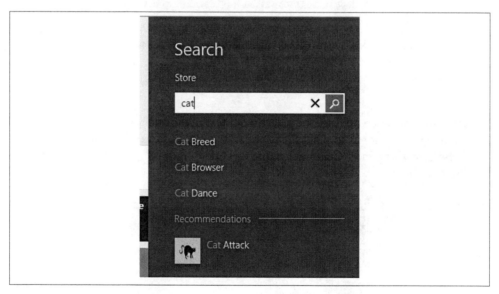

*Figure 8-7. Three suggestions, one separator, and a recommendation shown when searching the Store app*

### Finding suggestions

The first thing we'll look at is how to do the suggestions.

You're going to have to feel your way through for your own apps. While querying the database to get the suggestions is easy enough, actually tuning it to get the *right* suggestions is trickier. There's a reason why the suggestions on Google feel like magic—the developers have put massive amounts of engineering time and thought into it.

In our app, all we're going to do is take the query text and then find all of the report items in the cache that start with that value. We'll then return a distinct list of titles that are "stemmed" from the query text. We'll return the results as a `Dictionary<string, IEnumerable<ReportItem>>`. Although it seems logical to return just the strings, when we get to doing the recommendations we'll need to be able to dereference a suggestion string that surfaces a single item. (This will become clearer in the next section when we actually do this.)

Because we have a database, it makes sense to get it to do the heavy lifting for us in terms of returning the items. We'll use the `QueryAsync` method to do this. This method is a little blunt in that it requires us to provide SQL through, and as I mentioned before, when using an ORM it's better to get it to do the construction of the SQL. However, the only other method in sqlite-net that could do this (`Table`) won't build a `CONTAINS` query properly as of the time of writing.

Here's the method to return the search suggestions:

```
// Add method to ReportItem...
public static async Task<Dictionary<string, List<ReportItem>>>
GetSearchSuggestionsAsync(string queryText)
{
    // get everything and sort by the title...
    var conn = StreetFooRuntime.GetUserDatabase();
    var reports = await conn.QueryAsync<ReportItem>("select * from
ReportItem where title like ? order by title",
        new object[] { queryText + "%" });

    // walk and build a distinct list of matches...
    var results = new Dictionary<string, List<ReportItem>>(StringComparer
.CurrentCultureIgnoreCase);
    foreach (var report in reports)
    {
        // if we don't have a result with that title...
        if (!(results.ContainsKey(report.Title)))
            results[report.Title] = new List<ReportItem>();

        // add...
        results[report.Title].Add(report);
    }

    // return...
    return results;
}
```

Back when we looked at sharing in Chapter 7, you'll recall that we needed to use a *deferral* to tell Windows that it was going to take us a while to come up with the results. This needs to happen whenever you use async/await, so we'll need to use that same approach here. Once we have the deferral, we get our suggestions and pass them back through the object supplied as the event argument.

To answer the question of *where* we put this code, I propose that we create a new class called SearchInteractionHelper that we add to the UI-agnostic StreetFoo.Client project. The alternative is that we whack all of this code in the App class in the Windows Store app–specific project. This codebehind approach would make our MVVM abstraction harder to manage, thus my proposal of putting it in a new class.

Within the App class, I'm proposing that we do enough to set up the deferral and then pass it over to SearchInteractionHelper. My rationale for doing the deferral here is that the deferral is actually a Windows Store app–specific thing and hence more rightly lives in that project. Here's the code (you'll also need to change this method to be async):

```
async void search_SuggestionsRequested(SearchPane sender,
SearchPaneSuggestionsRequestedEventArgs args)
    {
        var deferral = args.Request.GetDeferral();
        try
        {
            await SearchInteractionHelper.PopulateSuggestionsAsync
(args.QueryText, args.Request.SearchSuggestionCollection);
        }
        finally
        {
            deferral.Complete();
        }
    }
```

Now we can turn our attention to the PopulateSuggestionsAsync method. Here's the code:

```
// Add method to SearchInteractionHelper...
public static async Task PopulateSuggestionsAsync(string queryText,
SearchSuggestionCollection results)
    {
        // if we don't have at least three characters to work with,
        // do nothing...
        if(queryText.Length < 3)
            return;

        // how many?
        int maxSuggestions = 5;

        // get the list...
        var suggestions = await ReportItem.GetSearchSuggestionsAsync
(queryText);
```

```
// sort the suggestions...
var titles = new List<string>();
foreach (var title in suggestions.Keys)
    titles.Add(title);
titles.Sort();

// add the suggestions...
foreach (var title in titles)
{
    results.AppendQuerySuggestion(title);

    // enough?
    if (results.Size == maxSuggestions)
        break;
}
}
```

Run the code now, and when you type into the search box you'll see some results. Figure 8-8 illustrates.

*Figure 8-8. Search suggestions appearing in search charm*

### Finding recommendations

The idea of recommendations is that if it's at all possible, if the user has entered enough of a search term to key into a single item, we should present that as a recommendation directly in the search pane. When the user clicks this recommendation, we need to take him or her directly to the item, circumventing the search page entirely. In a LOB app, you could rig this (for example) such that if the user keyed in a customer ID code you could present a link to the customer directly in the pane.

We've got most of the pieces that we need for this already. All we have to do is dig through our suggestion results and find the first one that only has one item. We'll then present that as the recommendation. If we display a recommendation, we're not allowed to display five search suggestions. We have to display three suggestions, one separator, and one recommendation (the idea being that we display only five "rows" in the UI).

The wrinkle to this is that recommendations have to have an image. Thus, when we find a recommendation we'll need to wrap it up in a `ReportViewItem` and pass it over to the `ReportImageCacheManager` class to get an image. (We first did this in Chapter 7.) Here's the modified version of `PopulateSuggestionsAsync`:

```
public static async Task PopulateSuggestionsAsync(string queryText,
SearchSuggestionCollection results)
{
    // if we don't have at least three characters to work with, do nothing...
    if(queryText.Length < 3)
        return;

    // how many?
    int maxSuggestions = 5;

    // get the list...
    var suggestions = await ReportItem.GetSearchSuggestionsAsync
(queryText);

    // sort the suggestions...
    var titles = new List<string>();
    foreach (var title in suggestions.Keys)
        titles.Add(title);
    titles.Sort();

    // do we have one that we can use as a recommendation?
    ReportItem recommendation = null;
    foreach (var title in titles)
    {
        if (suggestions[title].Count == 1)
        {
            recommendation = suggestions[title][0];
            break;
        }
    }

    // if we have a recommendation only show three suggestions...
    if (recommendation != null)
        maxSuggestions -= 2;

    // add the suggestions...
    foreach (var title in titles)
    {
        results.AppendQuerySuggestion(title);
```

```
            // enough?
            if (results.Size == maxSuggestions)
                break;
        }

        // add the recommendation...
        if (recommendation != null)
        {
            // we need an image...
            var viewItem = new ReportViewItem(recommendation);
            var imageUri = await new ReportImageCacheManager().
GetLocalImageUriAsync(viewItem);

            // add the suggestion...
            results.AppendSearchSeparator("Recommendation");
            results.AppendResultSuggestion(recommendation.Title,
recommendation.Description, recommendation.Id.ToString(),
                RandomAccessStreamReference.CreateFromUri(
                    new Uri(imageUri)), recommendation.Title);
        }
    }
}
```

Run the code, and you'll be able to surface a recommendation (as shown in Figure 8-9).

*Figure 8-9. Showing a recommendation in the search charm*

The only thing that's missing is that if you click on the recommendation, nothing happens. To fix this, we need to respond to the ResultSuggestionChosen event.

Much like on the search results proper, if we had a singleton page with the item details that we could navigate the user to, we'd do that here. However, for now, just to prove it works, we'll display a message box. Add a binding for the `ResultSuggestionChosen` event in the `OnLaunched` method of `App` and configure it to call this handler:

```
// Add method to App...
async void search_ResultSuggestionChosen(SearchPane sender,
    SearchPaneResultSuggestionChosenEventArgs args)
{
    var dialog = new MessageDialog("Chosen: " + args.Tag);
    await dialog.ShowAsync();
}
```

Run the search again, and you'll be able to click the recommendation. A message box will appear showing the ID of the report.

## Remembering Where We Were

The last thing we need to clean up relates to the situation where the user "reenters" the search function.

You can try this now. Access the StreetFoo search feature, search for something, and select a filter. From the charm, select another app (it doesn't matter which one). Then, reselect the StreetFoo app from the charm. The search will rerun, but the filter will be forgotten.

With the basic filters as per our implementation, this isn't much of a killer problem. However, in your own apps, which may have more complex filtering, this could be very frustrating. To that end, we'll build out this capability now.

There is a way to do this where we watch for suspension and resumption of the app and manage dumping our state to and from disk. However, given that we have a local SQLite database and a `SettingItem` class that lets us store persistent settings, we might as well (and it's easier to) use that. How this will work is that when we select a filter, we'll save the keyword of that filter into the settings. When we run a query, we'll look to see if the query text has changed. If it hasn't, we'll find the last used filter and select it, provided that it's still available. If the text has changed, we'll keep the All filter selected. We'll always revert to All when the text changes because it's confusing to have filter selections that survive the "mental switching" the user does when coming back to the search function. When the user comes back to search for something else, he or she is expecting a "blank sheet of paper" as opposed to something that's affected by choices made minutes, hours, or days ago.

To track those items, we'll need two constants to provide keys into the settings. Add these contacts to `SearchResultsPageViewModel`. (I've omitted code from this class for brevity.)

```
// Add constants to SearchResultsPageViewModel...
    public class SearchResultsPageViewModel : ViewModel,
ISearchResultsPageViewModel
    {
        // code omitted...

        // tracks the last used values...
        private const string LastQueryKey = "LastQuery";
        private const string LastFilterKey = "LastFilter";
```

As you know, the settings-in-SQLite functionality is all asynchronous, meaning that we need to modify our `HandleFilterActivated` method such that it becomes `async` and returns a `Task` instance. We'll also rename it so that we know it's supposed to be async. Here's the changed method:

```
// Modify method in SearchResultsPageViewModel...
    private async Task HandleFilterActivatedAsync(object args)
    {
        // walk...
        SearchFilter selected = null;
        foreach (var filter in this.Filters)
        {
            if (filter == args)
            {
                filter.Active = true;
                selected = filter;
            }
            else
                filter.Active = false;
        }

        // update...
        this.ApplyFilter();

        // save...
        if (selected != null)
            await SettingItem.SetValueAsync(LastFilterKey,
                selected.Keyword);
        else
            await SettingItem.SetValueAsync(LastFilterKey, null);
    }
```

When it's time to select a filter programmatically, we'll use the `ActivateFilter` method. This takes a keyword. Because there's a chance that a filter we supply isn't found, we'll rig the method to call back into itself with `null` in order to select the All filter. Here's the code:

```
// Add method to SearchResultsPageViewModel...
    private void ActivateFilter(string keyword)
    {
        // walk and set...
        bool found = false;
```

```
        foreach (var filter in this.Filters)
        {
            if (filter.Keyword == keyword)
            {
                filter.Active = true;
                found = true;
            }
            else
                filter.Active = false;
        }

        // did we do it? if not, activate the default one...
        if (keyword != null && !(found))
            this.ActivateFilter(null);
    }
```

Finally, we can then go back and look at the SearchAsync method. To recap, this needs to check to see if the query text has changed, and if it hasn't, reselect the filter that we used last time if it's still there. I've removed chunks of code from SearchAsync for brevity.

```
    private async Task SearchAsync(string queryText)
    {
        // flag...
        this.SearchDone = true;

        // set...
        this.QueryText = queryText;

          // code omitted...

        // do we have anything?
        this.Filters.Clear();
        if (this.MasterItems.Any())
        {
                // code omitted...
          }

        // do we need to select the filter?
        var lastQuery = await SettingItem.GetValueAsync(LastQueryKey);
        if (lastQuery == queryText)
        {
            // select the filter...
            var lastFilterName = await SettingItem.GetValueAsync
(LastFilterKey);
            if (!(string.IsNullOrEmpty(lastFilterName)))
                ActivateFilter(lastFilterName);
        }
        else
        {
            // update...
            await SettingItem.SetValueAsync(LastQueryKey, queryText);
        }
```

```
        // apply the filter...
        this.ApplyFilter();
    }
```

Run the app now, and you'll be able to flip in and out of the search results and have the filter selection preserved. Again, in this example our filters are very basic. In more complex arrangements—particularly with drop-down lists, which are fussy to use with touch—this approach becomes much more important.

Now that we have that, we can create our own converter:

```
public sealed class SearchArgsConverter:IValueConverter
    {
        public object Convert(object value, Type targetType, object parameter,
string language)
        {
            var args = (SearchBoxSuggestionsRequestedEventArgs)value;
            var displayHistory = (bool) parameter;
            if (args == null) return value;
            ISuggestionQuery item = new SuggestionQuery(args.Request,
args.QueryText)
            {
                DisplayHistory = displayHistory
            };
            return item;
        }

        public object ConvertBack(object value, Type targetType,
object parameter, string language)
        {
            return value;
        }
    }
```

In theory, we could just create the command in the view-model, but to avoid passing mysterious "object" parameters into our commands, we will create a generic delegate command so we can have a strongly typed command and know what sort of item we can expect:

```
public class DelegateCommand<T> : ICommand
{
    private readonly Predicate<object> _canExecute;
    private Action<T> _handler { get; set; }
    public event EventHandler CanExecuteChanged;

    public DelegateCommand(Action<T> handler, Predicate<object> canExecute)
    {
        this._handler = handler;
        _canExecute = canExecute;
    }
```

```
public void RaiseCanExecuteChanged()
{
    if (CanExecuteChanged != null)
        CanExecuteChanged(this, EventArgs.Empty);
}

public bool CanExecute(object parameter)
{
    return _canExecute == null || _canExecute(parameter);
}

public void Execute(object parameter)
{
    _handler((T)parameter);
}
}
```

And now we can create our command in the view-model and append the suggestions.
This code is just to give you an idea; you would want to abstract this further like we have
done in the rest of the application (see Figures 8-10 and 8-11):

```
public DelegateCommand<ISuggestionQuery> SuggestionRequest { get; set; }
public ViewModel()
{
    SuggestionRequest = new DelegateCommand<ISuggestionQuery>
(SuggestionRequestFor, o => true);
}

private void SuggestionRequestFor(ISuggestionQuery query)
{
    IEnumerable<string> filteredQuery = _data
        .Where(suggestion => suggestion.StartsWith(query.QueryText,
            StringComparison.CurrentCultureIgnoreCase));
    query.Request.SearchSuggestionCollection.AppendQuerySuggestions
(filteredQuery);
}

private readonly string[] _data = { "Banana", "Apple", "Meat", "Ham" };
```

Figure 8-10. All of the possible search suggestions

Figure 8-11. The typeahead search suggestions

## Using the SearchBox

The SearchBox was added in Windows 8.1 as it was a feature requested by many developers. The SearchBox allows the user to search from within the application and can be constrained to just one or several pages. The control itself isn't MVVM-friendly as is, as it relies heavily on events that can't be abstracted away. We need to access the event arguments to pass in, for example, search suggestions to the SearchSuggestionCollec tion, which is a property on the SearchSuggestionRequest object. Let's take a look at an MVVM implementation.

The first thing you would do is add the control to the page where you want to use it, or to a user control if you want to use the same control in several places:

```
<SearchBox SearchHistoryEnabled="False" x:Name="SearchBox" Width="500"
Height="50">
    </SearchBox>
```

The control has several events that give us access to the submitted query text (which can also be accessed through the QueryText property on the control) events to append suggestions and so on. The obvious problem for our MVVM purity is the reliance on events. We want to use commands. You can wire events to commands by using dependency properties or by creating custom behaviors, called attached behaviors.

Behaviors were introduced with Blend 3—XAML (and now also HTML and CSS in Windows Store apps) software that helps you with design, design time data, animations and storyboards, and behaviors.

Blend comes with Visual Studio as of Visual Studio 2012. Behaviors let you extend controls by adding behaviors to them. They let you encapsulate interaction in a reusable way, which then can be connected from the UI component to the code. In this case, we want to call a command when a certain event is triggered and access the event argument. To use behaviors you need to add a reference to the Blend SDK (see Figure 8-12).

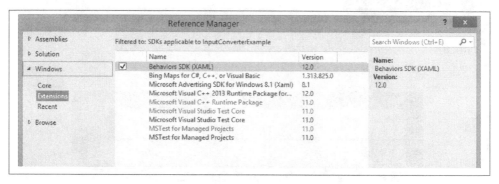

*Figure 8-12. Adding the behaviors SDK*

Once you've done that, you can go ahead with some behaviors that are already defined in the SDK. In this example, we'll look at wiring events to commands and accessing the event arguments. To show results, you use the `OnSearchSubmitted` event, bind it to a command, and from that command, you proceed as with the search charm. You can simply pass in the `QueryText` as a `CommandParameter` if you don't need to access the event arguments, and skip the converter. To make sure you don't get stuck, we'll cover how you access the event arguments, which you need to do when working with the collection of suggestions, for example:

```
<SearchBox SearchHistoryEnabled="False" x:Name="SearchBox" Width="500"
Height="50">
        <SearchBox.Resources>
            <local:SearchArgsConverter x:Name="ArgsConverter"/>
        </SearchBox.Resources>
        <interactivity:Interaction.Behaviors>
            <core:EventTriggerBehavior EventName="SuggestionsRequested">
                <core:InvokeCommandAction
                    Command="{Binding SuggestionRequest}"
                    InputConverter="{StaticResource ArgsConverter}"
                    InputConverterLanguage="en-US"
                    InputConverterParameter="{Binding ElementName=SearchBox,
Path=SearchHistoryEnabled}"/>
            </core:EventTriggerBehavior>
```

```
        </interactivity:Interaction.Behaviors>
    </SearchBox>
```

As you can see, we're listening for the `SuggestionRequested` event, and invoking a command when that event is triggered. In the following code, you'll see some input attributes. These are new to Windows Store apps, and are WinRT only. They let us access the event arguments through a converter and pass in language and a parameter as well.

*InputConverter*

> This gets or sets the converter used for the command. The command has to be of type `ICommand`, and the converter of the type `IValueConverter`.

*InputConverterLanguage*

> This gets or sets the language that is passed into the converter as a string.

*InputConverterParameter*

> This gets or sets the parameter passed into the converter. Notice that it's passed to the converter and not the command. Use this when you need to convert the parameter. Otherwise, use `CommandParameter`.

Because we don't want to pass in the event arguments as is to the `view-model` (this creates a coupling), we will create and interface a class so we can pass our own custom object instead. Here is an example of the interface and the class:

```
        public interface ISuggestionQuery
        {
            SearchSuggestionsRequest Request { get; }
            string QueryText { get; }
            bool DisplayHistory { get; set; }
        }
    public class SuggestionQuery : ISuggestionQuery
        {
            public SuggestionQuery(SearchSuggestionsRequest request, string
queryText)
            {
                Request = request;
                QueryText = queryText;
            }

            public SearchSuggestionsRequest Request { get; private set; }
            public string QueryText { get; private set; }
            public bool DisplayHistory { get; set; }
        }
```

## Other Best-Practice Notes

Microsoft publishes a number of recommendations for best practice within search, specifically around user experience. We've looked at most of them in this section. There are a couple of others.

One recommendation that comes up is *hit highlighting*. The idea here is that on the results page the part of the rendered result that matches the query text is highlighted. (For example, consider a search for *broken*—if a result says, "Fix broken light," the word *broken* is highlighted.) I did want to include this feature, but it's very difficult to implement in XAML. In fact, despite it being a recommendation from Microsoft, none of the built-in apps actually implement this feature! As a result, I've left it out. Search highlighting is helpful, however, so hopefully an easier way to implement it will come to the fore.

Other recommendations relate to appropriateness of use. One of them is to make sure that search is implemented via the charm, as opposed to via an option on the app bar. (Personally, I can see that in LOB apps, where data is more complex, actually being able to initiate an "advanced search" from the app bar is arguably helpful.) Another is not to confuse the operation of a global "find me stuff" option from the charm with "find me stuff within this thing I'm already looking at." The example Microsoft calls out in its best-practice documentation relates to a "find on page" function. That sort of thing should not be done using the charm.

# CHAPTER 9

# Settings

The last charm-based feature that we're going to look at is the settings charm, which allows you to define a set of commands that are presented along with one or two standard options within each app. Although originally defined within the Windows 8 experience vision as a common way to provide access for settings, a de facto standard has emerged whereby apps use it to provide access to their Help options. There is also a store requirement to provide easy access to a "privacy policy," and this should be done through the settings charm.

In this chapter, we're going to look at the standard options first and then add an option to jump out to the web browser to display the privacy policy. We'll build a *flyout* that can be used to host normal settings. (A flyout is a panel that winds in from the right side of the screen, similar to a pop up.) Within this flyout, we'll look at taking some marked-up text and rendering it in a "prettified" fashion. This will show us how we can render help content within the app if we aren't using HTML, and also show how we can render more richly formatted text within the app, where it's often impractical to host IE and render HTML.

## Adding Options

Let's now look at the basics of how to add options. As you may have guessed, this is an issue of asking WinRT to return a handler, whereupon we bind to events and feed back the information. In this case, we use WinRT's `SettingsPane` class and respond to the `CommandsRequested` event. When we do this, we need to create instances of `Settings Command` objects, one for each item that we want to appear in the settings view before the standard options.

## Standard Options

Each Windows Store app can display one or two default options in the settings charm. The one that you'll always get is the Permissions option. This will show the name of the app, provide an option for turning off push notifications (if applicable), and list any permissions that the app has. Figure 9-1 shows the permissions view for StreetFoo thus far.

*Figure 9-1. The standard permissions view*

If your app is installed via the store, you will also get a "Rate and review" option. You can see an example of this by looking in the settings for any built-in or downloaded app that you have.

## Adding Custom Options

The bare minimum that we can do to satisfy the requirement to provide a privacy statement within the app is to add an option that navigates to a web page.

 The Store requirement is such that the user should be able to access the statement from the app, but the whole text doesn't necessarily have to be in the app. I talk more about store requirements in Chapter 15.

Much like we did in the last chapter, we'll create a new class called `SettingsInteractionHelper` in the UI-agnostic project and wire it up to handlers in the Windows Store app–specific project.

Navigating to a URL is just a matter of using the `Windows.System.Launcher` class. This will dereference the default handler for a given protocol—in this case, `http:`, but it could equally be `mailto:` in order to launch the default email client—and then navigate to it. That same `Launcher` class can also open files using the `LaunchFileAsync` option.

The next code details a `SettingsInteractionHelper`, rigged with a method to display a "privacy statement." As the comment says, that's not a real privacy statement. I've also included an option to display some web-based help. Similarly, this is not a real help site.

```
public static class SettingsInteractionHelper
{
    public static async Task ShowPrivacyStatementAsync()
    {
        // this will just take the user off to a web page...
        // this isn't a real privacy statement, btw...
        await Launcher.LaunchUriAsync(new Uri
            ("http://programmingwindowsstoreapps.com/"));
    }

    internal static async Task ShowWebHelpAsync()
    {
        // again, not a real website...
        await Launcher.LaunchUriAsync(new Uri
            ("http://programmingwindowsstoreapps.com/"));
    }
}
```

As is by now a traditional approach, we'll hook up the settings charm handler from the `OnLaunched` method in App. The code is as follows (I've removed much of the code from the `OnLaunched` method for brevity):

```
// Modify method in App, add new handler method...
protected override async void OnLaunched(LaunchActivatedEventArgs args)
{
    // code omitted...

    // settings...
    var settings = SettingsPane.GetForCurrentView();
    settings.CommandsRequested += settings_CommandsRequested;
}

void settings_CommandsRequested(SettingsPane sender,
SettingsPaneCommandsRequestedEventArgs args)
{
    args.Request.ApplicationCommands.Add(new SettingsCommand
("PrivacyStatement", "Privacy Statement",
    async (e) => { await
```

```
    SettingsInteractionHelper.ShowPrivacyStatementAsync(); }));
}
```

If you now run the app, you'll see the Privacy Statement option appear in the settings charm. Select it, and IE will spring into life and navigate the user away. Figure 9-2 illustrates.

*Figure 9-2. The Privacy Statement option*

---

# Best Practice

It's worth calling out a couple of points about best practice.

There are no explicit guidelines about the casing of options on the charm. There isn't much in the way of consistency in this. OneNote MX uses sentence casing—for example, "Privacy and terms of use." IE uses title casing (e.g., Internet Options). Seeing as the default "Rate and review" is sentence-cased and also seeing that you can't change that, I'd go with sentence casing.

Microsoft's published guidelines also state that when you select an option, the current view should not be navigated—that is, the user should stay where he or she is. In the next section, we're going to create a settings flyout, which does exactly this. However, some of the built-in apps do navigate the page. The Store app is especially exuberant in this department.

In LOB apps, the settings charm is a decent place to put support tools and information —for example, functions that dump out diagnostic information, or that reset local caching. The same is possibly also true of consumer apps, although in consumer apps we have to be more careful not to blind the user with science.

---

# Implementing the Settings Flyout

The most common thing to do with the settings charm is to create a flyout that contains more options. I am going to present this here, even though we don't have much in the way of settings! What we'll do is present a view that isn't functional, concentrating on the process of building the flyout. Luckily for us, the WinRT API contains a Settings Flyout control that implements the basic behavior of winding in from the righthand side of the screen. All we have to do is create an instance of this control that is able to containerize specific settings panes. In this chapter, we're going to build two settings panes—one that displays some settings and another that displays a help message.

## Building a Settings Pane

The settings pane is a standard XAML surface. A lot of the examples you'll see of this on the Web use the UserControl class. However, we have to consider that right now our MVVM implementation is tied into using StreetFooPage by virtue of its implementation of IViewModelHost. Although the view-models don't know anything about the StreetFooPage, they do need to be able to "poke" back into the UI, which is why we've created the IViewModelHost route. If we choose to base our settings pane on something other than StreetFooPage, we'll need to extend that support forward into some expansion of UserControl. (Some people might argue that there's no need for any coupling like this at all—pragmatically, I think it's easier to have a degree of coupling while maintaining the spirit of a well-managed separation.)

I'm going to propose that we build an MvvmAwareControl based on UserControl. All that we really have to do here is implement IViewModelHost. The view-model implementations themselves won't care what they're based on. That's the point of the abstraction, after all.

You may recall that thus far we've used extension methods on the Page to drive additional functionality, such as displaying message boxes and initializing and dereferencing the view-model. We now have two classes that we need to provide this functionality to: StreetFooPage (which we did before) and MvvmAwareControl (which is new). This means we need to change those extension methods.

Weirdly—at least it seems slightly weird to me—we can just change the extension methods to extend IViewModel rather than Page, and suddenly all of that behavior becomes available to MvvmAwareControl. (This sort of thing is just one reason why extension methods are one of my favorite C# language features. What we're really doing here is creating a type of quasi-multiple-inheritance support.)

Now take a look at the revised version of PageExtender that contains the extension methods. (It may be worth renaming that class, but I've left it with the original name to save confusion for readers who may be comparing code across chapters.)

```
internal static class PageExtender
{
    internal static Task ShowAlertAsync(this IViewModelHost page, ErrorBucket
errors)
    {
        return ShowAlertAsync(page, errors.GetErrorsAsString());
    }

    internal static Task ShowAlertAsync(this IViewModelHost page, string
message)
    {
        // show...
        MessageDialog dialog = new MessageDialog(message != null ? message :
string.Empty);
        return dialog.ShowAsync().AsTask();
    }

    internal static void InitializeModel(this IViewModelHost page,
        IViewModel model)
    {
        // set up the data context...
        ((Control)page).DataContext = model;
    }

    internal static IViewModel GetModel(this IViewModelHost page)
    {
        return ((Control)page).DataContext as IViewModel;
    }
}
```

Once we've done that, building MvvmAwareControl is a cinch. Here's the code:

```
public class MvvmAwareControl : UserControl, IViewModelHost
{
    public MvvmAwareControl()
    {
    }

    Task IViewModelHost.ShowAlertAsync(ErrorBucket errors)
    {
        return PageExtender.ShowAlertAsync(this, errors);
    }

    Task IViewModelHost.ShowAlertAsync(
        string message)
    {
        return PageExtender.ShowAlertAsync(this, message);
    }

    public void ShowView(Type viewModelInterfaceType)
    {
        throw new NotImplementedException();
    }
```

```
        public void HideAppBar()
        {
            throw new NotImplementedException();
        }
    }
}
```

I've assumed in this code that supporting ShowView and HideAppBar is out of scope for this class.

We have to decide what we're going to call these controls. There's precedent for calling them *panes*—thus far, we've seen SearchPane and SettingsPane, which sit in the same physical place in the real estate. However, we can't call it SettingsPane, as this would clash with the WinRT class of the same name. My proposition, then, is that we call our new control MySettingsPane.

Using the Add New Item dialog, add a new UserControl called MySettingsPane. You'll get some XAML that looks like this:

```
<UserControl
    x:Class="StreetFoo.Client.UI.MySettingsPane"
    xmlns="http://schemas.microsoft.com/winfx/2006/xaml/presentation"
    xmlns:x="http://schemas.microsoft.com/winfx/2006/xaml"
    xmlns:local="using:StreetFoo.Client.UI"
    xmlns:d="http://schemas.microsoft.com/expression/blend/2008"
    xmlns:mc="http://schemas.openxmlformats.org/markup-compatibility/2006"
    mc:Ignorable="d"
    d:DesignHeight="300"
    d:DesignWidth="400">

    <Grid>

    </Grid>
</UserControl>
```

There are two things we need to change in that default XAML. We need to change the UserControl declaration to local:MvvmAwareControl. (We'll also need to change the base class, which we'll do in a moment.) We also need to change the width. Settings panes can be 346 pixels or 646 pixels in width. I find that 346 tends to be a bit narrow, so set this to 646. Here's the amended code:

```
<local:MvvmAwareControl
    x:Class="StreetFoo.Client.UI.MySettingsPane"
    xmlns="http://schemas.microsoft.com/winfx/2006/xaml/presentation"
    xmlns:x="http://schemas.microsoft.com/winfx/2006/xaml"
    xmlns:local="using:StreetFoo.Client.UI"
    xmlns:d="http://schemas.microsoft.com/expression/blend/2008"
    xmlns:mc="http://schemas.openxmlformats.org/markup-compatibility/2006"
    mc:Ignorable="d"
    d:DesignHeight="646"
```

```
        d:DesignWidth="400">

    <Grid>

    </Grid>
</local:MvvmAwareControl>
```

As mentioned, you'll also need to change the base class in the codebehind file, like so:

```
[ViewModel(typeof(IMySettingsPaneViewModel))]
public sealed partial class MySettingsPane : MvvmAwareControl
{
    private IMySettingsPaneViewModel ViewModel { get; set; }
    public MySettingsPane()
    {
        this.InitializeComponent();
        this.InitializeViewModel();
    }
}
```

All of these styles let us build our layout properly. As mentioned, we're not putting real controls on here—I've used a ToggleSwitch because it's one of the cooler new controls in Windows 8. Notice that the back button has a command binding to DismissCommand; we'll get to that soon. Here's the layout of MySettingsPane in its entirety:

```
<local:MvvmAwareControl
    x:Class="StreetFoo.Client.UI.MySettingsPane"
    IsTabStop="false"
    xmlns="http://schemas.microsoft.com/winfx/2006/xaml/presentation"
    xmlns:x="http://schemas.microsoft.com/winfx/2006/xaml"
    xmlns:local="using:StreetFoo.Client.UI"
    xmlns:d="http://schemas.microsoft.com/expression/blend/2008"
    xmlns:mc="http://schemas.openxmlformats.org/markup-compatibility/2006"
    mc:Ignorable="d"
    Width="646" Height="200">

    <Border Style="{StaticResource SettingsBorderStyle}">
        <Grid>
            <Grid.RowDefinitions>
                <RowDefinition Height="50"></RowDefinition>
                <RowDefinition Height="*"></RowDefinition>
            </Grid.RowDefinitions>

            <Grid Style="{StaticResource SettingsCaptionStyle}">
                <StackPanel Orientation="Horizontal">
                    <Button Style="{StaticResource SettingsBackButtonStyle}"
                      Command="{Binding DismissCommand}"/>
                    <TextBlock Grid.Row="1" Style="{StaticResource
                      SettingsCaptionTextStyle}">Settings</TextBlock>
                </StackPanel>
            </Grid>

            <Grid Grid.Row="2" Margin="10,10,10,10">
```

```
        <StackPanel>
            <ToggleSwitch Grid.Row="2" Header="The cows look small
                because..." OnContent="They are small" OffContent=
                "They are far away"></ToggleSwitch>
        </StackPanel>
    </Grid>
    </Grid>
</Border>

</local:MvvmAwareControl>
```

## Building MySettingsFlyout

To do this, add a new `SettingsFlyout` item to the project. Call it *MySettingsFlyout*.

This flyout will contain some default XAML. We need to change this so that the default text within the `StackPanel` instance doesn't exist, and give the `StackPanel` instance an `x:Name` attribute so that we can address it from code. Here's the XAML:

```
<SettingsFlyout
    x:Class="StreetFoo.Client.UI.MySettingsFlyout"
    xmlns="http://schemas.microsoft.com/winfx/2006/xaml/presentation"
    xmlns:x="http://schemas.microsoft.com/winfx/2006/xaml"
    xmlns:local="using:StreetFoo.Client.UI"
    xmlns:d="http://schemas.microsoft.com/expression/blend/2008"
    xmlns:mc="http://schemas.openxmlformats.org/markup-compatibility/2006"
    mc:Ignorable="d"
    IconSource="Assets/SmallLogo.png"
    Title="SettingsFlyout1"
    d:DesignWidth="346">

    <!-- This StackPanel acts as a root panel for vertical layout of the content
    sections -->
    <StackPanel VerticalAlignment="Stretch" HorizontalAlignment="Stretch" >

        <!-- The StackPanel(s) below define individual content sections -->

        <!-- Content Section 1-->
        <StackPanel x:Name="StackPanel" Style="{StaticResource
    SettingsFlyoutSectionStyle}">
        </StackPanel>

        <!-- Define more Content Sections below as necessary -->

    </StackPanel>
</SettingsFlyout>
```

In terms of the code, when we create a new instance of the settings flyout, we'll pass in an instance of one of the user controls that drives the pane. We'll then dynamically add this control to the `StackPanel` instance defined in the XAML. Here's the code:

```
public sealed partial class MySettingsFlyout : SettingsFlyout
{
    private UserControl UserControl { get; set; }

    public MySettingsFlyout()
    {
        this.InitializeComponent();
    }

    public MySettingsFlyout(UserControl control)
        : this()
    {
        // set the user control...
        this.UserControl = control;
        this.StackPanel.Children.Add(control);

        // subscribe...
        this.Loaded += OnLoaded;
    }

    private void OnLoaded(object sender, RoutedEventArgs routedEventArgs)
    {
        // set the title and the width...
        this.Title = ((IViewModel)this.UserControl.DataContext).Caption;
        this.Width = this.UserControl.Width;
    }
}
```

All that remains now is to rig up a way of showing the pane. We'll do this by adding another command to the settings command collection. Here's the change to App:

```
// Modify method in App...
void settings_CommandsRequested(SettingsPane sender,
SettingsPaneCommandsRequestedEventArgs args)
{
    args.Request.ApplicationCommands.Add(new SettingsCommand
("PrivacyStatement", "Privacy Statement",
            async (e) => { await SettingsInteractionHelper.
ShowPrivacyStatementAsync(); }));
    args.Request.ApplicationCommands.Add(new
        SettingsCommand("MySettings", "My Settings",
        (e) => {
            var flyout = new MySettingsFlyout(new MySettingsPane());
            flyout.Show();

        }));
}
```

Again, run the project and you'll now be able to access the new pane through the settings charm.

# Developing a Help Screen

Now, let's go through the relatively basic requirement of displaying help content on the screen. It's emerging as a standard approach within Windows Store apps to put a Help option on the settings pane, at least for those apps that provide help. We will rig Help to display when the user presses F1. (Although pressing F1 to access a help function is not necessarily current fashion, I want to show how you can handle keyboard events.)

Although we're going to see how to use this to represent help text, the rendering portion of this can be used anywhere in your app to render richer blocks of bigger text. For example, in LOB apps you may want to render product descriptions, or summaries of a customer's order history. In retail apps, you may want to render downloaded content.

Hypothetically, if you want to present text within the app, you want some formatting control. HTML is an obvious choice for this. And you can render HTML content using the `WebView` control. (This control containerizes IE.) This supports a `NavigateTo String` method into which you can feed a string containing the HTML to render. Or, you can use the `Navigate` method and give it a URL. (However, the `ms-appx` and `ms-appdata` protocols are not supported by `WebView`, so you need to load the data first and feed it in through `NavigateToString`.)

The problem with the IE-based approach is that it's a little blunt. Back in the olden days, this would not have been at all pretty. It's a better and more lightweight approach now, but it doesn't provide the sort of granularity and control you might need when rendering small portions of text.

Let's go down a different route and show you how to build up formatted content without using `WebView`. We're going to build a control called a `MarkupViewer` to which we can give some marked-up text and have it create XAML objects that present the text in a "prettified" way.

## Creating a Help Pane

I'm not going to go through how you create the structure of `HelpPane` in detail, as it's the selfsame job as creating the `MySettingsPane`. The more interesting aspect is in creating a control called `MarkupViewer` that will be responsible for rendering the help content.

What will normally happen with help content is that you'll have it loaded locally on the device, most likely in a Windows 8 world by having the content available in the ~/*Assets* folder of the project. (What we're not going to do here is build a complex, context-sensitive help system—all we're going to do is put some help content on the screen.) I'm assuming that we have one file called ~/*Assets/HelpText.txt*. You can put whatever you like in this file.

What we're going to do with our `IHelpPaneViewModel` is have it expose a command whereby the user can jump off to a website to get proper help, and a `Markup` property that will have the content to render. Here's the code:

```
public interface IHelpPaneViewModel : IViewModel, IDismissCommandSource
{
    ICommand WebHelpCommand { get; set; }

    string Markup { get; }
}
```

The implementation, then, looks like this:

```
public class HelpPaneViewModel : ViewModel, IHelpPaneViewModel
{
    // commands...
    public ICommand DismissCommand {
        get { return this.GetValue<ICommand>(); }
        set { this.SetValue(value); } }
    public ICommand WebHelpCommand {
        get { return this.GetValue<ICommand>(); }
        private set { this.SetValue(value); } }

    public HelpPaneViewModel()
    {

        WebHelpCommand = new DelegateCommand(async (args) => await
SettingsInteractionHelper.ShowWebHelpAsync());
    }

    // property for holding the markup...
    public string Markup { get { return this.GetValue<string>(); } set
{ this.SetValue(value); } }

    // loads the markup from disk when we're activated...
    public override async void Activated(object args)
    {
        base.Activated(args);

        // load...
        var file = await StorageFile.GetFileFromApplicationUriAsync(new Uri
("ms-appx:///Assets/HelpText.txt"));
        this.Markup = await FileIO.ReadTextAsync(file);
    }
}
```

You'll notice that we have the `FileIO` class read the help contents from disk.

In the next section, we're going to build a control called `MarkupViewer`. This will have a `Markup` property that's bound to the `Markup` property on the view-model. Similarly, we'll have a `HyperlinkButton` that will have its `Command` property bound to the `Web`

`HelpCommand` property on the view-model. Here's the XAML that shows those two controls within *HelpPane.xaml*:

```
<!-- snippet from HelpPane... -->
<Grid Grid.Row="1">
    <StackPanel Margin="10,10,10,10">
        <local:MarkupViewer Markup="{Binding Markup}" />
        <HyperlinkButton
Content="Visit our website to get more help"
Command="{Binding WebHelpCommand}"></HyperlinkButton>
    </StackPanel>
</Grid>
```

As is common practice, you'll need to modify the constructor of `HelpPage` so that it obtains and sets up the view-model. You'll also need to add a command into the `set tings_CommandRequested` handler in App. I'm proposing creating a static method for showing help, as we're going to activate this view through more mechanisms than just the settings pane. Here's the code:

```
// Modify method and add new method in App...
void settings_CommandsRequested(SettingsPane sender,
SettingsPaneCommandsRequestedEventArgs args)
{
    args.Request.ApplicationCommands.Add(new SettingsCommand
("PrivacyStatement", "Privacy Statement",
        async (e) => { await SettingsInteractionHelper.
ShowPrivacyStatementAsync(); }));
    args.Request.ApplicationCommands.Add(
        new SettingsCommand("MySettings", "My Settings",
        (e) => {
            var flyout = new MySettingsFlyout(new MySettingsPane());
            flyout.Show();
        }));
    args.Request.ApplicationCommands.Add(new SettingsCommand("Help",
"Help", (e) => { ShowHelp(); }));
}

internal static void ShowHelp()
{
    var flyout = new MySettingsFlyout(new HelpPane());
    flyout.Show();
}
```

You won't be able to compile yet, as we still have to build the `MarkupViewer` control.

## Handling the F1 Key

Handling the keypress is very easy to do—just override the `OnKeyUp` method in `StreetViewPage` to respond to the F1 key. Here's the code:

```
// Add method to StreetViewPage...
protected override void OnKeyUp(Windows.UI.Xaml.Input.
```

```
        KeyRoutedEventArgs e)
{
    if (e.Key == VirtualKey.F1)
        App.ShowHelp();
    else
        base.OnKeyUp(e);
}
```

That's it—if we could compile and run the app, we could then see that.

# Rendering Markup

Before we build the `MarkupViewer` control, let's consider how we render the content.

As we know by now, XAML is definitely not HTML. Whereas HTML is designed with text/document rendering as its primary function, XAML is not. If we want to render flowing text with formatting, we have to build up a control tree to do it. We can use `RichTextBox` to create a container for the text, and then put `Paragraph` and `Run` objects in it to build up the representation. For example, the following results in the representation shown in Figure 9-3:

```
<RichTextBlock FontSize="16">
<Paragraph>So, this is some text. And this word is
    <Run FontWeight="Bold">bold</Run>.
  </Paragraph>
  <Paragraph>And this text is
    <Run Foreground="Pink">pink</Run>.
    </Paragraph>
</RichTextBlock>
```

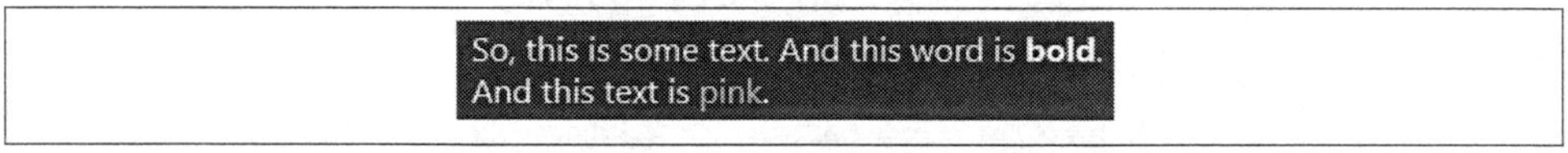

> So, this is some text. And this word is **bold**.
> And this text is pink.

*Figure 9-3. Example RichTextBlock rendering*

What we're going to do is take the contents of our help text file and create `Paragraph` instances for each line. If we were building a more sophisticated markup processor, we would just have to add a more complex control structure depending on the directives in the markup. The principle, though, would remain the same.

We need somewhere to put the markup. For our control, we'll extend `ContentControl`. (Ultimately, we'll put a `RichTextBlock` instance in the `Content` property. We can't extend `RichTextBlock` because it's sealed.) Here's the code:

```
public class MarkupViewer : ContentControl
{
    // dependency property...
    public static readonly DependencyProperty MarkupProperty =
DependencyProperty.Register("Markup", typeof(string), typeof(MarkupViewer),
```

```
            new PropertyMetadata(null, (d, e) => ((MarkupViewer)d).Markup =
    (string)e.NewValue));

        public MarkupViewer()
        {
        }

        public string Markup
        {
            get
            {
                return (string)GetValue(MarkupProperty);
            }
            set
            {
                SetValue(MarkupProperty, value);
                this.RefreshView();
            }
        }

        private void RefreshView()
        {
            // tbd...
        }
    }
```

If you recall back in Chapter 5, that's the same pattern that we've been using for adding properties to our controls using dependency properties.

Before we run it, let's make it do something so that we can prove it works. Modify RefreshView so that it creates a button, like this:

```
// Modify method in MarkupViewer...
private void RefreshView()
{
    var button = new Button();
    button.Content = this.Markup;

    // set...
    this.Content = button;
}
```

Run the app and summon the help, and it'll render our text in a giant button. Figure 9-4 illustrates.

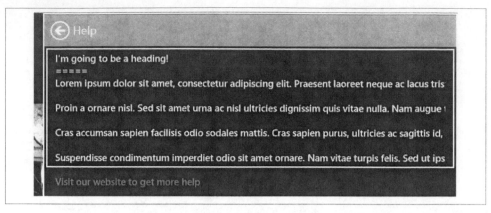

*Figure 9-4. Demonstrating that we've loaded the text and passed it through to Markup-Viewer*

Now we can do some processing on the text.

You'll notice from Figure 9-4 that the second line is a set of equals signs. I've borrowed this convention from Markdown. In Markdown, this notation is used to indicate that the preceding line should be a heading.

As I've mentioned, we're not going to do a proper Markdown implementation, but I want to do more than rendering flat text, hence the heading—we will support that.

The bits that we need to render the text are all in the `Windows.UI.Xaml.Documents` namespace. It works by combining *blocks* and *inlines*, all of which can be styled.

We'll create a root `RichTextBlock` instance, and add `Paragraph` instances to it. (Paragraphs are blocks.) To each paragraph we'll then add `Run` instances, a *run* being an inline.

When we start building our view, we'll take the CR+LF delimited text and break it down into lines. We'll walk through each line and look ahead to see if the next line is a heading. If it is, we'll adjust the styling of the paragraph that we're on and then skip the line. When we're done, we'll set the `Content` property to be the `RichTextBlock` instance that we created. Here's the code:

```
// Modify method in MarkupViewer...
private void RefreshView()
{
    // anything?
    if (string.IsNullOrEmpty(Markup))
    {
        this.Content = null;
        return;
    }

    // get the lines...
```

```csharp
var lines = new List<string>();
using (var reader = new StringReader(this.Markup))
{
    while(true)
    {
        string buf = reader.ReadLine();
        if (buf == null)
            break;
        lines.Add(buf);
    }
}

// walk...
var block = new RichTextBlock();
for (int index = 0; index < lines.Count; index++)
{
    string nextLine = null;
    if (index < lines.Count - 1)
        nextLine = lines[index + 1];

    // create a paragraph... and add it to the block...
    var para = new Paragraph();
    block.Blocks.Add(para);

    // create a "run" and add it to the paragraph...
    var run = new Run();
    run.Text = lines[index];
    para.Inlines.Add(run);

    // heading?
    if (nextLine != null && nextLine.StartsWith("="))
    {
        // make it bigger, and then skip the next line...
        para.FontSize = 20;
        index++;
    }
    else if (nextLine != null && nextLine.StartsWith("-"))
    {
        para.FontSize = 18;
        index++;
    }
}

// set...
this.Content = block;
}
```

Run the code and summon the help option, and you'll see something like Figure 9-5.

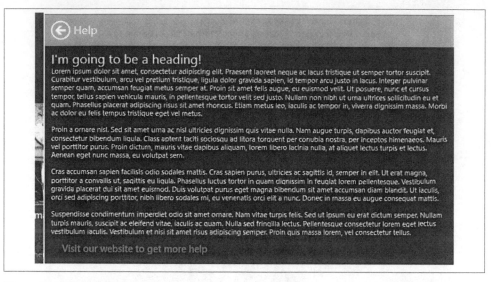

*Figure 9-5. "Prettified" markup*

There you go: nicely rendered text using a custom markup format, albeit quite a limited custom format. As I mentioned before, the easiest win here is that hopefully someone will port over Markdown or something similar. Either way, don't forget that this approach is not just valid for help text. It also applies to displays of complex text data in all sorts of data that you might present in your app. In fact, in the next chapter we'll use this same control to "prettify" rendering of the report description.

# CHAPTER 10

# Location

In all geo-capable apps, regardless of platform, there are three things you as a developer typically want to do. You want to determine where an asset is, present the user with some sort of visualization of location, or tag an activity to a point in space (and usually along with it a point in time). In this chapter, we're going to look primarily at the latter two. Although we'll also look briefly at getting a device's location, I'm keeping that discussion short because it's fairly straightforward and applies only in limited cases. However, we'll focus on mapping because a) it's helpful, and b) it's actually pretty cool! (My advice, if you want to sell a prototype project to your boss, is to put a map in it.)

We'll achieve the presentation of the actual maps by integrating Bing Maps. You will need a developer key to do this, but I'll go through that when we get to it. Before we do all that, though, we have to modify the app so that we actually have somewhere to present a map.

## Creating a Singleton View

To start the work that we need to do in this chapter, we need a page that we can put a map on. We'll create a *singleton view* that will display a single report from the local database. From a UI perspective we'll design this in classic Windows 8 style: a viewport that scrolls horizontally, presenting a "panorama" across the presentation. This will require us to use a ScrollViewer and a Grid.

In XAML, a ScrollViewer is—as its name implies—a control that implements scrolling. We can apply a standard style called HorizontalScrollViewerStyle to implement this in the standard way to achieve the required Windows 8 experience (i.e., swiping from side to side with a finger, and using the mouse wheel).

Figure 10-1 shows us what we're ultimately looking to achieve. Let's get started.

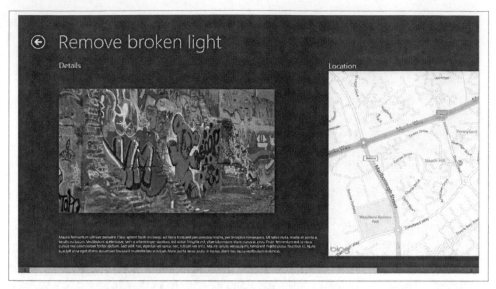

*Figure 10-1. Our objective: a singleton view showing the report details and a map*

## Creating the View-Model

Whether you're using MVVM or not, there are three common UI metaphors that you'll tend to see. You are usually either looking at a view that shows a list of related items, a view that's mainly displaying information about an item, or a view that falls into neither of this categories. At this point we've seen a view implementation that falls into the list model (the list of reports), and a view that falls into neither (the register page, settings page, etc.). What we're going to do in this section is look at how to create a base view-model when we want to create a singleton presentation of a piece of domain data.

To do this, we'll create a `ViewModelSingleton<T>` class that will expose a property called `Item` of type `T`. The advantage of this approach is that it gives us a common way of representing items on views such as this. It also creates a place to put common setup and error-handling code. If you're of a mind to, it can also act as a place to pin roll-your-own framework functionality.

Although I won't cover how to do so in these pages, we can do something similar with `ViewModelList<T>`, which we could use as a base for the view-model that we've created for the Reports page and the search results page.

Figure 10-2 shows a UML sketch of the implementation—although, to reiterate, we're only going to build the singleton view now. I've also omitted the interfaces from the sketch, but we'll have `IViewModel`, `IViewModelSingleton<T>`, and `IViewModelList<T>`.

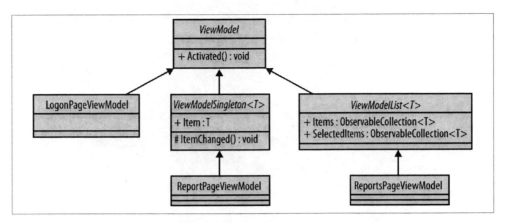

*Figure 10-2. UML static structure sketch showing ViewModelSingleton<T> and others*

Here's the code for `IViewModelSingleton<T>`. Note the type constraint indicating the T must be of type `ModelItem`:

```
public interface IViewModelSingleton<T> : IViewModel
    where T : ModelItem
{
    T Item { get; }
}
```

When we come to use one of these view-models, we'll need to give it the item to display. In the basic way in which XAML is used, outside of any MVVM cleverness we put in, we can pass an optional argument. In Chapter 8 we used this to pass around the search query that the user entered. In our case now, we can use that to pass in the item that we want to display. Related to this, we need to defend against not being passed an item or being passed an item of the wrong type. We'll also implement an `ItemChanged` method that we can override in order to set up the item when the view-model is activated. Here's the code:

```
public abstract class ViewModelSingleton<T> : ViewModel,
    IViewModelSingleton<T>
    where T : ModelItem
{
    // holds the base item that we're mapped to...
    private T _item;

    protected ViewModelSingleton(IViewModelHost host)
        : base(host)
    {
    }

    public T Item
    {
        get
```

```
        {
            return _item;
        }
        set
        {
            _item = value;
            this.OnPropertyChanged();

            // reload...
            this.ItemChanged();
        }
    }

    protected virtual void ItemChanged()
    {
        // no-op...
    }

    public override void Activated(object args)
    {
        base.Activated(args);

        // check...
        if (args == null)
            throw new InvalidOperationException(
                "An item was not supplied.");
        if(!(typeof(T).GetTypeInfo().IsAssignableFrom(args.GetType()
        .GetTypeInfo())))
        {
            throw new InvalidOperationException(string.Format(
            "An item of type '{0}' was supplied, but an item of type
            '{1}' was required.",
                args.GetType(), typeof(T)));
        }

        // are our arguments initializing our item?
        this.Item = (T)args;
    }
}
```

At this point, we don't need to do much with the new `ReportPageViewModel`. We do need to add an `OpenMapCommand`, which we'll use in the last section to open Bing Maps from within our application. Therefore, `IReportPageViewModel` just looks like this:

```
public interface IReportPageViewModel : IViewModelSingleton<ReportViewItem>
{
    ICommand OpenMapCommand { get; }
}
```

The actual `ReportPageViewModel` has some additional complexity in that we have to initialize the `ImageUri` property exposed by `ReportViewItem`. Here's the code—note how it reuses the `ReportImageCacheManager` that we first saw in Chapter 4.

```
    public class ReportPageViewModel : ViewModelSingleton<ReportViewItem>,
IReportPageViewModel
    {
        public ReportPageViewModel(IViewModelHost host)
            : base(host)
        {
        }

        protected override async void ItemChanged()
        {
            // set up our image...
            var manager = new ReportImageCacheManager();
            await this.Item.InitializeAsync(manager);
        }
    }
```

Now that we have the view-model logic built, we can turn our attention to creating the view.

## Creating the View

A key part of the Windows 8 experience is wide views that the user pans across left to right to reveal information. From a design perspective, the idea here is that the user is not fiddling around with panels and tabs to reveal information. It's all there, just not within the current viewport. When working with touch, grabbing anywhere and swiping is easier than zeroing in on and successfully hitting a target. For our report singleton view, we want to display some basic details about the report, and then display a map. We build such a view by creating a Grid control with the different panels on it, and then wrapping it using a ScrollViewer that provides the scrolling functionality.

What I'm proposing is that we create two panels—one for the image and description, and another for a map. To get started, create a new Basic Page called ReportPage. As usual, this page will have a header with a back button. We need to create our Scroll Viewer so that it goes in the second row of the grid that we were given by Visual Studio when the page was created. When we create our grid to go into the ScrollViewer, we create a thin column on the left that's the same width as the column used to accommodate the back button on the caption row. This aligns the left side of the first real panel with the left side of the caption text. In a moment, we'll build a new style called PanoramaPa nel that adjusts the spacing. You should note that the really important part of the ScrollViewer definition is to include the HorizontalScrollViewerStyle, which we need in order to get the Windows 8 experience. The base behavior of ScrollViewer is to act like a Win32 autoscroll control.

In terms of the data binding, we're going to use multipart expressions that use dot notation. For example, {Binding Item.ImageUri} can be used on the Image control. The DataContext for the page is our ReportPageViewModel. We know that this has an

Item property exposed by ViewModelSingleton<ReportViewItem>; from there, it's obvious that ImageUri is the already defined property on ReportViewItem.

We're also going to use the MarkupViewer control that we built in Chapter 9. Although we won't gain any direct benefit from using it here, I wanted to include it to underscore how such a thing can be used in regular data display. (In Chapter 9, I signaled that we can use the control for that, as opposed to it just rendering help text.)

We're going to use a XAML control called ScrollViewer to present the list. This needs to be configured with a style that tells it to scroll horizontally, rather than the Windows default of vertically. Add this style to StandardStyles.xaml to achieve this:

```
<!-- Add to StandardStyles.xaml -->
<Style x:Key="HorizontalScrollViewerStyle" TargetType="ScrollViewer">
    <Setter Property="HorizontalScrollBarVisibility" Value="Auto"/>
    <Setter Property="VerticalScrollBarVisibility" Value="Disabled"/>
    <Setter Property="ScrollViewer.HorizontalScrollMode" Value="Enabled" />
    <Setter Property="ScrollViewer.VerticalScrollMode" Value="Disabled" />
    <Setter Property="ScrollViewer.ZoomMode" Value="Disabled" />
</Style>
```

Here's the XAML that needs to be added to ReportPage:

```
<!-- Add to ReportPage -->
<ScrollViewer Style="{StaticResource HorizontalScrollViewerStyle}"
Grid.Row="1">
        <Grid>

            <Grid.ColumnDefinitions>
                <ColumnDefinition Width="120"></ColumnDefinition>
                <ColumnDefinition Width="800"></ColumnDefinition>
                <ColumnDefinition Width="800"></ColumnDefinition>
            </Grid.ColumnDefinitions>

            <ContentControl Grid.Column="1" Style="{StaticResource
PanoramaPanel}">
                <StackPanel>
                    <TextBlock Style="{StaticResource HeadingTextBlock}">
Details</TextBlock>
                    <Image Source="{Binding Item.ImageUri}"
HorizontalAlignment="Left" Width="640" Height="480" Stretch="Uniform"
                        Margin="0,0,0,10"></Image>
                    <local:MarkupViewer Markup="{Binding Item.Description}">
</local:MarkupViewer>
                </StackPanel>
            </ContentControl>

            <ContentControl Grid.Column="2" Style="{StaticResource
PanoramaPanel}">
                <StackPanel>
                    <TextBlock Style="{StaticResource HeadingTextBlock}">
Location</TextBlock>
```

```
                        <Button Content="We'll put a map in here eventually...">
    </Button>
                    </StackPanel>
                </ContentControl>

            </Grid>
        </ScrollViewer>
```

Another detail is that we need to change the caption to bind to the title of the report, as opposed to being the static "My Application" text. Here's that change:

```
        <!-- Back button and page title -->
        <Grid>
            <Grid.ColumnDefinitions>
                <ColumnDefinition Width="Auto"/>
                <ColumnDefinition Width="*"/>
            </Grid.ColumnDefinitions>
            <Button x:Name="backButton" Click="GoBack" IsEnabled="{Binding Frame.
CanGoBack, ElementName=pageRoot}"
Style="{StaticResource BackButtonStyle}"/>
            <TextBlock x:Name="pageTitle" Grid.Column="1" Text="{Binding
Item.Title}" Style="{StaticResource PageHeaderTextStyle}"/>
        </Grid>
```

To make this work, we just have to build the PanoramaPanel style. All that we're doing with this is adding some space between the panels. We need to add this to the *StandardStyles.xaml* file.

```
        <!-- Add to StandardStyles.xaml -->
    <Style x:Key="PanoramaPanel" TargetType="ContentControl">
        <Setter Property="Margin" Value="0,0,20,0"></Setter>
    </Style>
```

We can't run that yet—well, we can, but we can't actually reach that view through the frontend. Figure 10-3 shows what the designer looks like so that you know it's working. Note that the extent of the grid goes over the edge of the viewport. This is the effect that we want in order to create the panoramic scrolling.

We'll need to add an app bar to this page so that we have somewhere to put the command that will open up Bing Maps. Here's the markup for the app bar:

```
        <!-- Add markup to ReportPage.xaml -->
    <Page.BottomAppBar>
        <AppBar>
            <StackPanel HorizontalAlignment="Right" Orientation="Horizontal"
Grid.Column="2">
                <Button Style="{StaticResource EditAppBarButtonStyle}" Command=
"{Binding EditCommand}" />
                <Button Style="{StaticResource OpenMapAppBarButtonStyle}"
Command="{Binding OpenMapCommand}" />
            </StackPanel>
        </AppBar>
    </Page.BottomAppBar>
```

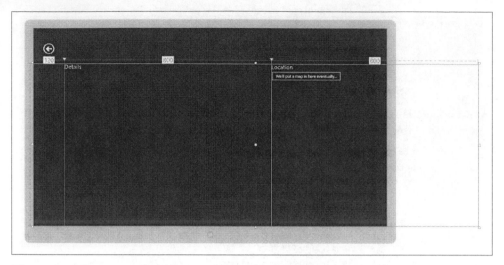

*Figure 10-3. Designer view of ReportPage*

Finally, to round off the code, we'll need to actually wire up the view-model. This is the same as we've done a few times now; the actual logic required in the pages is very light.

Here's the code:

```
public sealed partial class ReportPage : StreetFooPage
{
    private IReportPageViewModel ViewModel { get; set; }

    public ReportPage()
    {
        this.InitializeComponent();

        // set up the model...
        this.ViewModel = ViewModelFactory.Current.GetHandler
<IReportPageViewModel>(this);
        this.InitializeModel(this.ViewModel);
    }

        // code omitted...
}
```

## Navigating to the View

Now we need to get to a point where we can actually see our new view!

There are three routes into the view given the current state of the app: the current Reports page, the search results page, and the search recommendations view. (Recall in Chapter 8 that we were able to present a single report item on the actual search charm; this was a *search recommendation*.)

At the moment, the behavior of the Reports page is that when we touch on items, the selection changes. This has been fine up to now to demonstrate functionality, but more properly within the Windows 8 experience, when you touch on items they should open. You can see this behavior in the built-in apps.

Again, recall when we implemented search in Chapter 8, we built the view so that when you select an item it displays a message box. We did this by using the `IsItemClickEnabled` and `ItemClickedCommand` properties in `MyGridView`. All we have to do on `ReportsPage` is enable `IsItemClickEnabled` and bind `SelectionCommand` through to `ItemClickedCommand`. This will result in the raising of the `SelectionCommand` command when the user touches an item on the view. Here's the change:

```
<!-- Modify ReportsPage.xaml -->
<local:MyGridView
        x:Name="itemGridView"
        AutomationProperties.AutomationId="ItemsGridView"
        AutomationProperties.Name="Items"
        TabIndex="1"
        Margin="0,0,0,-4"
        Padding="116,0,116,46"
        ItemsSource="{Binding Source={StaticResource itemsViewSource}}"
        ItemTemplate="{StaticResource ReportItem250x250Template}"
        IsItemClickEnabled="true"
        ItemClickedCommand="{Binding SelectionCommand}"
        Grid.Row="1"
        />
```

We've already built a base type for commands called `NavigateCommand` that will automatically rattle a navigation request through to XAML. To make it work on `ReportsPageViewModel`, we just need to change the constructor to use it, as opposed to using `DelegateCommand` with a lambda expression. Here's that change:

```
// Modify constructor in ReportsPageViewModel...
public ReportsPageViewModel(IViewModelHost host)
    : base(host)
{
    // commands...
    this.RefreshCommand = new DelegateCommand(async (e) =>
    {
        this.Host.HideAppBar();
        await this.DoRefresh(true);

        // toast...
        string message = "I found 1 report.";
        if (this.Items.Count != 1)
            message = string.Format("I found {0} reports.",
this.Items.Count);
        var toast = new ToastNotificationBuilder(new string[] {
```

```
"Reports refreshed.", message });
            toast.ImageUri = "ms-appx:///Assets/Toast.jpg";
            toast.Update();
        });

        // open the singleton report view...
        this.SelectionCommand = new NavigateCommand<IReportPageViewModel>
(this.Host);
    }
```

Although we still have to cover the navigation behavior on the search operations, you
can run the project at this point to gain the satisfaction of seeing it working. Figure 10-4
illustrates.

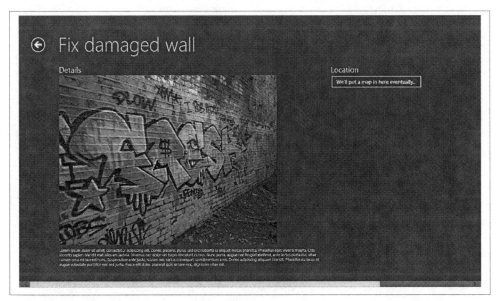

*Figure 10-4. The operational report singleton view*

We'll quickly round off the two search operations before we start looking at location
functionality proper.

The `SearchResultsPageViewModel` is the same trick as before. We just need to use
`NavigateCommand` on the `SelectionCommand`. Here's the code:

```
// Modify constructor in SearchResultsPageViewModel...
public SearchResultsPageViewModel(IViewModelHost host)
    : base(host)
{
    this.MasterItems = new List<ReportViewItem>();
    this.Results = new ObservableCollection<ReportViewItem>();
    this.Filters = new ObservableCollection<SearchFilter>();
```

```
        // command...
        this.SelectionCommand = new NavigateCommand<IReportPageViewModel>
(this.Host);
    }
```

The selection wiring on both the `ReportsPageViewModel` and `SearchResultsPageView`
`Model` implementations is easy: we have a `ReportViewItem`, and all we have to do is pass
it through the navigation. The search recommendation handler is a little trickier. In
Chapter 8 when we did this, we wrote this code to respond to the user selecting the
recommendation:

```
        async void search_ResultSuggestionChosen(SearchPane sender,
SearchPaneResultSuggestionChosenEventArgs args)
        {
            var dialog = new MessageDialog("Chosen: " + args.Tag);
            await dialog.ShowAsync();
        }
```

The `Tag` was set to the ID of the `ReportItem` in the local cache. What we need to do is
query it from SQLite and then navigate to the page. The method to get an object by ID
from the cache is just a matter of adding a new method to `ReportItem` and using sqlite-
net. Here's the code:

```
        // Add method to ReportItem...
        public static async Task<ReportItem> GetByIdAsync(int id)
        {
            var conn = StreetFooRuntime.GetUserDatabase();
            var query = conn.Table<ReportItem>().Where(v => v.Id == id);

            // return...
            return (await query.ToListAsync()).FirstOrDefault();
        }
```

Run the code, and you'll now be able to access the report singleton page from search
results.

 In Chapter 7, when we looked at sharing we added the share functionality to the Reports page. Because we can't select an item on the
Reports page anymore, in the code download you'll find that I've
moved the share functionality to the report singleton page.

Now that we have somewhere to put the options, we can finally look at the location
APIs!

# Retrieving a Current Location

We need to add an option to the app bar on the Reports page to get and display the current location. Luckily we can use an icon from Segoe UI Symbol to do this. We'll also need a button that shells out to the built-in Bing Maps app.

Here are the two styles that we need for our buttons. These need to be added to *Stand ardStyles.xaml*.

```
<!-- Add to StandardStyles.xaml -->
<Style x:Key="ShowLocationAppBarButtonStyle" TargetType="Button" BasedOn=
"{StaticResource AppBarButtonStyle}">
    <Setter Property="AutomationProperties.AutomationId" Value=
"ShowLocationAppBarButton"/>
    <Setter Property="AutomationProperties.Name" Value="Show Location"/>
    <Setter Property="Content" Value="&#xE128;"/>
</Style>

<Style x:Key="OpenMapAppBarButtonStyle" TargetType="Button" BasedOn=
"{StaticResource AppBarButtonStyle}">
    <Setter Property="AutomationProperties.AutomationId" Value=
"OpenMapAppBarButton"/>
    <Setter Property="AutomationProperties.Name" Value="Open Map"/>
    <Setter Property="Content" Value="&#xE139;"/>
</Style>
```

We can then create and add a new button to the app bar in the usual way, as we did in Chapter 4. (We'll build the command on the view-model in a moment.)

```
<!-- Modify ReportsPage.xaml -->
<Page.BottomAppBar>
    <AppBar>
        <Grid>
            <Grid.ColumnDefinitions>
                <ColumnDefinition Width="50*"/>
                <ColumnDefinition Width="50*"/>
            </Grid.ColumnDefinitions>
            <StackPanel Orientation="Horizontal" Visibility="{Binding
HasSelectedItems, Converter={StaticResource VisibilityConverter}}">
            </StackPanel>
            <StackPanel HorizontalAlignment="Right" Orientation="Horizontal"
Grid.Column="2">
                <Button Style="{StaticResource ShowLocationAppBarButtonStyle}"
Command="{Binding ShowLocationCommand}" />
                <Button Style="{StaticResource RefreshAppBarButtonStyle}"
Command="{Binding RefreshCommand}" />
                <Button Style="{StaticResource LogoutAppBarButtonStyle}"
Command="{Binding LogoutCommand}" />
            </StackPanel>
        </Grid>
    </AppBar>
</Page.BottomAppBar>
```

We also need to add the commands to our `IReportsPageViewModel`. Here's the code:

```
public interface IReportsPageViewModel : IViewModelList<ReportViewItem>
{
    ICommand RefreshCommand { get; }
    ICommand SelectionCommand { get; }
    ICommand ShowLocationCommand { get; }
}
```

 This listing reflects the change made in the code download to use `IViewModelList<T>`. That's not a change that we've made in the book, but it should be obvious to see what it does from the code.

When we actually want to get a location, we have to contend with two issues. First, the user may have turned location tracking off. In order to get any location capability at all, we need to indicate in our manifest that we intend to ask for it as part of the app's operation. When we try to get the location, Windows will display a pop up asking the user if she is sure she wants us to do that. If she says "no," we'll get an `UnauthorizedAc cessException`. If she says "yes," it *may* work. (I'll get to that in a moment.) However, if at one point she says "yes," she can still go into the permissions charm at a later date and turn it back off. Thus, each time we have to be careful to capture situations where location has been disallowed.

So, I said that location "may work." There are many reasons why it won't—for example, we might not have a GPS, or it may take too long to come back with a location fix. Similarly, then, we have to make sure we track those errors.

My proposal here is that we wrap the API that retrieves the location. (As we'll see, this happens to be done using `Windows.Devices.Geolocation.Geolocator`.) We'll create a `LocationHelper` class with a `GetCurrentLocationAsync` method. This will return a `LocationResult` containing the location in a `Geolocation` instance together with a `LocationResultCode` value that will tell us what happened.

`LocationResultCode` looks like this:

```
public enum LocationResultCode
{
    Ok = 0,
    AccessDenied = 1,
    UnknownError = 2
}
```

When we come to work with coordinates, there's a little bit of inconsistency in the APIs here. Geolocator returns instances of type Geocoordinate. The Bing Maps component we'll use later also used Geocoordinate. However, in Windows 8.1 there's a note against Geocoordinate that it's being deprecated. Because this deprecation is not complete—

i.e., other things in the Framework still use it, I've stuck with using the Geocoordinate class. Then, `LocationResult` looks like this:

```
public class LocationResult
{
    public LocationResultCode Code { get; private set; }
    public Geoposition Location { get; private set; }

    internal LocationResult(LocationResultCode code)
    {
        this.Code = code;
    }

    internal LocationResult(Geoposition location)
        : this(LocationResultCode.Ok)
    {
        this.Location = location;
    }
}
```

Finally, we can call down to the method to get the location. There isn't much to this—it's just deferring to a method that goes away and gets the location. Here's the code:

```
public static class LocationHelper
{
    public static async Task<LocationResult> GetCurrentLocationAsync()
    {
        try
        {
            var locator = new Geolocator();
            var position = await locator.GetGeopositionAsync();

            // return...
            return new LocationResult(position);
        }
        catch (UnauthorizedAccessException ex)
        {
            Debug.WriteLine("Geolocation access denied: " + ex.ToString());
            return new LocationResult(LocationResultCode.AccessDenied);
        }
        catch (Exception ex)
        {
            Debug.WriteLine("Geolocation failure: " + ex.ToString());
            return new LocationResult(LocationResultCode.UnknownError);
        }
    }
}
```

To call that, we need to add a command to our `ReportsPageViewModel`. We'll need to add both commands, but we only need to implement one. Here's the change (I've omitted quite a bit of code for brevity):

```
    public class ReportsPageViewModel : ViewModelList<ReportViewItem>,
IReportsPageViewModel
    {
        public ICommand RefreshCommand {
            get { return this.GetValue<ICommand>(); }
            private set { this.SetValue(value); } }
        public ICommand SelectionCommand {
            get { return this.GetValue<ICommand>(); }
            private set { this.SetValue(value); } }
        public ICommand ShowLocationCommand { get { return this.GetValue
<ICommand>(); } private set { this.SetValue(value); } }

        public ReportsPageViewModel(IViewModelHost host)
            : base(host)
        {
        // commands...
        this.RefreshCommand = new DelegateCommand(async (e) =>
        {
            this.Host.HideAppBar();
            await this.DoRefresh(true);

            // toast...
            string message = "I found 1 report.";
            if (this.Items.Count != 1)
                message = string.Format("I found {0} reports.",
this.Items.Count);
            var toast = new ToastNotificationBuilder(new string[] {
"Reports refreshed.", message });
            toast.ImageUri = "ms-appx:///Assets/Toast.jpg";
            toast.Update();
        });

        // open the singleton report view...
        this.SelectionCommand = new NavigateCommand<IReportPageViewModel>
(this.Host);

        // show the location...
        this.ShowLocationCommand = new DelegateCommand(async (e) =>
        {
            // get the location...
            var result = await LocationHelper.GetCurrentLocationAsync();
            if (result.Code == LocationResultCode.Ok)
            {
                await this.Host.ShowAlertAsync(string.Format("Lat: {0},
Long: {1}, Accuracy: {2}",
                    result.Location.Coordinate.Latitude,
result.Location.Coordinate.Longitude,
                    result.Location.Coordinate.Accuracy));
            }
            else
                await this.Host.ShowAlertAsync("Failed to get location: " +
result.Code.ToString());
```

```
        });
    }

    // code omitted...
}
```

 As per `IReportsPageViewModel`, this snippet contains the behind-the-scenes change to `ViewModelList<T>` that's in the code download but not in the book.

As mentioned, we can't get access to the location at all unless we modify the manifest. Figure 10-5 shows the Location capability in the manifest editor. You'll need to make this change if you want to get the location.

| Application UI | Capabilities | Declarations | Packaging |

Use this page to specify system features or devices that your app can use.

**Capabilities:**

☐ Documents Library Access
☐ Enterprise Authentication
☐ Home or Work Networking
☐ Internet (Client & Server)
☑ Internet (Client)
☑ Location
☐ Microphone
☐ Music Library
☐ Pictures Library Access
☐ Proximity
☐ Removable Storage
☐ Shared User-Certificates
☐ Text Messaging
☐ Videos Library Access
☐ Webcam

**Description:**

Enables access to the user's current location.

More information

*Figure 10-5. Setting Location capability in the manifest*

To test this, you don't need a device with GPS. Windows will have a go at getting the location back from your network connection on devices without GPS. The simulator can also be rigged to return a specific location. (We'll see this in the next section.) Either way, run the app and select the Show Location option. You'll first see a prompt, as per Figure 10-6. You'll then (hopefully) see the location, as per Figure 10-7.

*Figure 10-6. Windows asking the user to confirm location access*

*Figure 10-7. The determined location*

 If you want to confirm a value result from the location, access Google Maps and key in the latitude/longitude separated with a comma. The accuracy figure mentioned in Figure 10-7 is in meters and is unlikely to be very accurate without a GPS chip in the device.

## Using the Simulator with Location

Testing GPS functions is easier if you can feed test locations in, rather than relying on a physical GPS fix from where you are. If you're using the simulator, you can specify a location explicitly. On the simulator toolbar, click the globe option to do this. Figure 10-8 illustrates.

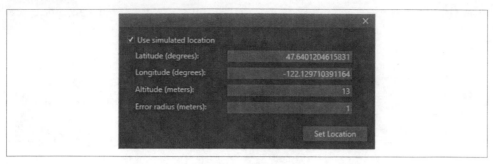

*Figure 10-8. Setting a location in the simulator*

Of course, a more practicable way to do this is to mock or fake the input into the classes that handle location. I talk more about unit testing in Appendix B.

# Integrating Maps

In the second half of this book, we'll look at integrating maps into our application. We'll discuss getting a map on the screen, and shelling out to the built-in Maps apps to get driving directions.

---

### Registering with Bing Maps

Before we can integrate maps into our application, we need to register for Bing Maps. I'm not going to go near pricing advice for using the Bing Maps API—you should take steps to ensure that you understand how the pricing structure works before you use it in your own applications. However, a test account is available for our use.

You can access the Bing Maps developer portal at the Bing Maps site (*https://www.micro soft.com/maps/developers/mobile.aspx*), or by running an online search for "bing maps developer." You're looking to create a new "trial" key, but obviously you may need to feel your way through the site.

The code download and these pages reference my key. You'll need to put your own key into your code, as there's no guarantee that my key will continue to work.

---

To display a map, we need to install the Bing Maps Visual Studio extension (VSIX). As of the time of writing, you can find this at the Visual Studio gallery (*http://visualstudio gallery.msdn.microsoft.com/*), or by searching online for "bing maps for windows store apps extension." Find, download, and install the VSIX.

When the VSIX is installed, you can add it to the StreetFoo.Client.UI project by right-clicking in Solution Explorer, selecting Add Reference, and opening up Windows→Extensions. You'll need to reference both Bing Maps for C#, C++, or Visual Basic (RP) and the Microsoft Visual C++ Runtime Package. (The latter is required to support the former.) Figure 10-9 illustrates.

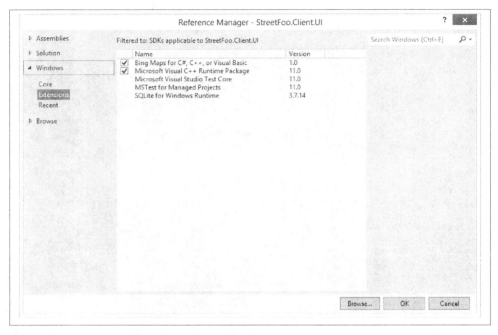

*Figure 10-9. Adding the Bing Maps extension*

## Adding the Bing Maps Control

We achieve integration by adding the Map control supplied with the library to the project. You can do this by editing the XAML in our code and adding a reference first to Bing.Maps and then to the control. The control is slightly fiddly in that by default it will take up all the space on the page, so we'll need to manually adjust the width and height.

As we do our work, we're going to want to extend the Map control to add functionality that binds in with our MVVM pattern. However, Map is sealed and thus we can't extend it directly. (You'll find this sort of thing happens a lot because of restrictions in WinRT's design.) Therefore, we'll create a new class called MyMap. This will extend ContentControl and containerize a map instance. This will also give us a way in which we can set the API key on the control centrally.

When we build this control, we need to override the ArrangeOverride method. This will tell us when our size within the container has been adjusted. We can react to this and adjust the dimensions of our containerized Map instance. Here's the code:

```
public class MyMap : ContentControl
{
```

```
        // containerized map...
        private Map InnerMap { get; set; }

        private const string BingMapsApiKey =
        "AhzHhvjTrVlqP1bs9D53ZWcLv5RsHkh_3BEFtTSfVoTjPxDl
        _PfkpbyfIh0a_H0a";

        // defines a standard zoom into street level...
        private const int StandardZoom = 15;

        public MyMap()
        {
            this.InnerMap = new Map();
            this.InnerMap.Credentials = BingMapsApiKey;

            // show it...
            this.Content = this.InnerMap;
        }

        protected override Windows.Foundation.Size ArrangeOverride
    (Windows.Foundation.Size finalSize)
        {
            this.InnerMap.Width = finalSize.Width;
            this.InnerMap.Height = finalSize.Height;
            return base.ArrangeOverride(finalSize);
        }
    }
```

We can now put that new map on the page. This needs to replace the button that we
added earlier as a placeholder. Here's the code:

```
<ContentControl Grid.Column="2" Style=
  "{StaticResource PanoramaPanel}">
    <StackPanel>
        <TextBlock Style="{StaticResource HeadingTextBlock}">
        Location</TextBlock>
        <local:MyMap Width="780" Height="550"></local:MyMap>
    </StackPanel>
</ContentControl>
```

That's actually all you have to do in order to add the map. If you run the project now,
you'll be able to go in and see the operational map, albeit at the default position and
zoom. Figure 10-10 illustrates.

*Figure 10-10. The default map embedded within ReportPage*

What we need to do next is zoom in and position the map on the item.

## Handling Input with the View

You'll have noticed that by default the map control will pick up mouse-wheel and mouse-button events, and will also sense your touching the control with your finger as you try to swipe the view from side to side.

This control has been designed to run full screen, so setting it as a thumbnail view is a little out of scope for how it's been constructed as of the time of writing. However, getting it to work as you might expect is a little fiddly. You can capture and override the mouse and pointer events to stop the scrolling, but then you need to capture and feed back those events to the container. As a specific example, pressing on the control with your finger and moving left or right shouldn't do nothing—it should scroll the container.

Moreover, there is a question as to whether you *want* to do this. If you look at how Google handles this on the normal search "application," you'll see it displays a map in the search results that you can't do anything with other than click, whereupon you end up at maps.google.com. If you want to do that, you can, and there are instructions at the end of this chapter about how to shell out to Bing Maps to do that. Alternatively, you may decide that it's actually helpful to be able to explore the map from within the app itself.

## Packaging Points for Display

Way back in Chapter 3, when we first downloaded reports from the server, we included a latitude and longitude for each item. These are in our SQLite database, but we haven't used them until now.

What we're going to do in this section is put a `Bing.Maps.Pushpin` control on the view and zoom it in. Specifically, we'll modify our `MyMap` control so that we can give it a named point to display. In a real implementation, it's more helpful to be able to provide a list of named points. However, this does make the problem more complex, so I'll show you how to add support for one via a property called `PushpinPoint`. When we set this property, we'll create a new `Bing.Maps.Pushpin` control and put it onto the map.

I'm proposing that we define a new class called `MappablePoint` and a new interface called `IMappablePoint` to do this. Implementation-wise, we already have two ways of representing points: `Windows.Devices.Geolocation.Geocoordinate` in WinRT, and `Bing.Maps.Location` in the Bing Maps library. These two are obviously implementation-specific, hence my proposal to create a new class that can cut across all of the platforms that we may want to implement against.

Generally, when you work with geolocation it's helpful to abstract everything out so that you're working with interfaces. (This isn't necessarily about mapping per se, but more about handling geodata in mobility scenarios.) This is why I've created `IMappablePoint`. We'll hit some wrinkles in terms of using interfaces with data binding in XAML, but I'll cover that.

`IMappablePoint` will have a lat/long pair, and a tag that we'll call `Name`. I've ignored the idea of altitude, as generally most business cases care only how to touch and manage things that are actually at a fixed and relatively close distance from the surface of the planet. Here's the code:

```
public interface IMappablePoint
{
    decimal Latitude { get; }
    decimal Longitude { get; }
    string Name { get; }
}
```

We're also going to need an `AdHocMappablePoint`. This will only really be used by the `MyMap` control, as there's an oddity in XAML whereby you can't create dependency properties that are based on interfaces. We have to use a concrete type, and we'll use `AdHocMappablePoint` to do that. `ReportView` and `ReportViewItem` will both support `IMappablePoint`, and we'll have to convert their geodata over to `AdHocMappablePoint` instances to get them onto the map.

Here's `AdHocMappablePoint`:

```
public class AdHocMappablePoint : IMappablePoint
{
    public decimal Latitude { get; private set; }
    public decimal Longitude { get; private set; }
    public string Name { get; private set; }

    public AdHocMappablePoint(IMappablePoint point)
        : this(point.Latitude, point.Longitude, point.Name)
    {
    }

    public AdHocMappablePoint(decimal latitude, decimal longitude,
        string name)
    {
        this.Latitude = latitude;
        this.Longitude = longitude;
        this.Name = name;
    }
}
```

 I decided to clone the supplied geodata in the first overload because
I wanted to take an immutable approach with that data for no other
reason than that I didn't want to deal with some dangling object
instance's data.

I mentioned that ReportView would support IMappablePoint. This class already has
compatible Latitude and Longitude properties. We do need explicit support for IMap
pablePoint.Name, however. Here's that change; I've removed a lot of code for brevity.

```
public class ReportItem : ModelItem, IMappablePoint
{
    // key field...
    [AutoIncrement, PrimaryKey]
    public int Id { get { return GetValue<int>(); }
        set { SetValue(value); } }

    // other fields...
    [Unique, JsonMapping("_id")]
    public string NativeId { get { return GetValue<string>(); }
        set { SetValue(value); } }
    public string Title { get { return GetValue<string>(); }
        set { SetValue(value); } }
    public string Description { get { return GetValue<string>(); }
        set { SetValue(value); } }
    public decimal Latitude { get { return GetValue<decimal>(); }
        set { SetValue(value); } }
    public decimal Longitude { get { return GetValue<decimal>(); }
        set { SetValue(value); } }

    public ReportItem()
```

```
        {
        }

        // code omitted...

        string IMappablePoint.Name
        {
            get
            {
                return this.Title;
            }
        }
    }
```

But, as we know, we don't show ReportItem instances in our presentation. We show ReportViewItem, so this also has to support IMappablePoint. This also needs to bring forward the geoproperties. Here's the code (again, I've omitted much of it):

```
    public class ReportViewItem : WrappingModelItem<ReportItem>, IMappablePoint
    {
        public ReportViewItem(ReportItem item)
            : base(item)
        {
        }

        public string NativeId { get { return this.InnerItem.NativeId; } }
        public string Title { get { return this.InnerItem.Title; } }
        public string Description { get { return this.InnerItem.Description; } }
        public decimal Latitude { get { return this.InnerItem.Latitude; } }
        public decimal Longitude { get { return this.InnerItem.Longitude; } }

        // code omitted...

        string IMappablePoint.Name
        {
            get
            {
                return ((IMappablePoint)this.InnerItem).Name;
            }
        }
    }
```

To recap, then, we're going to change MyMap so that it can support one point through a property called PushpinPoint. This property will be of type AdHocMappablePoint because, as I mentioned before, dependency properties cannot be of interface types.

The first thing we need to do is to create a custom data-binding converter that will take an "object" and work out how to transform it into an AdHocMappablePoint. Here's the code for IMappablePointConverter:

```
    public class IMappablePointConverter : IValueConverter
    {
```

```
        public object Convert(object value, Type targetType, object parameter,
        string language)
        {
            if(value == null)
                return null;

            if (value is AdHocMappablePoint)
                return (AdHocMappablePoint)value;
            else if (value is IMappablePoint)
                return new AdHocMappablePoint((IMappablePoint)value);
            else
                throw new NotSupportedException(string.Format("Cannot handle
                '{0}'.", value.GetType()));
        }

        public object ConvertBack(object value, Type targetType, object
        parameter, string language)
        {
            throw new NotImplementedException();
        }
    }
```

As you've done before, you'll need to go into *App.xaml* and globally enable that converter. Here's the change:

```
<!-- Modify App.xaml -->
<Application
    x:Class="StreetFoo.Client.UI.App"
    xmlns="http://schemas.microsoft.com/winfx/2006/xaml/presentation"
    xmlns:x="http://schemas.microsoft.com/winfx/2006/xaml"
    xmlns:local="using:StreetFoo.Client.UI"
    xmlns:common="using:StreetFoo.Client.UI.Common"
    >

    <Application.Resources>
        <ResourceDictionary>

            <common:BooleanToVisibilityConverter x:Key="VisibilityConverter" />
            <common:BooleanNegationConverter x:Key="NegationConverter" />
            <common:BooleanToVisibilityNegationConverter x:Key=
            "BooleanToVisibilityNegationConverter"/>
            <common:IMappablePointConverter x:Key="IMappablePointConverter" />

            <ResourceDictionary.MergedDictionaries>
                <ResourceDictionary Source="Common/StandardStyles.xaml"/>
            </ResourceDictionary.MergedDictionaries>

        </ResourceDictionary>
    </Application.Resources>
</Application>
```

Accepting that we've yet to build the `PushpinPoint` property on `MyMap`, here's the change to the XAML to bind up the property to the `Item` property exposed by the view-model, via our new converter:

```xaml
<ContentControl Grid.Column="2" Style="{StaticResource
PanoramaPanel}">
    <StackPanel>
        <TextBlock Style="{StaticResource HeadingTextBlock}">
        Location</TextBlock>
        <local:MyMap Width="780" Height="550"
                    PushpinPoint="{Binding Item, Converter=
                    {StaticResource IMappablePointConverter}}">
                    </local:MyMap>
    </StackPanel>
</ContentControl>
```

The final background bit that we need to do is provide a way for converting `IMappable Point` instances into `Bing.Maps.Location` instances. I'm going to propose something that's a little overkill, but I want to illustrate a technique.

If we create an extension method in `IMappablePoint` within the Windows Store app project (as opposed to the UI-agnostic project) called `ToLocation`, we can use this to create `Location` instances. It's overkill because we only have to do it once, but it is a helpful technique. `IMappablePoint` doesn't know anything about Bing Maps or Windows 8 apps, but we can extend it fluidly without much heartache through extension methods. Here's the code:

```csharp
public static class IMappablePointExtender
{
    public static Location ToLocation(this IMappablePoint point)
    {
        return new Location((double)point.Latitude, (double)point.Longitude);
    }
}
```

We can now finally write code to add the pushpin!

## Showing Points on the Map

Adding controls to the map surface is a little weird. The Bing Maps control will let you render *any* control on its surface. This makes it fantastically powerful. You're not limited to little icons and special things Microsoft happens to give you. Anything that inherits from `DependencyObject` (i.e., basically everything in XAML) you can render on a map.

The API is a little strange, however. You have to call a static method on `MapLayer`, passing in the object that you want to display and the location. You then add the object to the `Children` collection of the `Map` much as you normally would. Here's the code:

```csharp
// Add method to MyMap...
public Pushpin AddPushpin(IMappablePoint point)
```

```
{
    // create a pin and set its position...
    var pin = new Pushpin();
    pin.Text = point.Name;
    MapLayer.SetPosition(pin, point.ToLocation());

    // ...then add it...
    this.InnerMap.Children.Add(pin);

    // return...
    return pin;
}
```

However, if this is all we do, we'll just get a map showing the whole world with a tiny dot over the location. What we need to do is zoom the map in.

Normally, you would zoom the map in by giving it bounds of a lat/long square that you want to show in the viewport. This is easy enough to do if you have multiple points, but I'd say it is harder to do if you have only a single point. The reason I raise this is that the "zoom level" value that we need to supply when zooming doesn't have meaning in the real world. You have to fiddle with values until you find one that does what you want. (The zoom level is an internal value that has more to do with structuring and rendering the view than being something necessarily consumable from outside.) Back when we first defined MyMap, I added a constant called StandardZoom that was set to 15. This "felt" like the right value for what I was trying to do.

Here's the AddPushpinAndCenterAndZoom method:

```
// Add method to MyMap...
public void AddPushpinAndCenterAndZoom(IMappablePoint point, bool
animate = true)
{
    var pin = this.AddPushpin(point);

    // show...
    var duration = MapAnimationDuration.Default;
    if (!(animate))
        duration = MapAnimationDuration.None;

    // show...
    this.InnerMap.SetView(point.ToLocation(), StandardZoom, duration);
}
```

That method allows you to turn off the animation through the animate parameter. Animation is actually really helpful when rendering maps, as it clearly clues people into where things are in terms of their relative position in space. However, when we initialize the view it's distracting, so we'll turn animations off when we set PushpinPoint.

Finally, here's MyMap showing the dependency property implementation and the helper method that creates the pin:

```
    // Add members to MyMap...
    public class MyMap : ContentControl
    {
        // containerized map...
        private Map InnerMap { get; set; }

        // dependency properties...
        public static readonly DependencyProperty PushpinPointProperty =
            DependencyProperty.Register("PushpinPoint",
                typeof(AdHocMappablePoint), typeof(MyMap),
            new PropertyMetadata(null, (d, e) => ((MyMap)d).SetPushpinPoint
((AdHocMappablePoint)e.NewValue)));

        // credentials...
        private const string BingMapsApiKey =
"AhzHhvjTrVlqP1bs9D53ZWcLv5RsHkh_3BEFtTSfVoTjPxDl_PfkpbyfIh0a_H0a";

        // defines a standard zoom into street level...
        private const int StandardZoom = 15;

         // code omitted...

        public AdHocMappablePoint PushpinPoint
        {
            get { return (AdHocMappablePoint)GetValue(PushpinPointProperty); }
            set { SetValue(PushpinPointProperty, value); }
        }

        private void SetPushpinPoint(IMappablePoint point)
        {
            // set...
            this.ClearPushpins();

            // set...
            if (point != null)
                this.AddPushpinAndCenterAndZoom(point, false);
        }

        private void ClearPushpins()
        {
            this.InnerMap.Children.Clear();
        }
    }
```

Run the code now, and a pushpin will be created and the map centered and zoomed in
around it. Figure 10-11 illustrates.

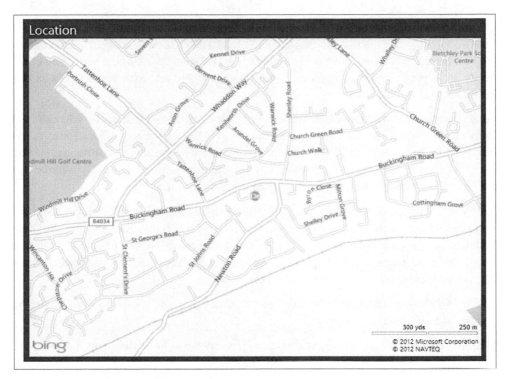

*Figure 10-11. The map and pushpin successfully rendered*

# Shelling to the Maps App

We're going to round off this discussion by having a look at how we can shell out of our app and into the built-in Bing Maps app.

A lot of apps that include mapping try to reproduce all possible mapping functionality within the app. My view is that this is a mistake, as it's often impractical to do as good a job of navigation as the built-in app on the device. (This happens regardless of device platform—this isn't a Windows-only thing.) Compare, for example, the number of apps that shell out to a browser to display a web page, as opposed to hosting a browser internally.

It is possible to get our app to open the Bing Maps app, and we can even have it plot driving directions for us by asking the app to open a URI with the bingmaps protocol. The Bing Maps app registers this protocol precisely for this sort of integration.

As of this writing, there aren't APIs within the Bing Maps library to do this, so we'll have to construct the URIs manually. However, I've heard this will be coming in later versions. So two things: first, watch out to see if there is an easier way to do this when you come to do it in production, and second, your mileage may vary with these URLs as this interface isn't documented.

One wrinkle we have, though, is that through this method—as it stands—you can't put pins on the map. Thus, if we use it just to zoom in to one of the report locations, it's not that helpful because all we'll see is a map; it's devoid of context and confusing. (If you see it, you have no sense as to why you opened the map to that location.) To make this work in a half-decent way, we'll actually ask for driving directions.

However, whereas in a normal app you're likely to be somewhere close to where these sample locations actually are, in this app you'll likely live in another country. So these illustrations get driving directions from a fixed point in the UK that happens to be close to all of the locations in the sample data. As I say, in a production app you'll want to use the result from `Geolocator.GetGeolocationAsync`.

We already have an app bar button defined that we can use to shell into Bing Maps. We just need to define the protocol.

The most straightforward thing to do is to ask for a point to be centered on the viewport. If we want to do that, we can issue a URI like this:

```
bingmaps://open/?cp=51.99437~-0.7322&lvl=15&trfc=1
```

That URL provides the point, a zoom level (15, again), and an indication as to whether we want to see traffic info (we do). The only real weirdness there is that the lat/long pair is split by a tilde (~), whereas you'd normally use a comma.

Without the ability to put a pushpin on the map, the only way to give context as to why we've shown the map is with driving directions. It so happens that all of the sample points in the database are near the geek-friendly Bletchley Park in the UK, so we'll get driving directions from there. The coordinates of Hut 1 at Bletchley Park are 51.9972, −0.7422.

To do that, we'll need a URL like this:

```
bingmaps://open/?rtp=pos.51.99720_-0.74220~pos.51.99437_-0.72629&trfc=1
```

We'll create a method called `OpenMapsAppAsync` to `LocationHelper` that will construct that URI and then issue it. Here's the code:

```
// Add method to LocationHelper...
internal static async Task OpenMapsAppAsync(IMappablePoint from,
IMappablePoint to, bool showTraffic = true)
    {
        string trafficFlag = "0";
        if (showTraffic)
            trafficFlag = "1";
```

```
                // create the URI...
                var uri = string.Format
("bingmaps://open/?rtp=pos.{0:n5}_{1:n5}~pos.{2:n5}_{3:n5}&trfc={4}",
from.Latitude, from.Longitude,
                to.Latitude, to.Longitude, trafficFlag);
            Debug.WriteLine("Navigating: {0}", uri);

            // open...
            await Launcher.LaunchUriAsync(new Uri(uri));
        }
```

All that we have to do then is rig it into the ReportPageViewModel class. We've already got a command for it defined, and we've already bound up the app bar on the report page to the command. Thus, this change is all we have to do, and we're golden:

```
            // Modify constructor in ReportPageViewModel...
            public ReportPageViewModel(IViewModelHost host)
                : base(host)
            {
                this.OpenMapCommand = new DelegateCommand(async (args) => {
                    var from = new AdHocMappablePoint(51.9972M, -0.7422M,
                        "Bletchley");
                    await LocationHelper.OpenMapsAppAsync(from, this.Item);
                });
            }
```

Run the code now and open a report. Open the app bar and press the Open Map button. You'll see something like Figure 10-12.

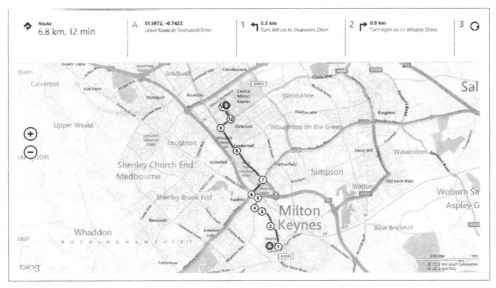

*Figure 10-12. Driving directions in the launched Bing Maps*

And that's it. As I said, it's likely there will be some refinements to the way that we integrate with Bing Maps down the line, but we can at least integrate proper mapping into our applications.

# CHAPTER 11

# Using the Camera

In this chapter, we're going to look at using the camera. While in previous chapters I've endeavored to make the examples applicable to both retail and LOB app use, basic use of the camera is more LOB than retail.

The issue with the camera in retail is that just taking a photo is actually very easy. All you need to use is the `CameraCaptureUI`, and it'll return a file containing the photo. (You can also use this class to capture video, although we won't be looking at that in detail in this chapter.)

In LOB applications, or more specifically in *field service applications* (i.e., people in the field undertake work for the organization), there are some basic use cases for the camera. You typically need to use the camera to capture work that needs to be done (e.g., inspectors visit an estate and proactively look for problems to solve like graffiti or trash), or to capture the state of something before and/or after work has been done (e.g., you take a photo of a broken sink before you fix it, and again after you fix it). A common related use case is to capture a photograph of the premises if the operative gets to the site but cannot gain access.

All of those scenarios follow roughly the same process: take a photo, store it on a device, and send it to the server when you can.

This chapter will mainly center on building out the functionality to create new problem reports, which will include, among other things, capturing a photo and storing on disk, as well as storing our problem report data in the local SQLite database—that is, staging the new report so that it is ready for upload. (We won't do the actual upload until Chapter 15.)

We'll also look at how we can resize the image to make storing quantities of images "gentler" in terms of device storage and bandwidth for transmission.

# Capturing Photos

In the last chapter, we created ReportPage to create a singleton read-only view of a page. In this chapter, we're going to create EditReportPage, which will be used to create an editable view of the report. We'll either pass this a blank, new ReportViewItem instance to create a new item, or pass it an instance created from the database data to edit an existing item.

We do, however, need to think first about how we're going to get these new problem reports up to the server, although, as mentioned, we're not actually going to do this until Chapter 15.

At the moment, if we have a report in our SQLite database we know that it will have originated on the server. If we are able to locally create new items, we'll have some items that are from the server and some items that are not. I'm proposing creating a new field on the report called Status that will indicate (among other things) whether the report is on the server or not. This property will use an enumeration that at this point has the values of Unchanged (i.e., the server gave it to us) or New (i.e., we created it locally).

Similarly, if we have changed an item in the local SQLite database that is marked as New we need to be able to indicate that it has been Updated. The final case is that we need to be able to indicate that a local item has been Deleted.

When we get to Chapter 15, we'll write code that examines this Status property to determine whether we need to send up new or changed items, or delete existing items, depending on the value of that property.

Where this is relevant to this chapter is that we already know that in order to put the photo on the screen on the Reports page, we use the native ID of the item to build up the filename. (Remember, if we have a native ID ABCDEF, the local path on disk where the image gets downloaded is *~/LocalState/ReportImages/ABCDEF.jpg*.) When we insert a new report, we also need to store the image in *ReportImages*, but we won't have an ID to go with it, as we're currently dependent on the server supplying one. Thus, for items in state New we'll set the NativeId property to be a new GUID. This gives us a valid, noncolliding value from which to dereference the image. So the process will be:

1. Create a new ReportViewItem and pass it into EditReportPage and EditReport PageViewModel.

2. Do data binding as normal to populate the fields.

3. At user request, we'll use CameraCaptureUI to get a photo from the camera. This image will be stored on disk as *TempState* until it's time to be used. (See Chapter 7 if you need a refresher on how to work with files.)

4. When the user clicks Save, we'll validate the data. If the item is new, we'll set its status to New and its native ID to the value returned by Guid.NewGuid(), and then store the image in *ReportImages*.

5. Ultimately, when we're able we'll call up to the server with the report data and the new image.

 What we haven't covered here—and actually we won't do this in the pages here, but the code download for this chapter will support it— is the scenario where the user goes in to edit a report, downloaded from the server, and takes a new photo. If we do this, we'll flag the fact that this has happened in another property called ImageUpda ted in ReportItem.

Let's get started with building out the UI.

# Creating EditReportPage

Structurally, EditReportPage will be very similar to ReportPage, which we built in the last chapter. As it is similar work, I'll try to work quite quickly through aspects you've already seen.

We're not going to worry about location so much in this chapter, other than to capture the location because we need it to create a valid record. What this means is that we won't put a map on the screen on the edit page, although in a production app you probably would want to in order to help the user understand that he had indeed captured the correct location. (You can use the Bing Maps control that we used in the last chapter to do this if you need to.)

All we'll do is call LocationHelper.GetCurrentLocationAsync (which we built in the last chapter) and render the coordinates on the screen.

What we're looking to build is something like Figure 11-1.

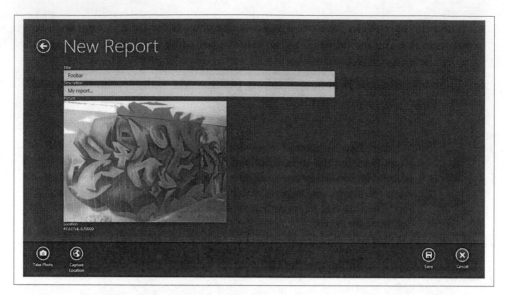

*Figure 11-1. The objective: creating a new report*

## Building EditReportPageViewModel and Its View-Model

Our new view-model interface will extend IViewModelSingleton<ReportViewItem> in the same way that we saw in the last chapter. In addition, we'll have two commands— one for handling taking a photo, and one for updating the location. We also need to expose an image that we can render on the page. This requires loading the image into a BitmapImage instance.

To make our lives easier, we'll add a property that indicates whether the item is new or not. (We'll use this when we want to display a different caption when we are in new or edit mode.)

Here's the definition of IEditReportPageViewModel:

```
public interface IEditReportPageViewModel : IViewModelSingleton
<ReportViewItem>
{
    ICommand TakePhotoCommand { get; }
    ICommand CaptureLocationCommand { get; }

    // are we new?
    bool IsNew { get; }

    // image presentation...
    BitmapImage Image { get; }
    bool HasImage { get; }
}
```

Going over the XAML side, we'll need a new `EditReportPage` created, and we'll need to create some styles for the app bar buttons. On the app bar we'll need options for Save and Cancel, as well as Take Photo and Capture Location. We already have a style for the Save button (Visual Studio creates it for us), so we only need to create the other three. We can use icons defined in the Segoe UI Symbol font. Here are the styles to add to *StandardStyles.xaml*:

```xml
<!-- Add styles to StandardStyles.xaml -->
<Style x:Key="SaveAppBarButtonStyle" TargetType="Button" BasedOn=
"{StaticResource AppBarButtonStyle}">
    <Setter Property="AutomationProperties.AutomationId" Value=
"SaveAppBarButton"/>
    <Setter Property="AutomationProperties.Name" Value="Save"/>
    <Setter Property="Content" Value="&#xE105;"/>
</Style>
<Style x:Key="CancelAppBarButtonStyle" TargetType="Button" BasedOn=
"{StaticResource AppBarButtonStyle}">
    <Setter Property="AutomationProperties.AutomationId" Value=
"CancelAppBarButton"/>
    <Setter Property="AutomationProperties.Name" Value="Cancel"/>
    <Setter Property="Content" Value="&#xE10A;"/>
</Style>

<Style x:Key="TakePhotoAppBarButtonStyle" TargetType="Button" BasedOn=
"{StaticResource AppBarButtonStyle}">
    <Setter Property="AutomationProperties.AutomationId" Value=
"TakePhotoAppBarButton"/>
    <Setter Property="AutomationProperties.Name" Value="Photo"/>
    <Setter Property="Content" Value="&#xE114;"/>
</Style>

<Style x:Key="CaptureLocationAppBarButtonStyle" TargetType="Button"
BasedOn="{StaticResource AppBarButtonStyle}">
    <Setter Property="AutomationProperties.AutomationId" Value=
"CaptureLocationAppBarButton"/>
    <Setter Property="AutomationProperties.Name" Value="Capture Location"/>
    <Setter Property="Content" Value="&#xE128;"/>
</Style>
```

We can now put the app bar on the page. Because the app bar is integral to the operation of the form, and because the user can't actually do anything with his editing until he presses Save, we can make the app bar "sticky" and open it from the start. We can do this in markup on the page. Here's the markup for the app bar:

```xml
<!-- Add markup to EditReportPage.xaml -->
<Page.BottomAppBar>
    <AppBar IsSticky="true" IsOpen="true">
        <Grid>
            <Grid.ColumnDefinitions>
                <ColumnDefinition Width="auto"/>
                <ColumnDefinition Width="50*"/>
```

```
                </Grid.ColumnDefinitions>
                <StackPanel Orientation="Horizontal">
                        <Button Style="{StaticResource TakePhotoAppBarButtonStyle}"
Command="{Binding TakePhotoCommand}" />
                        <Button Style="{StaticResource
CaptureLocationAppBarButtonStyle}" Command="{Binding CaptureLocationCommand}" />
                </StackPanel>
                <StackPanel HorizontalAlignment="Right" Orientation="Horizontal"
Grid.Column="1" Margin="0,1,5,-1">
                        <Button Style="{StaticResource SaveAppBarButtonStyle}"
Command="{Binding SaveCommand}" />
                        <Button Style="{StaticResource CancelAppBarButtonStyle}"
Command="{Binding CancelCommand}" />
                </StackPanel>
            </Grid>
        </AppBar>
    </Page.BottomAppBar>
```

I've chosen to split the items onto the left and right to create a logical separation of their
function. It's convention to put controls relating to save/close/cancel on the right. A side
effect of splitting them in this way across the whole width of the device is that a user
holding the device and working the screen with her thumbs can access both sets of
buttons equally well. (Besides, as discussed in Chapter 5 this is actually in Microsoft's
user interface guidelines for Windows Store apps.)

For the caption, we're going to have two TextBlock labels that will indicate whether the
view is in create mode or edit mode. I've done it like this for localization and separation
of concerns. When we get to localization in Chapter 15, you'll see the advantage there
—the XAML subsystem is able to swap out the localized string on the UI surface with
slightly less lifting than if we did it in the view-model programmatically. This segues
nicely into the point that if we did it in the view-model we're slightly muddying our
concerns, in that it's better not to have the view-model making presentation decisions
if we can help it.

Here's the caption that can show one of a pair of labels depending on the value of IsNew:

```
        <!-- Modify markup in EditReportPage.xaml -->
        <!-- Back button and page title -->
        <Grid>
            <Grid.ColumnDefinitions>
                <ColumnDefinition Width="Auto"/>
                <ColumnDefinition Width="*"/>
            </Grid.ColumnDefinitions>
            <Button x:Name="backButton" Click="GoBack" IsEnabled="{Binding Frame
.CanGoBack, ElementName=pageRoot}" Style="{StaticResource BackButtonStyle}"/>
            <TextBlock Grid.Column="1" Text="New Report" Style="{StaticResource
PageHeaderTextStyle}" Visibility="{Binding IsNew, Converter={StaticResource
BooleanToVisibilityConverter}}"/>
            <TextBlock Grid.Column="1" Text="Edit Report" Style="{StaticResource
PageHeaderTextStyle}" Visibility="{Binding IsNew, Converter={StaticResource
```

```
BooleanToVisibilityNegationConverter}}"/>
     </Grid>
```

We saw the form itself in Figure 11-1. What we didn't see was that where the image sits on the design surface, we will actually have two controls. We'll show a `TextBlock` control if the user has not specified an image, or we'll show an `Image` control if she has. We'll use the value of the `HasImage` property on the view-model to choose which one to display.

Here's the markup for that:

```
<!-- Add markup to EditReportPage.xaml -->
<Grid Grid.Row="1">
    <Grid.ColumnDefinitions>
        <ColumnDefinition Width="120"/>
        <ColumnDefinition Width="800"/>
    </Grid.ColumnDefinitions>

    <StackPanel Grid.Column="1">
        <TextBlock Text="Title"></TextBlock>
        <TextBox Text="{Binding Item.Title, Mode=TwoWay}"></TextBox>
        <TextBlock Text="Description"></TextBlock>
        <TextBox Text="{Binding Item.Description, Mode=TwoWay}">
</TextBox>

        <TextBlock Text="Picture"></TextBlock>

        <!-- the placeholder -->
        <Border Width="480" Height="360" BorderThickness="2" BorderBrush=
"White" HorizontalAlignment="Left"
                Visibility="{Binding HasImage, Converter={StaticResource
BooleanToVisibilityNegationConverter}}">
            <TextBlock HorizontalAlignment="Center" VerticalAlignment=
"Center">(No picture)</TextBlock>
        </Border>

        <!-- the image -->
        <Image Width="480" Height="360" HorizontalAlignment="Left"
Source="{Binding Image}"
                Visibility="{Binding HasImage, Converter={StaticResource
BooleanToVisibilityConverter}}">
        </Image>

        <TextBlock Text="Location"></TextBlock>
        <TextBlock Text="{Binding Item.LocationNarrative}"></TextBlock>
    </StackPanel>

</Grid>
```

The only thing that we haven't discussed is `LocationNarrative`. This just needs to return the latitude/longitude pair separated by a comma for display. We can add this now. While we're there, we also need a method to set the coordinates internally within a `ReportViewItem` instance from an `IMappablePoint` instance. (We'll see this in action later.) However, when the coordinates change, we also need to signal that the narrative has changed. We can do this by overriding OnPropertyChanged and listening for changes to the Latitude and Longitude properties. You'll note that this method is inefficient—we raise two signals that LocationNarrative has changed per pair of co-ordinates. An alternative approach—and actually a better approach if you want a cleaner class design—is to build a custom converter class that you can bind to instead of creating this separate property. Although we're not going to use a custom converter class, I wanted to show you this alternative approach that you could use as a shortcut.

Here's the code:

```
// Add method and property to ReportViewItem...
internal void SetLocation(IMappablePoint point)
{
    this.InnerItem.SetLocation(point);

    // update...
    this.OnPropertyChanged("LocationNarrative");
}

public string LocationNarrative
{
    get
    {
        if (this.Latitude != 0 && this.Longitude != 0)
            return string.Format("{0:n5},{1:n5}", this.Latitude,
this.Longitude);
        else
            return string.Empty;
    }
}
```

However, the ReportItem doesn't have SetLocation defined. Here's that change:

```
// Add method to ReportItem...
internal void SetLocation(IMappablePoint point)
{
    this.Latitude = point.Latitude;
    this.Longitude = point.Longitude;
}
```

Another little thing to do: we need to set up the view-model on the EditReportPage code. Here's that change:

```
// Modify EditReportPage...
public sealed partial class EditReportPage : StreetFooPage
{

    public EditReportPage()
    {
        this.InitializeComponent();
```

```
        this.InitializeViewModel();
    }

    // code omitted...
```

Let's now turn our attention back toward completing the implementation of `EditRe portPageViewModel`.

In terms of fields in the class, we'll need to store the two commands and also store a reference to the image on disk when we capture one from the camera. As mentioned, `CameraCaptureUI` will create an image on disk in *TempState* for us to use. Here's the first part of the view-model:

```
    public class EditReportPageViewModel : ViewModelSingleton<ReportViewItem>,
IEditReportPageViewModel
    {
        public ICommand TakePhotoCommand {
            get { return this.GetValue<ICommand>(); }
            private set {  this.SetValue(value); } }
        public ICommand CaptureLocationCommand {
            get { return  this.GetValue<ICommand>(); }
            private set { this.SetValue(value); } }

        // holds the image in TempState that we're displaying...
        private IStorageFile TempImageFile { get; set; }

        public EditReportPageViewModel(IViewModelHost host)
            : base(host)
        {
            // set up the commands...
            this.TakePhotoCommand = new DelegateCommand(async (args) => await
this.CaptureImageAsync());
            this.CaptureLocationCommand = new DelegateCommand(async (args)
                => await this.CaptureLocationAsync());
        }
    }
```

The first thing we'll handle is the location code. This will be updated when the view is activated, and from time to time if the user explicitly asks for it to be done via the app bar button. Here's the code; notice how we're reusing `LocationHelper` from Chapter 11:

```
    // Add methods to EditReportPageViewModel...
    public override async void Activated(object args)
    {
        base.Activated(args);

        // capture...
        await CaptureLocationAsync();
    }

    private async Task CaptureLocationAsync()
    {
```

```
        var result = await LocationHelper.GetCurrentLocationAsync();
        if (result.Code == LocationResultCode.Ok)
            this.Item.SetLocation(result.ToMappablePoint());
    }
```

The last thing we'll do in this section is to add the code that handles changing the caption depending on whether the item is new or not. The IsNew property will have to handle the situation where it's called before the Item property is initialized. We'll also flag that the property has changed when the item initialization happens. Here's the code:

```
// Add property and method to EditReportViewItem...
public bool IsNew
{
    get
    {
        // we may not have an item yet...
        if (this.Item == null)
            return true;
        else
            return this.Item.Id == 0;
    }
}

protected override void ItemChanged()
{
    base.ItemChanged();

    // update the caption...
    this.OnPropertyChanged("IsNew");
}
```

Before we go on to taking the picture, let's look at adding functionality to the base class to allow us to save and cancel.

## Saving and Canceling

One of the points of creating ViewModelSingleton<T> was so that we could add in functionality that's typical when working with a view of a single item. An example of this sort of functionality is a common approach to canceling, saving, and validating when we're in the sort of edit mode that we're in now. Thus, we'll go ahead and add methods to support those.

This will illustrate an interesting situation with async/await. Let's say you want to create a Save virtual method on a base class, the signature being protected virtual void Save(). A class that specializes from that base class may need to call async methods from the override of that method. The developer can do that by decorating the method with the async keyword. However, because the method returns void and not Task, it cannot be awaited. Without the await part, you still get asynchrony, but you also get in a total mess because you cannot control the process. You'll end up "lost in space" insofar as the holistic operation goes.

What we can do, then, is create our overrideable methods as "async friendly" without necessarily needing async functionality. We can do this by making them return a Task instance and then using Task.FromResult<T> to get a task to return. That returned task is effectively faked—it'll contain a result and appear to the caller that it has been completed already. The important part is that it allows the caller to do an await.

In these methods, we will create a ValidateAsync method that will return an Error Bucket instance containing problems. That method will be virtual so that the specializing class can do the validation. The SaveAsync method won't be virtual. It will call ValidateAsync using await and then defer to a virtual helper method that will do the actual work.

Here's the code to add to ViewModelSingleton<T>:

```
// Add methods to ViewModelSingleton<T>...
protected virtual Task<ErrorBucket> ValidateAsync()
{
    // return an empty error bucket (i.e. "success")...
    return Task.FromResult<ErrorBucket>(new ErrorBucket());
}

protected async Task<bool> SaveAsync()
{
    // validate...
    var result = await ValidateAsync();
    if (result.HasErrors)
    {
        await this.Host.ShowAlertAsync(result);
        return false;
    }

    // ok...
    await DoSaveAsync();
    return true;
}

protected virtual Task DoSaveAsync()
{
    return Task.FromResult<bool>(true);
}
```

Notice that DoSaveAsync returns a value from Task.FromResult<bool>(true). Because the method isn't marked as async, we have to return something; however, the only implementation on FromResult provided by WinRT requires a type argument. A common trick is to return a Boolean value in this way. It really doesn't matter what you return as the method is defined as returning a Task instance that doesn't have type parameters; the caller won't be expecting a particular type, as the method returns a vanilla Task.

The default operation of CancelAsync will be to call the host and tell it to GoBack. Again, we'll use the "Boolean task" trick from before, as this method doesn't actually await anything.

```
// Add method to ViewModelSingleton<T>...
protected virtual Task CancelAsync()
{
    // go back...
    this.Host.GoBack();

    // return...
    return Task.FromResult<bool>(true);
}
```

We'll need a way of calling those, and one way to do this is to create standard commands on the view-model that defer to the methods. That's exactly what we'll do.

In the IViewModelSingleton interface, we can define the properties for the commands:

```
public interface IViewModelSingleton<T> : IViewModel
    where T : ModelItem
{
    ICommand SaveCommand { get; }
    ICommand CancelCommand { get; }

    T Item { get; }
}
```

And in the actual class, we can implement them. Here's the code (I've omitted parts of ViewModelSingleton<T> for brevity):

```
public abstract class ViewModelSingleton<T> : ViewModel,
    IViewModelSingleton<T>
    where T : ModelItem
{
    // save and cancel commands...
    public ICommand SaveCommand { get { return this.GetValue<ICommand>(); }
private set { this.SetValue(value); } }
    public ICommand CancelCommand { get { return this.GetValue<ICommand>();
} private set { this.SetValue(value); } }

    // holds the base item that we're mapped to...
    private T _item;

    protected ViewModelSingleton(IViewModelHost host)
        : base(host)
    {
        this.SaveCommand = new DelegateCommand(async (args) => await
SaveAsync());
        this.CancelCommand = new DelegateCommand(async (args) => await
```

```
        CancelAsync());
        }

        // code omitted...
    }
```

We'll now look at how to display the form and ultimately take a picture.

# Adding the New Option

We'll add a button to the app bar on the Reports page that allows us to create a new item. Oddly, although we are given an app bar style called AddAppBarButtonStyle, which happens to have the caption "Add," the convention in the built-in Windows 8 apps is that the option to create new items should be labeled "New." Hence, the first thing to do is create a new style called NewAppBarButtonStyle that will use the same icon:

```
<!-- Add to StandardStyles.xaml -->
<Style x:Key="NewAppBarButtonStyle" TargetType="Button" BasedOn=
"{StaticResource AppBarButtonStyle}">
        <Setter Property="AutomationProperties.AutomationId" Value=
"NewAppBarButton"/>
        <Setter Property="AutomationProperties.Name" Value="New"/>
        <Setter Property="Content" Value="&#xE109;"/>
</Style>
```

I won't go through how to add the button to the app bar, or how to wire up a command, as we've done it a few times—take a look at Chapter 5 for the first run-through of this. I also won't show how to create a command called NewCommand in IReportsPageView Model. I'll assume that you can make those changes to the Reports page, although of course you'll find it properly implemented in the code download.

The actual implementation of that command could take some explanation, though, as we haven't seen it before. EditReportPageViewModel requires an instance of a Report ViewItem, and we'll need to create a blank one to use. Here's the modified constructor of ReportsPageViewModel. I've omitted some code for brevity.

```
        public ReportsPageViewModel()
        {
            // code omitted...

            // add...
            this.NewCommand = new DelegateCommand((e) => this.Host.ShowView
(typeof(IEditReportPageViewModel), new ReportViewItem(new ReportItem())));
        }
```

# Handling Temporary Files

So we know that we can use `CameraCaptureUI` to take a picture, and we know that picture will get stored on disk in *TempState*.

One of the problems with *TempState* is that it's not automatically cleaned up for us. Should the device's disk come under pressure, Windows will treat any files that it finds in any *TempState* folder belonging to any installed Windows 8 apps as fair game for deletion, but it's certainly possible for us to misuse *TempState* to the point where we're not creating a great experience for the user not just for our app, but systemwide. (Our massive temporary state could prevent the user from downloading his email mailbox, for example.)

Personally, I think it would have been better to have Windows manage these folders for us. It would have been easy enough to clear down this folder when the app stopped, and to rig in some sort of proactive cleanup mechanism within the OS. However, such a thing would take precious cycles, especially on Windows RT devices. To that end, we have to manage all of this ourselves.

What we need to do is be careful not to create orphaned temporary files as part of the photo-taking process. For example, if we take a photo and then take another photo, we can safely delete the first one, as it's been implicitly discarded. These images in the 1280×720 resolution that I was using took up about 150KB each, which may not seem like a lot, but over many months of heavy use could easily clog up the device unnecessarily.

In addition, if the user cancels the edit operation, we also have to be careful to remove any file that we may have taken during the aborted process. Although we'll talk more about application lifetime in Chapter 15, we aren't told when our process is unloaded; thus, if we happen to have a temporary image at the time when we're unloaded from memory, that file will be orphaned. Plus, you can't rely on a "suspend" notification here, because if you Alt-Tab between apps you'll get suspended and incorrectly delete any photo that got taken—an image the user may want.

The best approach would actually be to track the temporary filepath in the SQLite database and explicitly look to see if there was one on disk to clean up on application start.

I have, however, ignored this subtlety—it seemed to me to be acceptable to omit it for the sake of not overloading this chapter. I belabor the preceding point so that it's on your radar for your own production apps.

# Changing the Manifest

In order to take pictures, we need to turn on the appropriate capability in the manifest. Specifically, we need to turn on the Webcam capability. Open the manifest editor and do this now. Figure 11-2 illustrates.

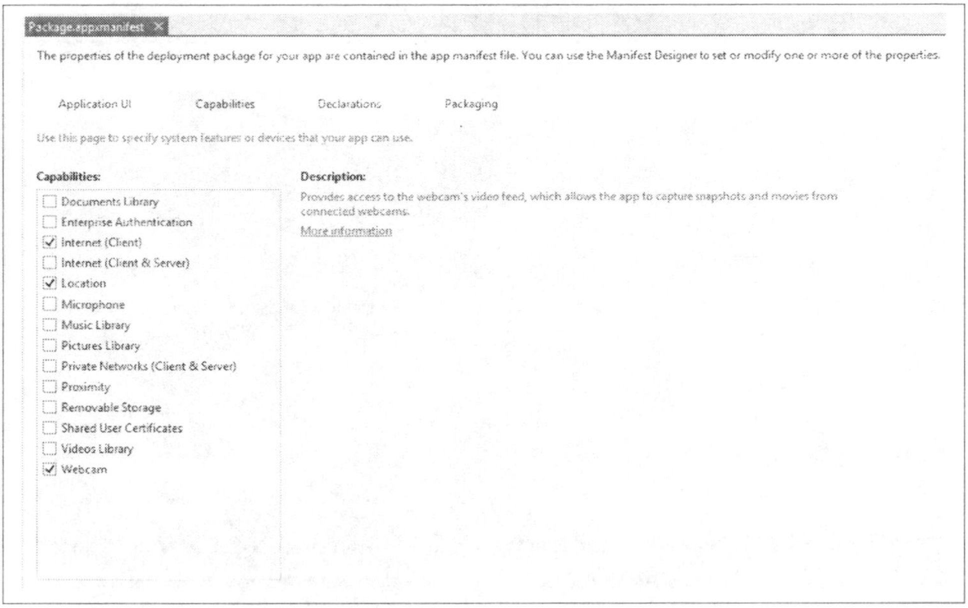

*Figure 11-2. The Webcam capability*

## Taking Pictures

Back when we built the basic structure of ReportPageViewModel, we rigged the Take PhotoCommand to call a method called CaptureImageAsync. We now need to build this method.

The first thing this method does is to call the WinRT photo capture methods—specifically, it will create a new CameraCaptureUI instance and call CaptureFileAsync. By default, this will return a JPEG file.

We'll store the file we capture in the TempImageFile property. However, we may already have one of those, so we'll call a method called CleanupTempImageFileAsync to get rid of any old one that we might have.

In order to put the file on the screen, we need to provide the XAML subsystem with an object that contains it. We'll create a new BitmapImage instance and load up the image data from the supplied file. We'll then set the Image property (which ultimately will go through and trigger a data-binding update so that the image displays on the form), and we'll store the reference to the file.

Here's the code:

```
// Add method to EditReportPageViewModel...
private async Task CaptureImageAsync()
{
```

```
// get the image...
var ui = new CameraCaptureUI();
var file = await ui.CaptureFileAsync(CameraCaptureUIMode.Photo);

// did we get one?
if (file != null)
{
    // do we have an old one to delete...
    await CleanupTempImageFileAsync();

    // load the image for display...
    var newImage = new BitmapImage();
    using (var stream = await file.OpenReadAsync())
        newImage.SetSource(stream);

    // set...
    this.Image = newImage;
    this.TempImageFile = file;
}
}
```

By way of supporting members, we've already spoken about CleanupTempImage FileAsync. Here's that method:

```
// Add method to EditReportPageViewModel...
private async Task CleanupTempImageFileAsync()
{
    try
    {
        if (this.TempImageFile != null)
            await this.TempImageFile.DeleteAsync();
    }
    catch
    {
        // ignore errors...
    }
    finally
    {
        this.TempImageFile = null;
    }
}
```

This method is written so that failed deleted operations are ignored. (This might happen if you have some weird file locking happening on the device.) This is usually a good approach if the main operation is impacted by whether or not the old file was deleted.

The HasImage and Image properties will look like this:

```
// Add properties to EditReportPageViewModel...
public bool HasImage
{
    get
    {
```

```
            return this.Image != null;
        }
    }

    public BitmapImage Image
    {
        get
        {
            return this.GetValue<BitmapImage>();
        }
        set
        {
            // set...
            this.SetValue(value);

            // update the flag...
            this.OnPropertyChanged("HasImage");
        }
    }
}
```

At this point, the application will run and we can take a photo. However, before we do that, we'll just override the `CancelAsync` method, the objective being to clean up any image file that we may have when we quit via that option. Here's the code:

```
// Add method to EditReportPageViewModel...
protected override async Task CancelAsync()
{
    // remove the temp image...
    await this.CleanupTempImageFileAsync();

    // base...
    await base.CancelAsync();
}
```

Now you can run the project and access the New page to add an item. If you take a photo, you'll find it in the *TempState* folder of your deployed package. (If you need to find that, go to *C:\Users\<User>\AppData\Local\Packages* and sort by Date Modified. Find the one with the most recent modification date, and it's likely yours.) Figure 11-3 shows File Explorer displaying the new image.

*Figure 11-3. The captured image in the TempState folder*

Of course, you'll actually see the image on the page, as illustrated back in Figure 11-1.

The next thing we need to look at is how we can actually save the image when we've finished working with it.

# Implementing Save

The objective here is to commit the changes to the underlying `ReportItem` to the database, and to position the image in the proper place on disk. The image itself will likely be too big, so we're going to look at resizing it so that it takes up less space on disk and —relevantly—is smaller for network transmission.

 In this book, I'm only going to take you through creating new items. In the code download, you'll find that `EditReportPageViewModel` is also able to update existing items.

## Validating and Saving

The first thing that we have to do is validate the data. We built a method called `ValidateAsync` into `ViewModelSingleton<T>` to support this. We just need to override it.

In the method, we'll check the `Title` and `Description` fields, we'll check that we have an image, and we'll check that we have a location. The location check is a little hacky— all we'll do is make sure we haven't got 0,0 as a coordinate. (Seeing as that point on the planet is in the middle of the ocean, it's probably OK. A better approach would be to track whether the user had actually updated the location.) Here's the code:

```
// Add method to EditReportPageViewModel...
protected override Task<ErrorBucket> ValidateAsync()
{
    var bucket = new ErrorBucket();
    if (string.IsNullOrEmpty(this.Item.Title))
        bucket.AddError("Title is required.");
```

```
        if (string.IsNullOrEmpty(this.Item.Description))
            bucket.AddError("Description is required.");
        if (!(this.HasImage))
            bucket.AddError("An image is required.");
        if (this.Item.Latitude == 0 && this.Item.Longitude == 0)
            bucket.AddError("A position is required.");

        // return...
        return Task.FromResult<ErrorBucket>(bucket);
    }
```

Note here that we use the `Task.FromResult<T>` "trick" to allow us to design the base class to support asynchrony without having asynchrony in the deriving classes.

We'll build the method to create the `ReportItem` in the database in a moment, but for now we can override the `Save` method similarly. As mentioned before, in these pages we're only going to build the `insert` functionality. In the download, `update` is also supported.

```
// Add method to EditReportPageViewModel...
protected override async Task DoSaveAsync()
{
    // save...
    if (this.IsNew)
    {
        // create a new one...
        await ReportItem.CreateReportItemAsync(this.Item.Title,
this.Item.Description, this.Item,
                this.TempImageFile);
    }
    else
    {
        // update an existing one...
        throw new InvalidOperationException("Implemented in the
download, not the book...");
    }

    // cleanup...
    await this.CleanupTempImageFileAsync();

    // return...
    this.Host.GoBack();
}
```

Note here that we clean up the temporary file. That's intentional—by design, `CreateReportItemAsync` (which we're about to build) won't assume it owns the file that it's been given to work with and hence it's not its responsibility to delete it.

For the save operation itself, we need to create a new `ReportItem` instance in the database and flag its status so that we know it needs to be transmitted up to the server when we get to that in Chapter 15. To this end, we need to set the `Status` property to `New` and set the NativeId to be a newly created GUID. I'll go through the CreateReportItemAsync method in stages, starting with that:

```
// Add method to ReportItem...
internal static async Task<ReportItem> CreateReportItemAsync(string
title, string description,
    IMappablePoint point, IStorageFile image)
{
    var item = new ReportItem()
    {
        Title = title,
        Description = description,
        NativeId = Guid.NewGuid().ToString(),
        Status = ReportItemStatus.New
    };
```

Once we've created the basic item, we can set the Latitude and Longitude fields via the SetLocation call that we built earlier:

```
item.SetLocation(point);
```

Then, we can do the actual insert:

```
// save...
var conn = StreetFooRuntime.GetUserDatabase();
await conn.InsertAsync(item);
```

With the basic database change made, we can turn our attention to the image. The idea here is that we "stage" the image into the ~/LocalState/ReportImages folder, just as if it had been downloaded from the server. We can do this by making up a filename based on the NativeId that we created before and then copying the supplied image over to that new location.

```
// stage the image...
if (image != null)
{
    // new path...
    var manager = new ReportImageCacheManager();
    var folder = await manager.GetCacheFolderAsync();

    // create...
    await image.CopyAsync(folder, item.NativeId + ".jpg");
}
```

Finally, we can return the item:

```
// return...
return item;
}
```

At this point, the operation will work and we can save reports. More importantly, we can go back to the Reports page and actually see our new report, as Figure 11-4 shows.

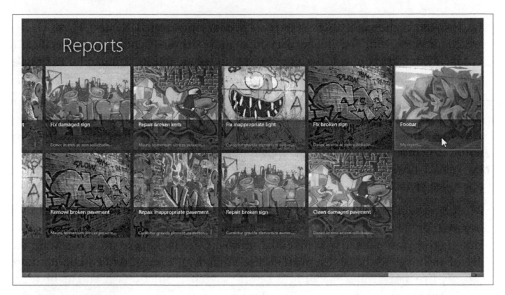

*Figure 11-4. The new Foobar report on the Reports page*

## Resizing Images

The last thing that I want to cover with regard to images is resizing. The default image configuration that's created on my machine is a 1280×720-pixel, JPEG-formatted image that happens to fit into a file of around 150KB.

Although that's not a big file, there are a couple of reasons why in LOB scenarios you may wish to control file size. If each operative does 10 visits a day, that's 31MB of transfer just on image data. Over cellular networks, this can end up as significant, especially if you have a lot of users all working in the same way.

Second—and this is a weirder problem—over time, devices tend to increase their default capture size. Whereas you can deploy some software on day one where the images are 150KB, on a typical new device deployed a couple years hence, it's not unusual to find the file size doubled. And while processor speed and memory tends to ramp up quickly, network transfer speeds are slower to roll out.

My recommendation is that in all cases you pick the size of image that the business demands and make your app always return that, rather than rely on the vagaries of the device.

This is one area of WinRT where things are quite different in the .NET world. A common way to resize images with .NET was to use GDI+. Specifically, you loaded a bitmap, created a new bitmap, created a device context over that new bitmap, and used GDI+ to scale and render the source into the target. However, that approach was not supported on servers; on the server we were supposed to use classes in the System.Windows.Me dia.Imaging namespace, such as BitmapEncoder and related classes. These classes worked directly with the image data in a more server-friendly way. Specifically, BitmapEncoder knew how to write out raster file data, and its companion BitmapDecoder knew how to read it.

In Windows 8 apps, you don't have access to GDI+ at all. Plus, the image manipulation functions have moved to the Windows.Graphics.Imaging namespace. As is often the case when things move from the .NET world into WinRT, their baseline functionality and/or structure also gets changed. So, although we have BitmapEncoder et al. in the new WinRT library, there are various bits missing. If you're used to using these APIs, your mileage may vary.

We're going to create a new method called ResizeAndSaveAsAsync in a new class called ImageHelper. This will take an input file, an output file, and a single "target dimension" value. Taking one value may seem odd, but what we're looking to do is constrain the edge of an image to the largest possible size. A landscape image will end up no more than, say, 640 pixels wide. That same image in portrait orientation will end up no more than 640 pixels high. The aspect ratio will be preserved.

The first thing we need to do is open up the source file. This will be the camera data file in our *TempState* folder.

We then create a BitmapDecoder. This will interpret the data in the file and tell us metrics about the file (e.g., how wide it is). BitmapDecoder will also surface the *pixel data*, which is the actual data that makes up the file. (In fact, BitmapDecoder understands files in terms of *frames*. We only have one frame in our file, which happens to be the picture that we took.)

Next, we open a stream to where we want the resulting image to go. This can be directed to disk (which is what we're going to do), or to memory (using an InMemoryRandomAccessStream instance). Once we have the stream, we need a BitmapEncoder. You can create these in various ways, but the one we're going to use is a *transcoder*, which converts from one format to the other.

Once we have the transcoder, we can specify the new dimensions of the image via the object exposed by the BitmapTransform property. (If we wanted to, we could also crop and rotate the image here.) Once that's done, we commit the transcoder by calling FlushAsync, and our new file will be written to disk.

I'll present ResizeAndSaveAsAsync in steps. I'm proposing creating a new class called ImageHelper to host this method. Here's the code; the first thing we do is open the source stream and get the decoder:

```
public static class ImageHelper
{
    internal static async Task ResizeAndSaveAsAsync
    (IStorageFile source, IStorageFile destination, int targetDimension)
```

```
    {
        // open the file...
        using(var sourceStream = await source.OpenReadAsync())
        {
            // step one, get a decoder...
            var decoder = await BitmapDecoder.CreateAsync(sourceStream);
```

Once we've done that, we can create the output stream and create the transcoding encoder. This requires the output stream and the source decoder:

```
            // step two, create somewhere to put it...
            using(var destinationStream =
                await destination.OpenAsync
                (FileAccessMode.ReadWrite))
            {
                // step three, create an encoder...
                var encoder = await BitmapEncoder.CreateForTranscodingAsync
                            (destinationStream, decoder);
```

The next stage is to configure the transformation. To do this, we need to determine if the image is portrait or landscape and calculate the aspect ratio. Depending on the orientation, we'll use a different calculation for the final dimension:

```
                // how big is it?
                uint width = decoder.PixelWidth;
                uint height = decoder.PixelHeight;
                decimal ratio = (decimal)width / (decimal)height;

                // orientation?
                bool portrait = width < height;

                // step four, configure it...
                if (portrait)
                {
                    encoder.BitmapTransform.ScaledHeight =
                    (uint)targetDimension;
                    encoder.BitmapTransform.ScaledWidth =
                    (uint)((decimal)targetDimension * ratio);
                }
                else
                {
                    encoder.BitmapTransform.ScaledWidth =
                    (uint)targetDimension;
                    encoder.BitmapTransform.ScaledHeight =
                    (uint)((decimal)targetDimension / ratio);
                }
```

Finally, we can write the image:

```
                // step five, write it...
                await encoder.FlushAsync();
            }
        }
```

```
        }
    }
```

Before we can test it, we need to change the `CreateReportItemAsync` method that we wrote earlier to use this "resize and save" method rather than the original code that moved the file. Here's the change:

```
internal static async Task<ReportItem> CreateReportItemAsync
(string title, string description,
    IMappablePoint point, IStorageFile image)
{
    var item = new ReportItem()
    {
        Title = title,
        Description = description,
        NativeId = Guid.NewGuid().ToString(),
        Status = ReportItemStatus.New
    };
    item.SetLocation(point);

    // save...
    var conn = StreetFooRuntime.GetUserDatabase();
    await conn.InsertAsync(item);

    // stage the image...
    if (image != null)
    {
        // new path...
        var manager = new ReportImageCacheManager();
        var folder = await manager.GetCacheFolderAsync();

        // save it as a file that's no longer than
        // 640 pixels on its longest edge...
        var newImage = await folder.CreateFileAsync
                    (item.NativeId + ".jpg");
        await ImageHelper.ResizeAndSaveAsAsync(image, newImage, 640);
    }

    // return...
    return item;
}
```

Run the code now, and you'll find that the image files are smaller. Open them up, and you'll notice the dimensions are restricted to 640 pixels along the longest edge.

## A Word About Capturing Video

I've limited this chapter's discussion to basic image capture only—as mentioned, that's the most common use in LOB apps, and retail app use of this feature is likely to be more advanced.

You can also allow capture video. Obviously, this will eat disk space and battery. The key reason why I didn't include this is because in field service applications it's a nightmare dealing with video uploads over cellular service, and as a result it tends to be quite specialized. However, you certainly can do it. If you want to capture video, though, you need to enable the Microphone capability in the manifest.

# CHAPTER 12

# Responsive Design

Windows Store apps allow you to run several applications side by side in the foreground, which allows you to multitask without having to switch between fullscreen applications. This feature appears popular with early adopters of Windows 8, and this is a trend we predict will continue. If you were planning a weekend trip to London, you could have a map application, weather application, and a travel application open to check nearby travel destinations. There are many cases in which being able to run applications side by side is helpful. Figure 12-1 shows the three applications: Map, Weather, and Travel.

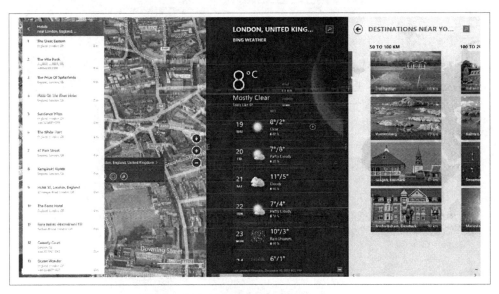

*Figure 12-1. Map, Weather, and Travel side by side*

The three applications have adjustable dividers between them to give us control of how much screen real estate they get. The default minimum width of an application is 500 pixels, but there is an even smaller size that was previously referred to as the "Snapped" mode. The smallest size is 320 pixels and applications have to opt in for that.

With two applications that support the smallest size, we let the third application fill out the rest of the screen (illustrated in Figure 12-2). This is really the trick with the view— we need to build a UI that can either adapt from being in the responsive view or the smallest view, or we have to provide a secondary UI that will be used for the smallest view. (The intent here is that every app has to be useful in either mode. Microsoft is keen to ensure that it isn't the case that one mode is "more special" than the other.)

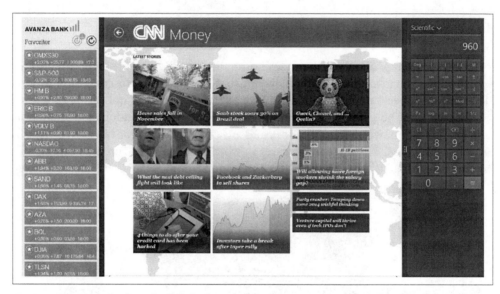

*Figure 12-2. On both sides of the screen, we have applications that support the 320-pixel width*

This is actually much easier to do with a proper MVVM model like the one that we have taken the time to build thus far. From time to time, we'll have to duplicate sets of controls for the smallest versus the responsive size view, but that's fine because all we have to do is configure the duplicated controls with the same bindings. The view model is sufficiently abstracted from the view that it doesn't care whether we're in either mode, nor does it care how many bindings each control has.

You need to have a display that has a width greater than or equal to 1024 pixels to be able to run several applications at the same time.

If you are developing on a machine with a lower screen resolution than that, use the simulator because it allows you to simulate resolutions higher than your base hardware.

Charms are enabled for the application you are using at the moment, which is indicated by a small white line in the middle of the divider closest to the application being used.

The general rule of snapped view is that the app should actually be functional when in that mode. It doesn't have to be fully functional—not every function has to be carried over—but it should not be a struggle for the user to use a snapped app. You may also encounter development requirements that mean that the smallest view makes no sense at all. I'm a fan of it. It's well worth implementing, and it's a great differentiator from the iPad.

# Updating the Grid View

By using a fluid layout that lets the application adapt to various screen sizes, we already have great support for the default minimum width—500 pixels. We do, however, want to support the smallest size as well, which might make the user bring our application to the foreground more often and interact with it. Support for the 320-pixel width is set in the app manifest under minimum width.

## The VisualStateManager

All of this work hinges on the VisualStateManager class within WinRT. The purpose of this class is to handle state changes, one example of which is the transition from the "Default" state (which includes scaling down to 500 pixels in width) to the "Small" state (320 pixels wide).

The VisualStateManager class has been around for a while—even before WinRT—and is worth learning well. The manager class handles states, and the states allow us to get a specific appearance of a control when it is in a specific state.

For the register page, we could define some visual states like the following:

```
<VisualStateManager.VisualStateGroups>
    <VisualStateGroup>
        <VisualState x:Name="Default"/>
        <VisualState x:Name="Small">
            <Storyboard>
                <ObjectAnimationUsingKeyFrames Storyboard.TargetName=
"backButton" Storyboard.TargetProperty="Style">
                    <DiscreteObjectKeyFrame KeyTime="0" Value="
{StaticResource SnappedBackButtonStyle}"/>
                </ObjectAnimationUsingKeyFrames>
```

```
                        <ObjectAnimationUsingKeyFrames Storyboard.TargetName=
"pageTitle" Storyboard.TargetProperty="Style">
                                <DiscreteObjectKeyFrame KeyTime="0" Value="
{StaticResource SnappedPageHeaderTextStyle}"/>
                        </ObjectAnimationUsingKeyFrames>

                        <ObjectAnimationUsingKeyFrames Storyboard.TargetName=
"helpText" Storyboard.TargetProperty="Visibility">
                                <DiscreteObjectKeyFrame KeyTime="0" Value="Visible"/>
                        </ObjectAnimationUsingKeyFrames>

                        <ObjectAnimationUsingKeyFrames Storyboard.TargetName=
"registrationForm" Storyboard.TargetProperty="Visibility">
                                <DiscreteObjectKeyFrame KeyTime="0"
Value="Collapsed"/>
                        </ObjectAnimationUsingKeyFrames>
                    </Storyboard>
                </VisualState>
            </VisualStateGroup>
        </VisualStateManager.VisualStateGroups>
```

Let's take a look at what is going on here. First of all, we define the `VisualStateManag
er.VisualStateGroups` element inside the element where we want to add the changes.
When using visual states for managing the resizing of the application, it will most often
be inside the outermost grid. Inside `VisualStateManager.VisualStateGroups`, we
create a group of states, and we give them appropriate names so we can access them
from our code. We then create a storyboard, which is a container timeline that lets us
animate dependency properties from one state to another. This is similar to how styles
work: you get a list of directives and the XAML subsystem walks through each one and
affects the dependency properties. In the storyboard directives that we have in the preceding code snippet, the first two change the styles of the button and caption to make
them smaller. The third one changes the visibility of a `TextBox` from collapsed to visible,
and the fourth one changes the visibility of the registration form from visible to collapsed. On the register and logon page, we'll just tell the user that this view doesn't work
in the smallest mode, whereas the Reports and Report page will support the 320 pixel
size. Notice how we don't define any storyboards for the default state. We don't have to
reverse the actions done in the other states.

When the Reports page was created, we used a grid page template. Whenever we use
this template, Visual Studio creates a `GridView` control with the name `itemsGridView`
and a `ListView` control with the name `itemsListView`. Both controls were bound to
the same data source, however, the `ListView` one was hidden. Throughout the life of
the app, we've been able to snap it from one side to the other. It's just that it wouldn't
have worked properly because we hadn't created working snap views. To make the logon
page work properly in snapped view, we need to do two things. The `ListView` uses
templates just like the `GridView`, and so we need a new template. If you recall, back in

Chapter 4 we built `MyGridView` so we could eventually host commands for use with the MVVM approach—commands like `ItemClickedCommand`. Next we'll build `MyList View` so we can do the same to the list view.

## Creating MyListView

The implementation of `ItemClickedCommand` on `MyListView` will be identical to the one we built on `MyGridView` in Chapter 8. Thus, I'll just present the code without going through it in detail. Here it is:

```
public class MyListView : ListView
{
    // as per the grid...
    public static readonly DependencyProperty ItemClickedCommandProperty =
        DependencyProperty.Register("ItemClickedCommand", typeof(ICommand),
typeof(MyListView),
        new PropertyMetadata(null, (d, e) => ((MyListView)d).
ItemClickedCommand = (ICommand)e.NewValue));

    public MyListView()
    {
        this.ItemClick += MyListView_ItemClick;
    }

    void MyListView_ItemClick(object sender, ItemClickEventArgs e)
    {
        if (this.ItemClickedCommand == null)
            return;

        // ok...
        var clicked = e.ClickedItem;
        if (this.ItemClickedCommand.CanExecute(clicked))
            this.ItemClickedCommand.Execute(clicked);
    }

    public ICommand ItemClickedCommand
    {
        get { return (ICommand)GetValue(ItemClickedCommandProperty); }
        set { SetValue(ItemClickedCommandProperty, value); }
    }
}
```

Again, as per Chapter 8, now that we've replicated the `ItemClickedCommand`, we also need to replicate the template that we created for displaying report items in the grid. This new template will be used for showing those same report items, but in a list.

Here's the template. Note how it uses the same bindings as the main report template. That's the point of snapped view—all we do is change the declaration of the UI and it should all just work:

```xml
<!-- add to StandardStyles.xaml -->
<DataTemplate x:Key="ReportItem80SnappedItemTemplate">
    <Grid Margin="6">
        <Grid.ColumnDefinitions>
            <ColumnDefinition Width="Auto"/>
            <ColumnDefinition Width="*"/>
        </Grid.ColumnDefinitions>
        <Border Background="{StaticResource
ListViewItemPlaceholderBackgroundThemeBrush}" Width="60" Height="60">
            <Image Source="{Binding ImageUri}" Stretch="UniformToFill"/>
        </Border>
        <StackPanel Grid.Column="1" Margin="10,0,0,0">
            <TextBlock Text="{Binding Title}" Style="{StaticResource
ItemTextStyle}" MaxHeight="40"/>
            <TextBlock Text="{Binding Description}" Style="{StaticResource
CaptionTextStyle}" TextWrapping="NoWrap"/>
        </StackPanel>
    </Grid>
</DataTemplate>
```

Finally, just a quick change to the list control. We need to change its type, change the template, and bind up the `ItemClickedCommand`. Note that we reuse the same command in the view-model. Again, we don't need to change the view-model at all for this to work. Here's the change:

```xml
<!-- Modify ReportsPage.xml -->
<local:MyListView
    x:Name="itemListView"
    AutomationProperties.AutomationId="ItemsListView"
    AutomationProperties.Name="Items"
    TabIndex="1"
    Grid.Row="1"
    Visibility="Collapsed"
    Margin="0,-10,0,0"
    Padding="10,0,0,60"
    ItemsSource="{Binding Source={StaticResource itemsViewSource}}"
    ItemTemplate="{StaticResource ReportItem80SnappedItemTemplate}"
    IsItemClickEnabled="true"
    ItemClickedCommand="{Binding SelectionCommand}"
    />
```

In the preceding code, `Collapsed` is given for the `Visibility` property to indicate that the element should not be displayed. We have to manually switch between the states when the window's size changes, so before we add the states, let's go ahead and create a responsive base page that inherits from `StreetFooPage`. Inside that class, we'll listen for the `SizeChanged` event and use `VisualStateManager.GoToState` to switch state depending on the new screen size, like so:

```csharp
public class ResponsiveStreetFooPage : StreetFooPage
{
    public ResponsiveStreetFooPage()
    {
```

```
        SizeChanged += OnSizeChanged;
    }
    private const double SmallMode = 320;

    private void OnSizeChanged(object sender, SizeChangedEventArgs e)
    {
        VisualStateManager.GoToState(this, e.NewSize.Width <= SmallMode ?
"Small" : "Default", true);
    }
}
```

Then we simply let the views that we want to use states inherit from that class; for us that would be the `ReportsPage`, `ReportPage`, `LogonPage`, and `RegisterPage`.

# Modifying the App Bar

The app bar as currently configured won't work properly in snapped view on the Reports page. We need to adjust that. As mentioned, in snapped view, we can fit only three buttons on the app bar. One option is to hide a button by adding a transition to the state transition storyboard. In order to do this, we have to name the button by declaring an `x:Name` attribute on the control.

But when we first built this app bar in Chapter 4, we constructed it so that it had options on the left and right. This became irrelevant in Chapter 10 when we took the selection off and made a click on a report go to the report singleton page. If we strip out all the grid layout stuff and name the button that we want to get rid of the "show location" button, we get the following:

```
<!-- Modify markup in ReportsPage.xml -->
<Page.BottomAppBar>
    <AppBar>
        <StackPanel HorizontalAlignment="Right" Orientation="Horizontal"
Grid.Column="2">
            <Button Style="{StaticResource NewAppBarButtonStyle}" Command=
"{Binding NewCommand}" />
            <Button x:Name="appbarShowLocation" Style="{StaticResource
ShowLocationAppBarButtonStyle}" Command="{Binding ShowLocationCommand}" />
            <Button Style="{StaticResource RefreshAppBarButtonStyle}"
Command="{Binding RefreshCommand}" />
            <Button Style="{StaticResource LogoutAppBarButtonStyle}"
Command="{Binding LogoutCommand}" />
        </StackPanel>
    </AppBar>
</Page.BottomAppBar>
```

Now that the button has a name, we can address it within the storyboard and hide it when the storyboard is enacted. This "enacting" happens when the user tells Windows that she wants to move the app into snapped mode. Here's the code:

```
<!-- Modify markup in ReportsPage.xml -->
        <VisualState x:Name="Small">
            <Storyboard>
                <ObjectAnimationUsingKeyFrames Storyboard.TargetName=
"backButton" Storyboard.TargetProperty="Style">
                    <DiscreteObjectKeyFrame KeyTime="0" Value="
{StaticResource SnappedBackButtonStyle}"/>
                </ObjectAnimationUsingKeyFrames>
                <ObjectAnimationUsingKeyFrames Storyboard.TargetName=
"pageTitle" Storyboard.TargetProperty="Style">
                    <DiscreteObjectKeyFrame KeyTime="0" Value=
"{StaticResource SnappedPageHeaderTextStyle}"/>
                </ObjectAnimationUsingKeyFrames>

                <ObjectAnimationUsingKeyFrames Storyboard.TargetName=
"itemListView" Storyboard.TargetProperty="Visibility">
                    <DiscreteObjectKeyFrame KeyTime="0" Value="Visible"/>
                </ObjectAnimationUsingKeyFrames>
                <ObjectAnimationUsingKeyFrames Storyboard.TargetName=
"itemGridView" Storyboard.TargetProperty="Visibility">
                    <DiscreteObjectKeyFrame KeyTime="0"
Value="Collapsed"/>
                </ObjectAnimationUsingKeyFrames>

                <ObjectAnimationUsingKeyFrames Storyboard.TargetName=
"appbarShowLocation" Storyboard.TargetProperty="Visibility">
                    <DiscreteObjectKeyFrame KeyTime="0"
Value="Collapsed"/>
                </ObjectAnimationUsingKeyFrames>

            </Storyboard>
        </VisualState>
```

Run the app and open the app bar in snapped view on the Reports page and you'll see something like Figure 12-3.

*Figure 12-3. The app bar in snapped view*

There may be cases where you can't just reduce the number of buttons like this. In a later section, we'll look at how to create a More button with a pop-up menu.

# Updating Singleton Views

The next type of view that we're going to look at is exemplified in the report singleton page. In this situation, we're going to create an entirely new view. We'll swap out the old view and replace it with the new view using the storyboard.

The first thing to address is how to best use the XAML designer. This will then let us lay out the new view with minimal guesswork. This is done by bringing up the Device view via the Design→Device menu. At the top of this view, you can click Windows OS Edge and then use the slider to set the minimum size. In Figure 12-4, you can see the left selection in play. The hatched portion of the device viewport shows the region occupied by the splitter and the filled view. The device window doesn't know of our states and therefore cannot be used with them. In Blend, which comes with Visual Studio, you can select states and see how they look there and add any modifications that you want. We won't cover the use of Blend in this book, but it is an excellent piece of software that helps tremendously where the Visual Studio designer is lacking.

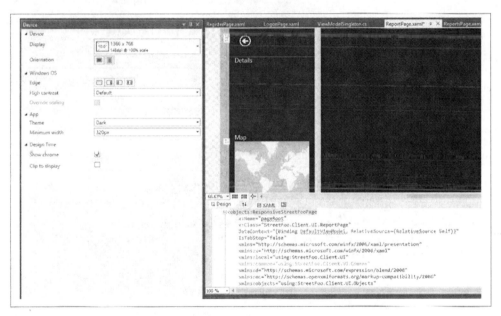

*Figure 12-4. Showing the application at 320 pixels wide to the left*

What you can see in the image is what we want to accomplish in the smallest width. For the screenshot, I simply cheated by changing the visibility of the containers, which I will talk more about in the following section.

What I'm proposing that we do here is approach this in a standard way. A first step is to let the page inherit from the new base page we mentioned earlier as you can see in the image. We'll assume that when we want to display a form in snapped view, we'll contain that form within a StackPanel. We'll also assume that the vertical extent of that StackPanel may go off the bottom edge of the screen. Thus we'll contain the StackPanel within a ScrollViewer configured to support this. Both of these controls will have styles applied, which we'll build in a moment. In terms of the actual view, because the view doesn't have any logic behind it and because everything is driven with data binding, we can just copy and paste the controls that we already had into the new container structure. Here's the change:

```
<!-- Modify markup in ReportPage.xaml -->
    <ScrollViewer x:Name="containerSnapped" Style="{StaticResource
SnappedContainerScrollViewer}" Grid.Row="1">

        <StackPanel Style="{StaticResource SnappedContainerStackPanel}">
            <TextBlock Style="{StaticResource HeadingTextBlock}">Details
</TextBlock>
            <Image Source="{Binding Item.ImageUri}" HorizontalAlignment=
"Left" Width="320" Height="240" Stretch="Uniform"
                                    Margin="0,0,0,10"></Image>
            <local:MarkupViewer Markup="{Binding Item.Description}">
</local:MarkupViewer>

            <TextBlock Style="{StaticResource HeadingTextBlock}"
Padding="0,10,0,0">Map</TextBlock>
            <local:MyMap Width="300" Height="300" ShowTraffic="true"
                        PushpinPoint="{Binding Item, Converter=
{StaticResource IMappablePointConverter}}"></local:MyMap>

        </StackPanel>

    </ScrollViewer>
```

Note that I've put an x:Name="containerSnapped" attribute on the ScrollViewer. This will be our convention for containers that are used in snapped mode. Similarly, on the ScrollViewer that we built in Chapter 10 to provide the panorama view, we'll add an x:Name="containerFill" attribute. Here's the change—I've presented the caption controls above the control by way of orientation:

```
<!-- Modify markup in ReportPage.xaml -->
    <Grid>
        <Grid.ColumnDefinitions>
            <ColumnDefinition Width="Auto"/>
            <ColumnDefinition Width="*"/>
        </Grid.ColumnDefinitions>
        <Button x:Name="backButton" Click="GoBack" IsEnabled="{Binding Frame.
CanGoBack, ElementName=pageRoot}" Style="{StaticResource BackButtonStyle}"/>
        <TextBlock x:Name="pageTitle" Grid.Column="1" Text="{Binding
Item.Title}" Style="{StaticResource PageHeaderTextStyle}"/>
    </Grid>
```

```
<ScrollViewer x:Name="containerFill" Style="{StaticResource
HorizontalScrollViewerStyle}" Grid.Row="1">
        <Grid>
```

Finally, we can change the storyboard to swap over the two containers:

```
<!-- Modify markup in ReportPage.xaml -->
    <VisualState x:Name="Small">
        <Storyboard>
            <ObjectAnimationUsingKeyFrames Storyboard.TargetName=
"backButton" Storyboard.TargetProperty="Style">
                <DiscreteObjectKeyFrame KeyTime="0" Value=
"{StaticResource SnappedBackButtonStyle}"/>
            </ObjectAnimationUsingKeyFrames>
            <ObjectAnimationUsingKeyFrames Storyboard.TargetName=
"pageTitle" Storyboard.TargetProperty="Style">
                <DiscreteObjectKeyFrame KeyTime="0" Value=
"{StaticResource SnappedPageHeaderTextStyle}"/>
            </ObjectAnimationUsingKeyFrames>

            <ObjectAnimationUsingKeyFrames Storyboard.TargetName=
"containerSnapped" Storyboard.TargetProperty="Visibility">
                <DiscreteObjectKeyFrame KeyTime="0" Value="Visible"/>
            </ObjectAnimationUsingKeyFrames>
            <ObjectAnimationUsingKeyFrames Storyboard.TargetName=
"containerFill" Storyboard.TargetProperty="Visibility">
                <DiscreteObjectKeyFrame KeyTime="0"
Value="Collapsed"/>
            </ObjectAnimationUsingKeyFrames>

        </Storyboard>
    </VisualState>
```

Run the app and you can snap the report singleton page as Figure 12-5 illustrates. What's quite cool is being able to move the slider between the smallest, the medium, and the full views and seeing the view adjust itself.

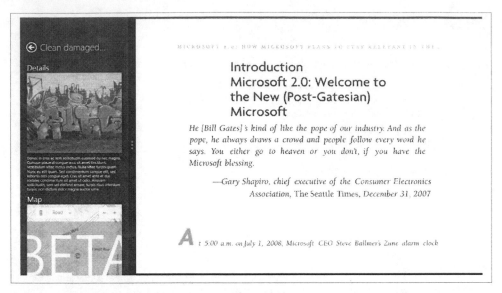

*Figure 12-5. The report singleton page in the smallest view*

## Adding a More Button to the App Bar

Modifying `EditReportPage` so that it supports the smallest view operates in a similar fashion to that of `ReportPage`; it is basically just a repeat of the work we just did. For that reason, I won't repeat it in these pages, but you'll find the code download has it working properly.

What I will go through is how to modify the app bar. At the moment, if you snap the edit page the app bar looks a little like Figure 12-6—i.e., the Save button is missing. Really what's happened is that it's been obscured by the Capture Location button.

*Figure 12-6. The edit page app bar with the Save button missing*

What we're going to do is, when we go into the smallest view, we'll hide the two buttons on the left and show a new button on the "right," labeled "More." I say "right" because it will appear this button is actually on the left of the view, but it's part of the set designated "right."

Don't be tempted to create smaller buttons on the app bar; they won't be user-friendly.

When the More button is pressed it'll display a pop up. This is done using the `Win dows.UI.Popups.PopupMenu` class. But there's a wrinkle—it's easier to build a `PopupMe nu` programmatically rather than doing it declaratively in XAML. And, even if you could declare it in XAML, when you show the pop up you have to give it a set of coordinates to use and that is much easier to manage programmatically.

To understand the problem, `PopupMenu` relies on you adding `UICommand` instances to a collection that it manages and then calling `ShowAsync`, passing in some coordinates.

Thus we have a dilemma; we've come so far without having to write traditional code-behind, do we really have to do it for this? There are two ways to go with this: we could create framework infrastructure within the view-model handler to expose out view-agnostic commands, and then create a special `MoreAppBarButton` control that understands how to use this infrastructure to create and show a `PopupMenu`. Or we could just code it up in the codebehind. I'm proposing doing it in the codebehind, for the simple reason that it's view-specific code. The view-model doesn't care how we've structured our app bar; that's a presentation-specific thing.

Turning back to the app bar, what we want to do is restructure that so that we have a named panel on the left that we can hide, and a More button on the right that we can show. Here's the code:

```
<!-- Modify markup in EditReportPage.xaml -->
<Page.BottomAppBar>
    <AppBar IsSticky="true" IsOpen="true">
        <Grid>
            <Grid.ColumnDefinitions>
                <ColumnDefinition Width="auto"/>
                <ColumnDefinition Width="50*"/>
            </Grid.ColumnDefinitions>
            <StackPanel Orientation="Horizontal" x:Name="appbarPanelLeft">
                <Button Style="{StaticResource TakePhotoAppBarButtonStyle}"
Command="{Binding TakePhotoCommand}" />
                <Button Style="{StaticResource
CaptureLocationAppBarButtonStyle}" Command="{Binding CaptureLocationCommand}" />
            </StackPanel>
            <StackPanel HorizontalAlignment="Right" Orientation="Horizontal"
Grid.Column="1" Margin="0,1,5,-1">
                <Button x:Name="appbarMore" Style="{StaticResource
MoreAppBarButtonStyle}" Visibility="Collapsed" Click="HandleMoreButton" />
                <Button Style="{StaticResource SaveAppBarButtonStyle}"
Command="{Binding SaveCommand}" />
                <Button Style="{StaticResource CancelAppBarButtonStyle}"
```

```
                  Command="{Binding CancelCommand}" />
                            </StackPanel>
                      </Grid>
              </AppBar>
        </Page.BottomAppBar>
```

Luckily, we are given a `MoreAppBarButtonStyle` by default. Notice that I've defined a `Click` attribute on the More button. This is to power the codebehind. In the editor view, double-click the More button and Visual Studio will create the handler for you. We'll do that in a moment.

Before we code up the handler, here's the change we need to make to the storyboard for transitioning into the smallest view. We hide the panel and show the button:

```
<VisualState x:Name="Small">
    <Storyboard>
        <ObjectAnimationUsingKeyFrames Storyboard.TargetName="backButton"
Storyboard.TargetProperty="Style">
            <DiscreteObjectKeyFrame KeyTime="0" Value="{StaticResource
SnappedBackButtonStyle}"/>
        </ObjectAnimationUsingKeyFrames>
        <ObjectAnimationUsingKeyFrames Storyboard.TargetName="titleNew"
Storyboard.TargetProperty="Style">
            <DiscreteObjectKeyFrame KeyTime="0" Value="{StaticResource
SnappedPageHeaderTextStyle}"/>
        </ObjectAnimationUsingKeyFrames>
        <ObjectAnimationUsingKeyFrames Storyboard.TargetName="titleEdit"
Storyboard.TargetProperty="Style">
            <DiscreteObjectKeyFrame KeyTime="0" Value="{StaticResource
SnappedPageHeaderTextStyle}"/>
        </ObjectAnimationUsingKeyFrames>

        <ObjectAnimationUsingKeyFrames Storyboard.TargetName="containerSnapped"
Storyboard.TargetProperty="Visibility">
            <DiscreteObjectKeyFrame KeyTime="0" Value="Visible"/>
        </ObjectAnimationUsingKeyFrames>
        <ObjectAnimationUsingKeyFrames Storyboard.TargetName="containerFill"
Storyboard.TargetProperty="Visibility">
            <DiscreteObjectKeyFrame KeyTime="0" Value="Collapsed"/>
        </ObjectAnimationUsingKeyFrames>

        <ObjectAnimationUsingKeyFrames Storyboard.TargetName="appbarPanelLeft"
Storyboard.TargetProperty="Visibility">
            <DiscreteObjectKeyFrame KeyTime="0" Value="Collapsed"/>
        </ObjectAnimationUsingKeyFrames>
        <ObjectAnimationUsingKeyFrames Storyboard.TargetName="appbarMore"
Storyboard.TargetProperty="Visibility">
            <DiscreteObjectKeyFrame KeyTime="0" Value="Visible"/>
        </ObjectAnimationUsingKeyFrames>

    </Storyboard>
</VisualState>
```

I didn't take you through the specifics of building the form as it should be obvious given the work we did previously, but in the page I have two forms: one for the default view and one for the smallest view. For consistency with ReportPage I've called one contain erFill and the other containerSnapped.

 You'll find that the code download shows fully implemented support for the smallest view size.

Previously, I mentioned that we need to create UICommand instances for use with Popup Menu. These take a display string and a delegate. We can just defer through to the commands on the view-model. Again, although we're doing codebehind here we don't want to break the separation of concerns provided by MVVM.

Here's the code—although I need to point out at this point that the "Take Picture" command will actually fail, but at least we'll be able to see the pop up:

```
// Add method to EditReportPage...
    private async void HandleMoreButton(object sender, RoutedEventArgs e)
    {
        var popup = new PopupMenu();
        popup.Commands.Add(new UICommand("Take Picture", (args) =>
this.ViewModel.TakePhotoCommand.Execute(null)));
    popup.Commands.Add(new UICommand("Capture Location", (args) =>  this.ViewModel.
CaptureLocationCommand.Execute(null)));

        // show...
        await popup.ShowAsync(((FrameworkElement)sender).
GetPointForContextMenu());
    }
```

The sender will come through as, obviously, the button. We'll need to use this to get a point to show the context menu. GetPointForContextMenu is an extension method on FrameworkElement that we need to build.

I'll present this without much comment as it's a little specialized for this book. This code needs to be added to the FrameworkElementExtender class that we built in Chapter 4 and modified again in Chapter 7.

```
// Add method to FrameworkElementExtender...
    internal static Point GetPointForContextMenu(this FrameworkElement
element)
    {
        GeneralTransform transform = element.TransformToVisual(null);
        Point point = transform.TransformPoint(new Point());
        return point;
    }
```

Run the code and bring up the app bar on the edit report page while in snapped view. You'll see something like Figure 12-7 when you press the More button.

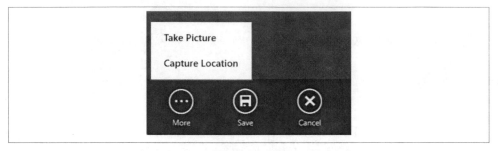

*Figure 12-7. The pop-up menu for the More button*

As mentioned, "Take Picture" will crash. Select the option and you'll get an exception message like this:

```
System.InvalidOperationException: A method was called at an unexpected time.
(Exception from HRESULT: 0x8000000E)
    at System.Runtime.CompilerServices.TaskAwaiter.ThrowForNonSuccess(Task task)
    at System.Runtime.CompilerServices.TaskAwaiter.HandleNonSuccessAndDebugger
Notification(Task task)
    at System.Runtime.CompilerServices.TaskAwaiter`1.GetResult()
    at StreetFoo.Client.EditReportPageViewModel.<CaptureImageAsync>d__17.MoveNext
() in c:\BookCode\Chapter13\StreetFoo.Client\StreetFoo.Client\Model\Instances\
EditReportPageViewModel.cs:line 84
--- End of stack trace from previous location where exception was thrown ---
    at System.Runtime.CompilerServices.TaskAwaiter.ThrowForNonSuccess(Task task)
    at System.Runtime.CompilerServices.TaskAwaiter.HandleNonSuccessAndDebugger
Notification(Task task)
    at System.Runtime.CompilerServices.TaskAwaiter.GetResult()
    at StreetFoo.Client.EditReportPageViewModel.<<.ctor>b__0>d__4.MoveNext() in
c:\BookCode\Chapter13\StreetFoo.Client\StreetFoo.Client\Model\Instances\
EditReportPageViewModel.cs:line 26
```

What this error is trying to tell you is that you can't take a photo when the application is in the smallest width.

We need to "unsnap" the view before we call the command. There are a few places where you can't access APIs from within snapped views. These normally occur when you would end up in a situation where the user might be unclear as to which app owned the helper UI. (The file pickers are another example of this.) This is down to the modality of the Windows 8 application model because you don't have a pop up to do the helper UI, the user can't "see" which application the helper UI is related to.

As we can't access this function, we'll just display a message telling the user this. Here's the change:

```
// Modify method in EditReportPage...
    private async void HandleMoreButton(object sender, RoutedEventArgs e)
    {
        var popup = new PopupMenu();
        popup.Commands.Add(new UICommand("Take Picture", (args) => {
            await this.ShowAlertAsync("Make the app full screen to use
the camera.");
        }));
        popup.Commands.Add(new UICommand("Capture Location", (args) =>
this.ViewModel.CaptureLocationCommand.Execute(null)));

        // show...
        await popup.ShowAsync(((FrameworkElement)sender).GetPointFor
        ContextMenu());
    }
```

Run the same operation again and the view will unsnap and you'll be able to take a photo.

# Handling Views That Don't Support 320-Pixel Width

From time to time you'll come across views that you don't want to have in the smallest width. That's fine—the application only has to remain mostly or "usefully" functional, not completely functional. In this situation it's helpful to put up a view that explains that the user is better off adjusting the width of the application to get the functionality (see Figure 12-8). This is what we did at the very beginning of this chapter when we talked about the visual states.

*Figure 12-8. The view presented when a page doesn't support the smallest width*

We did this simply by adding a TextBlock with the text and set the visibility to collapsed:

```
<TextBlock x:Name="helpText" Grid.Row="1" Grid.Column="1" Visibility="Collapsed"
Text="Logon cannot be used in this mode"/>
```

We then set it back to visible in the "Small" state:

```
<VisualState x:Name="Small">
    <Storyboard>
…
        <ObjectAnimationUsingKeyFrames Storyboard.TargetName="helpText"
Storyboard.TargetProperty="Visibility">
            <DiscreteObjectKeyFrame KeyTime="0" Value="Visible"/>
        </ObjectAnimationUsingKeyFrames>
…
    </Storyboard>
</VisualState>
```

# CHAPTER 13

# Resources and Localization

In this chapter we look at how we can *localize* our apps—that is, make them functional in different languages.

The general premise of localization remains unchanged from years gone by. Operationally, we have usually done this by creating a table containing strings, which are then used to replace static text on the UI. You then create copies of the table for each language that you want to support. Windows works out which table to use based on the user's systemwide language preferences.

The story in WinRT for handling strings is different from how it was in .NET. You now add *.resw* files to projects, rather than *.resx* files. The APIs for loading the strings are, as you've probably guessed, different. The process by which strings are packaged along with the app is also different. Strings are not embedded into the DLL but are combined into a *.pri* file that is deployed along with the app. So, we'll look in detail at how that works as we go.

Then, we'll look at how to replace strings in the XAML markup, how to explicitly load strings, and how we can localize images. We'll also cover a special feature that allows us to package multiple image resources that are selected out depending on the DPI of the display.

## .pri Files

*.pri* files, or Package Resource Index files, are the new file format used with WinRT and in Windows Store app development. They are a binary format that represents the hierarchy of resources used in your app and any dependencies. In Windows Store apps, we define resources by marking them with a Build Action of Content. All resources are included in this file, not just string resources.

If you have a standalone module with no dependencies other than *Windows.winmd* and .NET Core, you will end up with a *resources.pri* file on compilation that contains any strings that are defined within that app, as well as references to any resources. We define strings by adding one or more *Resources.resw* files into the app, one per required language locale.

Back in Chapter 8 we built some scratch applications to support that particular chapter's discussion. One of those was called ImageShareScratch. If you look in the build output of that, you'll find a *resources.pri* file. Figure 13-1 illustrates.

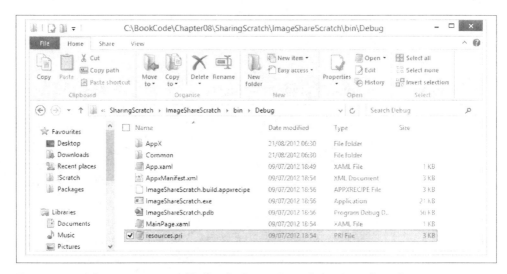

*Figure 13-1. The resources.pri file for the ImageScratch.exe Windows Store app*

The Windows 8 SDK ships with a utility called `makepri.exe` that can both make *.pri* files and dump out their contents. (I'll show you the command-line arguments you need to do this shortly.) If you dump out the contents of that *resources.pri*, you'll find all of the images and XAML files that were packaged along with the app. Here's a snippet of the output:

```
<?xml version="1.0" encoding="UTF-8" standalone="yes"?>
<PriInfo>
    <ResourceMap name="8c96f52a-1d50-4d5a-a5f5-27f950cf4765" version="1.0"
primary="true">
        <Qualifiers/>
        <ResourceMapSubtree name="Files">
            <NamedResource name="App.xaml"
uri="ms-resource://8c96f52a-1d50-4d5a-a5f5-27f950cf4765/Files/App.xaml">
                <Candidate type="Path">
                    <Value>App.xaml</Value>
                </Candidate>
            </NamedResource>
```

```
                <NamedResource name="MainPage.xaml"
    uri="ms-resource://8c96f52a-1d50-4d5a-a5f5-27f950cf4765/Files/MainPage.xaml">
                    <Candidate type="Path">
                        <Value>MainPage.xaml</Value>
                    </Candidate>
                </NamedResource>
                <ResourceMapSubtree name="Assets">
                    <NamedResource name="Logo.png"
    uri="ms-resource://8c96f52a-1d50-4d5a-a5f5-27f950cf4765/Files/Assets/Logo.png">
                        <Candidate type="Path">
                            <Value>Assets\Logo.png</Value>
                        </Candidate>
                    </NamedResource>

        <!-- file continues as you might expect... -->

        </ResourceMap>
    </PriInfo>
```

Where this story gets interesting is that as you combine modules to make bigger apps
—such as by including the Bing Maps component, the UI-agnostic StreetFoo.Client
assembly, JSON.NET, and so on—each dependency has its own *resources.pri* file, which
is used by makepri.exe to eventually build one master *resources.pri* file that contains
references that are universal across the whole install.

 It's worth remembering that if you're struggling to find the path to a
resource in your app, use makepri.exe to dump out the resource
structure. You can then find the resource path (or even just confirm
that it's there) and copy and paste the path. This is the best way to
troubleshoot resource references.

If you look in the XML I've just presented, you'll see one reference to a ResourceMap
and ResourceSubMap within. Each submap represents one component. Were we to run
makepri.exe and dump out the resources for the app as it exists in the last chapter, we'd
have entries as shown (rendered by IE) in Figure 13-2. (I'll just illustrate the output here
—I'll show you how to run makepri.exe in a moment. I've rendered it in IE so that I
can collapse sections down and make it easier to understand.)

```xml
<?xml version="1.0" encoding="UTF-8" standalone="true"?>
<PriInfo>
  <ResourceMap primary="true" version="1.0" name="569e8a16-efb8-4992-ada5-7407fecb3dee">
    <Qualifiers>
      <Language>EN, ZH-CN, PT-BR, JA, IT, FR, ES, DE</Language>
    </Qualifiers>
    <ResourceMapSubtree name="Bing.Maps">
    <ResourceMapSubtree name="Files">
      <NamedResource name="App.xaml" uri="ms-resource://569e8a16-efb8-4992-ada5-7407fecb3dee/Files/App.xaml">
      <NamedResource name="EditReportPage.xaml" uri="ms-resource://569e8a16-efb8-4992-ada5-7407fecb3dee/Files/EditReportPage.xaml">
      <NamedResource name="HelpPane.xaml" uri="ms-resource://569e8a16-efb8-4992-ada5-7407fecb3dee/Files/HelpPane.xaml">
      <NamedResource name="LogonPage.xaml" uri="ms-resource://569e8a16-efb8-4992-ada5-7407fecb3dee/Files/LogonPage.xaml">
      <NamedResource name="MySettingsPane.xaml" uri="ms-resource://569e8a16-efb8-4992-ada5-7407fecb3dee/Files/MySettingsPane.xaml">
      <NamedResource name="NotLoggedOnPage.xaml" uri="ms-resource://569e8a16-efb8-4992-ada5-7407fecb3dee/Files/NotLoggedOnPage.xaml">
      <NamedResource name="RegisterPage.xaml" uri="ms-resource://569e8a16-efb8-4992-ada5-7407fecb3dee/Files/RegisterPage.xaml">
      <NamedResource name="ReportPage.xaml" uri="ms-resource://569e8a16-efb8-4992-ada5-7407fecb3dee/Files/ReportPage.xaml">
      <NamedResource name="ReportsPage.xaml" uri="ms-resource://569e8a16-efb8-4992-ada5-7407fecb3dee/Files/ReportsPage.xaml">
      <NamedResource name="SearchResultsPage.xaml" uri="ms-resource://569e8a16-efb8-4992-ada5-7407fecb3dee/Files/SearchResultsPage.xaml">
      <NamedResource name="ShareTargetPage.xaml" uri="ms-resource://569e8a16-efb8-4992-ada5-7407fecb3dee/Files/ShareTargetPage.xaml">
      <NamedResource name="sqlite3.dll" uri="ms-resource://569e8a16-efb8-4992-ada5-7407fecb3dee/Files/sqlite3.dll">
      <NamedResource name="UnsnapWidget.xaml" uri="ms-resource://569e8a16-efb8-4992-ada5-7407fecb3dee/Files/UnsnapWidget.xaml">
      <ResourceMapSubtree name="Assets">
        <NamedResource name="HelpText.txt" uri="ms-resource://569e8a16-efb8-4992-ada5-7407fecb3dee/Files/Assets/HelpText.txt">
        <NamedResource name="Logo.png" uri="ms-resource://569e8a16-efb8-4992-ada5-7407fecb3dee/Files/Assets/Logo.png">
        <NamedResource name="LogoWide.png" uri="ms-resource://569e8a16-efb8-4992-ada5-7407fecb3dee/Files/Assets/LogoWide.png">
        <NamedResource name="SmallLogo.png" uri="ms-resource://569e8a16-efb8-4992-ada5-7407fecb3dee/Files/Assets/SmallLogo.png">
        <NamedResource name="SplashScreen.png" uri="ms-resource://569e8a16-efb8-4992-ada5-7407fecb3dee/Files/Assets/SplashScreen.png">
        <NamedResource name="StoreLogo.png" uri="ms-resource://569e8a16-efb8-4992-ada5-7407fecb3dee/Files/Assets/StoreLogo.png">
        <NamedResource name="Toast.jpg" uri="ms-resource://569e8a16-efb8-4992-ada5-7407fecb3dee/Files/Assets/Toast.jpg">
      </ResourceMapSubtree>
      <ResourceMapSubtree name="Bing.Maps">
      <ResourceMapSubtree name="Common">
      <ResourceMapSubtree name="StreetFoo.Client">
        <NamedResource name="sqlite3.dll" uri="ms-resource://569e8a16-efb8-4992-ada5-7407fecb3dee/Files/StreetFoo.Client/sqlite3.dll">
      </ResourceMapSubtree>
    </ResourceMapSubtree>
  </ResourceMap>
</PriInfo>
```

*Figure 13-2. The structure of the resources.pri file as per the app as it was at the end of Chapter 12*

Incidentally, the value shown in the URI after the `ms-resource:` protocol directive (`569e8a16-efb8-4992-ada5-7407fecb3dee`) is the package name as given in the manifest. We thus far haven't changed that package name from its default, which happens to be a GUID.

Hopefully, you can see how the entire app's state is laid out. We can now add strings into our project, and ultimately we'll see that reflected in the *resources.pri* data.

## Adding Strings

Start by creating a new Windows Store class library project called StreetFoo.Client.Resources.

Resources are managed by convention in WinRT. The convention for string resources is that you create a folder called *Strings* at the root of the project, and then folders per locale.

The way that locales are referenced in Windows hasn't changed for years. Locale codes —or more properly, Windows Language Code Identifiers (LCIDs)—typically look like this: en-US, fr-FR, de-DE, etc. The first part is the language code (which happens to adhere to ISO standard 639-1), and the second part is a country/region code (which happens to adhere to ISO standard 3166-1). For example:

*en-US*
   English language, United States country/region

*en-GB*

English language, Great Britain country/region

*fr-FR*

French language, France country/region

...and so on.

Why I'm belaboring this point is that Windows will "fail over" to languages depending on what the app supports and what your system supports. For example, I'm in the UK, so my machine is set to en-GB. If I have an app that defines resources for en-US but not en-GB, Windows will assume that en-US is a good enough match. Similarly, if I have an app that supports only fr-FR and a system set to en-GB, because Windows knows the app doesn't support any English language resources, it will use fr-FR because it has no other option.

What happens at a deeper level—which we'll see—is that Windows can be configured with a set of language preferences and will try to get the best fit out of what the machine supports, what the user chooses as her preferences, and what a given app can actually do.

Within the locale folders, you create a *Resources.resw* file. Figure 13-3 illustrates.

*Figure 13-3. Layout of the Resources project with an en-US resources file*

What we want to do first is prove that we can see strings that we create in the *resour ces.pri* file. Open up the *.resw* file and any string pair that you like. Figure 13-4 illustrates my choice.

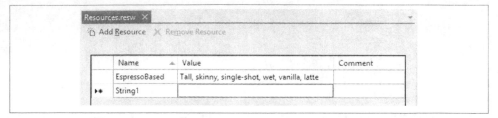

Figure 13-4. A resource string

If you're new to string translation, the "Comment" field is used for notes if you want to give the file over to a translation bureau for translation.

Now we need to reference the resources project from the main Windows Store app project. We do this in the usual way. Build the app, and a new *resources.pri* file will be created.

To run `makepri.exe`, you need to run the Developer Command Prompt for VS2012.

If you haven't done so already, it's worth pinning the Developer Command Prompt to your taskbar and setting it to run with administrator rights.

Run the prompt and navigate to the project directory. Execute this command line to create an XML file dump of the *resources.pri* contents. (Remember, this file will be in the ~/*bin/Debug* folder of the project.)

```
makepri dump /if resources.pri
```

This will create a *resources.pri.xml* file. You can open this in your favorite XML visualizer. Figure 13-5 shows the location of the new string.

*Figure 13-5. Our new string and ResourceMapSubTree*

The fact that the string exists in its own ResourceMapSubTree is important. When working in this mode, where resources are in a separate assembly, you have to fully qualify the identifiers in all cases. When you have resources in the same assembly, you generally don't have to do that. I'll explain more about that we as go on.

Now that we know how resources are collated and organized, let's look at how we can use them.

# Localizing Strings

Now, how can we actually localize strings within our apps? Let's look at how we can localize strings first in XAML using the automatic string replacement capability, and then how we can explicitly load up strings.

First, we need to look at an issue with the project setup.

## Default Project Locales

When the project is created in Visual Studio, Visual Studio takes the logged-on user's locale and writes it into the file as the default locale. You may need to manage that default; however, Visual Studio doesn't let you edit it through one of its tools. You need to change it using Notepad or a text editor of your choice.

In each of the three project files, open the *.csproj* and find the DefaultLanguage entry. (It'll be near the top.) For our purposes, as our default locale will be en-US, make sure it's en-US.

```
<DefaultLanguage>en-US</DefaultLanguage>
```

 When you do this, take care not to accidentally set Notepad to be the default handler for *.csproj* files. Nothing bad will happen, but it can be a pain.

You don't have to choose en-US on your projects—choose whichever is appropriate. The important point is that you control the locale, rather than assuming whatever one Visual Studio has set is correct.

## Localizing Strings in XAML

To test the string localization, we'll create a copy of the string table for French. (This is the fr-FR locale.) The first thing we'll do is change the caption at the top of the reports page.

We'll start by replacing the string in the language table. Rather than presenting screenshots when we do this, I'll present the string table as text. Table 13-1 shows the en-US table with the string. I'll discuss the naming shortly:

*Table 13-1. en-US string table*

| Name | Value |
| --- | --- |
| Reports_Caption.Text | Reports |

The easiest thing to do at this point is present how this works, and we'll then go back and talk about the naming convention.

The XAML replacement magic works by having you decorate controls with an x:Uid attribute. This is then used to find matching values in the string table. Notice I say "values" there. I've specified Text in Table 13-1. In fact, it can replace any property you like. This is helpful when you need to adjust the UI to accommodate language strings, but we'll get to that.

To see this working, we'll change the Reports page so that the caption is localized. To do this, we need to add the x:Uid attribute to the TextBlock control used for the caption. Here's the change:

```
<!-- Modify code in ReportsPage.xaml -->
<Grid>
    <Grid.ColumnDefinitions>
        <ColumnDefinition Width="Auto"/>
        <ColumnDefinition Width="*"/>
    </Grid.ColumnDefinitions>
    <Button x:Name="backButton" Click="GoBack" IsEnabled="{Binding Frame
.CanGoBack, ElementName=pageRoot}"
```

```
                Style="{StaticResource BackButtonStyle}"/>
                <TextBlock x:Name="pageTitle" Grid.Column="1" x:Uid=
        "/StreetFoo.Client.Resources/Resources/Reports_Caption" Text="Reports" Style="
        {StaticResource PageHeaderTextStyle}"/>
                </Grid>
```

When we specify the x:Uid, we have to provide a fully qualified resource path. The way we are doing it is slightly trickier as compared to most of the examples on MSDN and in the community because we have a separate resource assembly. If we had string resources directly within the Windows Store app project, we could just say ReportsCaption and let the resource loader infer the beginning of the path.

In either case, note that we don't specify the .*Text*. XAML is using the value to find all the strings with the same value prior to the dot. Anything after the dot is then the subject of data binding, with a dependency property being sought out and the value replaced. Note that there is no design-time support for this; hence, we still need to specify a static value for Text so that we can see it in the designer. To validate that the string replacement is working as a requirement, you may want to use the convention of prefixing the literal strings on the UI with an x. This will allow you to see at a glance which strings have not been enlisted in the localization.

Run the project and you won't see anything different. To see things done differently, we have to add new string tables.

To the resources assembly, add a locale for fr-FR and add a new *Resources.resw*. We then need to create a translation of the string that we had before. Figure 13-6 shows the solution structure. Table 13-2 shows the value of the replacement string in French.

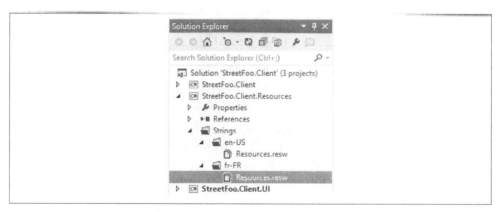

*Figure 13-6. The fr-FR locale string table in the Resources project*

*Table 13-2. fr-FR string table*

| Name | Value |
| --- | --- |
| Reports_Caption.Text | Déclarations |

In situations where Windows cannot find a string in a translated language table, but that string is in the default language table, Windows will fail over and use the default string.

If you build that, the *resources.pri* file will be changed. Here's the snippet of XML from that new *resources.pri* file where you can see the strings. The en-US and fr-FR strings are now available. Note too how the en-US one is shown as the default (isDefault).

```
<ResourceMapSubtree name="StreetFoo.Client.Resources">
    <ResourceMapSubtree name="Resources">
        <ResourceMapSubtree name="Reports_Caption">
            <NamedResource name="Text"
uri="ms-resource://569e8a16-efb8-4992-ada5-7407fecb3dee/StreetFoo.Client.
Resources/Resources/Reports_Caption/Text">
                <Candidate qualifiers="Language-FR-FR"
type="String">
                    <Value>Déclarations</Value>
                </Candidate>
                <Candidate qualifiers="Language-EN-US"
isDefault="true" type="String">
                    <Value>Reports</Value>
                </Candidate>
            </NamedResource>
        </ResourceMapSubtree>
    </ResourceMapSubtree>
</ResourceMapSubtree>
```

To try this, you need to change your language. It's difficult to write a book for a global audience and make assumptions about the languages that each reader has installed. I've based this on the assumption that you have English installed but no other languages.

The language selection is done from within Windows. WinRT will pick up the locale from Windows and choose the language that best fits based on those available and the default.

However, there's a problem. Although we can define multiple language tables in our languages assembly, the actual app doesn't know which languages are *supported*. This is also done by convention. We have to create blank *Resources.resw* files in the Windows Store app project that match the supported locales. Figure 13-7 shows this structure.

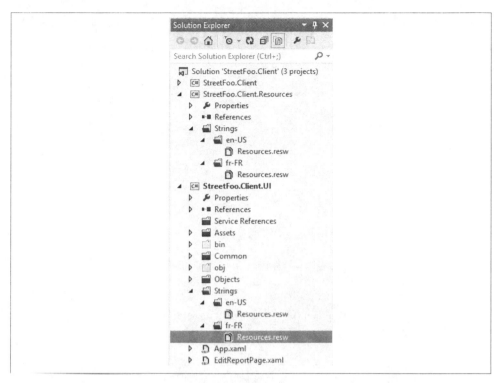

*Figure 13-7. Repeating the folder and file structure in the Windows Store app project*

To reiterate, the newly created *.resw* files in the StreetFoo.Client.UI project are blank.

You're now in a position to change your language preferences and see if the localization works. You do this through Control Panel—and the easiest way to access this in Windows 8 is to press Win+R, type **control**, and press Return. In the search box on the window, type **language** and you'll see an option for "Add a language." In Figure 13-8, I've added fr-FR, but more importantly I've made it my preferred language by putting it at the top. Windows will choose an application's language by cross-referencing the app's supported languages with the preference order defined in Control Panel.

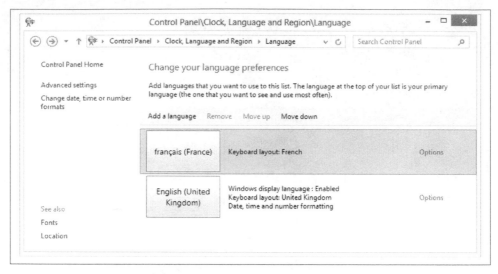

*Figure 13-8. Adding the fr-FR locale and making it preferred*

Run the app now, and the Reports page will have the French language caption. Figure 13-9 illustrates.

*Figure 13-9. The replaced string*

 Although I won't go through it here, I've added a de-DE language in the code download to give you more variations to play with.

## Conventions

Now that we've seen it working, we need to talk about conventions.

It's reasonably important to have some form of convention when working with language strings. With very complicated apps, you can end up with many hundreds of strings.

You should come up with your own convention that feels comfortable, but there are some restrictions. It's worth designing that convention so that you can see which UI aspect owns the string. In this case, I've proposed using Reports as the prefix for strings that relate to ReportsPage.

Because XAML uses dot notation to find properties to bind to, you cannot use dots in the part of the name that you own. Likewise, I'd recommend not using slashes because they are used in the paths that you specify to load the strings. What I've used in my strings is underscores.

You can also include elements—for example, perhaps you want messages that appear in MessageDialog pop ups to include *Message* in the name. Likewise, strings that apply to notifications might include Tile or Toast in the name.

The important thing is to have a convention; how that convention is structured is up to you.

## Changing Other Properties

One of the classic problems with localization is when you need to change the UI in order to accommodate a string. German is particularly prone to using words that are often longer than those used by other languages.

It's for this reason that the dot notation is included in the string name. You can reference any dependency properties that you like in there.

I won't show you how to do this in these pages, as it's obvious and there's nowhere to put it. However, in the code download I have a button on the Reports page that changes its height depending on the locale.

## Explicitly Loading Strings

To round off the discussion on strings, we need to look at how we can explicitly load strings for things like messages that are displayed in MessageDialogs and other notifications (i.e., those that are not necessarily expressed in markup).

Oftentimes when you load a string in this way you need to replace values in it—for example "I found 27 reports" may need to be replaced with "J'ai trouvé 27 déclarations." You can easily do this by loading a string and using the loaded string as the template for use with a normal string.Format call.

The approach I'm proposing here is to create a helper class that lets us load strings and optionally format them. Nothing about the string table setup will change.

We'll build a class called StringHelper with a method called Format. This will take a path to a string, load it, and then call string.Format on it, passing in any parameters (if we specified any).

Whereas before when we needed to put in the x:Uid attributes we specified the full string, in StringHelper, if we assume all the strings are in a single common assembly (which is a fair assumption), we can provide just the name of the string in the common assembly. When we come to load it, we'll assume the other elements of the path are static.

Here's the implementation for StringHelper. This uses a ResourceLoader bound to a specific resource map, the name of which is the name of our common language assembly. When we come to build the complete path, we need to specify that it's within the Resources branch, and then we just tack the name onto the end.

```
public static class StringHelper
{
    private const string ResourceMapName = "StreetFoo.Client.Resources";

    // loads a resource string and runs string.Format on it...
    public static string Format(string name, params object[] args)
    {
        var buf = new ResourceLoader(ResourceMapName).
            GetString("Resources/" + name);
        if (args.Any())
            return string.Format(buf, args);
        else
            return buf;
    }
}
```

To test it, we'll localize the text used in the toast displayed when we refresh the Reports page. We'll need one string for the toast caption, and then two strings to report back on the number of items that were loaded from the server.

The first step is to build up the string table. Tables 13-3 and 13-4 show the en-US and fr-FR tables.

*Table 13-3. en-US string table with toast strings*

| Name | Value |
| --- | --- |
| Reports_Caption.Text | Déclarations |
| Reports_Toast_ReportsRefreshed | Reports refreshed |
| Reports_Toast_IFound1Report | I found 1 report. |
| Reports_Toast_IFoundNReports | I found {0} reports. |

*Table 13-4. fr-FR string table with toast strings*

| Name | Value |
| --- | --- |
| Reports_Caption.Text | Déclarations |
| Reports_Toast_ReportsRefreshed | Déclarations rafraîchies |
| Reports_Toast_IFound1Report | J'ai trouvé 1 declaration. |
| Reports_Toast_IFoundNReports | J'ai trouvé {0} declarations. |

Using the strings is just how you'd imagine it might be. Rather than using literal strings, you load the appropriate string from the table using the new StringHelper class.

Here's the change to the constructor of ReportsPageViewModel, specifically where the RefreshCommand is initialized. I've omitted code from this class for brevity.

```
public ReportsPageViewModel(IViewModelHost host)
    : base(host)
{
    // commands...
    this.RefreshCommand = new DelegateCommand(async (e) =>
    {
        this.Host.HideAppBar();
        await this.DoRefresh(true);

        // toast...
        string message = StringHelper.Format("Reports_Toast_IFound1Report");
        if (this.Items.Count != 1)
            message = StringHelper.Format(
            "Reports_Toast_IFoundNReports", this.Items.Count);
        var toast = new ToastNotificationBuilder(new string[] {
StringHelper.Format("Reports_Toast_ReportsRefreshed"), message });
        toast.ImageUri = "ms-appx:///Assets/Toast.jpg";
        toast.Update();
    });

    // code omitted for brevity...
}
```

Run the project now with the fr-FR locale as your preferred locale, and you'll see the string on the toast in French rather than English. Figure 13-10 illustrates.

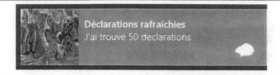

*Figure 13-10. Our toast notification from Chapter 6, but in French*

---

### Naming of StringHelper Methods

There's one last thing to discuss before we leave strings and move on to images. Our `StringHelper.Format` method doesn't have to take arguments. There is a line of thought that says that `Format` isn't the best name for this. You could create another method in `StringHelper` (e.g., `LoadString`) that didn't take arguments. All that would do, however, is defer to `Format`. Its sole purpose would be stopping your code from "looking funny" because of the preconceived perception that `Format` should take arguments.

---

# Localizing Images

In this next section, we'll look at how to work with localized image resources. This is helpful in situations where the image you're looking to convey has some localized meaning. However, the more interesting (and common) thing is how to vary the resource selection by display DPI.

We'll start by looking at varying the resource by locale.

## Varying Images by Locale

We've seen thus far that string resources are defined in our application using a convention-based approach. By virtue of the fact that we have resources in specific folders, `makepri.exe` knows that one string table belongs to the en-US locale, whereas another belongs to fr-FR.

That same convention-based approach flows through into all resource types. If we create an image with a given name (e.g., *Flag.png*), and if we put one in the *en-US* folder and another in the *fr-FR* folder, WinRT knows that we are defining a localized resource. Given where we are at the moment with our separate resource assembly, the easiest thing to do here is to continue this approach. (In fact, that's what we will do after this short diversion.)

There is another way to specify a localized resource file, which is to put the language identifier in the file itself. The rule is to put `.lang-<languageCode>` into the filename. Figure 13-11 shows this approach; however, this isn't the approach we're going to use in this book.

---

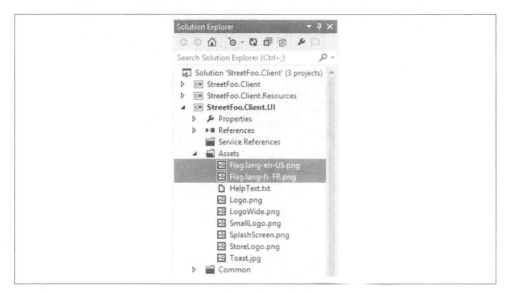

*Figure 13-11. Using the .lang-<languageCode> convention*

 One more thing: if you do use that approach, you may find you have to specify several language qualifiers in the string name. If you do this, separate them with underscores.

As mentioned, I don't want to go that way, as I want to show you how to do this using our separate resource assembly. We'll also use the approach of separating resources by locale-specific folder rather than using the filename. (You can still use the filename-based approach, but if you have a lot of resources to localize, splitting by folder can be more useful.)

Figure 13-12 shows the same flag files but in separate folders. I've created a root *Images* folder to do this.

To refer to these images in the XAML, nothing changes from the way we've done this before using the ms-appx: protocol in the URI.

Here's the change to the title block of ReportsPage to display an image. As you might expect, we don't have to do anything in order to specify that we want a localized value. It just works.

```
<!-- Back button and page title -->
<Grid>
    <Grid.ColumnDefinitions>
        <ColumnDefinition Width="Auto"/>
```

*Figure 13-12. Images broken down into specific language folders*

```
            <ColumnDefinition Width="*"/>
        </Grid.ColumnDefinitions>
        <Button x:Name="backButton" Click="GoBack" IsEnabled="{Binding Frame.
CanGoBack, ElementName=pageRoot}"
Style="{StaticResource BackButtonStyle}"/>
        <StackPanel Orientation="Horizontal" Grid.Column="1">
            <TextBlock x:Name="pageTitle" x:Uid=
"/StreetFoo.Client.Resources/Resources/Reports_Caption" Text="Reports"
Style="{StaticResource PageHeaderTextStyle}"/>
            <Image Source="ms-appx:///StreetFoo.Client.Resources/Images
/Flag.png" Width="25" Height="15" HorizontalAlignment="Left" Margin="0,30,0,0">
</Image>
        </StackPanel>
    </Grid>
```

Run the app in the en-US locale, and you'll see an image as shown in Figure 13-13.

*Figure 13-13. The en-US flag*

Change the locale to fr-FR and do the same thing (see Figure 13-14).

*Figure 13-14. The fr-FR flag*

That's all you have to do. WinRT will do the heavy lifting in terms of the resource selection.

## Varying Images by Display DPI

This section is challenging, as it's difficult to demonstrate different pixel density in a book. However, in order to make raster images look nice in your application, you need to handle display DPI.

DPI is a reasonably complex topic, and a detailed discussion is beyond the scope of this book. However, it has to do with scaling. Imagine you have a bitmap that fills the whole screen. When you develop it, you develop on a normal DPI resolution. The image will look fine to you. However, on deployment, if the end user uses a higher DPI screen, the OS will scale up that image and as a result it may not look as good. The idea, then, is that we provide multiple images in the application and allow Windows to use bigger images when appropriate and hence perform more appropriate scaling. (Scaling will always end up looking a little rubbish, as the whole point of it is to "invent" information that isn't there—we're aiming to get to "good enough.")

 This doesn't just affect full-screen renders. Windows will scale up the UI on higher DPI displays because otherwise targets get too small to touch accurately. This is why handling DPI is particularly important in Windows Store apps.

There is a sweeping recommendation with Windows Store apps that rather than using raster images at all, we're supposed to use vector images. In Chapter 5, for example, we tried where possible to use the vector images defined in the Segoe UI Symbol font. While this is true, it's naïve to assume the whole industry is going to pivot away from raster images to vector images for Windows Store apps. (Remember that I went into this topic in more detail in Chapter 5.)

To properly support high DPI displays, images need to be provided in 100% versions, 140% versions, and 180% versions. The 140% version is used when the DPI is between 174 and 239 DPI, and the 180% version is used for 240 DPI or above. The 100% version is for what (as of the time of writing at least) is considered to be a "normal," non-high-DPI display.

As you'd expect, the different images are specified using a convention-based approach —specifically, .scale-<percentage>. It's regarded as best practice to specify the 100% version explicitly. Figure 13-15 illustrates the flag resources in our solution with scale specified.

*Figure 13-15. Flag image resources specified with scale*

Again, in a book I can't really show you this. However, if you were to look at the output in *resources.pri*, you would see the different images in there, with each one having a defined Scale qualifier:

```
<ResourceMapSubtree name="StreetFoo.Client.Resources">
            <ResourceMapSubtree name="Images">
                <NamedResource name="Flag.png"
                uri="ms-resource://569e8a16-efb8-4992-ada5-7407fecb3dee
                /Files/StreetFoo.Client.Resources/Images/Flag.png">
                    <Candidate qualifiers="Language-FR-FR, Scale-180"
                      type="Path">
                        <Value>StreetFoo.Client.Resources\Images\fr-FR\
                        Flag.scale-180.png</Value>
                    </Candidate>
                    <Candidate qualifiers="Language-FR-FR, Scale-140"
                      type="Path">
                        <Value>StreetFoo.Client.Resources\Images\fr-FR\
                        Flag.scale-140.png</Value>
                    </Candidate>
                    <Candidate qualifiers="Language-FR-FR, Scale-100"
                      type="Path">
                        <Value>StreetFoo.Client.Resources\Images\fr-FR\
                        Flag.scale-100.png</Value>
                    </Candidate>
```

```xml
            <Candidate qualifiers="Language-EN-US, Scale-180"
             isDefault="true" type="Path">
                <Value>StreetFoo.Client.Resources\Images\en-US\
                Flag.scale-180.png</Value>
            </Candidate>
            <Candidate qualifiers="Language-EN-US, Scale-140"
             isDefault="true" type="Path">
                <Value>StreetFoo.Client.Resources\Images\en-US\
                Flag.scale-140.png</Value>
            </Candidate>
            <Candidate qualifiers="Language-EN-US, Scale-100"
             isDefault="true" type="Path">
                <Value>StreetFoo.Client.Resources\Images\en-US\
                Flag.scale-100.png</Value>
            </Candidate>
        </NamedResource>
    </ResourceMapSubtree>
</ResourceMapSubtree>
```

# CHAPTER 14

# Background Tasks and App Lifetime

In this chapter we're going to look at how we can make portions of our code run even when our app is not—a capability known as *background tasks*.

Background tasks are easy enough to work with, but they are one of the areas of Windows Store apps that is on the "difficult" end of the spectrum in terms of features in the API. This is because, with mobile, preserving battery life is paramount. Applications that can wake up and do whatever they like in the background are a problem, because without any form of control it'd be easy enough for the user to install some innocuous app, only to find that battery life on the device had halved without any real idea as to why.

In Windows 8/Windows RT, there are so many controls and restrictions on what background tasks can do that you could describe them as being openly hostile to apps that need to run in the background. The reason for this is that background tasks are designed to keep the device "fresh," but to do so within the context of a consumer/retail usage model. With LOB apps there is much more pressure on time, and it's this part that's not fantastically well served by the background tasks implementation as it stands at the time of writing. For example, a 10-minute delay in updates on a game is fine. If you have employees doing 20 jobs a day coordinated by your app with a 10-minute delay, however, that's a 3.3-hour delay per operative inserted into each working day just for idle time.

It's in this context that we're going to discuss background tasks: the classic "field worker" scenario. An operative is mobile all day, but from time to time will receive notifications of new jobs through his device. He will also complete jobs and have to send updates back to base. Connectivity may be sketchy, so although the user can click Add New Report (in our case) and the report will save locally, it could be many minutes or hours before the connection is sufficient to send the data back. The business usually requires data to be sent back in a timely manner—it's unusual that these systems in the real world are rigged to work on an "it's OK to sync when you get back to base" basis. The business will expect progress returned wirelessly throughout the day.

To this end, we're going to create a "synchronization" background task that will send up any pending updates, and download any new jobs.

What we'll do first is talk about app lifetime in Windows 8 and Windows RT. We'll then tackle building the background tasks that we need for our StreetFoo app. We'll look first at the general structure of the API and then go on to build our actual synchronization routines.

# App Lifetime

From first principles, you'd expect app lifetime to be quite a big topic in Windows Store app development. Practically, though, there's hardly anything to it, as the rules are so simple. If an app's running, it's taking up battery power—and the best approach that Windows can take is to make sure that if it's not being used, it's not running.

Any opportunity it has to do so, Windows will stop scheduling time for your process to run. When main memory comes under pressure, your app's memory working set can be dumped to disk and your process unloaded. When the user selects your app again, a new process is established, your working set reloaded, and CPU time scheduled to you. I offer this part as helpful information—as a developer you don't need to code anything special to support it, and as a user you shouldn't even notice that it's happening.

In total, you have three possible states for your app: `Running`, `Suspended`, and `NotRunning`. You get events, which you can access via `Application` and therefore your individual `App` class for `Suspending` (going from running to suspended) and for `Resuming` (going from suspended to running). You won't be told when you get dumped out of memory—you just get killed off. However, if you are running, you will go through the suspend phase before you do get killed off. Therefore, this is a good time to do any cleaning up or persisting of data that you need to do. (In fact, it's your only time.)

There is an important restriction with regards to suspending—you only get five seconds to do your work. If you take longer than that, you'll be unceremoniously killed. (And we're about to talk about CPU time, so I'm getting ahead of myself. This five seconds is as you would count them on your watch.)

 While we're here, it's worth mentioning the `OnActivated` and `OnLaunched` methods in `Application`. `OnLaunched` is called if the user launches your task from the Start screen via a tile. `OnActivated` is called if you start for any other reason. (If you recall, in a few places throughout this book we've had to do different behavior when we get launched by things like file association, share charms, etc.)

Underpinning all of this design is a new feature in Windows 8 and Windows RT called *connected standby* (CS). Prior to this computers were either "running normally," in "sleep mode" (main memory powered and controlled by the CPU, but no OS processes scheduled, no devices running), in "hibernate mode" (main memory contents entirely swapped to disk, computer off), or just "switched off."

CS is an operating system feature, and not necessarily a power management feature. In CS the system is still running as normal, it's just that Windows will stop doing as much as possible. If the hardware is appropriate (and I'll get to that), when the screen is off Windows is considered to be in CS. Windows Store apps are suspended as one step. As another step, normal Windows processes are suspended. There's this rather beautifully named step in the whole process called *quiescing*. This is why it's called CS—Windows is still running, as is the entire networking stack, hence Windows is *connected*. Your background tasks will still run in this mode, and when they are, everything will appear normal. After all, you're sandboxed off from everything so you never really know what the state of the rest of the system is in any case. Everyone else could be fast asleep, or processing a hard workload. You don't know, nor should you care.

Hardware-wise, in order for hardware to be CS-capable, the rules are that it has to have a certain flag set in firmware, it can't have spinning disks (as they could wake up to find themselves under heavy motion, which could break them), and it must be able to be cooled sufficiently via passive cooling. (One of the things that will wake the system is a thermal warning, so any problem there means the machine will hibernate and shut down fully.) For completeness, there is also a special capability you need on network adapters, but that's just a detail point.

In all, CS is a really decent Windows 8 feature, and what you're about to read may seem restrictive and strange—especially CPU quotas—but I hope as you reflect back on CS you'll realize why it's been built as it has.

# Background Tasks API

There are three basic concepts that you need to understand about background tasks. Learning how to implement background tasks to good effect is a matter of learning the subtleties and nuances of these three concepts. We'll talk about all of these aspects in more detail throughout the chapter.

- First, you have a *CPU usage quota*. The idea here is that you are given an amount of CPU to use—$n$ sections every $m$ minutes. Go over this, and your task is suspended until you "save up" more quota.

- Second, you have a set of *triggers* that you can use to kick off your tasks. Triggers also have *conditions*. For example, you can create a trigger to run every 15 minutes without conditions, or schedule the same thing but only on the condition that a user is logged on when it's time to run.

- Third, *background tasks are executed outside of the process of the main app*, regardless of whether the app is running or not. (This is a simplification—there are instances where they run inside your own app's process, but only certain types of tasks can do that, and those tasks are outside the scope of this book.) Restrictions also exist in that the class containing the task to execute must be in a WinRT component, not a normal .NET assembly. (WinRT components have the *.winmd* filetype.) We haven't looked this topic at all so far, but we will in this section.

Let's look at each of these three concepts in turn.

## CPU Usage Quota

I wanted to present this concept first because it's the one you need to have the best grasp of, but it's also the most woolly of all of them.

CPU usage quotas are quoted as follows:

- If you're running on the "lock screen," you get two seconds of CPU time every fifteen minutes.
- If you're not running on the "lock screen," you get one second of CPU time every two hours.

The first thing that needs defining here is *CPU time*. This is not the same measurement as SI units of time that you'd measure on your watch. This is often known as "clock on the wall" time.

For example, a method can start, run in five seconds of "clock on the wall time," and still come in under quota. CPU time is measured by Windows as time when the code is not blocking, and as we've seen with the asynchrony implementation throughout this book, there are plenty of times when your code is blocking. (Deep down, it relies on the Windows internal process timing instrumentation to work out how much time you've used.)

Simultaneously, this makes the CPU problem less pressing, but much weirder because it becomes harder to measure and understand without deep inspection. Coming back to connected standby, this restriction exists because the device never really ends up being "off." A laptop asleep in a bag being toted from site to site is in sleep, hibernate, or "off" mode. In any of those modes, user code doesn't run. As an OS designer, Microsoft needed to make sure that each app could only take "light sips" from the CPU when in CS.

Your strategy, then, should be to maximize the quota. The only ways you can do this are to a) do less, and b) put yourself on the lock screen. You should also note that the quota is shared across all of the background tasks tied to your app package—you don't get more quota by registering more tasks.

*Do less*

This becomes a normal optimization problem. If you have to download new work from a server, the background task would be better used to grab the data from the server, spool it to disk, and then stop as opposed to downloading it and processing it into the database. When the app resumes and you have no CPU quota in play, you can pick up the spooled data, and then update the database, complete all of the local processing, etc. (We'll implement this approach in our sync routine.)

*Putting yourself on the lock screen*

This is a good way of octupling your quota, but with much less direct control. Tasks on the lock screen appear as icons that can provide immediate feedback even if the device is off—for example, reporting on new emails or new calendar appointments. However, there are problems.

First, you can only request that the user puts your app on the lock screen—you can't make the user do it and you can't force it to happen. (We'll see this later during the implementation.) Second, you can only have seven apps on the lock screen in total. Third, if you go onto the lock screen, the user can remove you, and you don't get to keep asking her whether you can go back on it. Nor do you get to query whether you are still on the lock screen.

From a consumer app perspective, all of this is sensible. However, from a LOB app perspective, this could ideally do with less restriction. Having to train employees of the business that paid for the app not to remove LOB apps from the lock screen is pretty silly.

### Network constraints

Just as there are CPU constraints, there are also network constraints. Whereas the CPU constraints/quota apply whether the device is on AC power or battery power, network constraints only apply when on battery power.

I'm not going to go into detail on this; the restrictions are fairly roomy, and if you're doing "normal" communications (i.e., just shuttling bits of control data back and forth) you're unlikely to hit it. However, if you are planning to do large transfers on background tasks, you'll need to think about network constraints.

## Triggers and Conditions

Now that you understand the CPU quota, we can look at triggers.

`MaintenanceTrigger`

This is the simplest type of trigger to understand. You specify an interval (which can't be less than 15 minutes) and, provided that the device has AC power, the trigger will run. You don't have to be on the lock screen, but to reiterate, you will need AC power.

**TimeTrigger**

This is like a `MaintenanceTrigger`, but you don't need AC power and you do need to be on the lock screen. Being on the lock screen creates wrinkles in your implementation as per the previous explanation. Specifically, even for sideloaded LOB apps, you can't guarantee that you're on the lock screen. Again, the minimum interval is 15 minutes. (We'll talk about sideloading in Chapter 15.)

**SystemTrigger**

This is raised when certain system events happen, such as a user logging in or out, the Internet becoming available, and so on. I'm not going to repeat the MSDN documentation for this trigger in these pages, but it's worth having a look to see the sorts of things that you can do. (We'll use the `InternetAvailable` one in our example, though.) Some event types only apply if you're on the lock screen.

**PushNotificationTrigger**

This can be used to receive raw notifications. We didn't talk about these much in Chapter 5. To handle this sort of trigger, you'll need to be on the lock screen. (We're not going to go into detail on this here—refer to the MSDN for more information.)

**ControlChannelTrigger**

We're not going to talk about this one. This is for specialized networking activities that are beyond the scope of this book.

 It's the `PushNotificationTrigger` and `ControlChannelTrigger` that can be configured to run within your app's process. All of the others run in a standalone process.

As mentioned, each of these triggers can also accept conditions. The idea of these is that they let you ignore situations where it's pointless for you to run. You can decide whether you want to run if the user is `UserPresent` (meaning the device is unlocked) or `User NotPresent`, if you are `InternetAvailable` or `InternetNotAvailable`, or finally if you are `SessionConnected` (meaning the user is logged on) or `SessionDisconnected`.

The conditions can help save CPU quota. For example, if you have a periodic trigger that sends information to a server, you can choose not to do that if you have no Internet available. Then you can create a trigger that runs when the Internet comes back. By skipping the first one, you've saved $x$ amount of CPU quota by not calling up to the server. (Again, this is what we'll do in our actual example.)

If you're thinking about LOB apps, the seminal example is an operative in a truck who finishes a job at a location, hits Save, and puts the device on standby. You have two problems here: the operation may not have completed before he put the device on standby, or the device might not have had a good cellular collection at the time.

---

The inclination here is to use a maintenance trigger, but that trigger type has a problem in that it only runs when AC power is available. You could insist that operatives plug their device into the vehicle's power source whenever they are travelling. (In fact, on smartphone BYOD systems, this problem normally solves itself because the battery life is so poor that operatives get into the habit of doing this themselves anyway.) Alternatively, you could hope that the operative leaves the app on the lock screen.

The upshot here is that there essentially isn't a great way of solving this problem. In the olden days of the Windows Mobile platform, you could spin up a thread, your process would never die, and you could do what you want. On Android—a popular field-service app platform—you can create a background service that, again, runs in exactly the way that you want.

In the example we're going to create a maintenance trigger, a time trigger, and a system trigger to detect the Internet. These will send up changes and download new work whenever they run.

## Execution Model

So far in this book, we've skipped over the core differences between WinRT components and their libraries and .NET types and their assemblies. We've spoken about how there's a shared metadata model, and we know that WinRT underpins all of the work that we do, but I've generally avoided going into detail about this aspect because if you're working with .NET all of the time you generally don't care.

When we're using background tasks, however, we can't avoid proactively handling the boundary between the .NET and WinRT worlds; we have to deal with it head-on. Background task components must be created as WinRT components. You can still write them in .NET, it's just that rather than hosting them in a .NET assembly (the Class Library option in the project's properties), you have to host them as—as it's put in VS's project properties windows—a Windows Runtime Component. What you get at the end is a *.winmd* file rather than a *.dll*.

This sounds fine, but there's a problem. WinRT components have some rules that limit the richness that you can achieve with pure .NET. Compiling as a WinRT library will insist that exposed classes are sealed. There are also restrictions on overloads. These restrictions are down to restrictions in COM itself. A "hand-waving" answer as to why is that COM only supports interface inheritance, and in order to be in harmony with .NET it would also need to support implementation inheritance.

Again, this topic isn't something I want to dwell on in this book, because unless you're going cross-boundary (for example, creating C# components to consume in HTML/ JavaScript), you don't really need to worry about it.

When we come to our implementation, we're going to create a separate façade library that exposes our normal .NET task handling types out in a WinRT component library. This tends to be the easiest way of squaring the circle.

Background tasks are in virtually all cases hosted in a separate executable called `back groundTaskHost.exe`. (And yes—it has a lowercase *b*.) Any background tasks that you're ever likely to implement will run in this way.

From an OS design perspective, running the tasks in a separate process makes sense. You can run them at lower priority, you can kill them off, and you can keep track of what's happening in the universe of background tasks running on the device far more easily. From an app design perspective, it's also not a bad decision. The only situation you have to deal with is not having shared state between the running app and the background task. You'll have to deal with this aspect, but it's not difficult.

## Implementing a Sync Background Task

Now that we've been through the basics of how background tasks work, we'll take a look at actually implementing one.

We'll start by creating a task that has a `MaintenanceTrigger`. As mentioned previously, this needs to be hosted in a separate Windows Runtime component library. We'll make that library depend on the UI-agnostic StreetFoo library. In the UI-agnostic library we'll create a class that contains the logic called `BackgroundSyncTask`, and in the Windows Runtime component library we'll create a façade class called `BackgroundSyncTaskFa cade`. The easiest way to work with this stuff is to keep the Windows Runtime components as basic as possible so that you don't hit any of the design restrictions, and work as you naturally would back in the .NET world deferring from one to the other.

We'll also create a base class called `TaskBase`. When our task starts, we'll be running in a separate background process, so we'll need to boot up the app and log in the current user.

One of the tricky parts to get right when we register background tasks is that Windows will happily reregister the same task again and again. We have to manually go through and "reset" any task registrations that we want when we start the app.

To start, we'll need to stub out our `TaskBase` class. Here's the code:

```
public abstract class TaskBase
{
}
```

Next, we'll build `TaskHelper`. This class will be responsible for registering tasks.

Task registrations are held in the `BackgroundTaskRegistration` class. We can walk the `AllTasks` dictionary looking for an existing task to cancel. Tasks are identified by name, which is arbitrary. In our case we're going to create one task class pair (`Background SyncTask` and `BackgroundSyncTaskFacade`), and then create three tasks that can trigger it. We're going to create a `MaintenanceTrigger` (which will run every 15 minutes, but only on AC power), a `TimeTrigger` (which will run every 15 minutes, but only when we're on the lock screen), and a `SystemTrigger`. This last trigger will be configured to run whenever the device goes from having no Internet connectivity to having Internet connectivity.

Our `RegisterTaskAsync<T>` method will take the type of the task and the name, and also provide an `Action` callback that will be used to configure the task. (It's this part that will set up the trigger and the conditions.) When we come to build the task using a `BackgroundTaskBuilder`, it will require a value for its `TaskEntryPoint` property in the name of the façade class. We don't have direct metadata access to that, so we'll need to mangle the name ourselves. Specifically, this will be of the form `StreetFoo.Client.Tasks.<Name>Facade`.

Here's the code for `TaskHelper` that will do both the deletion of any existing registration, and creation of a new registration. The registration method will ultimately end up being async—for now we have to fake it using `Task.FromResult<bool>`:

```
public static class TaskHelper
{
    // registers a task with the given name...
    public static Task RegisterTaskAsync<T>(string name, Action
<BackgroundTaskBuilder> configureCallback)
        where T : TaskBase
    {
        // unregister any old one...
        UnregisterTask(name);

        // register the new one...
        var builder = new BackgroundTaskBuilder();
        builder.Name = name;

        // entry point is StreetFoo.Client.Tasks.<Name>Facade
        builder.TaskEntryPoint = string.Format("StreetFoo.Client.Tasks.
{0}Facade", typeof(T).Name);

        // configure...
        configureCallback(builder);

        // register it...
        builder.Register();

        // return a dummy task...
        return Task.FromResult<bool>(true);
    }

    // unregisters a task with the given name...
    private static void UnregisterTask(string name)
```

```
        {
            // find it, and unregister it...
            var existing = BackgroundTaskRegistration.AllTasks.Values.Where
(v => v.Name == name).FirstOrDefault();
            if (existing != null)
                existing.Unregister(true);
        }
    }
```

 This implementation ignores tasks that have been retired as you up-grade the app (e.g., you may have had a task in v1 that you don't need in v2). You'll need to unregister these too in order to be tidy, and to preserve any CPU quota that might get used up in handling the errors.

We'll need to call `RegisterTaskAsync<T>` whenever we boot the app—but there's a wrinkle. When we work like this, we have two ways in which we can boot. We can either boot interactively into the full Windows Store UI, or we can boot inside of `background` `TaskHost.exe`. If we're actually running in background mode, we don't want to change the task registration or things will get very confusing. As the task registration only makes sense when we're actually running the main app, my proposal is that we kick off this registration from the `App` class within the Windows Store app itself.

Background tasks are an area where a good logging infrastructure really pays dividends. To this end, I'm going to recommend adding the open source MetroLog library to our application. This project is loosely based on the popular .NET log4net and NLog projects, although it's hugely slimmed down in order to be sympathetic to the reduced capabilities in the WinRT API.

To add the MetroLog library to the project, right-click on the UI-agnostic Street-Foo.Client project and select Manage NuGet Packages. Search for MetroLog, and add this project. Figure 14-1 illustrates.

There is one problem that we need to deal with, which is that we need to wait for log messages to be written before we quit; otherwise, the whole process gets torn down and we don't have a chance to finish writing. (MetroLog's file writing capability is asynchronous because WinRT's file APIs are asynchronous.) We can use the `ILoggerAsync` interface on MetroLog to get hold of `Task` instances that relate to the write operations. We can collect all these and then use `Task.WaitAll` to flush them all through. To get an `ILoggerAsync`, all you have to do is cast a normal `ILogger` instance.

 You should note, though, that as of the time of writing there is a bug in MetroLog where pending write operations that are not actively tracked are not flushed on process shutdown—thus, things that we write as we go using the normal `ILogger` interface may not be flushed.

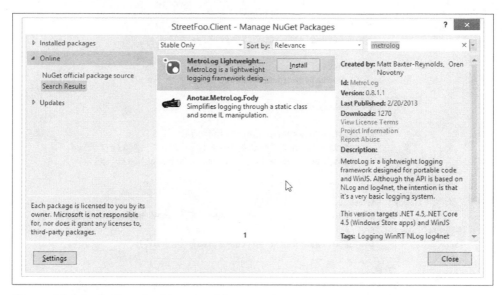

*Figure 14-1. Including the MetroLog Nuget package*

This is a lot to take on board, but there's just one more part...

In `TaskBase` we'll create a `RunAsync` method that will accept an `IBackgroundTaskIn stance` value. This is a WinRT interface, and an instance of this is given to us by the background task subsystem when the task runs. In the `RunAsync` method, we can boot the app and defer to an abstract method called `DoRunAsync`.

Here's the code:

```
public abstract class TaskBase
    {
        private ILogger _logger;

        // runs the operation...
        public async Task RunAsync(IBackgroundTaskInstance instance)
        {
            // logging is a bit tricky as we have to gather all of the messages
            // and flush them out...
            var logTasks = new List<Task<LogWriteOperation[]>>();

            // do some logging...
            var asyncLogger = (ILoggerAsync)this.Logger;
            logTasks.Add(asyncLogger.InfoAsync("Started background task '{0}'
(#{1})...",
                instance.Task.Name, instance.Task.TaskId));

            // run...
            try
```

```
            {
                // start the app...
                await StreetFooRuntime.Start("Tasks");

                // defer...
                await DoRunAsync(instance);
            }
            catch (Exception ex)
            {
                logTasks.Add(asyncLogger.FatalAsync(
                    string.Format("Background task '{0}' (#{1}) failed.",
                    instance.Task.Name, instance.Task.TaskId), ex));
            }

            // finish...
            logTasks.Add(asyncLogger.InfoAsync("Finished background task '{0}'
(#{1}).",

                instance.Task.Name, instance.Task.TaskId));

            // wait...
            await Task.WhenAll(logTasks);
        }

        // actual runner...
        protected abstract Task DoRunAsync(IBackgroundTaskInstance instance);

        // log...
        protected ILogger Logger
        {
            get
            {
                if(_logger == null)
                    _logger = LogManagerFactory.DefaultLogManager.GetLogger
(this.GetType());
                return _logger;
            }
        }
    }
```

The initial implementation of BackgroundSyncTask won't do much; it'll just write a
message to the log. Here's the code:

```
public class BackgroundSyncTask : TaskBase
{
    protected override Task DoRunAsync(IBackgroundTaskInstance instance)
    {
        this.Logger.Info("Called!");

        // short-circuit...
        return Task.FromResult<bool>(true);
    }
}
```

You can see here that we return a Task. We've seen this a few times now—it's easier to build framework components as asynchronous from the outset than to retrofit them later.

By convention we're going to create static ConfigureAsync methods in our task classes that will configure all of the triggers. In our example, we don't need to apply conditions —if you recall, conditions are things like "only when the user is logged on." We want all of our tasks to run regardless of state, and hence there are no conditions.

Here's the configuration code to add to BackgroundSyncTask. This method will create three separate background tasks as we discussed previously—one triggered by a Main tenanceTrigger, one triggered by a TimeTrigger, and one SystemTrigger that will respond when any Internet connection is restored.

```
// Add to BackgroundSyncTask...
public static async Task ConfigureAsync()
{
    // set up the maintenance task...
    await TaskHelper.RegisterTaskAsync<BackgroundSyncTask>
("BackgroundSyncMaintenance", (builder) =>
    {
        // every 15 minutes, continuous, when on AC...
        builder.SetTrigger(new MaintenanceTrigger(15, false));
    });

    // set up the time task...
    await TaskHelper.RegisterTaskAsync<BackgroundSyncTask>
("BackgroundSyncTime",
        (builder) =>
    {
        // every 15 minutes, continuous, when on lock screen...
        builder.SetTrigger(new TimeTrigger(15, false));
    });

    // set up the connectivity task...
    await TaskHelper.RegisterTaskAsync<BackgroundSyncTask>
("BackgroundSyncConnectivity", (builder) =>
    {
        // whenever we get connectivity...
        builder.SetTrigger(new SystemTrigger
(SystemTriggerType.InternetAvailable, false));
    });
}
```

You may have jumped ahead here and thought that it's possible for all of those tasks to run at the same time. That is indeed possible! (In fact, as the MaintenanceTrigger and TimeTrigger have the same interval, if we're on the lock screen and with AC power, these will run at the same time. Later, we'll look at a way of stopping this from happening by handling the race condition.)

To complete building out the task, we have to construct and register the façade. When we've done that, we can look at debugging and running the task.

## Building the Façade

To build the façade, we need to add a new project. Add a new Windows Store App→Class Library project to the solution called StreetFoo.Client.Tasks. When that's done, open the project properties and change the "Output type" value to Windows Runtime Component. Figure 14-2 illustrates.

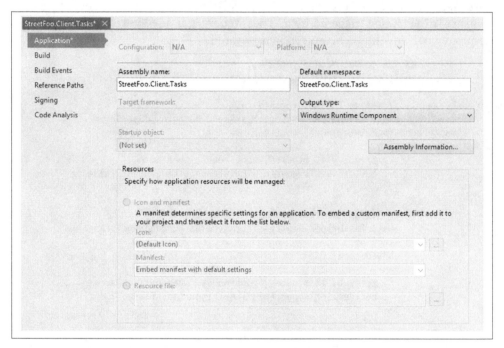

*Figure 14-2. Setting the project to emit a Windows Runtime component library*

When that's done, you'll need to make sure that the project is building in the x86 configuration. (Recall that we did this in Chapter 3; it's required to get the SQLite library to load properly.) Right-click on the solution, select Configuration Manager, and confirm that all projects are set to x86. Figure 14-3 illustrates.

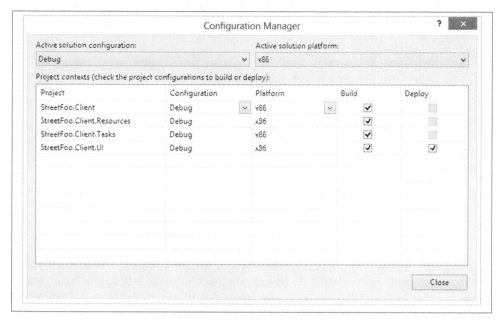

Figure 14-3. Confirming that the projects are set to build as x86

As a final step, we need to add references. First, add a reference to the StreetFoo.Client project from StreetFoo.Client.Tasks. Second, and very important, we need the app project to have a reference to the task façade project (otherwise, it won't get packaged). Add a reference to StreetFoo.Client.Tasks from StreetFoo.Client.UI.

Apart from the fact that it's contained within a Windows Runtime component library, we can build the BackgroundSyncTaskFacade class normally. The only thing we have to watch out for is that we need to abide by the rules. Again, I'm not going to dig into these rules too much, but in this instance we have to make sure the class is sealed. We also have to preserve the parameter name on the Run method, which is another WinRT rule. (Specifically, here it comes through as taskInstance. You're not allowed to rename it to instance, for example.)

The one thing we do have to handle in the façade project is a deferral. You may recall that we needed a deferral in Chapter 7 when looking at sharing, and in Chapter 8 when looking at searching. Deferrals are used in situations where Windows shells out to your app, but you need to run asynchronous methods. Because we do intend to drop into asynchronous methods to do what we need to do in this chapter, you will need to tell Windows that you're deferring. Without a deferral, Windows will assume you've finished your work and tear down your process. This can't be done in the base class, as the first await call we make will be in the façade; therefore, it has to be done in the façade.

Here's the code, which needs to be added to the StreetFoo.Client.Tasks project:

```
public sealed class BackgroundSyncTaskFacade : IBackgroundTask
{
    public async void Run(IBackgroundTaskInstance taskInstance)
    {
        var deferral = taskInstance.GetDeferral();
        try
        {
            // defer...
            var task = new BackgroundSyncTask();
            await task.RunAsync(taskInstance);
        }
        finally
        {
            deferral.Complete();
        }
    }
}
```

At this point, we just need to register the task. We do this using the Declarations tab of
the manifest editor. You have to do this exactly once for each façade you build, but in
each case you have to tell it the sorts of triggers that you want to support. Figure 14-4
shows the task declaration. In it I've said that it handles system events and timer events.

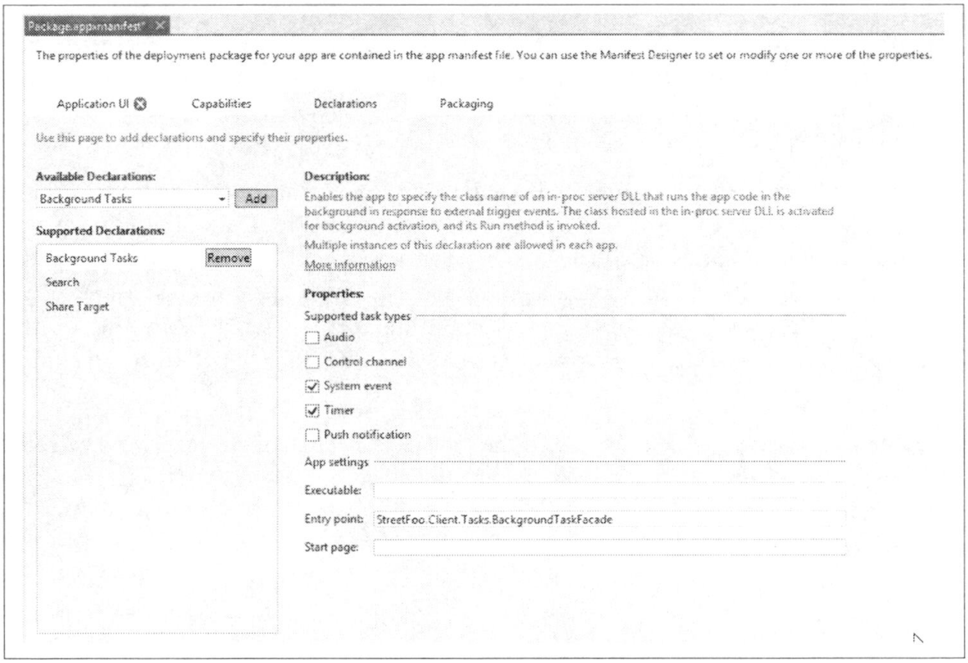

*Figure 14-4. Declaring the task in the manifest*

You might have noticed that when we declare the task, we get an error icon on the Application tab. The error is that we need to indicate whether we support lock screen notifications. We need to set this to Badge. This means "bring the badge number or glyph" forward. We can also bring forward the text from the tile, but I'll talk about that more when we look at the lock screen stuff (although you'd hardly ever want to bring tile text forward, as only one installed app can do this and the user would likely want to continue to use the default, which happens to be the calendar). When we indicate that we want to support lock notifications, we also need to specify an icon—specifically, the badge logo. This is a normal logo like the ones we've already seen, but needs to be 24×24 pixels. Figure 14-5 illustrates.

*Figure 14-5. The Notifications panel on the Application tab of the manifest editor with Badge enabled*

That's all we have to do to register the task. Now we just have to try it.

## Debugging the Task

Luckily for us, rather than having to wait 15 minutes for the events to trigger, we can ask Visual Studio to invoke the task for us manually.

Run the app and everything should be fine—the tasks will be registered, but you won't see anything different. In Visual Studio, locate the Debug Location toolbar—you may need to right-click on the toolbar and add this. You'll see a Suspend button, which you can use to manually suspend the task operations. (We're going to talk about application lifetime in the next chapter.) This button has a drop-down component: drop it down and you'll see the operations that you can invoke. Figure 14-6 illustrates.

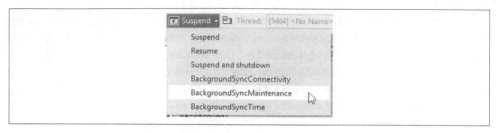

*Figure 14-6. Selecting a background task to invoke*

Invoke one—doesn't matter which—and your background task will run. Unless you set breakpoints, you won't see much. However, by default MetroLog will present some trace information that you can see in the Output window:

```
1|2012-10-10T09:48:17.6240993+00:00|TRACE|1|Created Logger
2|2012-10-10T09:48:17.6555459+00:00|INFO|1|BackgroundSyncTask|Started background
task 'BackgroundSyncMaintenance' (#4a758aea-46c6-48ee-8243-9cc998e532cd)...
3|2012-10-10T09:48:17.7957288+00:00|INFO|4|BackgroundSyncTask|Called!
4|2012-10-10T09:48:17.7957288+00:00|INFO|4|BackgroundSyncTask|Finished
background task 'BackgroundSyncMaintenance'
(#4a758aea-46c6-48ee-8243-9cc998e532cd).
```

From that, we can see that the background task is working properly.

In the version of the code that you can download, I've configured the logging system to use a `FileStreamingTarget` when booted to support tasks. This logging target streams messages through to a single file. If you look in the app's *LocalState* folder (see Chapter 6), you'll find that streamed output. The reason why I bring this up is that with the tasks registered, your tasks will keep running ad infinitum, or at least until the app is uninstalled. It's quite informative to go back and trace what happened over time. Here's the output from my machine over a short period of time:

```
3|2012-10-10T10:34:44.2550430+00:00|INFO|5|BackgroundSyncTask|Started background
task 'BackgroundSyncMaintenance' (#4d7df3e2-cd8b-4306-b1b6-08e9af2dbb25)...
2|2012-10-10T10:34:44.2550430+00:00|INFO|5|BackgroundSyncTask|Started background
task 'BackgroundSyncTime' (#5d6f778e-e6d3-49e1-b8d3-dd0bcf1f4793)...
2|2012-10-10T10:34:44.2550430+00:00|INFO|6|BackgroundSyncTask|Started background
task 'BackgroundSyncTime' (#5d6f778e-e6d3-49e1-b8d3-dd0bcf1f4793)...
3|2012-10-10T10:34:44.2550430+00:00|INFO|6|BackgroundSyncTask|Started background
task 'BackgroundSyncMaintenance' (#4d7df3e2-cd8b-4306-b1b6-08e9af2dbb25)...
4|2012-10-10T10:34:44.6447323+00:00|INFO|7|BackgroundSyncTask|Called!
4|2012-10-10T10:34:44.6447323+00:00|INFO|7|BackgroundSyncTask|Called!
5|2012-10-10T10:34:44.6447323+00:00|INFO|8|BackgroundSyncTask|Called!
6|2012-10-10T10:34:44.7071181+00:00|INFO|6|BackgroundSyncTask|Finished
background task 'BackgroundSyncMaintenance'
(#4d7df3e2-cd8b-4306-b1b6-08e9af2dbb25).
7|2012-10-10T10:34:44.7227041+00:00|INFO|6|BackgroundSyncTask|Finished
background task 'BackgroundSyncTime'
(#5d6f778e-e6d3-49e1-b8d3-dd0bcf1f4793).
5|2012-10-10T10:34:44.6447323+00:00|INFO|8|BackgroundSyncTask|Called!
```

```
7|2012-10-10T10:34:44.7227041+00:00|INFO|5|BackgroundSyncTask|Finished
background task 'BackgroundSyncTime' (
#5d6f778e-e6d3-49e1-b8d3-dd0bcf1f4793).
6|2012-10-10T10:34:44.7071181+00:00|INFO|5|BackgroundSyncTask|Finished
background task 'BackgroundSyncMaintenance'
(#4d7df3e2-cd8b-4306-b1b6-08e9af2dbb25).
```

What this shows is that the tasks can overlap—look for the cluster of "Called!" messages in the middle of that output. As mentioned before, we don't want this to happen because it's just a waste of our precious CPU time. After a quick look at troubleshooting background tasks, we'll discuss how to resolve this.

## Troubleshooting Background Tasks

If things aren't working for you, you can use the event log to do some troubleshooting. A common symptom of a broken task is when you try to break into it with Visual Studio and the entire app shuts down.

If you look in Event Viewer, you will find a whole collection of specialist event logs for working with Windows Store apps. Open Event Viewer and navigate to "Application and Services Logs"→Microsoft→Windows. If you're struggling with anything in Windows Store apps, you'll find diagnostic information to help at that location. If you're struggling with background tasks specifically, look in the `BackgroundTaskInfrastruc ture` log.

You'll find an Operational entry here. This is a straightforward informational trace on the load and run operations of the background tasks. If your task is failing, you should find references to it. (You can also turn on a diagnostic trace, but I've found this to be of limited use.)

Typically you will see two sorts of errors:

- 0x80040154 will be familiar to anyone who's worked with COM before. It means "class not registered." The most likely reason for this happening is that you have the class name wrong, either in the manifest, or when you referenced it during task registration.

- 0x80010008 is one that's caused me hours of wasted time when building Windows Store apps. This is a "generic failure" message. Things to check here are a) have you changed the project to Windows Runtime component library, b) have you targeted the appropriate processor (e.g., if you're using SQLite, you'll need x86, not Any CPU), and c) have you referenced the task project from the Windows Store app project?

## Restricting the Run Period

As we've mentioned a couple of times, we want to stop the tasks from overlapping. In our implementation, the `MaintenanceTrigger` is there really only as a backup to the `TimeTrigger` in case the user takes the application off of the lock screen. Likewise, there's nothing to stop the trigger that fires when connectivity changes from happening at the same moment as the timers. What I propose here is storing an "expiration time" in the SQLite database. If a task tries to run and the expiration is not in the past, it'll duck out early.

To finesse this, we'll also add a check to see if we have Internet connectivity. If we don't, we'll duck out early and wait for notification of when connectivity has been restored.

We can check connectivity using the `NetworkInformation` class. You'll either be told that you have no access, local access (i.e., LAN, but no Internet), Internet access, or *constrained access*. Constrained access is when you're using a WiFi hotspot and you hit a *captive portal*—that is, something you have to log into (usually involvement payment) before general Internet access is enabled.

Here's the property to add to `StreetFooRuntime` that will expose whether we have connectivity or not:

```
// Add property to StreetFooRuntime...
internal static bool HasConnectivity
{
    get
    {
        var profile = NetworkInformation.
            GetInternetConnectionProfile();
        return profile.GetNetworkConnectivityLevel() ==
NetworkConnectivityLevel.InternetAccess;
    }
}
```

Restricting the run period is tricky. As mentioned, we'll do this by setting an *expiration time* in the SQLite database. When a task runs, it will look to see if this expiration time is in the past. If it is in the past, it will run. It will also work on the assumption that if it is allowed to run, it's also responsible for setting the next expiration time.

However, if we set the next expiration time at 15 minutes, there's a chance that we could skip an entire period if we happened to come in at the exact second that the expiration was set for. So we need a period less than 15 minutes ideally.

Windows will schedule the task intervals roughly in sync—so we know they're run together at 15 minutes. I'm proposing setting the expiration period for five minutes. There is a slight wrinkle here in that the trigger that fires when we regain the Internet connection could collide with this expiration period too. Thus, if we detect that we have no Internet connection, we'll reset the expiration time. The upshot of this is that we'll always run if we are told that we have connectivity.

As a final step, we'll also check to see if we can log the user on. We did this before when we were activated in order to handle sharing requests in Chapter 7. To do anything useful in our sync method, we need to be logged in; thus, we'll return the result of `RestorePersistentLogonAsync` as the final arbiter of whether we can run or not.

There is a problem we need to deal with now. If we have two tasks scheduled with 15-minute intervals, they will run at the same time. This is certainly something that we don't want. What we need to do is treat this as a multithreading problem and impose a lock on the operation.

Windows will schedule each background task in its own discrete instance of `back groundTaskHost.exe`. This means that we can't rely on an in-memory synchronization primitive. What we'll need to do in this instance is create a lock file on disk. The way that I propose doing this is to bake the capability to handle lock files into `TaskBase`. We'll add a method to acquire a lock, and one to reset the lock. In fact, we're going to cheat here—this won't be a proper lock. A proper lock is supposed to wait until the lock is released. Our operation will be to simply abort the operation if the lock can't be acquired. I've proposed doing it this way because that sort of normal locking operation is hard in WinRT. Also, it wastes the CPU quota, as our desired outcome is to escape the task as quickly as possible if it's not appropriate to run.

The first operation is to create a lock file. We'll create static and instance versions of this so that we can control locks from both inside the object when it's running, and from outside the object when we're registering it. Here's the code—the operation is straight-forward. All we need to do is try to create a file based on the name of the type that we pass in. Any failure, and we'll assume a lock is already established:

```
// Add methods to TaskBase...
internal async static Task<bool> CreateLockFileAsync(Type type)
{
    try
    {
        var filename = GetLockFileName(type);
        await ApplicationData.Current.LocalFolder.
            CreateFileAsync(filename,
                CreationCollisionOption.FailIfExists);
        return true;
    }
    catch
    {
        // any exception - just return false...
        return false;
    }
}
```

```
protected Task<bool> CreateLockFileAsync()
{
    return CreateLockFileAsync(this.GetType());
}
```

To remove the lock, we'll need some methods to do this. Here's the code:

```
// Add methods to TaskBase...
internal async static Task ResetLockFileAsync(Type type)
{
    try
    {
        var filename = GetLockFileName(type);

        // get...
        var file = await ApplicationData.Current.LocalFolder.
GetFileAsync(filename);
        await file.DeleteAsync();
    }
    catch (FileNotFoundException)
    {
        // no-op...
    }
}

protected Task ResetLockFileAsync()
{
    return ResetLockFileAsync(this.GetType());
}
```

The reason why we have a static "reset" method is that we need to be able to smoothly recover in situations where the lock file exists on disk erroneously. (We have a static "create" method for consistency of design.) What we'll do is when we register a task, we'll reset the lock. This means that whenever the app is actually run, any locks are cleared. This design is a little wonky in that we could unlock at exactly the same moment a second task is trying to run, in which case we'll run two background tasks and potentially create resource conflict issues.

Here's the change to RegisterTaskAsync that will unlock the task. This is also where the method becomes a proper async method, too:

```
public static async Task RegisterTaskAsync<T>(string name, Action
<BackgroundTaskBuilder> configureCallback)
    where T : TaskBase
{
    // unregister any old one...
    UnregisterTask(name);

    // unlock it...
    await TaskBase.ResetLockFileAsync(typeof(T));

    // register the new one...
```

```
            var builder = new BackgroundTaskBuilder();
            builder.Name = name;

            // entry point is StreetFoo.Client.Tasks.<Name>Facade
            builder.TaskEntryPoint = string.Format("StreetFoo.Client.Tasks.
{0}Facade", typeof(T).Name);

            // configure...
            configureCallback(builder);

            // register it...
            builder.Register();
        }
```

Now that we've done all that, we can go back and modify the DoRunAsync method so that it includes both the locking check and the CanRun check. Note that we have the unlock call in the finally block, and also note that we can't await in a finally, so we'll get a warning here.

This is also where we'll see the expiration code for the first time. To recap, we'll try to get the time that the task expires, abort the request if it hasn't, and update the expiration time if it has. Finally, we'll log on the user and use the result of that as the final answer to whether we can run.

Here's the code (I've omitted the Configure method for brevity):

```
public class BackgroundSyncTask : TaskBase
{
    private const string SyncExpirationKey = "SyncExpiration";

    protected override async Task DoRunAsync(IBackgroundTaskInstance
        instance)
    {
        // try to lock...
        if (!(await CreateLockFileAsync()))
        {
            this.Logger.Info("Locked - skipping...");
            return;
        }

        try
        {
            // should we run?
            if (!(await CanRunAsync()))
                return;

            // log as usual...
          this.Logger.Info("Called!");
        }
        finally
        {
            // reset the lock file...
```

```
                ResetLockFileAsync();
            }
        }

        private async Task<bool> CanRunAsync()
        {
            // do we have connectivity?
            if (!(StreetFooRuntime.HasConnectivity))
            {
                this.Logger.Info("No connectivity - skipping...");

                // clear the expiration period...
                await SettingItem.SetValueAsync(SyncExpirationKey,
                string.Empty);

                // return...
                return false;
            }

            // check the expiration...
            var asString = await SettingItem.GetValueAsync
            (SyncExpirationKey);
            if (!(string.IsNullOrEmpty(asString)))
            {
                // parse...
                var expiration = DateTime.ParseExact(asString, "o",
                CultureInfo.InvariantCulture).ToUniversalTime();

                // if the expiration time is in the future, do nothing...
                if (expiration > DateTime.UtcNow)
                {
                    this.Logger.Info("Not expired (expiration is '{0}') -
                    skipping...", expiration);
                    return false;
                }
            }

            // we're ok - set the new expiration period...
            var newExpiration = DateTime.UtcNow.AddMinutes(5);
            await SettingItem.SetValueAsync(SyncExpirationKey,
            newExpiration.ToString("o"));

            // try to log the user in...
            var model = new LogonPageViewModel(new NullViewModelHost());
            return await model.RestorePersistentLogonAsync();
        }

        // code omitted...
    }
```

You can test this by setting breakpoints and using VS to trigger the tasks manually.

You should note in the code download that I've added a check to see if there is a debugger attached and skipped the expiration code. I did this to make debugging the actual syncing operation that we'll build later easier.

Here's some debug messages from an "organic" run of the system:

```
3|2012-10-12T20:14:12.7679692+00:00|INFO|5|BackgroundSyncTask|Started background
task 'BackgroundSyncTime' (#efc424e3-8d7c-405b-b1c1-c6c9d92b9871)...
2|2012-10-12T20:14:12.7629737+00:00|INFO|5|BackgroundSyncTask|Started background
task 'BackgroundSyncMaintenance' (#9bcd676b-825e-44d9-a0bb-bcfa8d6869f4)...
4|2012-10-12T20:14:13.2420173+00:00|INFO|8|BackgroundSyncTask|
Locked - skipping...
5|2012-10-12T20:14:13.2720318+00:00|INFO|8|BackgroundSyncTask|
Finished background task 'BackgroundSyncMaintenance'
(#9bcd676b-825e-44d9-a0bb-bcfa8d6869f4).
7|2012-10-12T20:14:13.3970527+00:00|INFO|6|BackgroundSyncTask|Called!
8|2012-10-12T20:14:13.8802410+00:00|INFO|5|BackgroundSyncTask|Finished
background task 'BackgroundSyncTime'
(#efc424e3-8d7c-405b-b1c1-c6c9d92b9871).
```

# Implementing the Sync Function

Now that we have the infrastructure in place, we can look at implementing the actual sync function.

This function will have two operations. First, it will send up to the server any new data that is waiting to go. If you're building field-service apps, it's important that this happens in the background. Oftentimes, work is actually signed off in poor signal areas. You then want to take advantage of the device traveling around to the next job to increase your chances of getting a working connection.

Second, the device needs to pull down new work to do. Again, in field service this is important, as you don't want the operatives idle, or indeed doing canceled work. Keeping the pending work list fresh is vital.

Coming back to the discussion at the start of this chapter, 15 minutes is probably too long to wait for either of these operations. If you have new work to do, my recommendation is to send a push notification to the device. This will prompt the user to open the app, whereupon you can explicitly go out because at that point the app will be running properly, and you can use a foreground activity to get the work to do from the server. This is, in my opinion, an acceptable compromise.

You may also recall that at the start of this discussion I said that to preserve CPU cycles we'd grab new work from the server, but not actually process it into the database. We'll save that new work to disk and process it when the app is back in the foreground.

# Sending Changes

We'll look first at how to send up changes. We laid the foundation for this work back in Chapter 11, when we implemented the report singleton view. We added a Status property to ReportItem that would track whether an item had to be sent to the server. We also created an ImageChanged property that would track whether the image had to be transmitted back up to the server.

We will now see how to handle sending up changes to the data, but in these pages I'm not going to go through uploading images. I've chosen not to make the server handle user images, for various and obvious reasons.

 You can transmit images using the HttpClient class that we have seen variously used in previous chapters.

The first thing we'll need is a proxy to call up to the server with the changes. Actually, we'll need two proxies, as the insert and update operations are separate. Specifically, we'll need to call HandleCreateReport and HandleUpdateReport. To keep things simple, we'll just look at inserts in these pages—the code download does support updates.

If you recall, each ReportItem has a local ID (Id) and a server-side ID (NativeId). In Chapter 11, when we added the ability to insert new reports into the local database, we set NativeId to be a GUID. At this point, when we upload the report to the server, we'll get back the newly allocated server-side ID. We'll have to patch this new value into the NativeId field of the local SQLite database after the insert operation completes.

To facilitate this, we'll create a CreateReportResult class. It's been a while since we built service proxies, but if you recall we have a convention whereby any responses from the server are wrapped in specialist "result objects" that extend ErrorBucket. We'll either get an error back from the server, or we'll get a native ID. Here's the implementation of CreateReportResult:

```
public class CreateReportResult : ErrorBucket
{
    public string NativeId { get; private set; }

    internal CreateReportResult(string nativeId)
    {
        this.NativeId = nativeId;
    }

    internal CreateReportResult(ErrorBucket bucket)
        : base(bucket)
    {
```

```
        }
    }
```

The next step is to create the interface for the service proxy. The CreateReport method will take primitives that map to the fields in the ReportItem class. Here's the code:

```
public interface ICreateReportServiceProxy
{
    Task<CreateReportResult> CreateReportAsync(string title,
string description,
        decimal longitude, decimal latitude);
}
```

Now we can look at the implementation. We've built a few service proxies now and they generally look the same, so I'll just quickly present this one. Please refer back to previous chapters if the construction is unclear:

```
public class CreateReportServiceProxy : ServiceProxy,
    ICreateReportServiceProxy
{
    public CreateReportServiceProxy()
        : base("CreateReport")
    {
    }

    public async Task<CreateReportResult> CreateReportAsync(string title,
string description, decimal longitude, decimal latitude)
    {
        // package up the request...
        var input = new JsonObject();
        input.Add("title", title);
        input.Add("description", description);
        input.Add("longitude", longitude.ToString());
        input.Add("latitude", latitude.ToString());

        // call...
        var executeResult = await this.Execute(input);

        // get the user ID from the server result...
        if (!(executeResult.HasErrors))
        {
            var reportId = executeResult.Output.GetNamedString("reportId");
            return new CreateReportResult(reportId);
        }
        else
            return new CreateReportResult(executeResult);
    }
}
```

Note how we're extracting the new server-side report ID out of the result. We'll use that later.

For the actual sync, we'll build the functionality for doing this in the `ReportItem` class and defer out to that from the `BackgroundSyncTask` class.

As mentioned, there will be two phases to this: we'll send changes first, and then we'll download new work. For the sending phase, we'll need to get the reports that have changed, and then decide which service proxy to call.

 This implementation has simplified error handling, compared to what you would need in production apps. In production scenarios, it's essential that you do not lose data that exists only on the device. This requires elegant error handling as well as complex and well-tested retry algorithms. In this implementation I've proposed being rather blunt—if you can't send the change, junk it. This really isn't good enough for production, but it's OK for our illustration. By the way, the hardest part of this problem is having sketchy connectivity (i.e., connectivity that comes and goes inconsistently) during the sync process. You have to handle each call carefully, trapping and handling errors and retrying appropriately. This is notoriously hard to test in the lab.

We need to handle the sending portion with multiple methods. We'll create a static database query method that will return all of the changed jobs. We'll create an instance method in `ReportItem` that will actually send the changes for us. We'll round this off with a static method that will coordinate all of that.

Here's the implementation of `GetLocallyChangedReportsAsync`:

```
// Add method to ReportItem...
private static async Task<IEnumerable<ReportItem>>
GetLocallyChangedReportsAsync()
{
    var conn = StreetFooRuntime.GetUserDatabase();
    return await conn.Table<ReportItem>().Where(v => v.Status !=
ReportItemStatus.Unchanged || v.ImageChanged).ToListAsync();
}
```

Next, the method that glues it all together. This will call out to get the changes and then defer to the individual per-report update method. I've added some logging in here so that you can get a better idea of what's happening. Here's the code:

```
// Add method to ReportItem...
internal static async Task PushServerUpdatesAsync()
{
    var logger = LogManagerFactory.DefaultLogManager.GetLogger
<ReportItem>();
    logger.Info("Pushing server updates...");

    // get all of the changed reports...
    var reports = await GetLocallyChangedReportsAsync();
```

```
// how many?
logger.Info("Found '{0}' changed report(s)...", reports.Count());

// if nothing, quit...
if (!(reports.Any()))
    return;

// otherwise...
var tasks = new List<Task>();
foreach (var report in reports)
    tasks.Add(report.PushServerUpdateAsync());

// wait...
await Task.WhenAll(tasks);

// finished...
logger.Info("Finished pushing updates.");
}
```

I haven't implemented this next recommendation for fear of making the code fussy, but a trick you can do with this sort of code is continually checking that you have connectivity before you go through each step.

For example, you might call out to get the local reports, but abort the operation if it turns out that you have no connection before you go out to PushServerUpdateAsync. This will reduce your CPU quota—or more rightly you can save it to such time as you know you have better connectivity.

Finally, we can look at the transmission portion. This is relatively easy—we examine the Status property and then branch accordingly. Here's the code:

```
// Add method to ReportItem...
internal async Task PushServerUpdateAsync()
{
    this.Logger.Info("Pushing update for #{0} ({1})...", this.Id,
this.Status);

    // what happened?
    if (this.Status == ReportItemStatus.Unchanged)
    {
        // no-op...
    }
    else if (this.Status == ReportItemStatus.New)
    {
        // insert...
        var service = new CreateReportServiceProxy();
        var result = await service.CreateReportAsync(this.Title,
this.Description, this.Longitude, this.Latitude);
```

```
                // patch back the native ID, if it worked...
                if (!(result.HasErrors))
                    this.NativeId = result.NativeId;
                else
                    this.Logger.Warn("Failed to insert report: " +
result.GetErrorsAsString());
            }
            else
                throw new NotSupportedException(string.Format("Cannot handle '{0}'.",
this.Status));

            // reset our flag...
            this.Status = ReportItemStatus.Unchanged;

            // set...
            var conn = StreetFooRuntime.GetUserDatabase();
            await conn.UpdateAsync(this);
        }
```

 This implementation only handles inserts. The code download handles updates and deletes as well.

Notice in the code how we reset the flag when we're done—this is the part that sets the Status property back to Unchanged. You can also see that we patch back the server-side report ID into the local copy, replacing our temporary ID.

To test this, run the app, log on, and create a new report. To upload it to the server, kick off the background task using Visual Studio. You'll be able to see what's happening using the Output window. If you really want to prove to yourself that the change has occurred, add a new report, sync, shut down the app, and uninstall the app. Deploy and run the app again, and when you've logged in and the reports have been downloaded from the server, the report that you added will come back again. Note that you'll get a stock image because we don't transmit any image that you've taken up to the server.

Another thing you can do is to create a new report and leave the app idle until the background task runs naturally. Or, you can create a new report—turn off your machine's network connection and then turn it back on. This will kick off the system connectivity trigger, and you'll see the update.

## Receiving New Work

Now that we know that we can trigger a task and send updates, we'll look at how we can adapt this to receive new work.

There is some subtlety here. I'm going to propose that we do this in quite a blunt fashion by downloading the entire set of reports from the server each time. In a production app, a better way to do this is to download a list of report IDs with version numbers. You can then check to see if you have new or changed reports and download them piecemeal. This saves both bandwidth and battery, and is a good thing to do. However, it makes the implementation quite complicated—more complicated than I would want it in this book.

Also, there is a problem in that our background task will always run whether the app is running or not. If new work is available and the app is running in the foreground, it would be ideal to signal the running app so that it can update the UI to indicate that new data is available. This is actually quite hard to do, and I'll talk more about that in the next section.

For now, we'll deal with the download. As we've discussed previously, to save our CPU quota we'll spool the report data to disk and pick it up again when we need it.

To start, we'll modify `BackgroundSyncTask` so that after it uploads any changes, it'll download the reports. We'll then use JSON.NET to stringify the reports that we download and store them in `TempState` in a file called *SpooledReports.json*. Here's the code:

```
public class BackgroundSyncTask : TaskBase
{
    private const string SyncExpirationKey = "SyncExpiration";
    internal const string SpoolFilename = "SpooledReports.json";

    protected override async Task DoRunAsync(IBackgroundTaskInstance
        instance)
    {
        // should we run?
        if (!(await CanRunAsync()))
            return;

        // send up changes...
        await ReportItem.PushServerUpdatesAsync();

        // still have connectivity?
        if (StreetFooRuntime.HasConnectivity)
        {
            this.Logger.Info("Getting reports from server...");

            // get...
            var proxy = ServiceProxyFactory.Current.GetHandler
<IGetReportsByUserServiceProxy>();
            var reports = await proxy.GetReportsByUserAsync();

            // errors?
            if(!(reports.HasErrors))
            {
                this.Logger.Info("Stashing reports on disk...");
```

```
                    // save...
                    var json = JsonConvert.SerializeObject(reports.Reports);
                    var file = await ApplicationData.Current.TemporaryFolder.
        CreateFileAsync(SpoolFilename, CreationCollisionOption.ReplaceExisting);
                    await FileIO.WriteTextAsync(file, json);
                }
            }
        }

        // code omitted...
    }
```

You'll note that I've added a check for connectivity (i.e., the call to `StreetFooRun time.HasConnectivity`). Again, this was something mentioned before; it's an easy check to do, and it quickly allows us to see if we're likely to be successful with the call and preserve our CPU quota if not.

Next we have to load up that spooled data. We have a method in `ReportItem` called `UpdateCacheFromServerAsync`. This method calls up to the server and updates the local database. My proposal is that if we have spooled data on disk, we short-circuit this operation and rather than go out to the network, we'll just parse the spooled JSON containing the reports.

 I must admit, I wondered about whether this was a good approach for a long time. It seems "impure" to work like this—we'd be hijacking an expected operation and doing something non-obvious and tricky to trace. However, in the end I got to a point where I felt it was pragmatic enough to use here, and also a decent example to show you.

The first thing we'll need is a method that loads up the spooled reports from disk. Here's the code:

```
    // Add method to ReportItem...
    private static async Task<IEnumerable<ReportItem>>
        GetSpooledReportsAsync()
    {
        IStorageFile file = null;
        try
        {
            file = await ApplicationData.Current.TemporaryFolder.
    GetFileAsync(BackgroundSyncTask.SpoolFil
    ename);
        }
        catch (FileNotFoundException)
        {
            return null;
        }
```

```
                // load...
                try
                {
                    var json = await FileIO.ReadTextAsync(file);
                    return JsonConvert.DeserializeObject<IEnumerable<ReportItem>>
(json);
                }
                finally
                {
                    // delete the file—we have to do this regardless, but we can't
                    // wait here...
                    file.DeleteAsync();
                }
            }
```

You'll notice here that we delete the file when we're done. There's a wrinkle here where we can't await in a finally, so we're just firing and forgetting the delete. (We saw the same thing when removing the lock file in TaskBase.) This could create a race condition where we collide the file. (Even though our app and the background tasks are running in separate isolated processes, the file effectively becomes shared memory and hence needs to be synchronized for multithread/multiprocess access.) This would lead us to the problems with locking with async—something that's beyond the scope of this chapter. If you use the normal locking routines (including the lock keyword), bad things will happen. There are ways that you can do this. Stephen Toub, a member of the Microsoft team that works on the asynchrony implementation, has a number of blog posts on this topic, including "Building Async Coordination Primitives," (*http://blogs.msdn.com/b/pfxteam/archive/2012/02/12/10266988.aspx*) of which AsyncLock is one example. My hope is that these primitives will end up in the full WinRT library over time.

But I digress: the trick is to delete the file so that this is a one-shot deal, as opposed to stopping the app from ever calling back to the server to get fresh data.

While we're here, we'll also need a method that indicates whether we have a file available on disk. Here's the code:

```
        // Add to ReportItem...
        internal static async Task<bool> HasSpooledReportsAsync()
        {
            try
            {
                await ApplicationData.Current.TemporaryFolder.GetFileAsync(
                    BackgroundSyncTask.SpoolFilename);
                return true;
            }
            catch (FileNotFoundException)
            {
                return false;
            }
        }
```

We can now modify the code that updates the cache to use the spooled file. Here it is:

```
// Modify method in ReportItem...
public static async Task UpdateCacheFromServerAsync()
{
    IEnumerable<ReportItem> reports = await GetSpooledReportsAsync();
    if (reports == null)
    {
        // create a service proxy to call up to the server...
        var proxy = ServiceProxyFactory.Current.GetHandler
<IGetReportsByUserServiceProxy>();
        var result = await proxy.GetReportsByUserAsync();

        // did it actually work?
        result.AssertNoErrors();

        // set...
        reports = result.Reports;
    }

    // update...
    var conn = StreetFooRuntime.GetUserDatabase();
    foreach (var report in reports)
    {
        // load the existing one, deleting it if we find it...
        var existing = await conn.Table<ReportItem>().Where(v =>
            v.NativeId == report.NativeId).FirstOrDefaultAsync();
        if (existing != null)
            await conn.DeleteAsync(existing);

        // create...
        await conn.InsertAsync(report);
    }
}
```

This will almost work end to end. The problem we have to fix now is that although this will run fine when we're in the background, when we navigate to the Reports page it'll use the data in SQLite (as the behavior we've had thus far is that unless we explicitly request a refresh, we'll "go local" and get the current version in SQLite).

This is why we needed the method to see if spooled reports were available. If we detect that they are, we can force a refresh whenever the Reports page is activated. This will flush through the changes at a point in time when it's most appropriate, and when we're in the foreground and hence not using up our CPU quota. Here's the code:

```
// Modify method in ReportsPageViewModel...
public override async void Activated(object args)
{
    base.Activated(args);

    // do we have spooled reports?
    var force = false;
```

```
        if (await ReportItem.HasSpooledReportsAsync())
            force = true;

        // refresh...
        await DoRefresh(force);
}
```

To test this, locate the app's *TempState* folder in File Explorer and you'll find there is no *SpooledReports.json*. Run the project and use Visual Studio to kick off the background operation. This will create the file; immediately terminate the app using Debug→Stop Debugging.

Start the app again, and when the Reports page displays you'll find the file has disappeared. The badge will also be updated on the app tile, although you may not notice that if you haven't added new reports. For extra points, you can create a report and then repeat the process. If you do this, you'll see the badge value change.

## Signaling the App from the Background Task

There's a gaping hole in the background task APIs—namely, that there's no elegant way to signal information from background tasks to any running tasks. As mentioned, if the Reports page is active and the background task triggers and discovers new jobs, it should be able to tell the Reports page to update itself. There is no standard mechanism in the APIs to do this. There is a mechanism for passing back numeric information to drive a progress bar, but that's it.

The documentation says that you're supposed to use persistent storage to do this, the implication being that you store a file on disk on one side, and detect it and respond on the other. Curiously, this is exactly what we've done with our *SpooledReports.json*—we create it in the background task and then ReportPageViewModel modifies its behavior because of its existence.

When I was prototyping the work for this chapter, I created a signaling system based on the "observer" design pattern. I haven't put it in these pages because of space constraints. The general shape of the solution looked like the following. You may care to build out your own implementation along these lines:

1. Create a base class called SignalBase. The idea is that developers would create specializations of these (e.g., NewReportsAvailableSignal).

2. When view-models start, they tell a manager class that they want to be told about signals. (This is the central part of the "observer" pattern.) View-models also implement an interface called ISignalSink if they want to participate in this activity.

3. Next, create a database entity called SignalItem. When background tasks want to send a signal, they create instances of SignalItem and store them in SQLite. The approach here is that each specialized signal class can contain read/write properties

that were JSON stringified into the SQLite database along with their owning class. Effectively what happens here is that the specialized signals end up being serialized into the database.

4. The manager creates a recurring ThreadPoolTimer. Every *n* seconds (I did 15), it will load up any SignalItem instances from SQLite, and then clear the table.

5. Each SignalItem is then examined in turn and a specialized signal instance created from it, along with any serialized data. The view-models that registered an interest in this are contacted in turn and passed the signal via the ISignalSink interface.

When I tried this, it worked very well. The background task would run and the app would automatically update itself. As mentioned, I didn't include it only because of space constraints.

## Putting the App on the Lock Screen

Finally, we need to put the app on the lock screen. We do this by calling the RequestLockScreenAsync method on the TaskHelper WinRT class. You can't check to see if you are on the lock screen; otherwise, you could keep nagging the user to add you, and that's the sort of behavior that Microsoft is not keen on from well-behaved apps. Here's the code (I've omitted code for brevity):

```
// Modify method in App...
protected override async void OnLaunched(LaunchActivatedEventArgs args)
{
    // Do not repeat app initialization when already running, just
ensure that
    // the window is active
    if (args.PreviousExecutionState == ApplicationExecutionState.
        Running)
    {
        Window.Current.Activate();
        return;
    }

      // code omitted...

    // configure tasks...
    await BackgroundSyncTask.ConfigureAsync();

    // ask about the lock screen...
    await TaskHelper.RequestLockScreenAsync();
}
```

If you run the code now, you'll be prompted to add the app to the lock screen. Figure 14-7 illustrates.

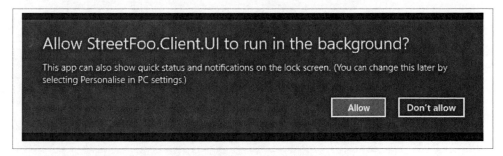

Figure 14-7. Prompting for permission to add to the lock screen

The app won't appear on the lock screen until the badge has changed. (You're supposed to show new notifications here, so any old badge value won't carry forward.) You can change the badge number by refreshing the Reports page. Once you add the app to the lock screen and refresh the reports, you'll see something like Figure 14-8.

Figure 14-8. The lock screen with the StreetFoo "pika" icon and badge

Now you'll find that your TimeTrigger tasks will also run. You'll also get more CPU quota, but that's difficult to measure!

# CHAPTER 15

# Sideloading and Distribution

The most basic form of distribution is a test distribution. You would most likely use this if you wanted to give a partner, customer, or other members of the team a version of your app to test.

You'll recall that when you start developing Windows Store apps in Visual Studio, the first thing that happens is you are asked to obtain a developer license. This is a form of *sideloading*. With a developer license installed, you can deploy any apps from any source onto that device.

There are two things to bear in mind with this. First, sideloading totally opens up the device to Windows Store malware by removing the deployment restrictions. Second, you are only permitted to use this approach for testing. You cannot use it for production deployment, and Microsoft is very strict about this. (One read of this is that Microsoft gets paid for the special licenses that you need to support production sideloading, but does not get paid for the developer licenses used for development sideloading.)

For my test, I created a separate virtual machine and installed Windows 8 Pro 32-bit. (I usually use 64-bit, and use 32-bit for variety more than anything.) What I wanted to do was have an entirely separate installation. I created the machine without a Microsoft Account association—that is, I used a local account to log on.

So let's do this for your application. The first thing you have to do is set the product build mode to Release. There are two reasons for this. First, in order to get the app certified, you have to build it in release mode. Second, there are certain dependencies on Win32 DLLs, both specifically through inclusion of the Visual C++ Runtime Package and also through SQLite. As is standard, Windows does not come installed with the debug bit.

Once we've set our app to release mode, we can create a package. In Solution Explorer, right-click on the project and choose Store→Create App Packages. You'll be presented with a wizard. In the first instance, we don't want to upload the package to the Store. Figure 15-1 illustrates.

*Figure 15-1. Indicating that we want to create a test package*

The next page of the wizard will ask where we want to create the package, what our version number is, and which configurations we wish to deploy. Figure 15-2 illustrates my choices. Notice that I've included both x86 and ARM support. This refers all the way back to Chapter 3, where the inclusion of SQLite first demanded that we think about which processor architectures we supported. Inclusion of Bing Maps also has an impact of sorts here; that, too, requires us to manage the processor targeting explicitly.

Incidentally, we are not creating an x64 package here. If you recall the discussion in Chapter 3, I mentioned this wasn't necessary, as an x86 implementation gets de facto coverage on x64 machines anyway. However, you certainly can create separate x64 packages if you wish. The one option we can't choose is Neutral (aka Any CPU), because SQLite and Bing Maps prevent the Any CPU selection.

Click the Create button and the packages will be created. The page that follows suggests that you run the Windows App Certification Kit. Don't do this—you don't need to do it for testing. As we'll see, it takes ages to run, and at this point it's a waste of time.

On disk you'll get a bunch of folders and files. Each folder relates to exactly one processor architecture package. Figure 15-3 illustrates the contents of one of the folders.

What you'll see in the folder is:

- A PowerShell script for installing the package.
- An *.appx* file containing the actual application.
- An *.appxsym* file containing debugging information.
- A *.cer* file containing a certificate. This will be installed on the target machine to validate the *.appx* file on deployment.
- The *Add-AppDevPackage.resources* folder containing string resources for, amazingly, the PowerShell install script (i.e., it's nothing to do with your app).

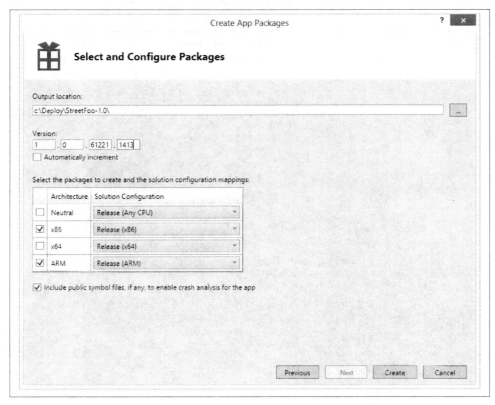

Figure 15-2. Defining package options

| Name | Date modified | Type | Size |
|---|---|---|---|
| Add-AppDevPackage.resources | 21/12/2012 14:19 | File folder | |
| Dependencies | 21/12/2012 14:19 | File folder | |
| Add-AppDevPackage.ps1 | 26/07/2012 19:08 | Windows PowerS... | 60 KB |
| StreetFoo.Client.UI_1.0.61221.1413_ARM.appx | 21/12/2012 14:19 | APPX File | 4,414 KB |
| StreetFoo.Client.UI_1.0.61221.1413_ARM.appxsym | 21/12/2012 14:19 | APPXSYM File | 25 KB |
| StreetFoo.Client.UI_1.0.61221.1413_ARM.cer | 21/12/2012 14:19 | Security Certificate | 1 KB |

Figure 15-3. Contents of the ARM package folder

- The *Dependencies* folder containing other *.appx* packages that need to be installed along with your app. In our instance, it's the Visual C++ Runtime Package.

All we have to do on the test VM is physically transfer that folder over to the target machine and run the PowerShell script. You can run the PowerShell script by right-clicking on the *.ps1* file and selecting "Run with PowerShell." The script actually needs admin rights to work, but the script will elevate rights for you if required.

Three things should happen next. If you don't have a developer license installed on the machine, you'll be prompted to get one. To test this, I created a new Microsoft Account at Outlook.com (*http://outlook.com*) and used that email address. Next, the script will install the certificate included with the bundle. Finally, it will install the actual app. This last part is done using the PowerShell script Add-AppxPackage.

 Not surprisingly, Remove-AppxPackage can be used to remove a package. Get-AppxPackage can be used to enumerate the packages on the device. These scripts are actually quite helpful—from time to time, you can get deployment failures. You can force-remove the bad package by getting the ID with Get-AppxPackage and then performing the removal with Remove-AppxPackage.

When the script is completed, you'll find the app on the Start screen and you can run it as normal.

As mentioned, the likelihood is that if you're doing this, you're giving it to someone else to test. If you need to, you can use the Remote Debugging tools that we discussed in Chapter 6 to connect to the remote machine.

## Using the Windows App Certification Kit

One of the big advantages of Windows 8 and Windows RT compared to other platforms is that you can do some of the validation for yourself using the Windows App Certification Kit. (This is often just called the WACK, pronounced "whack.") This is a tool that performs static and dynamic analysis of your code. Importantly, it runs the same tests as the Windows Store backend does when you upload your code. To this end, it's well worth running your code through the WACK before you submit it to the Store.

The reason I wanted to talk about the WACK *before* we talk about Store submissions generally is because of sideloading:

- If you intend to distribute your app publicly through the Store, Microsoft will only do so if your app passes Microsoft's run through its copy of the WACK. Thus, if you want to get your app on the Store, it's worth validating it yourself first.

- If you intend to distribute your app through production sideloading, but not through the store, it's Microsoft's recommendation that you still run the WACK.

I won't go into what the WACK actually does, as these rules are likely to change. Any errors that you'll get will be self-explanatory. However, the most common error that occurs when using the WACK is forgetting to set the solution to Release mode. Also, if you try to run the WACK with a Debug build, you can get false positives. In short, make sure you test a Release build.

All of this means that Microsoft will not allow a Debug build into the Store.

# Distribution Through Production Sideloading

Now, let's look at *production sideloading*, a more complex distribution method, because both the rules and the process are tricky. However, you have to do it in order to be properly licensed. The general process is that any Windows 8 or Windows RT device comes with sideloading capability switched off. You need to first turn this capability on, and then install your apps.

In this section I'm going to talk about Microsoft software licensing. You should know that I'm not an expert on licensing, and as a policy I don't give advice on licensing. What's presented here is guidance only—you should seek your own professional, qualified advice on licensing matters.

Windows 8 is available in three versions. The first is a vanilla, "home" version, which is simply called Windows 8. Ignore that version—we're not talking about that at all. The other versions are Windows 8 Pro and Windows 8 Enterprise.

You can find information on this whole process on TechNet (*http:// bit.ly/1jXhsyi*).

As I mentioned, we won't be discussing licensing or talking about what is best—however, I do need to present a bit of information about licensing to complete the picture of how and when you can sideload.

Microsoft prefers to sell software to businesses under what it calls Volume Licensing (VL). When an end user buys Windows software off the shelf, or preinstalled on a computer, that is a retail license and outside of VL. The idea behind VL is that due to a volume purchase a business will receive a discount, easier management, and certain rights.

One VL program, Software Assurance (SA), is a program that allows for the buying of software on a quasi-subscription basis. Sideloading *only* works on Windows systems that are SA-licensed copies, or that fit into other programs that have similar privileges to those granted by SA. The Enterprise Edition of Windows 8 cannot be bought other than through SA. What this means is that if you go and buy 50 laptops from Dell, Lenovo, or whomever, those will come with retail licenses of Pro that you have to upgrade or replace with SA licenses. So, if your situation allows for sideloading, read on.

## Turning on Sideloading on Windows 8

To turn on sideloading on Windows 8, you do one of these things. (I'll talk about Windows RT in a moment.)

- Take a Windows 8 Enterprise machine, join it to the Active Directory domain, and turn on a group policy item. This group policy item is called "Allow all trusted applications to install," and can be found in Computer Configuration→Administrative Templates→Windows Component→App Package Deployment.

- Take a Windows 8 Enterprise machine, don't join it to the domain, and then activate what's known as the *enterprise sideloading product key*.

- Take an SA-licensed Windows 8 Pro machine (it doesn't matter if it's joined to the domain or not), and then activate the enterprise sideloading product key.

- Take a non-SA-licensed Windows 8 Pro machine (it doesn't matter if it's joined to the domain or not), fix up the license to make it "comply with the rules," and then activate the enterprise sideloading product key.

It's this "complying with the rules" step that's difficult. Essentially, Microsoft wants you to be on SA. As of the time of writing, you can make a non-SA Pro license similar enough to an SA license by doing the following:

- Enlisting the device in Microsoft Intune. Intune is a cloud-based service that provides basic mobile device management (MDM) features. We'll talk about this again later.

- Enlisting the device in a Virtual Desktop Access (VDA) license.

- Enlisting the device in a Companion Device Licence (CDL) license.

 If you don't know what VDA or CDL licenses are, don't worry—most people don't. It just illustrates why you'd likely need specialist advice if you need to do this.

If you can't do any of those things, the stopgap is to buy the enterprise sideloading key. For reference, as of the time of writing, you could buy enterprise sideloading product keys in packs of 100 for $3,000 (i.e., about $30 per unit).

However, there is a risk associated with sideloading. Note that the description on the group policy items reads as follows:

```
If you enable this policy setting, you can install any trusted app package.
A trusted app package is one that is signed with a certificate chain that
can be successfully validated by the local computer.
```

## Installing Apps

Once you have the sideloading configured, you can install the app.

The expectation from Microsoft is that you do this installation through Intune. For Windows RT, this is essentially the only practicable way to do it. If you use Intune, what will happen is that you'll configure the device such that it is associated with your company's Intune account. You upload the application binaries to Intune and configure the policy items to decide who gets the app, and then the app is either automatically or manually downloaded by the users.

If you don't want to use Intune, there are two other ways that you can get your app installed.

The first way is to do as shown before and use the PowerShell scripts to install the apps. You can do this manually, or you can configure domain logon scripts to run the PowerShell scripts. (This would obviously be less easy with Windows RT, as you don't have domain logon on Windows RT.)

The second way to do this is to bake the app into any desktop image that you push out to desktops in your business.

# Distribution Through the Windows Store

So far we've considered delivery of test builds for debugging, or private builds of the app for internal use. Many people will want to deliver their apps through the public Windows Store.

I'm not going to go through all of the whys and wherefores of getting your app onto the Store—for one thing most of it is obvious, and for another Microsoft will likely keep changing the details of the process, rendering obsolete any screenshots that I present. However, I will take you through the fundamentals.

You will need a developer account on the Store. You will need to pay for this, although as of the time of writing MSDN subscribers get a paid developer account for free.

You'll need to "reserve the name" for your app on the Store website. This tells Microsoft that you intend to use the name and stops others from claiming it. You can reserve a name for 12 months. If you don't use it in that period, others can claim it.

Once you have reserved the name, you can associate the Windows Store project in Visual Studio with the name in the Store. To do this, right-click on the project in Solution Explorer and select Store→Associate App with the Store.

You'll be asked to log in to your Store account. Once you do this, you'll be asked to select the name of the app from the names registered against your account. In Figure 15-4, you can see that I have reserved the name StreetFoo.

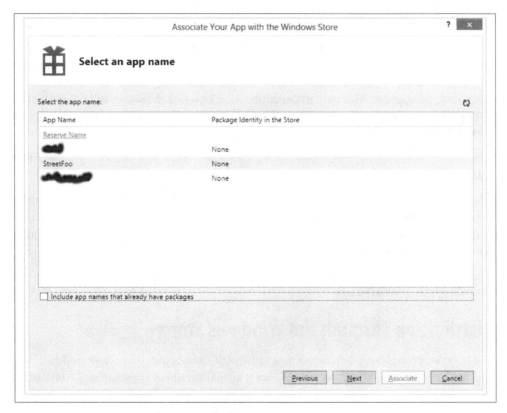

*Figure 15-4. Associating the app with the store*

Click Next, and then Associate to associate the project. This involves changing the project settings, and also downloading and installing your private developer certificate from the Store.

If you look in the Packaging tab of the manifest editor, you'll see that the application details have been changed to those you entered on the Store. In Figure 15-5, you can see that the name of the publisher is given as AMX Software Ltd (the name of my business), and that the package name is given as mbrit.StreetFoo. These replace any placeholder values used for debugging.

*Figure 15-5. Modified manifest settings*

 The name mbrit.StreetFoo is actually a mistake I made when registering the name in the Store. Ideally, this should be a Java-style reversed domain name. My domain is mbrit.com, so the name should really be com.mbrit.StreetFoo.

Once you've done the association, you need to go through the packaging steps. This is essentially the same process we went through at the beginning of the chapter. However, this time when you start the wizard, choose Yes for the question "Do you want to build packages to upload to the Window Store?" Other than that, the process is the same.

With the packages created, go back onto the Store and complete the store listing. As part of that process, you will be invited to upload the packages. Upload the packages for both the x86 and ARM processors. Figure 15-6 illustrates.

*Figure 15-6. Uploading the packages*

And that's it! Once you complete the listing, Microsoft will set about validating the app. Once it's satisfied that the rules have been followed, your app will be live in the Store.

# Cryptography and Hashing

In this appendix we'll talk about SSL (Secure Sockets Layer), device security, and encryption in SQLite, and then look at practical examples of hashing, generating random data, and symmetric encryption.

## SSL

I will touch on SSL first. It goes without saying that all communication with your server/ servers should be done over SSL. There's no excuse for this not to be the case.

## Device Security

In a business context, what project sponsors are really worried about are devices getting lost with sensitive information on them. The way to square the circle is to rely on the device to be secure and for your apps to rely on that security. Baking your own security into the app may not actually get you very far, which is one of the reasons why this topic isn't a central thrust of this book despite its importance in the problem domain. You shouldn't need to think about it, or do anything special in order to make it happen.

Mobile devices are supposed to be managed via something called *mobile device management* (MDM). MDM is provided in two parts. One part is provided by the platform vendor and describes "policies" on the device that support device management and security. For example, the platform vendor may bake in a policy that can be turned on or off that indicates whether the user has a passcode on the device, another that specifies whether the device is wiped after *n* incorrect passcodes, and so on. The second part of MDM is a management tool that pushes down policy to those devices. Examples of MDM vendors at the time of writing include AirWatch, MobileIron, Good Technology, and Microsoft Intune. As an aside, MDM products also have "value adds," things like secure document lockers and mobile application management (MAM), which is usually interpreted as private app stores operated by a company for its employees.

In enterprise environments, what customers are typically most worried about is data loss. The easiest way to handle this is to encrypt the device. On Windows 8 Pro and Enterprise you have BitLocker support, so all you have to do here is turn that on. (The baseline edition of Windows 8 intended for home use—that is, not the Professional or Enterprise editions—doesn't have BitLocker support, but you'd rarely find that in business.) On the Windows RT side, there isn't a thing called "BitLocker," but the device encryption that you can activate is actually BitLocker under the hood.

With both of those technologies, you should be "safe" if a machine is lost in the field in terms of not leaking the data. What seems to be missing as of the time of writing is the ability to remote-wipe the *entire* machine. Although information is due to come out on this, it appears remote wipe on Windows RT only kills off messaging-related data and not application data generally. With Windows 8 the story is slightly different, as MDM products have more freedom in what they can do.

The upshot: always make sure you have encryption switched on so that if you do lose a device, it's less of a problem than it could be.

## SQLite

SQLite has no practical way built in to lock down access to data contained within.

> There is support for encrypting data within SQLite databases—if you search online for it, you can find a number of open source and commercial solutions.

However, this brings me back to my original point: you are better served relying on the security on the device to keep your data safe, rather than trying to bash your app into implementing security that will unavoidably be poorer.

## Hashing

In the first of three practical examples that we'll look at in these pages, we're going to explore hashing.

I'm not going to try to cover the advantages or disadvantages of different hashing algorithms—I'm just going to explain the basics of how to call them. I'm also not going to get into how to apply them to common usage patterns, and particularly here I'm talking about hashing with regards to password security. The reason why I'm ducking this is a) it's complicated, and b) if you're reading this even just two years after I wrote it, industry best practice would likely not be what it is today.

The hash algorithms that you are given in WinRT are MD5, SHA-1, SHA-256, SHA-384, and SHA-512. In these pages, I'm going to show you SHA-512. In normal .NET, you get those just enumerated, and you also get RIPEMD160. To be honest, and I'm not sure this is necessarily valid logic, I'd never heard of RIPEMD160 until I wrote this paragraph, so I don't think it'll be sorely missed in Windows Store app development.

For this exercise, we're going to create a new Windows Store app project that can accept some text to be hashed. We'll then hash it using SHA-512, both to a base-64 string and a hex dump of the underlying bytes. In the project, we won't create a complex app with MVVM abstraction, etc. We'll just create a little proof-of-concept app.

Create a new Visual C# – Windows Store – Blank App project called HashScratch. To `MainPage`, add a `StackPanel` control, three `TextBlock` controls, a `Button` control, and three `TextBox` controls, as shown in Figure A-1. The `TextBox` controls need `x:Name` values of `textInput`, `textBase64`, and `textHex`.

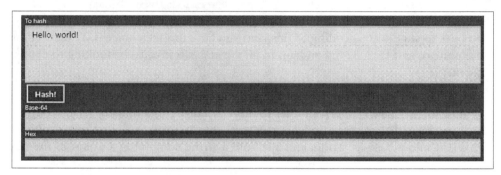

*Figure A-1  The layout of our scratch project*

For clarity, here's the XAML representing the layout of the controls.

```
<StackPanel Margin="10,10,10,10" Width="800"
        HorizontalAlignment="Left">
    <TextBlock Text="To hash"></TextBlock>
    <TextBox x:Name="textInput" Text="Hello, world!" Height="100"
AcceptsReturn="true"></TextBox>
    <Button Content="Hash!" Click="HandleHashClick"></Button>
    <TextBlock Text="Base-64"></TextBlock>
    <TextBox x:Name="textBase64" AcceptsReturn="true"></TextBox>
    <TextBlock Text="Hex"></TextBlock>
    <TextBox x:Name="textHex" AcceptsReturn="true"></TextBox>
</StackPanel>
```

You'll notice in the XAML that I've defined a `Click` method for the button. You can either do this, or just double-click on the button on the design surface to create a default handler.

In Chapter 6, when we were working with files, we saw that we worked directly with WinRT classes that replaced the .NET file I/O class that we'd been used to previously. In the .NET world, you'll be familiar with the various stream classes that we were given to work with file data and also other forms of data. In WinRT there are new types for dealing with streams, which you can find in the `Windows.Storage.Streams` namespace. Also in this namespace you'll find an interface called `IBuffer`. This is used to represent a "lightweight stream." In .NET we would have often just used a `byte[]` value. (I'll talk more about that in a moment.)

When we're working with hashing, we use two classes. We use `HashAlgorithmProvider` to get a worker class that will actually do the hashing, and we use `CryptographicBuffer` to marshal data into and out of `IBuffer` instances. `CryptographicBuffer` isn't a buffer in its own right—it's a static class with a bunch of static helper methods. `CryptographicBufferHelper` would actually be a better name.

There are classes in `CryptographicBuffer` to convert strings to binary—specifically, they act to emit an `IBuffer` instance containing the binary representation of the string. You have to supply an encoding to this, and you have limited choice: UTF-8, UTF-16 little endian, and UTF-32 big endian. In all normal cases, you'd be looking to choose UTF-8.

Once you have your `IBuffer`-wrapped input, you can then pass it over to the algorithm of your choice. This will return another `IBuffer` instance containing the hashed output. Once you have that, you can do what you want with it. In our scenario we're going to convert it into a base-64 string, and also into a string containing a dump of the hex values.

 One "top tip" for .NET developers is this. You may find that you need to convert your `IBuffer` into a `byte[]` array. From first principles this is pretty difficult, but there are extension methods that you can access that do all of this lifting for you. However, they are quite well buried; you need to include the `System.Runtime.InteropServices.WindowsRuntime` namespace.

Here's the code for our hashing operation:

```
// Add method to MainPage...
private void HandleHashClick(object sender, RoutedEventArgs e)
{
    // get the text...
    var inputText = this.textInput.Text;

    // put the string in a buffer, UTF-8 encoded...
    IBuffer input = CryptographicBuffer.ConvertStringToBinary(inputText,
        BinaryStringEncoding.Utf8);
```

```
        // hash it...
        var hasher = HashAlgorithmProvider.OpenAlgorithm
(HashAlgorithmNames.Sha512);
        IBuffer hashed = hasher.HashData(input);

        // format it...
        this.textBase64.Text = CryptographicBuffer.
EncodeToBase64String(hashed);
        this.textHex.Text = CryptographicBuffer.EncodeToHexString(hashed);
    }
```

Obviously in that method we're processing the output twice—once to get a base-64 string, and then again to get a hex dump. You'd almost certainly never do this in the real world; it's just for illustration so that we can see both types of output.

Run the project and click the button, and you'll see a result like Figure A-2. You can compare the output by running the same input string through various websites that will compute hashes from arbitrary strings. Search online for "calculate sha-512 hash" to find one you like.

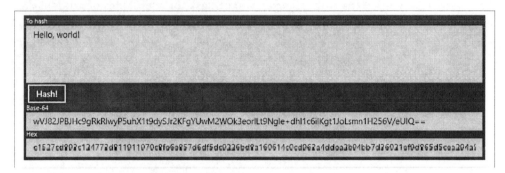

*Figure A-2. A successful run of the SHA-512 hash algorithm*

# Generating Random Data

I won't take you through building this, as it's very simple. You'll find a RandomSpike project in the downloads for this appendix.

Random data is used frequently in cryptography, but there are also plenty of examples where having good-quality random data in your software is a good thing. The random-number generator provided by System.Random is a classic pseudorandom number generator and isn't particularly random. It compromises randomness for speed. The random numbers used in cryptography have to be as close to "organically random" as possible, and generators used for this purpose will take longer to run and use more processor horsepower.

Generating a random number is easy—there's a method in `CryptographicBuffer` that will give you an integer value. Here's an example:

```
private void HandleRandomInteger(object sender, RoutedEventArgs e)
{
    this.buttonInteger.Content = CryptographicBuffer.GenerateRandomNumber()
.ToString();
}
```

We can also create a random block of data using the `GenerateRandom` method. This will return back an `IBuffer`, which we can work with in the usual way. Here's an example:

```
private void HandleRandomData(object sender, RoutedEventArgs e)
{
    var buffer = CryptographicBuffer.GenerateRandom(1024);
    this.textRandom.Text = CryptographicBuffer.
        EncodeToHexString(buffer);
}
```

Now that we know how to generate arbitrary blocks of data, you can use this to generate other numeric primitives through the expedient of creating enough bytes to make one. For example, if you want a 64-bit integer, you can ask for eight bytes of random data and then convert it to a primitive type using the standard .NET `BitConverter` class. To get a `byte[]` value out of an `IBuffer` instance, you can use the extension methods that become available when you include the `System.Runtime.Interop.WindowsRuntime` namespace. Here's an example:

```
private void HandleRandomLong(object sender, RoutedEventArgs e)
{
    // get eight bytes of data...
    var buffer = CryptographicBuffer.GenerateRandom(8);

    // convert it...
    ulong val = BitConverter.ToUInt64(buffer.ToArray(), 0);
    this.buttonLong.Content = val.ToString();
}
```

That's all there is to generating random data. Let's round off this chapter by talking about symmetric encryption.

# Symmetric Encryption

Symmetric encryption is the process whereby you can take a block of data, encrypt it using a key, and then decrypt it back to the original data using that same key.

I've made an assumption in this chapter that asymmetric encryption is less interesting to readers of this book. Asymmetric encryption tends to have very specific use cases, and as a developer you generally have to abide by the implementation rules in order to do anything with it. Symmetric encryption is much more of a helpful, ad hoc concept to have around.

In this section we're going to create another scratch project, EncryptionScratch, and add a `TextBox` control containing data that we can encrypt.

Figure A-3 shows the layout that we're aiming for.

*Figure A-3. Encryption scratch app layout*

Here's the XAML for the form:

```
<StackPanel Margin="10,10,10,10" HorizontalAlignment="Left" Width="400">
    <TextBlock Text="Text to encrypt"></TextBlock>
    <TextBox AcceptsReturn="true" Height="150" Text="Hello, world."
x:Name="textData"></TextBox>
    <StackPanel Orientation="Horizontal">
        <Button Content="Encrypt" Click="HandleEncryptClick"></Button>
        <Button Content="Decrypt" Click="HandleDecryptClick"></Button>
    </StackPanel>
</StackPanel>
```

When we do asymmetric encryption, we need to provide both a key and an *initialization vector* (IV). Although it looks like that's just a password in two parts, they are very different. The key is supposed to be your super-secret; only you know its value. The IV is "less secret"—its purpose is to randomize the input stream so that the same key yields different output. (And thus it's a little similar to the concept of a salted hash—it makes it harder to discover the underlying values used as part of the data-hiding process.)

In the sample you can download, I created two random values using the `Cryptogra phicBufffer.GenerateRandom` method that we saw before. One of these we'll use for the key, and the other we'll use for the IV.

The approach to using the symmetric encryption calls is similar to that used in hashing: we create a buffer containing the input data, get the algorithm that we want, create a key from the "key material," and then call CryptographicEngine, passing everything in.

Here's the code to encrypt the text:

```
            private const string keyAsHex =
  "d1ee5548bae50c6c52e785dbee523f022a1f39eb316dad2d2d50cc72957da4ef";
            private const string ivAsHex =
  "b2ba13011d845de7be1a246331a46f5d56ceea4bb6e81fde547b54440ad6d415";

            private void HandleEncryptClick(object sender, RoutedEventArgs e)
            {
                // input...
                var input = CryptographicBuffer.ConvertStringToBinary(this.textData
  .Text, BinaryStringEncoding.Utf8);

                // create...
                var keyMaterial = CryptographicBuffer.DecodeFromHexString(keyAsHex);
                var iv = CryptographicBuffer.DecodeFromHexString(ivAsHex);

                // encrypt...
                var encryptor = SymmetricKeyAlgorithmProvider.OpenAlgorithm(
                    SymmetricAlgorithmNames.AesCbcPkcs7);
                var key = encryptor.CreateSymmetricKey(keyMaterial);
                var encrypted = CryptographicEngine.Encrypt(key, input, iv);

                // show...
                this.textData.Text = CryptographicBuffer.EncodeToHexString(
                    encrypted);
            }

            private void HandleDecryptClick(object sender, RoutedEventArgs e)
            {
                // we'll do this in a moment...
            }
```

In that code, the algorithm name that I've proposed using is AesCbcPkcs7. In .NET we used to just ask for the RijandaelManaged encryption class (which does AES encryption, like the one we've selected here). You could then set properties on this instance to devise the cipher model (CBC in our example) and the padding mode (PKCS #7 in this example). In WinRT, you don't get to set properties on the encryption worker as we did before; you have to ask for a qualified object that matches what you want.

If you run the preceding code, you can try encrypting some text. Figure A-4 shows a result.

*Figure A-4. A successful encryption call*

The decryption routine is the reverse of all that. Here's the code:

```
private void HandleDecryptClick(object sender, RoutedEventArgs e)
{
    // input...
    var input = CryptographicBuffer.DecodeFromHexString(this.textData.Text);

    // create...
    var keyMaterial = CryptographicBuffer.DecodeFromHexString(keyAsHex);
    var iv = CryptographicBuffer.DecodeFromHexString(ivAsHex);

    // decrypt...
    var decryptor = SymmetricKeyAlgorithmProvider.OpenAlgorithm(
        SymmetricAlgorithmNames.AesCbcPkcs7);
    var key = decryptor.CreateSymmetricKey(keyMaterial);
    var decrypted = CryptographicEngine.Decrypt(key, input, iv);

    // show...
    this.textData.Text = CryptographicBuffer.ConvertBinaryToString
(BinaryStringEncoding.Utf8, decrypted);
}
```

Now you can run the project and both encrypt and decrypt text. To test this properly, enter some plain text to encrypt and press the Encrypt button a multiple, but known, number of times. The string will get longer and longer as you do this. Once you're satisfied, click the Decrypt button the same number of times, and you'll eventually get back to the plain-text value that you entered originally.

# Unit Testing Basics for Windows Store Apps

I'm being very careful to call this section "Unit Testing Basics," emphasis on the "Basics." Describing unit testing is beyond the scope of this book, and my objective here is to provide a basic outline of unit testing for total newbies. Specifically, I'm looking to show how the integrated unit-testing features work in Visual Studio 2012, and finally demonstrate that what we've done in the book is unit-testable.

We've gone to great lengths in our project to use MVVM—a very common objective of which is to provide unit-testing vectors. The question is, does it work?

## Unit Testing for Newbies

If you're not using unit testing in your day-to-day work, you should be. Unit testing is like having a savings account and the spare cash and discipline to put a little aside each month. There's a little upfront pain, but when you need it, you'll be extremely glad it's there.

The principle of unit testing is based on the truism of software engineering that "system in known state plus known value yields predictable result." So, if you have a method that multiplies two values together, you can create a unit test that plugs in two known values and checks against a known result. The principle is that if you happen to break that method somewhere down the line, you'll be told about it before it ends up in the customer's hands.

So a typical test might look like this:

```
// test the results of multiply...
private void TestMultiply()
{
  // make sure that the Multiply things method returns an expected result...
  Assert.AreEqual(77, MyMagicClass.Multiply(7, 11));
}
```

That's a contrived example, but the principle behind it is sound. What you're really looking to do is build up a set of functions that are able to go through and exercise all of the individual parts of the app. There are all sorts of benefits to unit testing, such as easier refactoring, and having the tests operate as a type of documentation. Another strong advantage—which is a big thing I like about it—is that if you build your tests first you can get all of the sides of a problem expressed in test "stubs" before you start coding. For example, if you are writing tests to check the functionality of code that emails invoices to customers, you can go ahead and block out tests for "what happens if there's no email address," "what happens if there are no invoices," "what happens if the email address is there, but invalid," and so on. This "test first" approach makes development easier as well as making your code more likely to pass acceptance testing first time.

Anyway, it's not my intention here to teach you everything about unit testing or why it's a good thing. If you're new to it, all you need to know to follow along is that we're going to produce test functions that are able to exercise different aspects of the code that we've built so far.

## Creating a Test Project

Creating a test project is much as you would imagine: simply add a new Windows Store Unit Test Library project into the solution. Figure B-1 illustrates.

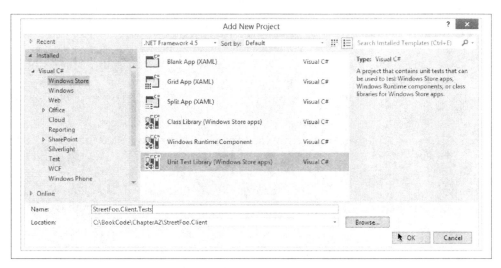

*Figure B-1. Adding a new Unit Test Library project*

You'll need to modify the references for the test project to include the UI-agnostic project.

# Testing RegisterServiceProxy

The reason why we built all of the MVVM stuff in this book was so we could do things like decouple the view-model and service proxies from the actual service implementation when we were undertaking unit testing.

This concept applies equally well to databases as it does to web services. The principle behind decoupling comes back to the central premise of unit testing—that is, "system in known state plus known value yields predictable result."

For example, if the remote service is unavailable when your tests are running, all of your tests that rely on it being available will fail. That situation would create a whole swath of invalid test results. Moreover, this assumes that the service's persistent store is in a known state when you start—for example, you might try to register a user with a given username that happens to work the first time, as the username hasn't been used, but would fail on subsequent attempts. (This point also applies to local databases or file stores—having a persistent state between runs can really muck up unit testing, or at least make it difficult to revert to a known state on start.)

The way to get around this is to create a simulated implementation of the service and call that simulation rather than the real thing.

The easiest thing to do is create a "fake" implementation. This involves building a new object that implements whatever interface or interfaces the originally consumed object did. You can then make that object return whatever you fancy depending on what you are testing. Faking is the method that we're going to use here.

In .NET, it is common to create mock objects. Usually this involves using a library; a popular one to do this with .NET is called Moq (*https://github.com/Moq*). However, for security reasons, Windows Store apps do not support the technology that enables Moq to emit new assemblies and consume them using `System.Reflection.Emit`. Thus, for all intents and purposes, mocking is currently impossible in Windows Store apps.

To get started, the first thing to do is create a class called `FakeRegisterServiceProxy`. This will implement `IRegisterServiceProxy`, but its implementation of the `RegisterAsync` method will not call the server. The following code simply returns a GUID if the supplied username is mbrit; otherwise, it'll return an error. Note that we have to obtain a `Task` to return to the caller.

```
public class FakeRegisterServiceProxy : IRegisterServiceProxy
{
    public Task<RegisterResult> RegisterAsync(string username, string email,
string password,
        string confirm)
    {
        if (username == "mbrit")
            return Task.FromResult<RegisterResult>(new RegisterResult
(Guid.NewGuid().ToString()));
```

```
        else
        {
            var error = new RegisterResult(new ErrorBucket());
            error.AddError("Invalid username.");
            return Task.FromResult<RegisterResult>(error);
        }
    }
}
```

There are two more things that we need to do in order to make this functional. We need to get TinyIoC to return the fake implementation rather than the real one, and we need to get the unit tests to handle `async` methods.

## Starting the Runtime and Handling async Methods

We already have a method for starting the runtime—namely, the `Start` method in `StreetFooRuntime`. We need to make sure this is called whenever our test is initialized.

Visual Studio will create a unit-test class called `UnitTest1` for us when we create a new project. Rename this class as `RegisterServiceProxyTests` and then add a `Setup` method to get the test started. Decorating this with the `TestInitialize` attribute ensures that Visual Studio's test runner will confirm that this method completes before executing any discovered tests.

Visual Studio's test runner has support for asynchronous test and setup methods. As per our discussion on asynchronous methods in Chapter 2, we have to give the unit-test runner a chance of understanding that our method will run asynchronously. As you might expect, we can do this by marking the method as `async` and having it return a `Task` instance.

As part of the setup, we need to override the default behavior of the TinyIoC's automatic registration such that when we ask for a handler for `IRegisterServiceProxy`, we get our faked implementation back. We do this by calling the `SetHandler` method on the `ServiceProxyRuntime` singleton. Here's the code:

```
[TestClass]
public class RegisterServiceProxyTests
{
    [TestInitialize]
    public async Task Setup()
    {
        await StreetFooRuntime.Start("Tests");

        // set...
        ServiceProxyFactory.Current.SetHandler(
            typeof(IRegisterServiceProxy),
            typeof(FakeRegisterServiceProxy));
    }
}
```

Next we need to actually test the method. As this method uses asynchronous methods, we again have to mark it as `async` and have it return a `Task` instance. It's the `Task` instance that makes this all magically work—it tells the Visual Studio test runner that it has to handle the asynchrony.

```
    // Add method to RegisterServiceProxyTests...
[TestMethod]
public async Task TestRegisterOk()
{
    var proxy = ServiceProxyFactory.Current.GetHandler
<IRegisterServiceProxy>();

    // ok...
    var result = await proxy.RegisterAsync("mbrit",
        "matt@amxmobile.com", "Password1", "Password1");
    Assert.IsFalse(result.HasErrors);
}
```

To run the tests, select Test ⁎ Run ⁎ All Tests from the menu. The Test Explorer will open and you'll see the results of your tests. Figure B-2 illustrates.

*Figure B-2. A successful test run*

# Testing the View-Models

That's the basics of the unit testing covered. The view-models need a little bit more work, as these are dependent on having a `IViewModelHost` to use. Luckily, this was built with unit testing in mind, so all we need to do is to create a fake implementation of that too.

The Visual Studio test runner can run tests in parallel, so we can't use a static singleton for this class. We'll have to create a new instance of it for each test. This is easily done. The functionality that I'm proposing putting into this example will just keep track of how many messages have been displayed. With invalid data, we'll validate that we got an error. With valid data, we'll validate that we did not. We'll have to capture the message shown, as we'll need to do specific validation on this to determine whether the operation worked or not. In a production implementation, you'd want to be more nuanced than this.

Here's the code for FakeViewModelHost. For this illustration, I've left some of the methods as throwing a "not implemented exception":

```
internal class FakeViewModelHost : IViewModelHost
{
    public int NumMessagesShown { get; private set; }
    public string LastMessage { get; private set; }

    internal FakeViewModelHost()
    {
    }

    public IAsyncOperation<IUICommand> ShowAlertAsync(ErrorBucket errors)
    {
        return ShowAlertAsync(errors.GetErrorsAsString());
    }

    public IAsyncOperation<IUICommand> ShowAlertAsync(string message)
    {
        // update the number of messages...
        this.NumMessagesShown++;
        this.LastMessage = message;

        // return...
        return Task.FromResult<IUICommand>(null).AsAsyncOperation
<IUICommand>();
    }

    public void ShowView(Type viewModelInterfaceType, object args = null)
    {
        throw new NotImplementedException("This operation has not been
implemented.");
    }

    public void ShowAppBar()
    {
        throw new NotImplementedException("This operation has not been
implemented.");
    }

    public void HideAppBar()
    {
        throw new NotImplementedException("This operation has not been
implemented.");
    }

    public void GoBack()
    {
        throw new NotImplementedException("This operation has not been
implemented.");
    }
}
```

Finally, here are our two tests:

```
[TestClass]
public class RegisterPageViewModelTests
{
    [TestInitialize]
    public async Task Setup()
    {
        await RegisterServiceProxyTests.SharedSetup();
    }

    [TestMethod]
    public void TestRegisterCommandWithInvalidPasswords()
    {
        var host = new FakeViewModelHost();
        var model = ViewModelFactory.Current.GetHandler
<IRegisterPageViewModel>(host);

        // set...
        model.Username = "mbrit";
        model.Email = "mbrit@mbrit.com";
        model.Password = "foobar";
        model.Confirm = "barfoo";

        // check...
        Assert.AreEqual(0, host.NumMessagesShown);

        // run - this will fail validation on the password...
        model.RegisterCommand.Execute(null);

        // check...
        Assert.IsFalse(host.LastMessage.Contains("The new user has been
created."));
    }

    [TestMethod]
    public void TestRegisterCommandWithOk()
    {
        var host = new FakeViewModelHost();
        var model = ViewModelFactory.Current.GetHandler
<IRegisterPageViewModel>(host);

        // set...
        model.Username = "mbrit";
        model.Email = "mbrit@mbrit.com";
        model.Password = "F00bar";
        model.Confirm = "F00bar";

        // check...
        Assert.AreEqual(0, host.NumMessagesShown);

        // run - this will fail validation on the password...
        model.RegisterCommand.Execute(null);
```

```
        // check...
        Assert.IsTrue(host.LastMessage.Contains("The new user has been
created."));        }
    }
```

And that's it. Now if we run our tests, all three will pass (as illustrated in Figure B-3).

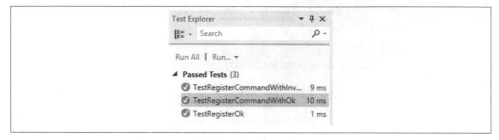

*Figure B-3. Our successful unit tests*

# Index

*We'd like to hear your suggestions for improving our indexes. Send email to index@oreilly.com.*

## K

Krueger, Frank, 84

## L

language support (see localization)
languageCode convention, 402
latitude/longitude display, 350
    (see also location services)
licenses, 447, 451
lifetime, of apps, 410
line-of-business (LOB) applications, x
Ling methods, 111
local access networks (LAN), 428
local notifications
    asynchrony and, 167
    badges, 164, 167
    functionality of, 155
    notification builders, 157
    tiles, 170–177
    toast, 158–167
    turning off/on, 156
    XML templates for, 156
local persistent data
    caching data locally (see data, caching local-
      ly)
    clean up during suspended phase, 410
    database uses, 83
    SQLite overview, 84
    SQLite use, 85–89
    storing settings, 89
localization
    basics of, 387
    conventions for, 398
    of images, 402–406
    .pri files for, 387–393
    of strings, 393–401
location services
    capability in manifest editor, 326
    map integration, 328–338
    permissions, 323, 327
    retrieving current location, 322–328
    shelling to Bing Maps, 339–342
    singleton view for, 311
    uses for, 311
LocationNarrative, 350
lock screen, 412, 425, 444
logon pages
    building, 70–75

layout of, 71
    modifying view, 97
    service proxy for, 68
LogonPageViewModel, 97
loose coupling, benefits of, 48

## M

Mail app, 12, 124, 229
maintenance, of background tasks, 425
    (see also debugging)
MaintenanceTrigger, 413
makepri.exe utility, 388
malware, 193, 447
Manage NuGet Packages dialog box, 49, 91
managed code environment, 1, 7, 13
manifest editor, 183, 197, 252, 326, 356, 366, 424
mapping, 100
maps
    Bing Maps control, 329
    Bing Maps registration, 328
    feature salability, 311
    input defaults, 331
    showing points on, 336
Markdown notation, 308
markup extensions, 22
memory, 410
MessageDialog class, 37
metadata, 4
Metro-style projects
    creating new, 5
    native UI technology for, 12
MetroLog library, 418
Micro-ORM (object-relational mapping), 87
Microphone capability, 366
Microsoft Account Connected, 206, 447
Microsoft Intermediate Language (MSIL), 92
mobile application management (MAM), 457
mobile device management (MDM), 457
Model-View-Controller (MVC), 25
Model/View/View Model (MVVM), 25, 68, 370
Modern UI projects
    description of, ix
    Items Page, 105
    reductionist approach in, 109
ms-appdata URI protocol, 217
ms-appx: protocol handler, 150
mscorlib, 8
multi-select grids, 126
multi-threading, 217

transcoders, 364
triggers, and background tasks, 413
typed overloads, 73

## U

U.S. English language support, 390
    (see also localization)
unit testing
    Build - Deploy, 198
    decoupling service interfaces for, 60, 469
    example of successful, 473
    introduction to, 467
    IoC and, 48
    of image sharing, 254
    recommendations for, 27
    RegisterServiceProxy, 469
    runtime and async, 470
    test packages, 447
    test project creation, 468
    of view-models, 471
updaters, 157
updates, syncing, 438
URIs (uniform resource identifiers), 217
usage quotas, 412
user accounts, push notifications and, 179
user experience (UX), 12, 55
user interface (UI)
    basic pages, 15–25
    interface tracks, 11
    Model/View/View-Model (MVVM), 25
    MVVM and inversion of control, 28–38
    secondary for snapped view, 370
    view-model and running the app, 38
    WPF and Silverlight, 26
    XAML parsing, 14, 265
user-specific data, 103

## V

validation, with WACK, 450
values, reading/writing of, 96
video, 366
view-model
    creation of, 38, 312, 346
    DataTransferManager hook-up, 224
    decoupling from view, 48
    DoRegistration method, 42
    IViewModelHost, 41
    running the app, 43

testing of, 471
views
    bi-panel, 315
    navigation to, 318
    snapped view, 369–385
Visual Studio
    Blend design software, 290, 377
    creating projects in, 5
    Debug tab, 242
    Manage NuGet Packages dialog box, 49
    Output window, 244
    package editor, 183
    Professional vs. Express, xiv
    search result template, 270
VisualStateManager class, 371
Volume Licensing (VL), 451
VSIX installer dialog box, 84

## W

Webcam capability, 356
wide tiles, 171
WiFi hotspots, 428
WIMP (windows, icons, menus, pointer) interface, 119
Win32 API, 1
Windows 8, 1
Windows 8 UX guidelines
    button position, 15
    filesystem restrictions, 193, 196
    search function, 276
Windows App Certification Kit (WACK), 450
Windows event log, 243
Windows Phone, 14, 83
Windows Presentation Foundation (WPF), 13, 26
Windows Push Notification Service (WNS)
    app registration, 183
    process of, 177
    sending to, 182, 188
    troubleshooting, 191
Windows RT, 1
Windows Runtime (WinRT)
    app lifetime in, 410
    asynchrony in, 55–59
    component libraries, 422
    file representation in, 196
    limitations on .NET, 415
    metadata system, 4–9
    photo capture methods in, 357

# X

# Y

## About the Authors

**Matt Baxter-Reynolds** (@mbrit) is a mobile software development consultant, mobile technology industry analyst, author, blogger, and technology sociologist with 20 years of experience in server-side and mobile client software development.

**Iris Classon** (@IrisClasson) is a C# MVP, Pluralsight author, and well-known speaker and blogger. She holds a dozen certificates in .NET development with a specialization in client app development and Windows Phone development.

## Colophon

The animal on the cover of *Programming Windows Store Apps with C#* is a pika (*Ochotona princeps*). The name *pika* can refer to any number of mammal in the Ochotonidae family, including rabbits and hares. This particular species also goes by the name "whistling hare" because of its characteristic high-pitched call that is used as an alarm when diving into its burrow.

Native to cold climates, pikas can be found mostly in Asia, North America, and areas of Eastern Europe. Many species inhabit areas with crevices that provide shelter—primarily rocky mountain sides. Still others live in crude burrows, while pikas in Eurasia sometimes share burrows with snowfinches. Pikas do not hibernate, and spend much of the warmer months hunting and gathering food to eat during the winter.

This small mammal is compact, with short limbs, round ears, and no external tail. They grow to between 15 to 23 cm (5.9 to 9.1 in) in length and can weigh up to 120 to 350 g (4.2 to 12.3 oz). These mammals are herbivores, feeding primarily on plant matter—forbs, grasses, sedges, shrub twigs, moss, and lichen. Pikas who live in rocks have small litters, with fewer than five young. Burrowing pikas tend to have larger litters and more frequently.

The cover image is from *Shaw's Zoology, Volume 2.1*. The cover font is URW Typewriter and Guardian Sans. The text font is Adobe Minion Pro; the heading font is Adobe Myriad Condensed; and the code font is Dalton Maag's Ubuntu Mono.

# Have it your way.

   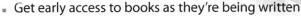

CPSIA information can be obtained at www.ICGtesting.com
Printed in the USA
BVOW07s2244160214

344846BV00004B/4/P